# SCIENCE FOR CHILDREN

# SCIENCE FOR CHILDREN

*Resources for Teachers*

NATIONAL SCIENCE RESOURCES CENTER

Smithsonian Institution • National Academy of Sciences

NATIONAL ACADEMY PRESS

WASHINGTON, D.C. 1988

The photograph on the front cover is of a painting, *Will Wonders Never Cease*, 1969, by the California-based painter, Jess. This painting, one of a series of oils called *Translations*, was inspired by an engraving derived from an 1887 painting by J. Dvorak, *The First Butterfly in the Net*. The words are from Gertrude Stein's *The Making of the Americans*. The original painting by Jess is in the permanent collection of the Hirshhorn Museum and is reproduced here by permission of the museum and the artist. (Photograph by Lee Stalsworth, courtesy of the Hirshhorn Museum and Sculpture Garden, Smithsonian Institution, The Joseph H. Hirshhorn Purchase Fund, 1986.)

The National Science Resources Center (NSRC) was established in 1985 as a joint undertaking of the Smithsonian Institution and the National Academy of Sciences. The NSRC's mission is to contribute to the improvement of science and mathematics teaching in the nation's schools by establishing a science and mathematics curriculum resource center and information database, developing and disseminating resource materials for science and mathematics teachers, and offering a program of outreach and leadership-development activities.

The Smithsonian Institution was created by act of Congress in 1846 in accordance with the will of the Englishman, James Smithson, who in 1826 bequeathed his property to the United States of America, "to found at Washington, under the name of the Smithsonian Institution, an establishment for the increase and diffusion of knowledge among men." The Smithsonian has since evolved into an institution devoted to public education, research, and national service in the arts, sciences, and history. This independent federal establishment is the world's largest museum complex and is responsible for public and scholarly activities, exhibitions, and research projects nationwide and overseas.

The National Academy of Sciences was chartered by Congress in 1863 as a private, nonprofit organization dedicated to the furtherance of science and engineering for the public welfare. In 1916 the National Research Council was organized, enabling the Academy to draw upon the entire American scientific and technical community in the pursuit of its mandate to provide independent advice to the nation on critical scientific and technical questions.

The views expressed in this book are solely those of its contributors and do not necessarily reflect the views of the Smithsonian Institution or the National Academy of Sciences.

**Library of Congress Cataloging-in-Publication Data**

Science for children.

Includes indexes.
1. Science—Study and teaching (Elementary)—
Bibliography. I. National Science Resources
Center (U.S.)
Z5818.S3S38  1988  [LB1585]  372.3'5044  88-25445
ISBN 0-309-03934-7

*First Printing, October 1988*
*Second Printing, April 1989*
*Third Printing, August, 1989*
*Fourth Printing, May 1990*
*Fifth Printing, April 1991*
*Sixth Printing, January 1992*

Printed in the United States of America

Additional copies of SCIENCE FOR CHILDREN are available as follows:

| Quantity | Price |
| --- | --- |
| 1 | $9.95 ea. |
| 2-9 | $8.50 ea. |
| 10 or more | $7.95 ea. |

Order from National Academy Press, 2101 Constitution Avenue, NW, P.O. Box 285, Washington, DC 20055. All orders must be prepaid with delivery to a single address. No discounts. Prices are subject to change without notice.

*Science is not simply a collection of facts; it is a discipline of thinking about rational solutions to problems after establishing the basic facts derived from observations. It is hypothesizing from what is known to what might be, and then attempting to test the hypotheses.*

*Taught properly, science can be part of the curriculum of the preschool as well as of the elementary-school child. The teaching of science at this level does not require complicated, expensive apparatus. It does require a teacher imbued with a love for logical thinking and the imagination to design simple experimentation that permits the child to think of himself or herself as an investigator.*

*The love for logical thinking must come first; the facts can later fall into place.*

Rosalyn S. Yalow, member of the National Academy of Sciences, Nobel laureate, and distinguished professor-at-large at the City University of New York's Mount Sinai School of Medicine, speaking at commencement, 1988, Drew University.

Centennial School District, Multnomah Education Service District, Portland, Oregon
*Photograph by Craig Walker*

# FOREWORD

Recently a drive has begun to improve science instruction in the nation's elementary schools. New and innovative science curriculum projects are starting up. Schools are increasing their emphasis on science in the elementary curriculum and providing more time to teach it. It is vital that this time be spent in accomplishing something that is lasting and significant for children.

The need for improved elementary science teaching has never been more clear. Science instruction in the United States has failed to keep up with the needs of our high-technology society. Although a number of large-scale federally funded projects in the post-Sputnik era attempted to improve science instruction, elementary science remains a textbook-only subject for most students in the early grades, if they study science at all.

Despite a flurry of excitement associated with the seminal elementary science projects of the sixties, few elementary schools now have hands-on science programs. Moreover, most elementary teachers have little formal science training and are hesitant to teach science beyond what is laid out in the textbook. Too often this textbook science offers little more than rote memorization. Instead of interesting children in science, it convinces them that science is tedious and difficult to understand and should be avoided.

Meanwhile, national reports continue to bemoan our lack of qualified graduates to fill math, science, and engineering jobs. In international competitions, even our best students score below students of other industrialized nations. For all our efforts to attract women and minorities to careers in science and technology, their representation in these fields is small and declining. This waste of talent comes about, in part, because the adult society does not encourage most youngsters to pursue careers in scientific or technical fields. Science literacy is at a low level in our culture.

We *can* do better. Moreover, we cannot afford to miss the opportunity to improve elementary science education. We must put good science-instruction material in teachers' hands from the start. They have the conviction; what they need is assistance in locating the resources they can then tailor to suit their classroom needs. *Science for Children* is designed to help them do this.

Frank Press
President
National Academy of Sciences

Robert McC. Adams
Secretary
Smithsonian Institution

Milwaukee Public Schools, Milwaukee, Wisconsin
*Photograph by Robert Zeman*

# ACKNOWLEDGMENTS

*Science for Children: Resources for Teachers* has been a major undertaking and a gratifying one. Like most such efforts, it could not have been accomplished without the hard work and cooperation of a core group of staff, combined with the advice and generous assistance of a large number of consultants, volunteers, and other professionals.

The information database on which this guide is based was compiled with support from the U.S. Department of Education and the Department of Defense. The bulk of the research and writing was done by Mary Dickinson Bird and JoAnn DeMaria, both science educators on the staff of the National Science Resources Center. They created the database on which this guide is based, with the assistance of Caroline Acker and Elizabeth Robelen. A number of the curriculum annotations were written by teachers Stephen Baumann, Joanne Goodwin, Ella Miller, Gary Miller, and Blanche Wine. Timothy Falb, NSRC computer specialist, formatted the guide and prepared it, through countless iterations, for publication. Adeline Naiman served as editor of the resource guide, working closely with Sally Shuler, NSRC program director.

Many individuals gave us materials, classroom photographs, and professional assistance. We are especially grateful to these contributors:

Judi Backman, Math/Science Coordinator, Highline Public Schools, Seattle, Washington

James Bird, Reference Librarian, McKeldin Library, University of Maryland, College Park, Maryland

Angela Cooper, Manager of Museum-To-Go Kits and Outreach, Franklin Institute, Philadelphia, Pennsylvania

Robert DeMaria, Mars, Inc., McLean, Virginia

Mary Duru, Assistant Professor, Early Childhood Education, University of Maryland, Baltimore County, Baltimore, Maryland

Neal Eigenfeld, Science Curriculum Specialist, Milwaukee Public Schools, Milwaukee, Wisconsin

Elizabeth Fenske, Elementary Science Special Projects Teacher, Fairfax County Public Schools, Fairfax, Virginia

George Franz, Teacher, The Computer School, New York City Public Schools, New York, New York

Johnnie Hamilton, Science Curriculum Coordinator, Fairfax County Public Schools, Fairfax, Virginia

Richard McQueen, Specialist, Science Education, Multnomah Education Service District, Portland, Oregon

Harold Pratt, Executive Director of Science and Technology, Jefferson County Public Schools, Golden, Colorado

Wayne Ransom, Vice President and Director of Education and Programs, Franklin Institute, Philadelphia, Pennsylvania

Larry Small, Science/Health Coordinator, Schaumburg School District 54, Schaumburg, Illinois

Susan Sprague, Director of Science and Social Studies, Mesa Public Schools, Mesa, Arizona

Myra Vachon, Curriculum and Instruction Supervisor, Milwaukee Public Schools, Milwaukee, Wisconsin

Emma Walton, President, National Science Supervisors Association; Science Program Coordinator, Anchorage School District, Anchorage, Alaska

Susan Wolff, Computer Specialist, Fairfax Country Public Schools, Fairfax, Virginia

Robert Zeman, Teacher, Milwaukee Public Schools, Milwaukee, Wisconsin

We wish to thank also the museums, science-technology centers, zoological parks, aquariums, nature centers, and professional organizations that contributed information and assistance.

We have been particularly fortunate in the assistance we received from the *Science for Children* review panel. These individuals, listed below, gave generously of their time by thoughtfully reviewing the guide in manuscript. We benefited much from their knowledge, positive criticisms, suggestions, and support.

Robert E. Anastasi, Education Programs Specialist, National Association of Elementary School Principals, Alexandria, Virginia

Ann I. Bay, Director, Office of Elementary and Secondary Education, Smithsonian Institution, Washington, DC

Gordon Cawelti, Executive Director, Association for Supervision and Curriculum Development, Alexandria, Virginia

Audrey Champagne, Senior Program Director, American Association for the Advancement of Science, Washington, DC

Hubert Dyasi, Director, City College Workshop Center, New York, New York

James Ebert, Vice President, National Academy of Sciences, Washington, DC; Director, Chesapeake Bay Institute, Johns Hopkins University, Baltimore, Maryland

Arnold Fege, Director of Government Relations, National Congress of PTA's, Fairfax, Virginia

Elsa Feher, Exhibits Director, Fleet Science Center, San Diego, California

Jack Goldstein, Professor of Physics, Brandeis University, Waltham, Massachusetts

Joe Griffith, Principal, Thoreau School, Concord, Massachusetts

Charles Hardy, Curriculum Director, Highline Public Schools, Seattle, Washington

Gene Hickey, Elementary School Teacher, Garfield Math/Science Specialty School, Milwaukee, Wisconsin

Phyllis Marcuccio, Director of Publications, National Science Teachers Association, Washington, DC

Lynn Margulis, University Professor, Department of Biology, Boston University, Boston, Massachusetts

Ted Maxwell, Chairman, Center for Earth and Planetary Studies, National Air and Space Museum, Washington, DC

Perry Montoya, Elementary School Teacher, Johnson Elementary School, Mesa, Arizona

Philip Morrison, Professor of Physics, Massachusetts Institute of Technology, Cambridge, Massachusetts

Phylis Morrison, Public Broadcasting Associates, Cambridge, Massachusetts

Alice Moses, Program Director, Instructional Materials Development, National Science Foundation, Washington, DC

Jerome Pine, Professor of Physics, California Institute of Technology, Pasadena, California

Robert Ridky, Professor of Geology, University of Maryland, College Park, Maryland

Kent Rossier, Science Curriculum Supervisor, Department of Defense Dependents Schools, West Germany

Susan Snyder, Program Director, Science and Mathematics Education Network, National Science Foundation, Washington, DC

Lynne Strieb, Elementary School Teacher, John B. Kelly School, Philadelphia, Pennsylvania

Gloria Tucker, Director of Science, Beers Elementary School, Washington, DC

Bonnie VanDorn, Executive Director, Association of Science-Technology Centers, Washington, DC

Melvin Webb, Professor of Biology/Science Education, Clark College, Atlanta, Georgia

Judith White, Chief, Office of Education, National Zoological Park, Washington, DC

Karen Worth, Director, Boston Schools Program, Wheelock College, Boston, Massachusetts

For their patient help, we thank the staffs of the National Academy Press and the Smithsonian Institution Press.

Last, we would like to thank Robert McC. Adams, Secretary of the Smithsonian Institution; Frank Press, President of the National Academy of Sciences; and the NSRC Advisory Board for their vision and support in helping the NSRC to undertake this project.

Douglas M. Lapp
Executive Director
National Science Resources Center

# NATIONAL SCIENCE RESOURCES CENTER

## National Academy of Sciences—Smithsonian Institution

## Advisory Board

Albert Baez, President, Vivamos Mejor/USA

Peter Cannon, Vice President - Research and Chief Scientist, Rockwell International Corporation

Hubert Dyasi, Director, City College Workshop Center

James Ebert, Vice President, National Academy of Sciences

Elsa Feher, Exhibits Director, Reuben Fleet Science Center

Robert C. Forney (Chairman), Executive Vice President, E. I. du Pont de Nemours and Company

Robert Fuller, Vice President (retired), Johnson & Johnson

Samuel Gibbon, Executive Producer, *The Voyage of the Mimi*, Bank Street College of Education

Jack Goldstein, Professor of Physics, Brandeis University

Harry Gray, Professor of Chemistry, California Institute of Technology

Charles Hardy, Curriculum Director, Highline Public Schools

Robert Hoffmann, Assistant Secretary for Research, Smithsonian Institution

Ann Kahn, Immediate Past President, National Congress of PTA's

Amie Knox, Educational Consultant, Camille and Henry Dreyfus Foundation

William McCune, Chairman, Polaroid Corporation

Phyllis Marcuccio, Director of Publications, National Science Teachers Association

Lynn Margulis, University Professor, Department of Biology, Boston University

Ted Maxwell, Chairman, Center for Earth and Planetary Studies, National Air and Space Museum

Philip Morrison, Professor of Physics, Massachusetts Institute of Technology

Phylis Morrison, Public Broadcasting Associates

Jerome Pine, Professor of Physics, California Institute of Technology

Peter Raven, Director, Missouri Botanical Garden

Robert Ridky, Professor of Geology, University of Maryland

Ralph Rinzler, Assistant Secretary for Public Service, Smithsonian Institution

Irwin Shapiro, Director, Smithsonian Astrophysical Observatory

David Sheetz, Senior Vice President and Chief Scientist, Dow Chemical Company

Philip Smith, Executive Officer, National Academy of Sciences

Melvin Webb, Professor of Biology/Science Education, Clark College

Carolyn Wilson, Director of Planning and Development, Woodrow Wilson National Fellowship Foundation

Karen Worth, Director, Boston Schools Program, Wheelock College

## Staff

Douglas M. Lapp, Executive Director
Sally G. Shuler, Program Director
Adeline Naiman, Director of Publications
Shirley Ash, Administrative Officer
Timothy Falb, Program Assistant
Mary Dickinson Bird, Research Associate
JoAnn DeMaria, Research Associate

# CONTENTS

INTRODUCTION   1

HOW TO USE THIS RESOURCE GUIDE   2

I. CURRICULUM MATERIALS   7
    Life Science   7
    Health and Human Biology   34
    Earth Science   38
    Physical Science   44
    Multidisciplinary and Applied Science   60

II. SUPPLEMENTARY RESOURCES   81
    Science Activity Books   81
    Books on Teaching Science   92
    Science Book Lists and Other References   99
    Magazines for Children and Teachers   103

III. SOURCES OF INFORMATION AND ASSISTANCE   109
    Museums and Science-Technology Centers   109
    Professional Associations and Organizations   130
    Elementary Science Curriculum Projects—Past and Present   138
    Publishers   147
    Suppliers of Science Materials and Apparatus   152

INDEX   157
    Topic   157
    Title   164
    Author/Project   168
    Grade Level   171
    Grade Level by Category   172
    Sources of Information and Assistance   173

Community School District 3, New York City Public Schools, New York, New York

*Photograph by Stanley Chu*

# INTRODUCTION

*Science is not a list of facts and principles to learn by rote;
it is a way of looking at the world and asking questions.*

F. James Rutherford, Chief Education Officer
American Association for the Advancement of Science

*Science for Children: Resources for Teachers* is a guide designed to assist those who are working to improve elementary science education. The materials described here are recommended because they provide outstanding support for carrying out effective hands-on, inquiry-based programs.

*Science for Children* has been prepared by the National Science Resources Center, a joint effort of the National Academy of Sciences and the Smithsonian Institution in Washington, DC. The NSRC staff are developing new teaching materials for elementary classrooms; creating a national network of teachers, scientists, and science educators; providing leadership training; and assembling a collection and database of the best materials available for hands-on science teaching.

We at the NSRC believe that children begin to learn science from the moment they start to perceive their environment. They have an innate need to make sense of what happens. They make assumptions based on their perceptions, and they begin to predict what will happen and to test their predictions. Bit by bit, they form a useful model of the world around them.

Before children go to school, they exercise their natural curiosity daily. School can expand their universe and open new areas of inquiry for them. Or, it can close off their search for knowledge by presenting science as a set of words and rules to be memorized from the pages of a textbook.

The teacher plays a powerful role in deciding which route to follow. If a child asks, "Why?" the teacher can answer, "Because...," implying that the answers come from established authority and must be mastered. Alternatively, the teacher can turn questions back to the questioners: "How could you find out?" or "What do you think?" and thereby encourage them to persist in finding answers for themselves and to develop and test their own critical-thinking skills. This is the kind of science that we at the NSRC want to encourage.

Hands-on science means just that—learning from the materials and processes of the natural world through direct observation and experimentation. Professional scientists develop hypotheses and then test these ideas through repeated experiments and observations. They cannot simply "know" that something is so; they must demonstrate it. The education of children in science must also provide for this kind of experience, not simply to confirm the "right" answer but to investigate the nature of things and arrive at explanations that are satisfying to children and that make sense to them.

The elementary science materials included in this resource guide reflect this spirit. They offer students opportunities to experiment productively, to ask questions and find their own answers, and to develop patience, persistence, and confidence in their own ability to tackle and solve real problems.

1

# HOW TO USE THIS RESOURCE GUIDE

*Science for Children: Resources for Teachers* contains many of the resources for hands-on elementary science teaching that are currently available from publishers, distributors, libraries, and repositories of out-of-print materials. This guide does not attempt to be exhaustive, although it does represent considerable research.

The guide is divided into three major sections: **Curriculum Materials**, **Supplementary Resources**, and **Sources of Information and Assistance**.

The first section includes those print materials that are substantial enough to form the core of a curriculum—activity-based units upon which an elementary science program can be built.

The second section is devoted to outstanding science activity books, books about science teaching, science magazines for teachers and students, lists of recommended trade books, and other useful references. Although none of these entries can serve, by itself, as the centerpiece of an elementary science program, each offers philosophical or practical support for the implementation of hands-on science in the schools.

The third section provides a broad survey of institutional resources for elementary science teaching: museums and science-technology centers; professional associations and organizations that provide information, services, or materials; publishers and suppliers of instructional materials and apparatus; and descriptions of major funded projects intended to improve science education, both those of the past and those that are under way.

The quickest way to locate an entry in this guide is to consult one of the six alphabetical indexes at the back of the book. An entry can be located by its topic, title, author or project, grade level, grade level by category, or source. If you are interested in surveying what is available for the grade or subject you are teaching, the index is the best place to start. If you want to browse in order to get ideas for teaching, you may prefer to turn to the appropriate section of the guide, as listed in the Contents, and scan the entries.

## Section I.   Curriculum Materials

This is the largest section of the guide. The entries are divided into five categories commonly used in science teaching: **Life Science**, **Health and Human Biology**, **Earth Science**, **Physical Science**, and **Multidisciplinary and Applied Science**. A few entries appear in more than one category.

Each bibliographic entry consists of a citation, appropriate grade level, source for kits or materials, price, and a brief annotation, written by a teacher-reviewer.

The bibliographic citation includes title, author/project, location and name of publisher, ISBN, and publication date. The title is given first to enable you to browse through a section by topic. Some publications list the project as author; others name individual authors as shown on the title page. When an earlier edition is of historical interest, its date of publication, in parentheses, follows the date of the latest edition. Most publications cited are currently in print; consult the Sources index to locate publishers' addresses. We have also indicated sources for those items that are out of print but worth seeking out.

In some instances, we have suggested grade levels that differ slightly from the publisher's advertised levels. We have done this after careful use or examination of the materials, and the recommendation reflects our judgment of the levels for which the activities described will be most appropriate and successful.

We have made every effort to insure that the prices listed are current. We cannot guarantee them, however, and we urge you to check with distributors before you place an order.

We have included the ISBN (International Standard Book Number), if one was assigned, to help you order commercially distributed materials. Some publishers use different codes, however, so you may want to consult the publisher before you order an item.

The curriculum descriptions in this guide were written by experienced teachers. Each annotation contains a brief overview of the concepts taught and the activities suggested, as well as comments on the overall usefulness of the material. We have not attempted to rate the items, since what is ideal for one setting may not work in another. All, however, have been judged to be supportive of inquiry-based science teaching that fosters understanding of science concepts through hands-on student investigations.

## Section II.   Supplementary Resources

There are many kinds of publications that support the teaching of hands-on science. In this section, we provide annotated listings of several additional types of resource materials for teachers.

**Science activity books** for children to use in school or at home offer enrichment of the curriculum in engaging ways and call for readily available, low-cost materials. Helpful directions and illustrations are usually provided. These books can be found in bookstores or libraries or ordered from the publishers. Some may already be in your school library. Parents may be interested in knowing about these books for home activities.

**Books on teaching science** provide background material on the subject matter of elementary science and a broad range of pedagogical resources for good science teaching. The books described focus on inquiry-style, hands-on science teaching methods that support the educational philosophy of the NSRC. A selection of **science book lists** for children is also included, as well as directories of other kinds of resources.

**Magazines for children and teachers** round out this section of the guide. Some are useful for teachers, some for children, and some for both. Grade levels are indicated. Current subscription prices are given, together with publishers' names and addresses.

## Section III.   Sources of Information and Assistance

Educators who are looking for specific kinds of help and advice may want to get in touch with scientific and educational organizations that are working to improve science education. The third section of this guide lists institutional resources of this kind, as well as materials suppliers and publishers.

**Museums and science-technology centers** can be found in many localities and are excellent resources for informal, as well as classroom, instruction. Most welcome visits by teachers and students. Many produce their own hands-on teaching materials and circulate these through loan or purchase, regionally or nationally. We have included some of these materials in the curriculum section of this guide. A number of museums and centers offer courses or workshops for teachers on the use of their exhibits and materials, and on related science topics.

**Professional associations and organizations** are sources of sound information about their fields of specialization. Some can provide speakers for school presentations. Many of these organizations offer their own resource materials to enrich teaching, often free of charge. A great many publish magazines or newsletters to which one can subscribe with or without membership. We have given the names of permanent staff of the organization, rather than elected officers, where we could.

For informational purposes, we have also included in this section descriptions of **elementary science curriculum projects**, both those that are currently active and the major projects of the past. Most of these are of more than historical interest, since their products are still available and are described in the curriculum section.

We have given the names and addresses of **publishers** of the curriculum entries and also of the **suppliers of science materials and apparatus**. These are included as a handy reference, but the list is not exhaustive, since new suppliers are continually entering the arena.

## What This Guide Does Not Include

Several kinds of teaching resources are not reviewed in this guide. One is computer software for elementary science. Many publishers offer science software, and the quality of their programs is improving all the time. We plan to expand our study of such programs and include them among our resources in the near future. This guide does list a small sampling of software-review magazines that teachers have found useful, as well as a software directory.

We have also not attempted to review the vast array of audiovisual materials—films, videotapes, filmstrips, slides, posters, videodisks, multimedia programs, and the like—although many such excellent products exist and can play an important role in the science classroom. We plan to consider these in detail at a later date and to study ways in which the broad range of available media can be integrated with printed materials and kits to enrich science teaching.

Absent, as well, are reviews of the vast number of science trade books that enrich children's knowledge and understanding of science. Many teachers use such books as part and parcel of their science curriculum. We have supplied sources of book lists, and we urge teachers to supplement hands-on activities in the classroom with extensive reading.

Elementary science textbooks are also not reviewed in this resource guide. Many of the exemplary districts in our network tell us they have discontinued using elementary science textbooks, although some districts use texts as supplements to their activity-based science programs. Other districts have turned to the use of science trade books instead of traditional textbooks for science readings.

Yet many school districts do base their entire science curriculum on one of the elementary science textbook series available from commercial publishers. We believe, however, that an elementary science program should not be centered on the use of a textbook alone.

Science is a process and a way of thinking; both aspects require active participation by the individual learner. Students must have opportunities to carry out scientific investigations, using a wide variety of concrete materials. Students should learn to set up their own experiments, to change variables systematically, to make accurate observations and measurements, and to record and graph data.

Teachers are often under pressure to cover everything in the textbook on schedule and to "teach to the test." Nonetheless, research has shown that most children learn science better and sharpen their problem-solving skills most effectively through hands-on instruction. We recommend that teachers begin by introducing hands-on activities one at a time into their science classes, in order to become more comfortable with this style of teaching. We are certain that teachers will continue to expand their hands-on teaching when they see their students learning science in a way that engages them and offers lasting educational benefits.

We know that children take a natural delight in "doing" science. It is our profound hope that *Science for Children* will encourage more teachers to teach hands-on science and help them to do it successfully.


## A Special Request

This resource guide is a first attempt. We regard it as the beginning of a shared effort to make elementary science teaching more effective and enjoyable for teachers and children. Because the NSRC plans to produce a revised edition of this guide in the future, we welcome comments and recommendations.

Please send such contributions to the following address:

National Science Resources Center
Arts and Industries Building, Room 1201
Smithsonian Institution
Washington, DC 20560

# I. CURRICULUM MATERIALS

This section contains descriptions of printed curriculum materials—some with kits or suggested equipment—that can serve as the core of a hands-on elementary science program. Teacher's guides and activity packets have been selected because they give outstanding attention to activity-based learning. Each entry is substantial enough to function as a unit of study for specific concepts, science topics, or skills. All the materials are available, either as current publications or as archived documents anyone may consult. We are aware that our list is not exhaustive, despite our best efforts, and we welcome suggestions for additions we can acquire and review in future editions of this resource guide. For addresses of suppliers or publishers, consult the Sources index at the end of this guide, then the full listings in Section III.

Materials in this section are divided into five major categories: Life Science, Health and Human Biology, Earth Science, Physical Science, and Multidisciplinary and Applied Science. Some items have been included in more than one category because they incorporate activities relating to several topics. Curriculum materials containing activities that are general in nature or that deal with three or more topics have been included in the last category, Multidisciplinary and Applied Science.

Much research shows that hands-on science instruction can provide successful educational experiences for children with different skills, learning styles, and background knowledge. Accordingly, we have avoided designating materials as particularly appropriate for children with learning disabilities or special needs, for girls rather than both girls and boys, or for racial or ethnic minorities. Certain programs or publications were designed for children with physical handicaps, and those are noted in the Topic index. For all other annotated entries, we make the assumption that every schoolchild can benefit from working directly with the "stuff" of science and will enjoy the process. The teacher must make the decision about what is appropriate for the learning level of each class or student; we describe what is offered so as to help the teacher make that decision.

## Life Science

Included in the Life Science section are curriculum materials relating to plants, animals, ecology, and general biology.

The ADAPTATIONS module consists of seven activity folios: Animal Movement in Water, Desert Water Keepers, Food Grab, Hold It, Invent an Animal, Invent a Plant, and Seed Dispersal. Children discover how aquatic animals move through water and how different desert plants conserve water; investigate the food-gathering adaptations of animals and the water-holding power of organisms; design and construct animals and plants; and modify seeds and fruits for dispersal. Each folio contains background information, preparation hints, a list of materials needed, directions for the activities, and possible extensions. The folios are well organized and have useful illustrations and diagrams. The OBIS POND GUIDE supplements this module.

*ADAPTATIONS.* Outdoor Biology Instructional Strategies (OBIS). Nashua, NH: Delta, 1979, 1980.
Grade(s): 4,5,6,7,8
Supplies: Materials available locally.
Module: $15.60

*ALL AROUND*. Learning Through Science. Collis, Margaret, and Kincaid, Doug. London, England: Macdonald, 1982. ISBN 0-356-07553-2
Grade(s): 2,3,4,5
Supplies: Materials available locally or from commercial suppliers.
Activity Cards and Guide: $27.00 (Available in the U.S. from Teacher's Laboratory.)

In the ALL AROUND activity cards, the local environment becomes a training ground for the development of young naturalists. The skills of observation, using all the senses, are reinforced as children carry out explorations and investigations of the plant and animal life around their homes. By examining animal and plant habitats, children gain an awareness of the life needs, variability, and adaptability that exist in the living world. The teacher's guide contains no formal lesson plans but offers useful information. The 24 activity cards can be used independently but are more appropriate for teacher-directed lessons.

*AMAZING MAMMALS, PART I*. Ranger Rick's NatureScope. Washington, DC: National Wildlife Federation, 1986.
Grade(s): K,1,2,3,4,5,6,7
Supplies: Materials available locally.
Guide: $6.00

AMAZING MAMMALS, PART I introduces children to the general characteristics of mammals, their biology and behavior, and how they interact with humans. Through observations, experiments, games and simulations, creative writing, crafts, and large-motor activities, children learn to distinguish mammals from other vertebrate classes and investigate their importance to humans. The guide contains 22 lessons suitable for classroom or playground, with detailed background information, student activity sheets, and an excellent list of resources.

*AMAZING MAMMALS, PART II*. Ranger Rick's NatureScope. Washington, DC: National Wildlife Federation, 1986.
Grade(s): K,1,2,3,4,5,6,7
Supplies: Materials available locally.
Guide: $6.00

AMAZING MAMMALS, PART II is an interdisciplinary investigation of the specific characteristics of mammalian groups. Students participate in games and experiments that demonstrate the unique adaptations of primates, rodents, marine mammals, hoofed mammals, and carnivorous and insectivorous mammals. There are 24 lessons with detailed background information, student activity sheets, questions for further study, and a guide to supplemental resources.

*ANIMAL ACTIVITY*. Elementary Science Study (ESS). New York, NY: McGraw-Hill, 1969.
Grade(s): 4,5,6
Supplies: Materials available locally or from commercial suppliers, or homemade
Out of print. Available on SCIENCE HELPER K-8 or from ERIC (see Sources index).

ANIMAL ACTIVITY introduces children to techniques for observing and measuring the activity levels of small mammals, such as mice, gerbils, or hamsters. An exercise wheel in the animal's cage is linked to a counter that monitors the animal's activity. Children observe and record activity levels, investigating the effects of diet, age, temperature, time of day, size of cage, and classroom noise levels. The guide contains specifications for building an exercise wheel. A student guide, EXPERIMENTS ON ANIMAL ACTIVITY, accompanies the unit.

*ANIMAL BEHAVIOR*. Outdoor Biology Instructional Strategies (OBIS). Nashua, NH: Delta, 1979, 1980, 1981.
Grade(s): 4,5,6,7,8
Supplies: Materials available locally.
Module: $17.15

ANIMAL BEHAVIOR includes eight activities: Ants, For the Birds, Isopods, Jay Play, Leapin' Lizards, Scram or Freeze, The Old White Sheet Trick, and Web It. Children investigate the behavior, structure, and interaction of ants, pigeons, ducks, jays, isopods, lizards, animals that live under logs and rocks, flying insects, and spiders. Through conducting light-related experiments, spraying webs with mist, playing a "freeze" and "scram" game, constructing a "lizard rig," salting the jays' preferred-color food, and observing a variety of animals, children come to discuss and make predictions about animal behavior. Each activity folio contains background information, preparation hints, a list of materials needed, directions for the activities, and possible extensions. The folios are well organized and have useful illustrations. The OBIS LAWN GUIDE supplements this module.

In ANIMAL DEFENSES, children explore the defensive structures and behaviors of dinosaurs and familiar animals of today. Students create a defenseless animal and supply it with physical defense mechanisms. They then dramatize a meeting of their imaginary animals with a Tyrannosaurus rex. Successive activities focus on the physical characteristics and defense behaviors of dogs, cats, turtles, lizards, and other animals. Each lesson plan includes an overview, a suggested time frame, a list of materials, ideas for preparation, and directions for the activity. This guide also contains extensions and modifications for grades 1 and 2.

*ANIMAL DEFENSES.* Great Explorations in Math and Science (GEMS). Echols, Jean. Berkeley, CA: Lawrence Hall of Science, 1987.
Grade(s): K,1,2
Supplies: Materials available locally, from commercial suppliers, or from Lawrence Hall of Science.
Guide: $6.50

In ANIMALS IN ACTION, students investigate animal behavior by observing animals in action. By bringing animals into the classroom and enclosing them in a contained area, children learn to observe objectively, describe behaviors, test reactions to certain stimuli, and then apply these skills to experimentation with other common small animals. Background information, discussion of humane treatment of animals, easy-to-follow lesson plans, and an excellent small-animal resource guide are included in this book.

*ANIMALS IN ACTION.* Great Explorations in Math and Science (GEMS). Barrett, Katharine. Berkeley, CA: Lawrence Hall of Science, 1986.
Grade(s): 5,6,7,8,9,10,11,12
Supplies: Materials available locally, from commercial suppliers, or from Lawrence Hall of Science.
Guide: $7.50

ANIMALS IN THE CLASSROOM encourages teachers to keep animals of all kinds in the classroom and to use them in teaching language arts, mathematics, and social studies, as well as in science and nature study. The guide is divided into four sections. The first is an account of a year with desert animals in a primary classroom. The second section contains a checklist for care of a variety of animals. The third and fourth sections describe methods that have worked successfully in caring for gerbils and lizards. Some simple, inexpensive cages are described for use with small animals. A resource list is included, but owing to the age of this edition, it is somewhat outdated.

*ANIMALS IN THE CLASSROOM: A GUIDE FOR TEACHERS.* Elementary Science Study (ESS). New York, NY: McGraw-Hill, 1970.
Grade(s): 1,2,3
Supplies: Materials available locally. Out of print. Available from ERIC (see Sources index).

AQUATIC ANIMAL BEHAVIOR consists of seven activities: Animal Movement in Water, Attract a Fish, Damsels and Dragons, Hopper Circus, Salt Water Revival, Water Breathers, and Water Striders. Children discover how aquatic animals move through water, fish with different baits and lures, uncover clues to how dragonflies and damselflies react to flying decoys, use Action Cards to learn about hopping animals, create artificial high tides, investigate the currents made by animals when they breathe and move, and explore the movement and feeding behaviors of water striders. Each folio contains background information, preparation hints, a list of materials needed, directions for the activities, and possible extensions. The folios are well organized and have useful illustrations and diagrams. The OBIS POND GUIDE supplements this module.

*AQUATIC ANIMAL BEHAVIOR.* Outdoor Biology Instructional Strategies (OBIS). Nashua, NH: Delta, 1979, 1980, 1981.
Grade(s): 4,5,6,7,8
Supplies: Materials available locally.
Module: $15.60

The AUDUBON ZOO ACTIVITY BOOKS consist of six books: Asian Domain Activity Book, Grasslands of the World Activity Book, World of Primates Activity Book, World of Birds Activity Book, Wisner Children's Village Discovery Book, and Louisiana Swamp Exhibit Discovery Book. They have been designed to encourage the development of positive attitudes towards wildlife, thereby ensuring the future of wildlife worldwide. These books may be used in conjunction with a zoo visit or as independent classroom activities. Each book includes activities suitable to a variety of skill levels.

*AUDUBON ZOO ACTIVITY BOOKS.* Audubon Park and Zoological Garden. New Orleans, LA: Audubon Zoo, 1982, 1986.
Grade(s): 2,3,4,5,6
Supplies: Materials available locally.
Activity Book: $2.50

*BACKYARD*. Outdoor Biology Instructional Strategies (OBIS). Nashua, NH: Delta, 1979, 1980.
Grade(s): 4,5,6,7,8
Supplies: Materials available locally.
Module: $18.65

The BACKYARD module includes eight activities: Birdfeeder, Flower Powder, Food Grab, Invent an Animal, Isopods, Sticklers, Super Soil, and Water Holes to Mini-Ponds. Children build a bird feeder and observe bird behaviors, simulate flower pollination, design devices that can capture prey, create an animal compatible with the local environment, investigate isopods, compare soils, monitor water holes, and then play a simulation game about habitat and distribution and relate these concepts to real organisms. Each activity folio contains background information, preparation hints, a list of materials needed, directions for the activities, and possible extensions. The folios are well organized and have useful illustrations and diagrams. The OBIS POND GUIDE supplements this module.

*BEGINNINGS*. Science Curriculum Improvement Study (SCIS). Herrera, Sharon, and Thier, Herbert D. Nashua, NH: Delta, 1974.
Grade(s): K,1
Supplies: Materials from Delta.
Out of print. Available on SCIENCE HELPER K-8 (see Sources index).

BEGINNINGS offers a wide variety of activities and experiences in life and physical sciences. Students compare and group objects by color and shape, and describe objects by texture, size, odor, and sounds. They string beads, trace shapes, grow plants, sort leaves, observe animals, and pour liquids. The lessons can be used in any order and offer a comfortable hands-on introduction to science for young children.

*BEGINNINGS*. Science Curriculum Improvement Study (SCIIS/85). Thier, Herbert D.; Karplus, Robert; Lawson, Chester A.; Knott, Robert; and Montgomery, Marshall. Nashua, NH: Delta, 1986 (1979). ISBN 0-87504-400-X
Grade(s): K,1
Supplies: Kit from Delta.
Guide: $21.95, Kit: $355.00

The SCIIS/85 BEGINNINGS guide is the same as the original SCIS guide with one exception: the SCIIS/85 kit contains an aquarium and an order form to send away for living organisms. Students will be able to observe freshwater crabs, goldfish, newts, snails, and water plants.

*BEHAVIOR OF MEALWORMS*. Elementary Science Study (ESS). Nashua, NH: Delta, 1986 (1966).
Grade(s): 4,5,6,7,8
Supplies: Materials available locally, from commercial suppliers, or kit from Delta.
Guide: $8.00, Kit: $18.00, Activity Cards (35): $6.00, Readers (6): $9.50

In BEHAVIOR OF MEALWORMS, the study of larval insects provides an opportunity for children to develop skills in scientific inquiry. Unstructured observation of mealworms opens the unit, leading students to formulate questions about the biology and behavior of these organisms. In devising experiments to answer their questions, the children collect data, keep records, and come to conclusions that they can share with classmates. The guide contains extensive background information on mealworms, with instructions for their care and suggestions for further experimentation, evaluation, and classroom management.

*BIO-CRAFTS*. Outdoor Biology Instructional Strategies (OBIS). Nashua, NH: Delta, 1979, 1980.
Grade(s): 4,5,6,7,8
Supplies: Materials available locally.
Module: $18.65

Attention!; Birds Nests; Bugs, Worms and Others; Environmental Sun Prints; Food Grab; Invent an Animal; Invent a Plant; Seed Dispersal; and Web Weavers are the nine activities included in the BIO-CRAFTS module. Children create eye-catching designs, birds nests, make-believe organisms, photogram records of living and non-living objects, devices to catch prey, animals, plants, and spider webs. After design and construction are completed, the children observe the effect of these projects and similar materials in nature. They study the behaviors of the animals and plants that inhabit each environment. Each activity folio is well organized and has useful illustrations and diagrams. Background information, preparation hints, a list of materials needed, directions for the activities, and possible extensions are included in each folio.

BIRDS, BIRDS, BIRDS! provides an interdisciplinary introduction to the study of ornithology. Students participate in classroom and playground activities that encourage them to investigate the biological and behavioral characteristics of birds through observation, games and simulations, writing, and art. Ranging in appeal from kindergarten to intermediate grades, the guide contains 25 detailed lesson plans with background information and supplemental student activity sheets. There is an extensive appendix of resources and evaluation questions.

*BIRDS, BIRDS, BIRDS!* Ranger Rick's NatureScope. Washington, DC: National Wildlife Federation, 1986.
Grade(s): K,1,2,3,4,5,6,7
Supplies: Materials available locally.
Guide: $6.00

With BONES, children are encouraged to investigate similarities and differences in the skeletal structures of various animals. Students examine mystery bones, prepare and assemble skeletons, investigate the composition and properties of bones, and study the characteristics of joints. The guide contains helpful background information and suggestions for acquiring and preparing skeletons for classroom use. It is accompanied by two booklets: How to Make a Chicken Skeleton, and Bone Picture Book.

*BONES.* Elementary Science Study (ESS). St. Louis, MO: McGraw-Hill, 1968.
Grade(s): 1,2,3,4,5
Supplies: Materials available locally or from commercial suppliers.
Out of print. Available from ERIC (see Sources index).

BREAKWATERS AND BAYS consists of seven activities: Beach Zonation, Clam Hooping, Crawdad Grab, Flocking to Food, OBIS Oil Spill, Rock Pioneers, and Water Breathers. Children examine the distribution of organisms in a rocky intertidal zone, investigate the natural history of clams, and discover the currents created by aquatic animals when they move and breathe. Opportunities to build crawdad traps and artificial "beaks" are the focus of two activities. Additional experiences include using popcorn to simulate an oil spill and assess its impact on the environment, and conducting a population census of squirting clams. Each folio provides background information, a list of materials needed, preparation hints, directions for the activities, and possible extensions. The folios are easy to read and include useful illustrations and diagrams. The OBIS POND GUIDE supplements this module.

*BREAKWATERS AND BAYS.* Outdoor Biology Instructional Strategies (OBIS). Nashua, NH: Delta, 1979, 1980, 1982.
Grade(s): 4,5,6,7,8
Supplies: Materials available locally.
Module: $15.60

BRINE SHRIMP provides a simple, inexpensive way to introduce children to the study of living things and to the workings of a life cycle. Students maintain a saltwater environment in which these tiny crustaceans hatch, grow, and eventually produce offspring. Although designed for grades one and two, the unit also includes more formal experiments for third and fourth grades. Children are encouraged to observe carefully as they conduct simple activities to determine the effects of light, temperature, and salt concentrations. (Brine shrimp take about six weeks to mature, a factor teachers should consider in planning the unit.)

*BRINE SHRIMP.* Elementary Science Study (ESS). Nashua, NH: Delta, 1985.
Grade(s): 1,2,3,4
Supplies: Materials available locally or kit from Delta.
Guide: $4.50, Kit: $37.00, Activity Cards (30): $5.10, Readers (6): $9.50

In BUDDING TWIGS, children examine the structure of twigs brought into the classroom and observe the development of buds forced into leaf or bloom ahead of season. The children note external features of "bare" winter twigs: bark color and texture, leaf scars, thorns, and hairs. During development of buds, the students observe position, number, covering, and arrangement on the twig. They dissect buds and stems to reveal internal structure, and use colored water to observe water conduction in twigs. They also experiment with methods for accelerating bud development. The guide contains information on collecting, cutting, and caring for twigs. There are also drawings of common twigs and buds, and a budding sequence chart.

*BUDDING TWIGS.* Elementary Science Study (ESS). New York, NY: McGraw-Hill, 1970.
Grade(s): 4,5,6
Supplies: Materials available locally.
Out of print. Available from ERIC (see Sources index).

*BUTTERFLIES.* Elementary Science Study (ESS). New York, NY: McGraw-Hill, 1970.
Grade(s): K,1,2,3,4,5
Supplies: Materials available locally, from commercial suppliers, or kit from Delta.
Out of print. Available from ERIC (see Sources index).

BUTTERFLIES provides an opportunity for children to observe closely the life cycle and characteristics of these familiar insects. While witnessing the metamorphoses of the organisms from egg to adult, the children learn how to handle and care for them. Students are encouraged to generate their own questions about the butterflies and to seek answers through careful observation. The guide contains complete instructions on acquiring and caring for butterflies, provides information on common species and their habits, and offers advice on construction of nets and cages.

*BUZZING A HIVE.* Great Explorations in Math and Science (GEMS). Echols, Jean C. Berkeley, CA: Lawrence Hall of Science, 1987.
Grade(s): P,K,1,2
Supplies: Materials available locally, from commercial suppliers, or from Lawrence Hall of Science.
Guide: $11.00

In BUZZING A HIVE, children discover the complex social behavior, communication, and hive environment of the honeybee; the parts of a honeybee's body; and how bees adapt to the larger world. Students participate in artistic and dramatic activities, such as dramatizing the life in a beehive, performing bee dances, role-playing the pollen-gathering process, and creating a mural. The author includes suggestions for modifying this unit for preschool and kindergarten children. The plan for each of the six lessons contains an overview, time needed, a list of materials, suggestions for preparation and for setting up the room, directions for the activity, and extensions. Background information for teachers is in a separate section at the end of the guide.

*CAMPSITE.* Outdoor Biology Instructional Strategies (OBIS). Nashua, NH: Delta, 1979, 1980, 1981.
Grade(s): 4,5,6,7,8
Supplies: Materials available locally.
Module: $14.10

CAMPSITE comprises six activities: A Better Fly Trap, Ants, Jay Play, Silent Stalking, The Old White Sheet Trick, and Who Goes There? Children investigate the behavior of flies, ants, jays, night-flying insects, and other animals. Nighttime activities include using a flashlight and fluorescent bait to find evidence of animal activity, discovering the effects of light on insects, and playing a silent stalking game to explore the importance of this skill to predators and of sound detection to prey. Each activity folio provides background information, preparation hints, a list of materials needed, directions for the activities, and possible extensions. The folios are well organized and have useful illustrations and diagrams.

*THE CHESAPEAKE BAY.* Virginia Marine Science Museum. Virginia Beach, VA: Virginia Marine Science Museum, 1987.
Grade(s): 3,4
Supplies: Materials available locally.
Consult museum for price.

THE CHESAPEAKE BAY unit, though written to coincide with a trip to the Virginia Marine Science Museum, contains information and activities suitable for any class studying animal and plant life in a bay area. Background information is included about such habitats as fresh water, saltwater marshes, sandy beaches, shallow water, oyster beds, underwater structures, and open deep water. Students locate and explore the bay area and identify what lives there. The guide also has a bibliography and a list of sources of information.

*CHILD'S PLAY.* Outdoor Biology Instructional Strategies (OBIS). Nashua, NH: Delta, 1979, 1980.
Grade(s): 4,5,6,7,8
Supplies: Materials available locally.
Module: $15.60

CHILD'S PLAY consists of seven activities: Attention!, Envirolopes, Food Grab, Gaming in the Outdoors, Sound Off!, What Lives Here?, and Web Weavers. Children explore visual communication; hunt for a variety of textures, colors, odors, and evidence of organisms at a specific study site; create devices to capture prey or gather plants; go on a scavenger hunt; simulate animal sounds; observe and identify plants and animals at an aquatic site; and using string, reproduce the intricacies of different spider webs. Each guide contains background information, preparation hints, a list of materials needed, directions for the activities, and possible extensions. The folios are well organized and have useful illustrations and diagrams. The OBIS POND GUIDE supplements this module.

The COASTAL PLAIN RIVER unit was written to coincide with a field trip to the Virginia Marine Science Museum, but the activities and background information included in this guide would be helpful to any classroom teacher designing or implementing lessons about coastal or river life. This teacher's guide contains background information about amphibians, reptiles, snakes, fish, birds, and mammals; student activities, such as making dioramas and setting up a freshwater aquarium; student and teacher bibliographies; a list of learning objectives; and several worksheets of animal picture cards.

*COASTAL PLAIN RIVER CURRICULUM.* Virginia Marine Science Museum. Virginia Beach, VA: Virginia Marine Science Museum, 1987.
Grade(s): 1,2
Supplies: Materials available locally.
Consult museum for price.

The COMMUNITIES unit emphasizes the interdependent populations in any given area. Students dissect and identify parts of a seed, plant seeds in a terrarium, and learn about food chains. The children gradually add animals to their terrarium to discover plant eaters, animal eaters, and decomposers. They learn that plants are producers and animals are consumers within a given community. Finally, they look at a community where people control the environment.

*COMMUNITIES.* Science Curriculum Improvement Study (SCIS). Knott, Robert C.; Lanier, Mary Ann; Lawson, Chester A.; and Sheehan, Charlyn. Chicago, IL: Rand McNally, 1971.
Grade(s): 5
Supplies: Materials from Delta.
Out of print. Available on SCIENCE HELPER K-8 (see Sources index).

The COMMUNITIES, SCIS II unit remains essentially the same as the original version, with the addition of 16 lessons.

*COMMUNITIES.* Science Curriculum Improvement Study (SCIS II). Paldy, Lester G.; Amburgey, Leonard L.; Collea, Francis; Cooper, Richard; Maxwell, Donald E.; and Riley, Joseph W. Nashua, NH: Delta, 1986 (1970).
Grade(s): 5
Supplies: Kit from Delta.
Guide: $15.00, Kit: $360.20, Activity Cards: $17.50

This version of COMMUNITIES is basically the same as the SCIS and SCIS II guides, but it does include several additions. An appendix contains five well-constructed evaluation tools that focus on process. A supplement is added that offers a simplified format for the lessons.

*COMMUNITIES.* Science Curriculum Improvement Study (SCIIS/85). Thier, Herbert D.; Karplus, Robert; Lawson, Chester A.; Knott, Robert; and Montgomery, Marshall. Nashua, NH: Delta, 1985 (1970). ISBN 0-87504-410-7
Grade(s): 5
Supplies: Kit from Delta.
Guide: $26.95, Kit: $405.00

CONNECTIONS consists of six activity packets: Animal Families, Desert Communities, Creature Features, Winter Explorers, Magnificent Mammals, and Fresh from the Farm. Through a variety of games, puzzles, language arts, and large-motor activities, children learn that animals can be sorted according to certain characteristics, that they are adapted in special ways to their environments, and that there are many ways in which animals are important to humans. Although the packets were originally designed to enhance field trips to the zoo, their activities can be very effective in classroom study of animals. Study prints, color slides, and student activity sheets accompany informative teacher's guides.

*CONNECTIONS.* Brookfield Zoo. Brookfield, IL: Chicago Zoological Society, 1987. ISBN 0-913934-03-8
Grade(s): K,1,2,3,4
Supplies: Materials available locally.
Consult zoo for price.

*CRAYFISH*. Elementary Science Study (ESS). New York, NY: McGraw-Hill, 1969.
Grade(s): 4,5,6
Supplies: Materials available locally or from commercial suppliers.
Out of print. Available from ERIC (see Sources index).

In CRAYFISH, children conduct classroom investigations of the behavior of these freshwater crustaceans. They offer different types of food and note the animals' preference and, by making modifications to the animals' environment, discover not only which habitat the crayfish prefer but also how environment influences social structure. Opportunities for further observation and experimentation are encouraged, and background information is provided on gender differences, reproduction, and general care. The guide also suggests sources and techniques for collecting or buying crayfish and for preserving any classroom specimens that fail to survive.

*DESERT*. Outdoor Biology Instructional Strategies (OBIS). Nashua, NH: Delta, 1979, 1980.
Grade(s): 4,5,6,7,8
Supplies: Materials available locally.
Module: $17.15

The DESERT module consists of eight activities: Cactus Wheel, Cool It, Desert Hunt, Desert Water Keepers, Leapin' Lizards, Lichen Looking, Terrestrial Hi-Lo Hunt, and Water Holes to Mini-Ponds. These activities focus on habitats and the adaptations of the animals and plants within the desert, water hole, pond, and other environments. Children determine the population densities of desert plants; use the temperature variations at a specific site to try to keep a "lizard" from getting too hot or cold; design scavenger hunts; determine how different desert plants conserve water; investigate lizard feeding behavior and interactions; search for lichens; and monitor fertilized and unfertilized water holes. They locate the warmest and coolest, wettest and driest, windiest and calmest, and brightest and darkest sections of the environment and note the animals and plants within each area. Each activity folio contains background information, preparation hints, a list of needed materials, directions for the activities, and possible extensions. The folios are well organized and have useful illustrations and diagrams. The OBIS POND GUIDE supplements this module.

*DIGGING INTO DINOSAURS*. Ranger Rick's NatureScope. Washington, DC: National Wildlife Federation, 1984.
Grade(s): K,1,2,3,4,5,6,7
Supplies: Materials available locally.
Guide: $6.00

DIGGING INTO DINOSAURS introduces students and teachers to these extinct animals and the world in which they lived. Fossil evidence forms the basis for information and activities provided by the guide. In classroom and playground lessons that integrate science with mathematics, language arts, social studies, art, and physical education, students from kindergarten to the intermediate grades learn the comparative sizes of dinosaurs, how they were named, and what their lives might have been like. Background information is extensive, and the 24 detailed lesson plans are accompanied by student activity sheets. An appendix provides additional information on resources, evaluation, and current theories.

*DISCOVERING DESERTS*. Ranger Rick's NatureScope. Washington, DC: National Wildlife Federation, 1986.
Grade(s): K,1,2,3,4,5,6,7
Supplies: Materials available locally.
Guide: $6.00

DISCOVERING DESERTS introduces children to the ecology of arid lands. Students engage in interdisciplinary classroom and playground activities that explore the concepts of desert formation, conservation, and animal and human adaptation for arid climates. There are 23 carefully planned lessons, ranging from kindergarten through intermediate grades, with complete background information and supplemental student activity sheets. An appendix suggests questions for evaluation as well as additional resources.

DIVING INTO OCEANS introduces children to the physical properties of the sea, the variety of habitats from deep ocean floor to intertidal zone, and the interactions between people and the marine environment. Students conduct simulation experiments with salt water, play food web and symbiosis games, and engage in many other activities that integrate art, language arts, math, and social science with study of the ocean. The guide contains 19 well-organized lessons, with background information, student activity sheets, and an excellent resource list.

*DIVING INTO OCEANS*. Ranger Rick's NatureScope. Washington, DC: National Wildlife Federation, 1988.
Grade(s): K,1,2,3,4,5,6
Supplies: Materials available locally.
Guide: $6.00

With EARTHWORMS, children observe the developmental stages and investigate the behavioral patterns of these abundant and easy-to-care-for animals. Students design and carry out experiments to determine the kind of environment earthworms prefer: light or dark, moist or dry, warm or cool. They experiment with different soil types in the earthworms' habitat. By creating mini-environments in clear plastic tubes or boxes, they observe how worms move and what they do underground. Outdoor lessons provide an opportunity to compare classroom observation with the actual earthworm environment. Children test their classroom experiences by predicting where they will find earthworms outdoors. The guide provides information on collecting, purchasing, caring for, housing, and feeding earthworms.

*EARTHWORMS*. Elementary Science Study (ESS). Nashua, NH: Delta, 1971.
Grade(s): 4,5,6
Supplies: Materials available locally or kit from Delta.
Guide: $5.50, Kit: $41.00

In the Franklin Institute's ECOSYSTEMS unit, children construct an aquarium and a terrarium and investigate food webs, the water cycle, the oxygen-carbon dioxide cycle, and their interrelationships. Through these six activities, students reinforce the basic concepts of an ecosystem. The teacher's guide includes a motivating question, a list of materials, a step-by-step procedure, reproducible student worksheets, and possible extension activities for each lesson.

*ECOSYSTEMS*. Franklin Institute Museum-To-Go. Philadelphia, PA: Franklin Institute, 1988.
Grade(s): 4,5,6
Supplies: Materials available locally or kit from Science Kit, Inc.
Kit: $165.00

In ECOSYSTEMS, students build aquariums and terrariums; plant seeds; investigate moisture, condensation, evaporation, the water cycle, and the oxygen-carbon dioxide cycle; and then experiment with a mock chemical pollutant. The students study different organisms, such as crickets, algae, snails, and guppies, as these are introduced to, and interact with, their ecosystems.

*ECOSYSTEMS*. Science Curriculum Improvement Study (SCIS). Conard, David; Knott, Robert C.; Lanier, Mary Ann; Lawson, Chester A.; Peterson, Gordon E.; and Sheehan, Charlyn. Chicago, IL: Rand McNally, 1971.
Grade(s): 6
Supplies: Materials from Delta.
Out of print. Available on SCIENCE HELPER K-8 (see Sources index).

ECOSYSTEMS, SCIS II, is similar to the original version but expanded by 10 lessons.

*ECOSYSTEMS*. Science Curriculum Improvement Study (SCIS II). Paldy, Lester G.; Amburgey, Leonard L.; Collea, Francis; Cooper, Richard; Maxwell, Donald E.; and Riley, Joseph W. Nashua, NH: Delta, 1985 (1970). ISBN 0-8339-1602-5
Grade(s): 6
Supplies: Kit from Delta.
Guide: $15.00, Kit: $425.60, Activity Cards: $17.40

*ECOSYSTEMS.* Science Curriculum Improvement Study (SCIIS/85). Thier, Herbert D.; Karplus, Robert; Lawson, Chester A.; Knott, Robert; and Montgomery, Marshall. Nashua, NH: Delta, 1985 (1970).
Grade(s): 6
Supplies: Kit from Delta.
Guide: $18.00, Kit: $435.00

The SCIIS/85 version of ECOSYSTEMS easily adapts to a range of teaching styles and experience. It has several new lessons on types and modifications of ecosystems. Communities of plants and animals in seven distinctly different North American ecosystems are introduced, and human impacts on natural ecosystems are studied.

*EGGS & TADPOLES.* Elementary Science Study (ESS). Nashua, NH: Delta, 1985 (1969).
Grade(s): K,1,2,3,4,5,6
Supplies: Materials available locally or from commercial suppliers.
Guide: $5.50, Kit: $94.00

EGGS & TADPOLES provides the opportunity for children to examine frog eggs and observe their hatching into tadpoles and, if scheduling permits, their complete development into frogs. Children are encouraged to generate questions about the life cycle, behavior, and ecology of this amphibian; to develop their own strategies for observation and data collection in search of answers; and to discover new questions. The guide contains detailed information on collecting or purchasing eggs and on caring for the developing animal, and proper techniques for release.

*ENDANGERED SPECIES: WILD & RARE.* Ranger Rick's NatureScope. Washington, DC: National Wildlife Federation, 1987.
Grade(s): K,1,2,3,4,5,6,7
Supplies: Materials available locally.
Guide: $6.00

ENDANGERED SPECIES: WILD & RARE focuses on the process of extinction and the role of humans in destruction or conservation of plants, animals, and habitats. As they learn about the many kinds of threats facing plant and animal species, students participate in classroom and playground activities that integrate science with social studies, mathematics, language arts, drama, music, and art. There are 19 detailed lesson plans, student activity sheets, and excellent background information, as well as a useful resource guide.

*ENVIRONMENTS.* Science Activities for the Visually Impaired/Science Enrichment for Learners with Physical Handicaps (SAVI/SELPH). Berkeley, CA: Lawrence Hall of Science Center for Multisensory Learning, 1983.
Grade(s): 4,5,6,7
Supplies: Kit from Lawrence Hall of Science.
Folio Guide: $5.00, Complete Kit: $64.00, Economy Kit: $42.00

The ENVIRONMENTS module consists of four activities: Environmental Plantings, Sea What Grows, Isopods, and The Wanted Weed. Students investigate the concept of environment and learn what factors in an organism's environment make it an appropriate place in which to live. Controlled experiments test for water requirements and salt tolerance in plants, and for environmental preferences among isopods. A culminating activity takes children to the schoolyard for close observation of local weeds, their structure and habitat. The instructions contain science background, as well as helpful suggestions for creating successful learning experiences for students of varied physical abilities.

*ENVIRONMENTS.* Science Curriculum Improvement Study (SCIS). Conard, David; Knott, Robert C.; Lawson, Chester A.; and Sheehan, Charlyn. Chicago, IL: Rand McNally, 1970.
Grade(s): 4
Supplies: Materials from Delta.
Out of print. Available on SCIENCE HELPER K-8 (see Sources index).

To study ENVIRONMENTS, the students begin by designing and building their own terrariums. They then conduct experiments to determine the responses of the animals and plants to changes in such environmental factors as amount of light, heat, and moisture. The students learn about optimum range, as they record and interpret results and then use the information to plan a new and more favorable environment. An accompanying kit includes materials and class charts.

The teacher's guide for ENVIRONMENTS, SCIS II, remains the same as the original version, with the addition of lessons and changes in the types of organisms used.

*ENVIRONMENTS.* Science Curriculum Improvement Study (SCIS II). Paldy, Lester G.; Amburgey, Leonard L.; Collea, Francis; Cooper, Richard; Maxwell, Donald E.; and Riley, Joseph W. Nashua, NH: Delta, 1986 (1970).
Grade(s): 4
Supplies: Kit from Delta.
Guide: $15.00, Kit: $362.00, Activity Cards: $17.40

The teacher's guide for ENVIRONMENTS, SCIIS/85, has been revised to include a supplement prepared by teachers, reducing preparation time and providing a simplified lesson format. A lesson on "The Human Environment" has been added.

*ENVIRONMENTS.* Science Curriculum Improvement Study (SCIIS/85). Thier, Herbert D.; Karplus, Robert; Lawson, Chester A.; Knott, Robert; and Montgomery, Marshall. Nashua, NH: Delta, 1985 (1970). ISBN 0-87504-408-5
Grade(s): 4
Supplies: Kit from Delta.
Guide: $26.95, Kit: $510.00

The teacher's guide for ESTUARINE BIOLOGY includes information about the natural features of an estuary, the communities that make up an estuary, the life cycles of various estuarine organisms, the relationship of these natural systems to the economics of a specific area, and the need to protect and conserve this natural resource. The activities are written for the Chesapeake Bay area and refer to exhibits in the museum, but they may easily be adapted to the study of any water ecosystem. An excellent bibliography is part of this teacher's guide. Two other publications, SOUTHERN MARYLAND MARITIME HISTORY and THE FOSSILS OF CALVERT CLIFFS, are similar in usefulness.

*ESTUARINE BIOLOGY.* Calvert Marine Museum. Solomons, MD: Calvert Marine Museum [no date].
Grade(s): 5,6,7,8
Supplies: Materials available locally.
Guide: free

In FLOWERS AND POLLINATION, children dissect flowers to examine their structure and then investigate adaptations that enhance pollination. The guide contains a complete materials list, helpful background information, and ideas for additional activities.

*FLOWERS AND POLLINATION.* Missouri Botanical Garden (Suitcase Science). St. Louis, MO: Missouri Botanical Garden [no date].
Grade(s): 3,4,5,6
Supplies: Materials available locally or kit from Missouri Botanical Garden.
Kit: free local loan with $25.00 deposit

The FOR 8-TO-11-YEAR-OLDS module consists of nine activities: Ants; Attract a Fish; Bugs, Worms and Others; Great Streamboat Race; Invent an Animal; Isopods; Junk-in-the-Box; Plant Hunt; and Scram or Freeze. Children explore the behavior of ants, minnows, insects, isopods, animals that use people-made litter for food or shelter, and animals that live under logs and rocks. They create simulations, play games, make collections, discuss value judgments, conduct cork-steamboat races, and invent animals. Each activity folio contains background information, a list of materials needed, preparation hints, directions for the activities, and possible extensions. The folios are well organized and have useful illustrations and diagrams. The OBIS LAWN GUIDE supplements this module.

*FOR 8-TO-11-YEAR-OLDS.* Outdoor Biology Instructional Strategies (OBIS). Nashua, NH: Delta, 1979, 1980, 1981.
Grade(s): 4,5,6,7,8
Supplies: Materials available locally.
Module: $18.65

*FOR LARGE GROUPS*. Outdoor Biology Instructional Strategies (OBIS). Nashua, NH: Delta, 1979, 1980, 1981.
Grade(s): 4,5,6,7,8
Supplies: Materials available locally.
Module: $15.60

The FOR LARGE GROUPS module consists of six activities: Acorns, Food Chain Game, Invent an Animal, Population Game, Silent Stalking, and Sound Off! All of these activities use a game or simulation format for instruction. Children play a survival game and study the winter food storage strategies of squirrels; investigate food chains by assuming the roles of animals within a food chain; and participate in a feeding game to find out how many deer can survive in a herd's environment. They explore the importance of silent stalking skills to predators and the necessity of sound detection to prey, and they communicate secretly to partners, using animal sounds. Each activity folio contains background information, a list of materials, preparation hints, directions for the activities, and possible extensions. The folios are well organized and have useful illustrations and diagrams.

*FOR SMALL GROUPS & FAMILIES*. Outdoor Biology Instructional Strategies (OBIS). Nashua, NH: Delta, 1979, 1980, 1981.
Grade(s): 4,5,6,7,8
Supplies: Materials available locally.
Module: $17.15

The FOR SMALL GROUPS & FAMILIES module consists of eight activity folios: A Better Fly Trap, Ants, Attract a Fish, Birdfeeder, Damsels and Dragons, Great Streamboat Race, Leaf Living, and Leapin' Lizards. Small groups use a "lizard rig" to investigate the feeding behavior and interactions of lizards. They hide and attempt to navigate in a pile of leaves to experience the environment of certain animals, conduct cork-boat races to discover the rate and direction of currents in a stream, and present flying decoys to damselflies and dragonflies to study perching behavior. They construct a bird feeder to observe bird behavior, fish with a variety of baits and lures to explore the behavior of minnows, and build fly traps to investigate the behavior of flies. Each folio contains background information, a list of needed materials, hints for lesson preparation, directions for the activities, and possible extensions. The folios are well organized and have useful illustrations and diagrams. The OBIS LAWN GUIDE supplements this module.

*FOREST*. Outdoor Biology Instructional Strategies (OBIS). Nashua, NH: Delta, 1980, 1981, 1982.
Grade(s): 4,5,6,7,8
Supplies: Materials available locally.
Module: $15.60

The FOREST module contains seven activity folios: Jay Play, Leaf Living, Lichen Looking, Litter Critters, Logs to Soil, Sawing Away, and Tree Tally. Children learn about animals that live in a pile of leaves, in the ground, and on or in rotten logs. They look for the most common trees in an area and observe fallen logs to count tree rings and study patterns of growth. Additional activities include observing the habitats, shapes, and colors of lichens and discovering the food-color preference of jays and then altering the taste of favored food to see if food-gathering behavior changes. Each activity folio contains background information, a list of needed materials, preparation hints, directions for the activities, and possible extensions. The folios are well organized and have useful illustrations and diagrams.

*GAMES AND SIMULATIONS*. Outdoor Biology Instructional Strategies (OBIS). Nashua, NH: Delta, 1979, 1980.
Grade(s): 4,5,6,7,8
Supplies: Materials available locally.
Module: $15.60

The GAMES AND SIMULATIONS module consists of seven activities: Cool It, Flower Powder, Follow the Scent, Food Chain Game, Population Game, Sticklers, and Variation Game. By playing simple games or enacting simulations, children try to keep a "thermometer lizard" from overheating or getting too cold, use artificial bees and flower models to investigate pollination, discover one way animals use their sense of smell, and assume the roles of animals in a food chain. They find out how many deer can survive in a herd's home range, learn about habitat and distribution of organisms, and identify differences among individuals. Each activity folio provides background information, a list of materials, preparation hints, directions for the investigations, and possible extensions. The folios are easy to read and include useful illustrations and diagrams.

GROW LAB gives children the opportunity to participate in the planning and cultivation of a classroom garden. Students design a garden, examine seeds, then plant them and observe their growth and life cycles. The guide contains excellent background information on caring for classroom gardens, constructing light frames, and involving parents and community. There are complete instructions for all activities and a list of helpful resources.

*GROW LAB: A COMPLETE GUIDE TO GARDENING IN THE CLASSROOM.* National Gardening Association. Pranis, Eve, and Hale, Jack. Burlington, VT: National Gardening Association, 1988.
ISBN 0-915873-31-1
Grade(s): K,1,2,3,4,5,6
Supplies: Materials available locally or Grow Lab Garden from National Gardening Association.

THE GROWING CLASSROOM encourages teachers and children to use classroom gardening as a focus for activities that integrate life, earth, and physical sciences. Students design classroom gardens, plant seeds, and study the growth and life cycles of their developing plants, applying what they learn to problems in, and discussions of, ecology and conservation. The guide contains a bibliography, background information for teachers, and a list of recommended materials. Although designed for use in grades 2-6, the lessons can be adapted for younger and older children.

*THE GROWING CLASSROOM.* Appel, Gary; Cadoux, Margaret; Glick, Lisa; and Jaffe, Roberta. Capitola, CA: Life Lab Science Program, 1985.
Grade(s): K,1,2,3,4,5,6,7,8
Supplies: Materials available locally or from Let's Get Growing.
Consult Life Lab for new price.

Each USMES unit is based on a challenge that presents a school or community problem to be solved by the children. The GROWING PLANTS challenge: Grow plants for... [whatever the children decide, such as, for gifts, for transplanting into a garden, for selling]. The children's interest in growing plants leads to experimenting with plants under special conditions or transplanting plants into gardens or parks. The teacher's guide includes a range of possible activities; however, no specific lesson plans are provided. A list of questions is included to stimulate further investigation or analysis.

*GROWING PLANTS.* Unified Science and Mathematics for Elementary Schools (USMES). Newton, MA: Education Development Center, Inc., 1975.
Grade(s): 2,3,4,5,6
Supplies: Materials available locally.
Out of print. Available from ERIC (see Sources index).

GROWING SEEDS enables children not only to observe the life cycles of plants but also to engage in such scientific processes as classification, measurement, prediction, and experimentation. They begin by examining a collection of small items and establishing criteria for determining which of the objects are, in fact, seeds. They then sort, plant, and observe growth of these "seeds," collecting and sharing data with their classmates. The guide contains suggestions for classroom management, as well as a list of seeds and nonseeds that have been used effectively.

*GROWING SEEDS.* Elementary Science Study (ESS). Nashua, NH: Delta, 1986 (1967).
Grade(s): K,1,2,3
Supplies: Materials available locally or kit from Delta.
Guide: $6.20, Kit: $31.00, Activity Cards (23): $5.10, Readers (6): $9.50

The HABITATS unit consists of hands-on activities that may either accompany a trip to Marine World or be done as independent class projects. The guide also contains animal flash cards, suggestions for enrichment, a glossary, and a bibliography.

*HABITATS.* Marine World Africa USA. Vallejo, CA: Marine World Africa USA [no date].
Grade(s): K,1,2,3,4,5,6,7,8,9,10,11,12
Supplies: Materials available locally.
Guide: $1.50

*HAVE YOU BEEN TO THE SHORE BEFORE?* Northern New England Marine Education Project. Orono, ME: Northern New England Marine Education Project, University of Maine, 1980.
Grade(s): 6,7,8,9
Supplies: Materials available locally or from commercial suppliers.
Consult University of Maine for price.

HAVE YOU BEEN TO THE SHORE BEFORE? contains eight activities that introduce the complex interactions of life at the sea's edge. Students conduct ecological investigations of a classroom aquarium, then explore the coastal environment through field experiences. Extensive background information, a resource list, an annotated bibliography, and detailed field trip advice accompany the unit. Although the lessons are written for the North Atlantic coast, they can easily be adapted for other tidal areas.

*HIDE A BUTTERFLY.* Great Explorations in Math and Science (GEMS). Echols, Jean C. Berkeley, CA: Lawrence Hall of Science, 1986.
Grade(s): P,K,1,2,3
Supplies: Materials available locally, from commercial suppliers, or from Lawrence Hall of Science.
Guide: $6.50

In HIDE A BUTTERFLY, children learn about protective coloration and the behavior of birds and butterflies. Students make a mural, create butterfly and bird puppets, and perform a play, while coming to an understanding of how animals and insects adapt to their environments. The author has included special instructions for using this unit with younger preschool children and with children in grades 1, 2, and 3. The plan for each of the three lessons contains an overview, background information, time needed, a list of materials, step-by-step directions for preparation and for setting up the room, procedures for the activity, and extensions.

*HUMAN IMPACT.* Outdoor Biology Instructional Strategies (OBIS). Nashua, NH: Delta, 1980, 1981, 1982.
Grade(s): 4,5,6,7,8
Supplies: Materials available locally.
Module: $15.60

The HUMAN IMPACT module consists of seven activities: Can Fishing, Junk-in-the-Box, OBIS Oil Spill, Out of Control, Plants Around a Building, Too Many Mosquitoes, and Trail Impact Study. Children investigate how people and events affect the environment. They discover the kinds of animals that live in and on submerged cans and people-made litter, use popcorn to simulate an oil spill, observe the changes in a lawn released from human control, and investigate how the environment around a building affects the growth of plants. The students learn about biological control by identifying predators that eat mosquito larvae, and they lay out the course of a footpath that has the least impact on the study site. Each activity folio provides background information, preparation hints, a list of needed materials, directions for the activities, and possible extensions. The folios are well organized, with useful illustrations and diagrams. The OBIS LAWN GUIDE supplements this module.

*INCREDIBLE INSECTS.* Ranger Rick's NatureScope. Washington, DC: National Wildlife Federation, 1986.
Grade(s): K,1,2,3,4,5,6,7
Supplies: Materials available locally.
Guide: $6.00

INCREDIBLE INSECTS provides an introduction to the biology and behavior of these diverse and multitudinous organisms. Activities range from kindergarten to intermediate grades, integrating science with language arts, mathematics, social studies, physical education, and art. Through simulations, games, classroom experiments, and playground activities, children investigate the characteristics of insects and learn about their interactions with humans. The guide contains extensive background information for teachers, with student activity sheets and 34 well-organized lesson plans. An appendix provides additional information on evaluation, resources, and construction of useful equipment.

*INCREDIBLE INSECTS (Discovery Pac).* Ranger Rick's NatureScope. Washington, DC: National Wildlife Federation, 1988.
Grade(s): K,1,2,3,4,5,6,7
Supplies: Materials available locally.
Discovery Pac: $10.95

The Discovery Pac to accompany INCREDIBLE INSECTS contains many activities that supplement the lessons in the original volume. Children engage in community investigations, visit discovery stations to learn about various species, study insect adaptations, and read fiction or biographies about insects and the people who interact with them. The guide is well organized and is accompanied by a packet of color photographs for study.

In the INSECTS AND OTHER CRAWLERS unit, children investigate beetles, ants, ladybugs, butterflies, moths, and grasshoppers. They explore how these insects move, eat, and adapt to their environments. Students make homes for their bugs and construct an ant farm. They examine spiderwebs, wasps nests, and beehives; listen to insect sounds; and observe and compare many other aspects of insects and other crawlers. Each of the 28 activities includes a learning objective, process skills, a list of materials, suggested questions, directions for the exploration, and extensions.

*INSECTS AND OTHER CRAWLERS (Windows on Science series).* Westly, Joan. Sunnyvale, CA: Creative Publications, 1988. ISBN 0-88488-706-5
Grade(s): K,1,2
Supplies: Materials available locally, commercial suppliers, or kit from Creative Publications.
Guide: $8.25, Complete Kit for Windows on Science series: $250.00

The LAWN AND FIELDS module comprises nine activities: Animal Diversity, Animals in a Grassland, Hopper Herding, Mystery Marauders, Plant Hunt, Roots and Shoots, Silent Stalking, Web It, and Web Weavers. Children investigate the variety of animals that live in a managed lawn and a weedy area, count and identify the different kinds of insects discovered, and determine which of these are plant eaters. They simulate stalking skills, observe the behavior of spiders, and replicate the intricacies of their webs. The students determine the species of plants that grow in a particular study site and identify "mystery plants." Each activity folio provides background information, a list of needed materials, preparation hints, directions for the activity, and possible extensions. The folios are well organized with useful illustrations and diagrams. The OBIS LAWN GUIDE supplements this module.

*LAWNS AND FIELDS.* Outdoor Biology Instructional Strategies (OBIS). Nashua, NH: Delta, 1980, 1981, 1982.
Grade(s): 4,5,6,7,8
Supplies: Materials available locally.
Module: $18.65

LET'S HEAR IT FOR HERPS! is an interdisciplinary approach to the study of reptiles and amphibians, their characteristics, life cycles, and interactions with humans. Students engage in classroom and playground experiments, games, and simulations that introduce the variety of reptiles and amphibians and their adaptations for survival. They investigate the history of these animals and explore scenarios for the future, including problems of predation, overhunting, and habitat destruction. There are 20 lessons, accompanied by excellent background information, student activity sheets, and a detailed resource guide.

*LET'S HEAR IT FOR HERPS!* Ranger Rick's NatureScope. Washington, DC: National Wildlife Federation, 1987.
Grade(s): K,1,2,3,4,5,6,7
Supplies: Materials available locally.
Guide: $6.00

In LIFE CYCLES, students start by searching for seeds in various fruits and vegetables. Seeds are planted, and their germination is observed. As the plants reach maturity, produce flowers, and form a new generation of seeds, children study and record growth and development. They observe life cycles and metamorphosis of animals, such as fruit flies, frogs, and mealworms. Finally, students investigate the concept of biotic potential, the normal production of offspring occurring without any deaths.

*LIFE CYCLES.* Science Curriculum Improvement Study (SCIS). Conard, David; Fletcher, Sandra; and Lawson, Chester A. Chicago, IL: Rand McNally, 1970.
Grade(s): 2
Supplies: Materials from Delta.
Out of print. Available on SCIENCE HELPER K-8 (see Sources index).

Frogs have been replaced by butterflies in SCIS II LIFE CYCLES. Also, duplicating masters for plant and animal growth data are included, to aid record keeping for both students and teachers.

*LIFE CYCLES.* Science Curriculum Improvement Study (SCIS II). Paldy, Lester G.; Amburgey, Leonard L.; Collea, Francis; Cooper, Richard; Maxwell, Donald E.; and Riley, Joseph W. Nashua, NH: Delta, 1986 (1970).
Grade(s): 2
Supplies: Kit from Delta.
Guide: $15.00, Kit: $351.00, Activity Cards: $17.40

*LIFE CYCLES*. Science Curriculum Improvement Study (SCIIS/85). Thier, Herbert D.; Karplus, Robert; Knott, Robert; Lawson, Chester A.; and Montgomery, Marshall. Nashua, NH: Delta, 1985.
ISBN 0-87504-404-2
Grade(s): 2
Supplies: Kit from Delta.
Guide: $24.95, Kit: $435.00

The SCIIS/85 LIFE CYCLES guide differs from the SCIS and SCIS II guides on the same topic. Classification of plants and animals has become an introductory activity, and several valuable appendices provide strategies for teaching and evaluating hands-on science. A supplement offers teachers a simplified format that reduces preparation time, but because it lacks background information, it cannot be used in place of the basic materials.

*THE LIFE OF BEANS AND PEAS*. Elementary Science Study (ESS). New York, NY: McGraw-Hill, 1969.
Grade(s): 1,2,3,4
Supplies: Materials available locally. Out of print. Available from ERIC (see Sources index).

THE LIFE OF BEANS AND PEAS offers children the opportunity to observe the life cycle of plants from seed to second generation. Quick-growing, hardy legume seeds are examined, sprouted, and planted, and their growth is monitored. Following the appearance of flowers and the production of seed pods, the children harvest their crop, using some of the seeds for eating and others for further planting. Children can use data from the first generation to make predictions about the second, comparing the life cycle and growth rates. The guide suggests grocery store sources for seeds of various kinds and contains helpful information concerning classroom plant care.

*LIVING IN WATER*. National Aquarium in Baltimore. Chase, Valerie; Aspinwall, Karen; Campbell, Lee Anne; Nichols, Martha; and Tillett, Martin. Baltimore, MD: National Aquarium in Baltimore, 1987.
Grade(s): 4,5,6
Supplies: Materials available locally or from commercial suppliers.
Guide: $4.00

LIVING IN WATER consists of 36 activities exploring the nature of the aquatic environment and the relationships among organisms that live there. Children investigate the physical properties of fresh and salt water and conduct observations and experiments to determine the impact of these properties on the biological and behavioral adaptations of aquatic animals and plants. They examine predator-prey relationships, and they research the role of humans in maintaining the balance and quality of life in aquatic environments. Each lesson is presented in both narrative and outline form for ease of use by teachers of diverse interests or needs. A detailed materials list, a directory of resources, extensive background information, and student activity sheets are included.

*MAKING DO WITH PLANTS*. Missouri Botanical Garden (Suitcase Science). St. Louis, MO: Missouri Botanical Garden [no date].
Grade(s): 2,3
Supplies: Materials available locally or kit from Missouri Botanical Garden.
Kit: free local loan with $25.00 deposit

MAKING DO WITH PLANTS offers investigations of the many uses of plants. Children create crafts from plant materials, make natural dyes, and learn of medicinal value of some plants. They study Native American plant lore as well. The guide contains a great deal of helpful background information and a complete materials list. Although it was written to accompany a kit, it can be used independently with locally obtained materials.

*MAPPING ANIMAL MOVEMENTS*. Great Explorations in Math and Science (GEMS). Barrett, Katharine. Berkeley, CA: Lawrence Hall of Science, 1987.
Grade(s): 5,6,7
Supplies: Materials available locally, from commercial suppliers, or from Lawrence Hall of Science.
Guide: $6.50

In MAPPING ANIMAL MOVEMENTS, students carry out hands-on experiences with animals and learn research techniques used by biologists to study animal behavior. Children practice a sampling system, using the classroom as a habitat. They then use this skill to observe, track, map, graph, and identify patterns in the movements of a variety of animals, such as crickets and hamsters. The guide includes easy-to-follow lesson plans for each activity, suggestions for the care and handling of animals, and reproducible student data sheets.

In MAPPING FISH HABITATS, students set up a fish tank, map fish movements, identify the home range, and brainstorm ideas for experimentation and monitoring fish movements. The guide includes useful information about setting up an aquarium and interesting fish facts, as well as specific lesson plans for each activity.

*MAPPING FISH HABITATS*. Great Explorations in Math and Science (GEMS). Barrett, Katharine, and Sneider, Cary. Berkeley, CA: Lawrence Hall of Science, 1987.
Grade(s): 5,6,7,8
Supplies: Materials available locally, from commercial suppliers, or from Lawrence Hall of Science.
Guide: $7.50

MICROGARDENING introduces children to the nature of molds and how they grow. Children learn about sterile procedures and conduct experiments with common materials to discover where molds come from, influences on their growth rates, and how they can be used. The guide contains substantial background information, as well as thorough instructions for preparing and completing experiments.

*MICROGARDENING, AN INTRODUCTION TO THE WORLD OF MOLD*. Elementary Science Study (ESS). Nashua, NH: Delta, 1985 (1968).
Grade(s): 4,5,6
Supplies: From commercial suppliers or kit from Delta.
Guide: $24.30, Kit: $66.00

In MINIBEASTS: STAGES 1 AND 2, a comprehensive plan is presented for the location, capture, care, and study of land and water invertebrates. Children observe with a keen eye, then record and discuss the characteristics of the creatures that are collected. Investigations are designed to help students learn how these small animals move, eat, and reproduce, and why they behave in certain idiosyncratic ways. Strategies are presented to help keep the creatures alive so that observations can be made at all stages of their development. The guide includes an identification chart, as well as suggestions for constructing appropriate habitats.

*MINIBEASTS: STAGES 1 AND 2*. Science 5/13. Parker, Sheila. London, England: Macdonald, 1973.
ISBN 0-356-04106-9
Grade(s): K,1,2,3,4,5,6,7
Supplies: Materials available locally or from commercial suppliers.
Guide: $9.00 (Available in the U.S. from Teacher's Laboratory.)

MOSQUITOES introduces children to the life cycle of these abundant and much maligned, but fascinating, insects. Students construct miniature habitats in which mosquito eggs hatch and larvae develop. Using background information from the guide, they study the biology and behavior of the adult insects. The guide contains instructions for care and handling of mosquitoes and ideas for experimentation.

*MOSQUITOES: A RESOURCE BOOK FOR THE CLASSROOM*. Elementary Science Study (ESS). New York, NY: McGraw-Hill, 1971.
Grade(s): 4,5,6,7,8
Supplies: Materials from commercial suppliers.
Out of print. Available from ERIC (see Sources index).

The NEIGHBORHOOD WOODS module consists of eight activities: Bird Nests, Creepers and Climbers, Lichen Looking, Mystery Marauders, Sensory Hi-Lo Hunt, Shake It!, Snug as a Bug, and Swell Homes. Children design bird nests, place them at a site, and try to locate and identify one another's nests. They look at the structure and climbing patterns of vines; learn about the habitat, shapes, and colors of lichens; identify plant eaters; and find extremes of environmental variables. Students construct homes for imaginary insects; retrieve insects from different trees, plants, and shrubs; and compare simulated and natural environments. Each activity folio provides background information, preparation hints, a list of materials, directions for the activities, and possible extensions. The folios are well organized and have useful illustrations and diagrams.

*NEIGHBORHOOD WOODS*. Outdoor Biology Instructional Strategies (OBIS). Nashua, NH: Delta, 1980, 1982.
Grade(s): 4,5,6,7,8
Supplies: Materials available locally.
Module: $17.15

*NIGHTTIME.* Outdoor Biology Instructional Strategies (OBIS). Nashua, NH: Delta, 1980, 1981.
Grade(s): 4,5,6,7,8
Supplies: Materials available locally.
Module: $15.60

The NIGHTTIME module consists of seven activities: Night Eyes, Night Shine, Silent Stalking, Sound Off, The Old White Sheet Trick, Web It, and Who Goes There? Children explore mysterious eyes, aquatic animals, the stalking skills of predators, animal sounds, night-flying insects, and animals active at night. There are many activities on how light affects the behavior of organisms. Each activity folio provides background information, a list of needed materials, preparation hints, directions for the activities, and possible extensions. The folios are well organized with useful illustrations and diagrams. The OBIS POND GUIDE supplements this module.

*OBIS LAWN GUIDE.* Outdoor Biology Instructional Strategies (OBIS). Falk, John. Nashua, NH: Delta, 1980.
Guide: $2.30

The OBIS LAWN GUIDE helps teachers identify some of the most common organisms found in and around lawns, fields, pastures, vegetable or flower gardens, and vacant lots. Plants and animals that may be seen by the naked eye or simple magnification are included. The plant section is in two parts: grass and nongrass. Animals are in three groups: small flying animals, small crawling and hopping animals, and big animals. The text provides a useful introduction to organisms of lawn and field, and its illustrations are realistic. The OBIS LAWN GUIDE is useful with the following modules: ANIMAL BEHAVIOR, FOR 8-TO-11-YEAR-OLDS, FOR SMALL GROUPS & FAMILIES, HUMAN IMPACT, and PAVEMENT AND PARKS.

*OBIS POND GUIDE.* Outdoor Biology Instructional Strategies (OBIS). Buller, Dave. Nashua, NH: Delta, 1980.
Guide: $3.00

The OBIS POND GUIDE helps teachers identify animal and plant life in ponds and other aquatic sites. Only those organisms have been included that may be seen with the naked eye or with simple magnification. The guide divides the animal kingdom into invertebrates and vertebrates, with each group organized by phylum or class. Common, rather than scientific names, have been used. The plant section is organized by growing area—shore, emergent, floating, and submerged. The text provides a useful introduction to pond life, and the illustrations are realistic. This guide is useful with the following OBIS modules: ADAPTATIONS, AQUATIC ANIMAL BEHAVIOR, BACKYARD, BREAKWATERS AND BAYS, CHILD'S PLAY, DESERT, NIGHTTIME, OUTDOOR STUDY TECHNIQUES, PONDS AND LAKES, SEASHORE, and STREAMS AND RIVERS.

*OBIS SAMPLER.* Outdoor Biology Instructional Strategies (OBIS). Nashua, NH: Delta, 1979.
Grade(s): 4,5,6,7,8
Supplies: Materials available locally.
Module: $11.00

The OBIS SAMPLER module includes four activities: Food Chain Game, Seed Dispersal, Sticklers, and Water Breathers. Children role-play animals in a food chain, disperse seeds, investigate where organisms live, and discover the currents created by aquatic animals when they move and breathe. Each folio provides background information, a list of materials needed, preparation hints, step-by-step directions for the activities, and possible extensions. The folios are easy to read and include useful illustrations and diagrams.

*ORGANISMS.* Science Curriculum Improvement Study (SCIS). Fletcher, Sandra; Lawson, Chester A.; and Rawitscher-Kunkel, Erika. Chicago, IL: Rand McNally, 1970.
Grade(s): 1
Supplies: Materials from Delta.
Out of print. Available on SCIENCE HELPER K-8 (see Sources index).

In ORGANISMS, students describe different seeds, germinate the seeds, and grow plants. They set up an aquarium with guppies, snails, and water plants, in order to observe and discuss birth, growth, and death of organisms. Detritus, the decaying matter in the aquarium, offers another learning opportunity as it is used to fertilize plants. Students then explore the schoolyard or nearby parks to learn firsthand about natural habitats.

The SCIS II version of ORGANISMS differs from the original by the addition of 13 lessons.

*ORGANISMS*. Science Curriculum Improvement Study (SCIS II). Paldy, Lester G.; Amburgey, Leonard L.; Collea, Francis; Cooper, Richard; Maxwell, Donald E.; and Riley, Joseph W. Cambridge, MA: American Science and Engineering (AS&E), 1978 (1970).
ISBN 0-8339-1102-3
Grade(s): 1
Supplies: Kit from Delta.
Guide: $12.25, Kit: $294.70, Activity Cards: $17.40

The SCIIS/85 Teacher's Guide offers a revised format that simplifies the use of the ORGANISMS unit. The addition of several appendices offers teachers five evaluation activities and a helpful discussion of attitudes in science.

*ORGANISMS*. Science Curriculum Improvement Study (SCIIS/85). Lawson, Chester A.; Knott, Robert; Karplus, Robert; Thier, Herbert D.; and Montgomery, Marshall. Nashua, NH: Delta, 1985 (1970). ISBN 0-87504-402-6
Grade(s): 1
Supplies: Kit from Delta.
Guide: $24.95, Kit: $325.00

OUR WONDERFUL WORLD: SOLUTIONS FOR MATH + SCIENCE contains 19 sequenced investigations in environmental studies, covering the following topics: air, water, water transport, soil, plants, animals, and insects. The students engage in such activities as analyzing the volume of snow, comparing habitats, exploring natural selection and camouflage, and testing clothes as insulators. Each investigation contains a specific lesson plan, including materials and time needed, background information, procedures, discussion questions, and extensions. Several reproducible student pages are provided with each investigation.

*OUR WONDERFUL WORLD: SOLUTIONS FOR MATH + SCIENCE*. Activities to Integrate Mathematics and Science (AIMS). Beakes, Norris; Beck, Janet; Deruiter, Henry Richard; Dewey, John; and Freeman, Thomas L. Fresno, CA: AIMS, 1986.
Grade(s): 5,6,7,8
Supplies: Materials available locally.
Guide: $10.95

The OUTDOOR STUDY TECHNIQUES module includes ten activities: Bean Bugs, Fly a Leaf, How Many Organisms Live Here?, Mapping a Study Site, Moisture Makers, Pigment Puzzles, Plant Patterns, Shake It!, Water Snails, and Who Goes There? Children take a census of a population of organisms too numerous to count. They fly and race leaves to determine which catch more wind, estimate the number of organisms living in a small pond sample, map a study site, test different leaves for moisture content, and explore leaf and flower colors using chromatography. They investigate the insect population of trees, plants, and shrubs; discover snails' preferred habitats; and find evidence of animals active at night. Each activity folio provides background information, a list of needed materials, preparation hints, directions for the activities, and possible extensions. The folios are well organized and have useful illustrations and diagrams. The OBIS POND GUIDE supplements this unit.

*OUTDOOR STUDY TECHNIQUES*. Outdoor Biology Instructional Strategies (OBIS). Nashua, NH: Delta, 1980, 1981, 1982.
Grade(s): 4,5,6,7,8
Supplies: Materials available locally.
Module: $20.20

*PAVEMENT AND PARKS*. Outdoor Biology Instructional Strategies (OBIS). Nashua, NH: Delta, 1980.
Grade(s): 4,5,6,7,8
Supplies: Materials available locally.
Module: $17.15

The PAVEMENT AND PARKS module consists of eight activities: Ants, Envirolopes, Environmental Sun Prints, For the Birds, Junk-in-the-Box, Plant Hunt, Plants Around a Building, and Sound Off! In this series of activities, children explore the urban environment to locate a variety of organisms, examine their behaviors and habitats, and record information in usable and creative ways. Students observe birds, ants, animals that live in people-made litter, and plants in a variety of settings. Each activity folio provides background information, a list of needed materials, preparation hints, directions for activities, and possible extensions. The folios are easy to understand and have useful illustrations and diagrams. The OBIS LAWN GUIDE supplements this module.

*PEOPLE AND THE SEA*. Virginia Marine Science Museum. Virginia Beach, VA: Virginia Marine Science Museum, 1987.
Grade(s): 5,6
Supplies: Materials available locally.
Consult museum for price.

The PEOPLE AND THE SEA unit was written to accompany a field trip to the Virginia Marine Science Museum but contains information and activities that would be useful to any classroom teacher designing or implementing lessons about fishing. The guide includes background information about the fishing habits of the Indians and the English colonists, commercial fin fishing, commercial shellfishing, and sportfishing; activities, such as identifying the uses of the sea and its resources and writing original fish stories; student and teacher bibliographies; a list of sources; learning objectives; and several student worksheets.

*POND WATER*. Elementary Science Study (ESS). New York, NY: McGraw-Hill, 1969.
Grade(s): 3,4,5,6
Supplies: Materials available locally.
Out of print. Available from ERIC (see Sources index).

POND WATER introduces children to the wide variety of life in a pond. By using hand lenses and microscopes, children discover that pond water is teeming with tiny living creatures whose behavior can be observed easily. The guide contains complete information on collecting pond water, with suggestions for observations and experiments. Accompanying activity cards provide detailed instructions for building and maintaining an aquarium, for preparing slides, and for recognizing and caring for pond organisms.

*PONDS AND LAKES*. Outdoor Biology Instructional Strategies (OBIS). Nashua, NH: Delta, 1979, 1980, 1981.
Grade(s): 4,5,6,7,8
Supplies: Materials available locally.
Module: $17.15

The PONDS AND LAKES module consists of eight activities: Animal Movement in Water, Attract a Fish, Can Fishing, Habitats of the Pond, Too Many Mosquitoes, Water Breathers, Water Holes to Mini-Ponds, and What Lives Here? Children observe and identify plants and animals that live in ponds, lakes, and water holes. They study animal behavior and how changes in the environment affect the lives of these organisms. Specific investigations include using a variety of baits and lures to attract minnows, monitoring life at a water hole or pond over a period of eight-to-ten weeks, and finding predators that eat mosquito larvae. Each activity folio provides background information, preparation hints, a list of materials, directions for the activities, and possible extensions. The folios are well organized and have useful illustrations and diagrams. The OBIS POND GUIDE supplements this unit.

*POPULATIONS*. Science Curriculum Improvement Study (SCIS). Conard, David; Knott, Robert C.; Lanier, Mary Ann; and Lawson, Chester A. Chicago, IL: Rand McNally, 1972.
Grade(s): 3
Supplies: Materials from Delta.
Out of print. Available on SCIENCE HELPER K-8 (see Sources index).

While studying the POPULATIONS unit, students construct aquariums and terrariums and chart increases or decreases in population by tracking the numbers of daphnia and aphids over a two-week period of time. The pupils study and experiment with these populations to learn about food chains, relationships between predators and prey, plant eaters, and animal eaters. This investigation of interdependent populations leads students to a definition of "community."

The SCIS II version of POPULATIONS differs from the original by the addition of nine lessons.

*POPULATIONS*. Science Curriculum Improvement Study (SCIS II). Paldy, Lester G.; Amburgey, Leonard L.; Collea, Francis; Cooper, Richard; Maxwell, Donald E.; and Riley, Joseph W. Cambridge, MA: American Science and Engineering (AS&E), 1978 (1970).
ISBN 0-8339-1302-6
Grade(s): 3
Supplies: Kit from Delta.
Guide: $15.00, Kit: $357.00, Activity Cards: $17.40

The teacher's guide for SCIIS/85 POPULATIONS is very similar to SCIS and SCIS II with a few additions. Several appendices offer evaluation activities and a helpful discussion of attitudes in science. A supplement provides a simplified format that reduces preparation time, but since it lacks background information it cannot be used alone.

*POPULATIONS*. Science Curriculum Improvement Study (SCIIS/85). Thier, Herbert D.; Karplus, Robert; Lawson, Chester A.; Knott, Robert; and Montgomery, Marshall. Nashua, NH: Delta, 1978 (1970). ISBN 0-87504-406-9
Grade(s): 3
Supplies: Kit from Delta.
Guide: $26.95, Kit: $395.00

PROJECT SEASONS introduces elementary students to cycles in nature, demonstrating the interconnectedness of living things with their environments. Children engage in classroom and playground activities that integrate language arts, math, science, and social studies, as they investigate the natural phenomena of the changing seasons. The guide contains 82 well-planned lessons arranged by season and grade level and accompanied by supplementary information and ideas for extensions.

*PROJECT SEASONS: SEASONAL TEACHING IDEAS K-6*. The Stewardship Institute. Shelburne, VT: The Stewardship Institute, 1986.
Grade(s): K,1,2,3,4,5,6
Supplies: Materials available locally.
Guide: $29.95

The PROJECT WILD AQUATIC EDUCATION ACTIVITY GUIDE consists of 40 activities that explore the world of water. Children investigate life in aquatic habitats from classroom aquariums to nearby puddles, ponds, or streams. Integrating science with language arts, social studies, and math, the children engage in games, crafts, and experiments that demonstrate the complex connections between aquatic organisms and the environments that support them. Detailed lesson plans are accompanied by excellent background information, suggestions for classroom management, and ideas for evaluation and extension. Indices and appendices are exhaustive.

*PROJECT WILD AQUATIC EDUCATION ACTIVITY GUIDE*. Project WILD. Boulder, CO: Project WILD, 1987.
Grade(s): K,1,2,3,4,5,6,7,8
Supplies: Materials available locally.
Free with workshop

The PROJECT WILD ELEMENTARY ACTIVITY GUIDE contains 81 lessons that investigate the biology, behavior, and ecology of animals. Classroom and outdoor activities integrate science with language arts, mathematics, and social studies, as children engage in observations, experiments, crafts, and games that demonstrate the complex relationship between animals and their environment. The lessons are very well planned, with helpful background information, advice on classroom management, ideas for extension and evaluation, and suggested resources. Indices and appendices are exhaustive.

*PROJECT WILD ELEMENTARY ACTIVITY GUIDE*. Project WILD. Sacramento, CA: Project WILD, 1983, 1985, 1986.
Grade(s): K,1,2,3,4,5,6,7,8
Supplies: Materials available locally.
Free with workshop

*RAINFORESTS*. Marine World Africa USA. Vallejo, CA: Marine World [no date].
Grade(s): K,1,2,3,4,5,6,7,8,9,10,11,12
Supplies: Materials available locally.
Guide: $1.50

The RAINFORESTS teacher's guide includes activity sheets, flash cards, and hands-on investigations. Background information, directions for activities, and conservation tips are given for each grade level. Children make bird feeders, play games, and role-play to decide the fate of an area at the edge of a lush rainforest where planning is under way for construction of a paved road. A glossary and a list of conservation organizations are provided.

*SCHOOL ZOO*. Unified Science and Mathematics for Elementary Schools (USMES). Newton, MA: Education Development Center, Inc., 1975.
Grade(s): K,1,2,3,4,5,6,7
Supplies: Materials available locally.
Out of print. Available from ERIC (see Sources index).

Each USMES unit is based on a challenge that presents a school or community problem to be solved by the children. The SCHOOL ZOO challenge: Find ways to collect and maintain a variety of animals in the classroom or school area as a learning resource. Children are involved in all aspects of maintaining and displaying animals. They devise means of conveying information to other people about the care and keeping of animals. The teacher's guide includes a range of possible unit activities; however, no specific lessons are provided. A list of questions is included to stimulate further investigations or analysis.

*SCHOOLYARD*. Outdoor Biology Instructional Strategies (OBIS). Nashua, NH: Delta, 1979.
Grade(s): 4,5,6,7,8
Supplies: Materials available locally.
Module: $15.60

A Better Fly Trap, Food Chain Game, Invent a Plant, Metric Capers, Seed Dispersal, Sticklers, and Terrestrial Hi-Lo Hunt are the seven activities included in the SCHOOLYARD module. Children construct a fly trap to observe the behavior of flies, role-play animals in a food chain, create new plants, measure environmental objects, and discover how seeds are adapted for dispersal. They play a simulation game that introduces the concepts of habitat and distribution, and they consider a variety of environmental variables, identifying specific sections of a study site. Each activity folio provides background information, a list of needed materials, preparation hints, directions for activities, and possible extensions. The folios are well organized and have useful illustrations and diagrams.

*SEALS, SPOUTS, AND SANDPIPERS*. Manomet Bird Observatory. Albright, Janis; Bird, Mary D.; and Faulds, Ann. Manomet, MA: Manomet Bird Observatory, 1987.
Grade(s): 3,4,5,6,7
Supplies: Materials available locally or from commercial suppliers.
Guide: $29.00

SEALS, SPOUTS, AND SANDPIPERS is an introduction to marine ecology, offering activities that relate to whales, seals, and the coastal environment. Students conduct simulations, play games, and engage in many other activities that integrate the study of marine mammals and shorebirds with arts, language arts, and social science. Flashcards, stickers, and posters accompany this guide.

*SEASHORE*. Outdoor Biology Instructional Strategies (OBIS). Nashua, NH: Delta, 1979, 1980, 1981.
Grade(s): 4,5,6,7,8
Supplies: Materials available locally.
Module: $14.10

The SEASHORE module is made up of six activities: Animal Movement in Water, Beachcombing, Hopper Circus, Salt Water Revival, Seas in Motion, and Water Breathers. Children investigate aquatic environments and observe the organisms found at each study site. They discover how aquatic animals move through water and how this movement and breathing are affected by currents. They search for evidence of plant and animal life on a sandy beach and discuss the possible origins of their finds. They watch beach hoppers, grasshoppers, and frogs; create an artificial high tide and note its effect on marine life; and use simple devices to simulate the movements and currents of the sea. Each activity folio provides background information, a list of materials, preparation hints, directions for activities, and possible extensions. The folios are well organized and have useful illustrations and diagrams. The OBIS POND GUIDE supplements this module.

SEEDS introduces young children to similarities and differences among seeds and to the life cycles of common plants. Students compare seeds and nonseeds, devising criteria for classification. They dissect seeds to find out what's inside, they investigate adaptations for seed dispersal, and they plant seeds and observe growth. The guide contains a complete list of materials, helpful background information, and ideas for extending seed study and integrating it with mathematics and language arts. Although the guide is written to accompany the Suitcase Science Seed Kit, its activities can be very effective with locally available materials.

*SEEDS*. Missouri Botanical Garden (Suitcase Science). St. Louis, MO: Missouri Botanical Garden [no date].
Grade(s): P,K,1,2
Supplies: Materials available locally or kit from Missouri Botanical Garden.
Kit: free local loan with $25.00 deposit, Consumable materials: $.50/student

In the SEEDS AND WEEDS unit, children examine and compare many different types of seeds. They investigate seeds in their own environment and explore the various ways seeds travel and plant themselves. Students plant seeds, cook seeds, dissect seeds, and use seeds to make musical instruments. Each of the 28 activities lists a learning objective, process skills, materials, suggested questions, directions for the exploration, and extensions.

*SEEDS AND WEEDS (Windows on Science series)*. Westly, Joan. Sunnyvale, CA: Creative Publications, 1988. ISBN 0-88488-710-3
Grade(s): K,1,2
Supplies: Materials available locally, from commercial suppliers, or kit from Creative Publications.
Guide: $8.25, Complete Kit for Windows on Science series: $250.00

SEEDS ON SAFARI encourages children to investigate adaptations of seeds and the life cycles of plants. Children discover how adaptations affect seed dispersal and enhance production of plants. They plant seeds and observe the growth and development of the resulting plants. The guide contains many ideas for additional activities, as well as helpful background information. Although it is written to accompany a Suitcase Science Kit, it can be used independently.

*SEEDS ON SAFARI*. Missouri Botanical Garden (Suitcase Science). St. Louis, MO: Missouri Botanical Garden [no date].
Grade(s): 3,4,5
Supplies: Materials available locally or kit from Missouri Botanical Garden.
Kit: free local loan with $25.00 deposit, Consumable materials: $.50/student

In SMALL THINGS, children discover the microscopic world through use of water-drop lenses, hand lenses, and microscopes. They explore the concept of magnification and become acquainted with various tools and techniques for magnifying small objects. They learn to make and stain slides, examining onion cells and single-celled organisms. Emphasis is placed on independent investigation, on careful observation of similarities and differences among specimens, and on recording and discussing results. There are 11 sequential lessons with student worksheet masters.

*SMALL THINGS: AN INTRODUCTION TO THE MICROSCOPIC WORLD*. Elementary Science Study (ESS). Nashua, NH: Delta, 1987 (1967).
Grade(s): 4,5,6
Supplies: Kit from Delta.
Guide: $16.40, Teacher's Kit: $68.00, Kit (for 6 students): $53.00

In STARTING FROM SEEDS, children experiment with various types of seeds, containers, and growth media to explore questions about how plants develop. They investigate the effects of moisture or lack of moisture, discover what happens when plants are grown in the dark, and find ways to change the direction of plant growth. Ideas for further experimentation include the effects of salt or temperature, the presence of parasitic insects, the impact of making cuttings, and attempts to grow plants from parts other than seeds. The unit emphasizes independent inquiry and encourages students to develop their own strategies for collecting, analyzing, and sharing data. The guide also contains helpful information about classroom gardening techniques and problems.

*STARTING FROM SEEDS*. Elementary Science Study (ESS). New York, NY: McGraw-Hill, 1971.
Grade(s): 1,2,3,4,5,6
Supplies: Materials available locally.
Out of print. Available from ERIC (see Sources index).

*STREAMS AND RIVERS.* Outdoor Biology Instructional Strategies (OBIS). Nashua, NH: Delta, 1980, 1981, 1982.
Grade(s): 4,5,6,7,8
Supplies: Materials available locally.
Module: $17.15

The STREAMS AND RIVERS module includes eight activities: Crawdad Grab, Damsels and Dragons, Great Streamboat Race, Hold It, OBIS Oil Spill, Water Snails, Water Striders, and What Lives Here? In these activities, children observe and identify crawdads, damselflies, dragonflies, snails, water striders, and other aquatic plant and animal life. They conduct cork-boat races, create popcorn oil spills, and design cork or sponge creatures. Each activity folio provides background information, a list of materials, preparation hints, directions for the activities, and possible extensions. The folios are well organized and have useful illustrations and diagrams. The OBIS POND GUIDE supplements this module.

*STRUCTURES OF LIFE.* Science Activities for the Visually Impaired/Science Enrichment for Learners with Physical Handicaps (SAVI/SELPH). Berkeley, CA: Lawrence Hall of Science Center for Multisensory Learning, 1982.
Grade(s): 4,5,6,7
Supplies: Kit from Lawrence Hall of Science.
Folio Guide: $5.00, Complete Kit: $119.00, Economy Kit: $87.00

The STRUCTURES OF LIFE unit consists of seven activities: Origin of Seeds, Seed-Grams, The Sprouting Seed, Growing Further, Roots, Meet the Crayfish, and Crayfish at Home. Children experiment with living organisms, searching for seeds in familiar fruits and vegetables, using histograms to record data, examining sprouting seeds, planting roots, and observing behavioral characteristics of crayfish. The module contains scientific background information, as well as instructions for facilitating successful learning among all types of students, including visually impaired, orthopedically impaired, and learning disabled.

*TRACKS.* Elementary Science Study (ESS). New York, NY: McGraw-Hill, 1971.
Grade(s): 3,4,5,6
Supplies: Materials available locally.
Out of print. Available from ERIC (see Sources index).

In TRACKS, children learn to recognize similarities and differences among tracks left by people, tires, and animals. The students observe and compare various tracks in the classroom and in the field, learning how to estimate the size of the animal that left them and the speed at which it was traveling. They make casts and prints and create stories about the sources of tracks they have seen. The guide contains helpful information on identifying tracks and is accompanied by track cards, animal photos, and the Track Picture Book.

*TRAIL.* Outdoor Biology Instructional Strategies (OBIS). Nashua, NH: Delta, 1980, 1982.
Grade(s): 4,5,6,7,8
Supplies: Materials available locally.
Module: $14.10

The TRAIL module consists of six activities: Cardiac Hill, Gaming in the Outdoors, Hold a Hill, Shake It!, Trail Construction, and Trail Impact Study. Children participate in activities that increase their awareness of the environment and how people and events may alter it. They use heart rate to determine the maximum steepness for a footpath, scavenge in order to become more familiar with the environment, and determine the relationship between erosion and slope. The students match a "mystery community" with animals that are shaken from different trees and shrubs, select the best trail-construction technique for a specific study site, and lay out a footpath that will have the least impact on the environment. Each activity folio provides background information, a list of materials, preparation hints, directions for the activities, and possible extensions. The folios are well organized and have useful illustrations and diagrams.

*TREES ARE TERRIFIC!* Ranger Rick's NatureScope. Washington, DC: National Wildlife Federation, 1985.
Grade(s): K,1,2,3,4,5,6,7
Supplies: Materials available locally.
Guide: $6.00

TREES ARE TERRIFIC! is an interdisciplinary guide to the biology of trees and forest ecology. Through observations, experiments, games, and simulations, students from kindergarten through intermediate grades investigate the characteristics of trees, their growth and reproduction, and their influence on human life. There are 26 carefully detailed lessons, accompanied by extensive background information and student activity sheets, as well as evaluation questions and suggested resources.

In TREES: STAGES 1 AND 2, the observation and investigation of this most abundant and important resource provides limitless opportunities to engage children in the basic processes of science. Examination begins with activities using leaves, fruits, and seeds. Children choose a tree and come to know it through the seasons by exploring its structure, noticing changes, and finding out about the animal community that lives in, on, and around it. Information abounds that continually encourages children to see the special place that trees occupy in the environmental scheme.

*TREES: STAGES 1 AND 2.* Science 5/13. Parker, Sheila. London, England: Macdonald, 1973. ISBN 0-356-04347-9
Grade(s): K,1,2,3,4,5,6,7
Supplies: Materials available locally or from commercial suppliers.
Guide: $9.00 (Available in the U.S. from Teacher's Laboratory.)

URBAN GARDENING is a two-volume curriculum unit designed for grades K-4 and 5-9. Students at all levels are encouraged to consider the environment of the city around them, to plan an efficient garden, and to plant seeds and monitor their growth. Activities integrate science with other content areas, as students care for their gardens and study the small ecosystems they have created. The guides contain complete materials lists, helpful background information, and many useful ideas for extensions.

*URBAN GARDENING.* Missouri Botanical Garden (Suitcase Science). St. Louis, MO: Missouri Botanical Garden [no date].
Grade(s): K,1,2,3,4,5,6,7,8,9
Supplies: Materials available locally.
Kit: free local loan with $25.00 deposit, Consumable materials: $.50/student

In USING THE ENVIRONMENT 1: EARLY EXPLORATIONS, outdoor experiences are used as the basis for introducing children to the fundamental processes of science. Activities encourage children to use their senses to become aware of the spatial and numerical aspects of their surroundings. Many opportunities to observe and record in the out-of-doors culminate in children's use of their creative processes to write, draw, or communicate about what they have learned. Language development is stressed equally with the acquisition of scientific skills. The guide includes a valuable narrative account of successful outdoor experiences that other teachers have directed.

*USING THE ENVIRONMENT 1: EARLY EXPLORATIONS.* Science 5/13. Collis, Margaret. London, England: Macdonald, 1974. ISBN 0-356-04353-3
Grade(s): K,1,2,3,4
Supplies: Materials available locally or from commercial suppliers.
Guide: $9.00 (Available in the U.S. from Teacher's Laboratory.)

In USING THE ENVIRONMENT 2: INVESTIGATIONS, PART 2, children investigate weather, plant and animal growth, soil, birds, and the science of school playground equipment. Many diagrams are provided to serve as models for equipment, gauges, and materials that will be helpful with the investigations. Record keeping is emphasized, and a variety of charts are provided as examples of possible formats for recording information. The guide includes a valuable section that suggests various ways of getting children to write about their experiences in the environment.

*USING THE ENVIRONMENT 2: INVESTIGATIONS, PART 2.* Science 5/13. Collis, Margaret. London, England: Macdonald, 1974. ISBN 0-356-04355-X
Grade(s): 3,4,5,6,7
Supplies: Materials available locally or from commercial suppliers.
Guide: $9.00 (Available in the U.S. from Teacher's Laboratory.)

In USING THE ENVIRONMENT 3: TACKLING PROBLEMS, PART 1, activities lead to the design of controlled experiments that investigate some major biological ideas and relationships. Initial studies concentrate on the interdependence of living things by looking at the survival rates of seeds and the relationships among predators, prey, and parasites. Later experiments focus on the relationship between form and function in both plants and animals. As in earlier grades, the basic processes of collecting and classifying are emphasized, but under more difficult circumstances, where children look for evidence of variation and adaptation in both plants and animals. Many opportunities are provided for the use of charts and graphs to represent findings.

*USING THE ENVIRONMENT 3: TACKLING PROBLEMS, PART 1.* Science 5/13. Collis, Margaret. London, England: Macdonald, 1974. ISBN 0-356-04356-8
Grade(s): 6,7,8,9
Supplies: Materials available locally or from commercial suppliers.
Guide: $9.00 (Available in the U.S. from Teacher's Laboratory.)

*USING THE ENVIRONMENT 3: TACK-LING PROBLEMS, PART 2.* Science 5/13. Collis, Margaret. London, England: Macdonald, 1974. ISBN 0-356-05000-9
Grade(s): 6,7,8,9
Supplies: Materials available locally or from commercial suppliers.
Guide: $9.00 (Available in the U.S. from Teacher's Laboratory.)

In USING THE ENVIRONMENT 3: TACKLING PROBLEMS, PART 2, children investigate environmental factors that affect the distribution of living things both on land and in water. Students begin with experiences that allow them to approximate the number of living things to be found at any study site. In-depth investigations seek to determine the effect that various weather conditions, terrestrial features, and people-made intrusions have upon the living things in any one area. Strategies are provided for applying advanced measuring techniques to help in the gathering of environmental information. The guide is comprehensive, but teachers will still need a strong background in directing environmental investigations.

*USING THE ENVIRONMENT 4: WAYS AND MEANS.* Science 5/13. Collis, Margaret. London, England: Macdonald, 1975. ISBN 0-356-05001-7
Supplies: Materials available locally or from commercial suppliers.
Grade(s): K,1,2,3,4,5,6,7,8,9
Guide: $9.00 (Available in the U.S. from Teacher's Laboratory.)

USING THE ENVIRONMENT 4: WAYS AND MEANS provides valuable suggestions for equipment, materials, and facilities that can involve children in outdoor investigations. Plans are detailed to turn a school into outdoor study sites. Methods are described to help with organization of field trips, as well as design and development of successful environmental experiments. Additional information is presented that will ease the job of extending the work accomplished outdoors, when the children return to the classroom. This guide will be invaluable to any teacher who wants to make environmental education a part of the classroom curriculum.

*WADING INTO WETLANDS.* Ranger Rick's NatureScope. Washington, DC: National Wildlife Federation, 1986.
Grade(s): K,1,2,3,4,5,6,7
Supplies: Materials available locally.
Guide: $6.00

WADING INTO WETLANDS provides an interdisciplinary introduction to the ecology of these tremendously productive habitats. Students participate in classroom and field experiences, observing flora and fauna, and conducting experiments, games, writing, art, and math activities that demonstrate the unique characteristics of wetlands and their importance to humans. There are 20 well-organized lessons, accompanied by useful background information, student activity sheets, and a detailed list of resources.

*WATER WORLD.* Virginia Marine Science Museum. Virginia Beach, VA: Virginia Marine Science Museum, 1987.
Grade(s): K,1,2
Supplies: Materials available locally.
Consult museum for price.

The WATER WORLD unit examines sea stars, horseshoe crabs, whelks, and other marine animals. Though written to accompany a field trip to the museum, the activities are applicable to any kindergarten class interested in investigating aquatic animals. The guide includes background information about echinoderms, mollusks, arthropods, and tunicates; student activities, such as making animal word cards and aquatic puppets; student and teacher bibliographies; appendices of learning objectives; ideas for making equipment; suggestions for planning a field trip; and animal picture cards.

*WESTERN NEW YORK FRESHWATER ECOLOGY STUDY GUIDE.* Aquarium of Niagara Falls. Niagara Falls, NY: Aquarium of Niagara Falls, 1982.
Grade(s): 3,4,5,6,7,8
Supplies: Materials available locally.
Guide: free

The FRESHWATER ECOLOGY STUDY GUIDE is designed to introduce students to the forms of life found in freshwater habitats. It can supplement any unit on pond life or aquatic plants and animals. Included in this book are background information about amphibians, reptiles, fish, and other organisms; suggestions for exploring a pond; paper-pencil activities; a glossary; and a bibliography.

The WINTERTIME module consists of six activities: Acorns, Animal Anti-Freeze, Birdfeeder, Population Game, Scent Tracking, and Wintergreen. Children role-play squirrels and deer and learn how to survive. They search for a hibernation site for a make-believe animal, construct a bird feeder, and investigate the behavior of birds. They simulate prey scents and play a game where a predator tracks prey by following its scent. Students locate green plants under the snow and determine the light and temperature conditions of the environment. Each activity folio provides background information, a list of materials, preparation hints, directions for the activities, and possible extensions. The folios are well organized with useful illustrations and diagrams.

*WINTERTIME.* Outdoor Biology Instructional Strategies (OBIS). Nashua, NH: Delta, 1979, 1980, 1981, 1982.
Grade(s): 4,5,6,7,8
Supplies: Materials available locally.
Module: $15.60

YOUR NEIGHBORS: THE TREES invites children to take a closer look at these familiar plants. Students map the area around the school, indicating the location of nearby trees. They make leaf prints, study uses of trees, identify the various parts of a tree, and are encouraged to learn to recognize different tree species. The guide contains ideas for activities that integrate science with art and social studies, as well as helpful background information and a complete materials list.

*YOUR NEIGHBORS: THE TREES.* Missouri Botanical Garden (Suitcase Science). St. Louis, MO: Missouri Botanical Garden [no date].
Grade(s): 4,5,6,7
Supplies: Materials available locally or kit from Missouri Botanical Garden.
Kit: free local loan with $25.00 deposit

# Health and Human Biology

Included in this section are curriculum materials on the topics of human biology, health, and personal safety.

*ACTION/REACTION*. Health Activities Project (HAP). Buller, David; Carter, Lynne; Gipsman, Sandra; Jacobson, Mark; Lee, Rhona; and Schneider, Livingston. Northbrook, IL: Hubbard, 1980.
Grade(s): 4,5,6,7,8
Supplies: Kit from Hubbard.
Guide: $6.50, MiniKit (2-6 students): $94.50, Class Kit: $455.00

The ACTION/REACTION module contains three activity folios: Reaction Time, Improving Reaction Time, and Let's Manipulate. In the first activity, students chart the speed of their responses to light, sound, and touch stimuli. They compare their responses to the different stimuli and attempt to identify factors contributing to these results. In the second activity, students repeat the stimulus-response experiments for five consecutive days, seeking evidence of improved reaction time. They graph their results and compute percent improvements. In the final activity, students practice eye-hand coordination activities, collecting and comparing data to determine the effects of practice on performance. The module contains student data sheets and useful background information for the teacher, as well as suggestions for classroom management and follow-up activities.

*BALANCE IN MOVEMENT*. Health Activities Project (HAP). Buller, David; Carter, Lynne; Gipsman, Sandra; Jacobson, Mark; Lee, Rhona; and Schneider, Livingston. Northbrook, IL: Hubbard, 1980.
Grade(s): 4,5,6,7,8
Supplies: Kit from Hubbard.
Guide: $8.50, MiniKit (2-6 students): $72.50, Class Kit: $340.00

BALANCE IN MOVEMENT contains six sequential activity folios: Balance and Vision, Rope Walk, Stability in Movement, Exploring Balance Boards, Balance Experiments, and Balance and Fatigue. Students conduct experiments to determine how vision affects their balance while they are standing still or moving. They explore the stability of different body positions and then, standing on balance boards, test their ability to balance under various circumstances: with eyes fixed or moving, with feet apart or together, with arms free or folded, and before or after exertion. Emphasis is on collection and analysis of data and application to familiar situations. The module contains helpful information and hints for classroom management, as well as student data sheets.

*BREATHING FITNESS*. Health Activities Project (HAP). Buller, David; Carter, Lynne; Gipsman, Sandra; Jacobson, Mark; Lee, Rhona; and Schneider, Livingston. Northbrook, IL: Hubbard, 1980.
Grade(s): 4,5,6,7,8
Supplies: Kit from Hubbard.
Guide: $9.50, MiniKit (2-6 students): $69.95, Class Kit: $340.00

The BREATHING FITNESS module consists of six activity folios: Exploring Breath Rates, Breath Recovery, Breath Control, Measuring Lung Volume, Measuring Breath Volume, and Gas Exchange. Students learn how to measure their breathing rates; investigate the relationship between lung volume and height; and conduct experiments on the effects of breathing styles, breath holding, exercise, and rest. They also measure relative amounts of carbon dioxide in air students exhale while at rest and after exercise. Emphasis is on collection and analysis of data, and application to familiar situations. There is extensive background information for teachers, with student data sheets and suggestions for classroom management.

*CONSUMER HEALTH DECISIONS*. Health Activities Project (HAP). Buller, David; Carter, Lynne; Gipsman, Sandra; Jacobson, Mark; Lee, Rhona; and Schneider, Livingston. Northbrook, IL: Hubbard, 1980.
Grade(s): 4,5,6,7,8
Supplies: Kit from Hubbard.
Guide: $7.50, Class Kit: $215.00

The CONSUMER HEALTH DECISIONS module contains four activity folios: Consumers' Choice, Madison Avenue, Puzzling It Out, and Yellow Pages. Students conduct taste tests and analyze advertisements to investigate the effects of information, advertising, and expectation on consumer decisions. A team game provides practice in making safety-oriented decisions, and a scavenger hunt through the telephone book familiarizes children with the health and safety resources of their local community. The activities focus on situations relevant to students' lives. There is extensive background information for teachers, with classroom management hints and student activity sheets.

The ENVIRONMENTAL HEALTH AND SAFETY module contains five activity folios: Fallout, Epidemic, Turn Around, Turning Response and Age, and Testing Depth Perception. Students investigate the presence of pollutants in the air and conduct simulations to trace the spread of "disease" (nontoxic fluorescent paste) by direct and indirect contact. They test depth perception and turning responses, and they apply their findings to such activities as riding a bicycle or driving a car. Data collection and analysis are emphasized and hypotheses encouraged. The module includes student data sheets and background information for teachers, as well as specific suggestions for classroom management.

*ENVIRONMENTAL HEALTH AND SAFETY.* Health Activities Project (HAP). Buller, David; Carter, Lynne; Gipsman, Sandra; Jacobson, Mark; Lee, Rhona; and Schneider, Livingston. Northbrook, IL: Hubbard, 1980.
Grade(s): 4,5,6,7,8
Supplies: Kit from Hubbard.
Guide: $8.50, MiniKit (2-6 students): $78.50, Class Kit: $440.00

FLEXIBILITY AND STRENGTH consists of five activity folios: Limber Up, Grip Strength, Up and Away, Splint Relay, and Stiff Joints. Students conduct experiments that test their range of movement and grip strength, and they assess improvement resulting from practice. They investigate the relationship between their heights and the distances they can jump vertically and horizontally. Wearing splints on various joints, they learn the effects of limited mobility. Students are encouraged to collect, analyze, and compare data, and to apply their findings to familiar situations. Student data sheets are included, as are complete classroom management instructions and background information.

*FLEXIBILITY AND STRENGTH.* Health Activities Project (HAP). Buller, David; Carter, Lynne; Gipsman, Sandra; Jacobson, Mark; Lee, Rhona; and Schneider, Livingston. Northbrook, IL: Hubbard, 1980.
Grade(s): 4,5,6,7,8
Supplies: Kit from Hubbard.
Guide: $8.50, MiniKit (2-6 students): $89.50, Class Kit: $395.00

FROM HEAD TO TOE: RESPIRATORY, CIRCULATORY, AND SKELETAL SYSTEMS contains 12 investigations. The students participate in such activities as creating a heart model, analyzing information about activity and blood pressure, using ratio and proportion to make skeletal systems, and graphing lung capacity. Each investigation contains a specific lesson plan, including materials and time needed, background information, procedures, discussion questions, and extensions. Several reproducible student pages are provided with each investigation.

*FROM HEAD TO TOE: RESPIRATORY, CIRCULATORY, AND SKELETAL SYSTEMS.* Activities to Integrate Mathematics and Science (AIMS). Akers, Art; Greco, Jim; Pasley, Ann; Dupree, Lois; Owen, Steve; Rogers, George; and Rojas, Yolanda. Fresno, CA: AIMS, 1986.
Grade(s): 5,6,7,8
Supplies: Materials available locally.
Guide: $10.95

GROWTH TRENDS contains four activity folios: Equals, Size and Age, The Way We Grow, and Maturity Perceptions. Students investigate body proportions by taking measurements, then analyze their data to discover growth trends among their classmates. They compare their data to measurements of typical newborn infants, to determine how proportions change with maturation. They discuss distinctions between having the physical capability and getting permission to perform certain tasks, such as driving a car. Data collection and analysis are encouraged, with emphasis on teamwork and applicability to students' lives. Background information for teachers and suggestions for classroom management are included.

*GROWTH TRENDS.* Health Activities Project (HAP). Buller, David; Carter, Lynne; Gipsman, Sandra; Jacobson, Mark; Lee, Rhona; and Schneider, Livingston. Northbrook, IL: Hubbard, 1980.
Grade(s): 4,5,6,7,8
Supplies: Kit from Hubbard.
Guide: $7.50, MiniKit (2-6 students): $74.95, Class Kit: $240.00

*HEART FITNESS*. Health Activities Project (HAP). Buller, David; Carter, Lynne; Gipsman, Sandra; Jacobson, Mark; Lee, Rhona; and Schneider, Livingston. Northbrook, IL: Hubbard, 1980.
Grade(s): 4,5,6,7,8
Supplies: Kit from Hubbard.
Guide: $8.50, MiniKit (2-6 students): $38.50, Class Kit: $190.00

HEART FITNESS consists of five activity folios: Exploring Heartbeats, Exploring Pulse, Pulse Recovery, Shape Up, and Extra Weight. The students locate their hearts and pulse points, listening to each and comparing data collected from various positions and during different states of activity. They investigate the relationship between heartbeats and pulse, test their pulse recovery rate after exercise, then develop a simple training program to improve recovery rate. Activities conducted with and without weighted backpacks illustrate the effect of extra weight on pulse rate. The collection and comparison of data engage students in careful examination of their exercise habits. The module contains student data sheets, extensive background information for teachers, and classroom management suggestions.

*JAW BREAKERS AND HEART THUMPERS*. Activities to Integrate Mathematics and Science (AIMS). Courtney, Barry; Crossley, Helen; Dixon, Susan; Hill, Loretta; House, Kathleen; Rudig, Anne; Wiebe, Ann; Wiens, Gina; and Williams, Nancy. Fresno, CA: AIMS, 1984.
Grade(s): 3,4
Supplies: Materials available locally.
Guide: $10.95

In JAW BREAKERS AND HEART THUMPERS, there are 18 investigations relating to the human body and foods. Children participate in such activities as measuring heart rates, observing patterns in fingerprints, and calculating amounts of sugar in bubble gum. Each investigation contains a specific lesson plan, including materials and time needed, background information, procedures, discussion questions, and extensions. Several reproducible student pages accompany each investigation, making it convenient for students to gather and record data for graphing.

*NUTRITION/DENTAL HEALTH*. Health Activities Project (HAP). Buller, David; Carter, Lynne; Gipsman, Sandra; Jacobson, Mark; Lee, Rhona; and Schneider, Livingston. Northbrook, IL: Hubbard, 1980.
Grade(s): 4,5,6,7,8
Supplies: Kit from Hubbard.
Guide: $9.50, Class Kit: $440.00

NUTRITION/DENTAL HEALTH consists of six activity folios: Jaws, Trouble Spots, Cavities, Slim Chance, Lunch Time, and Eating Awareness. Students make casts of their teeth and use them to investigate size, shape, and function. With the aid of a nontoxic dye, they locate tooth surfaces in their own mouths where plaque deposits can cause cavities, then test strategies for reducing plaque. Students investigate the nutritive value of foods, planning and scoring menus and examining their snacking habits. A simulation game illustrates the ongoing conflict between tooth decay and oral hygiene, and a board game relates diet and exercise to healthy weight. The module emphasizes collection and analysis of data and encourages extension of classroom activities to the home environment. There is extensive background information for teachers, with student data sheets and detailed suggestions for classroom management.

*OURSELVES*. Learning Through Science. Richards, Roy, and Kincaid, Doug. London, England: Macdonald, 1981. ISBN 0-356-07549-4
Grade(s): K,1,2,3,4
Supplies: Materials available locally or from commercial suppliers.
Activity Cards and Guide: $27.00 (Available in the U.S. from Teacher's Laboratory.)

In the OURSELVES activity cards, children develop science process skills as they investigate the variations and attributes associated with the human senses. Gathering and recording information are emphasized as children measure, then compare, the results of investigations that test the capabilities of the sensing organs. Pinpointing sounds, determining leg strength, experiencing the relationship between taste and smell, and learning about the skeletal and digestive systems lead children to understand more about themselves. The teacher's guide contains no formal lesson plans but offers useful information. The 24 activity cards are designed so that they may be used independently by children or as a guide for a total classroom lesson.

In OURSELVES: STAGES 1 AND 2, children investigate the many facets that make up their uniqueness as individuals. Working together with their classmates, children measure and record information about their body parts. They compare their findings and discuss the variation that is seen among all human beings. Many opportunities are provided for children to write about their findings. The guide suggests activities that involve children in scientific investigations that will give them a better understanding of their place in the human race.

*OURSELVES: STAGES 1 AND 2.*
Science 5/13. Richards, Roy. London, England: Macdonald, 1973.
ISBN 0-356-04349-5
Grade(s): K,1,2,3,4
Supplies: Materials available locally or from commercial suppliers .
Guide: $9.00 (Available in the U.S. from Teacher's Laboratory.)

The PERSONAL HEALTH DECISIONS module contains five activity folios: Change a Habit, Habits Anonymous, On the Spot, Risky Business, and Stress Management. Students investigate the impact of individual and social behaviors on health. They identify habits they would like to break or beneficial habits they would like to develop, keeping records of each and engaging in behavior modification techniques to reinforce change. Group games demonstrate how peer pressure affects individual actions and how risk-taking can affect personal health. Students learn the impact of stress and develop strategies for conscious relaxation in stressful situations. Student sheets are included to facilitate collection and analysis of data. There are also complete instructions for classroom management, and background information for teachers.

*PERSONAL HEALTH DECISIONS.*
Health Activities Project (HAP). Buller, David; Carter, Lynne; Gipsman, Sandra; Jacobson, Mark; Lee, Rhona; and Schneider, Livingston. Northbrook, IL: Hubbard, 1980.
Grade(s): 4,5,6,7,8
Supplies: Kit from Hubbard.
Guide: $8.50, MiniKit (2-6 students): $63.50, Class Kit: $225.00

SIGHT AND SOUND consists of six activity folios: Mask Relay; Field of Vision; Animal Masks; Pinhole Viewer; Look, Listen, and Find; and Where Are You? Students conduct experiments and play games that define the field of vision and demonstrate its importance to daily life. Wearing masks of various types, students learn the effects of changed or reduced field of vision, and discover how, in the case of animals, it necessitates certain behavior. The students assemble pinhole viewers and use lenses to investigate how the amount of light and type of refraction affect images that reach the eye. Additional activities explore the use of visual cues for communication and the advantage of having two ears. Student data sheets and challenge cards are included in the module, as are background information for teachers and instructions for classroom management.

*SIGHT AND SOUND.* Health Activities Project (HAP). Buller, David; Carter, Lynne; Gipsman, Sandra; Jacobson, Mark; Lee, Rhona; and Schneider, Livingston. Northbrook, IL: Hubbard, 1980.
Grade(s): 4,5,6,7,8
Supplies: Kit from Hubbard.
Guide: $9.50, MiniKit (2-6 students): $44.95, Class Kit: $290.00

The SKIN TEMPERATURE module consists of four activity folios: Map Your Temperature, Out in the Cold, The Great Heat Escape, and Heat Traps. Students make predictions about the skin temperature at various points on their bodies, then test their predictions by using strip thermometers to measure temperature at these sites. They conduct experiments to discover how long it takes skin temperature to recover from exposure to cold and devise strategies for speeding recovery time. They also investigate heat loss by measuring the temperature of the air around them, measure the effects of exercise on skin temperature, and test the insulation properties of different types of clothing fabric. The background information is very helpful for teachers, as are the classroom management suggestions and student data sheets.

*SKIN TEMPERATURE.* Health Activities Project (HAP). Buller, David; Carter, Lynne; Gipsman, Sandra; Jacobson, Mark; Lee, Rhona; and Schneider, Livingston. Northbrook, IL: Hubbard, 1980.
Grade(s): 4,5,6,7,8
Supplies: Kit from Hubbard.
Guide: $7.50, MiniKit (2-6 students): $25.00, Class Kit: $180.00

# Earth Science

The Earth Science section contains curriculum materials relating to geology, geography, weather, and astronomy.

*ADVENTURES ALONG THE SPECTRUM*. Hansen Planetarium. Salt Lake City, UT: Hansen Planetarium, 1985.
Grade(s): 4,5,6,7,8
Supplies: Materials available locally.
Guide: $4.00

ADVENTURES ALONG THE SPECTRUM includes excellent background information for the teacher. It delineates important concepts and suggests activities and motivating questions that make learning fun and successful. Children make a spectroscope, experiment with prisms and light, investigate the relationship between a star's color and its temperature, and apply new knowledge to common objects and events. A list of resources for teachers, including astronomy periodicals and calendars, and a bibliography are part of this guide.

*ASTRONOMY*. Franklin Institute Museum-To-Go. Philadelphia, PA: Franklin Institute, 1988.
Grade(s): 4,5,6
Supplies: Materials available locally or kit from Science Kit, Inc.
Kit: $145.00

The ASTRONOMY unit consists of eight activities that offer children the opportunity to explore the world beyond earth. They investigate the sun, the nine planets of our solar system, and the stars, and they identify the forces that determine the position of these bodies in space. The teacher's guide includes a motivating question, a list of materials, a step-by-step procedure, reproducible student worksheets, and possible extension activities for each lesson.

*ASTRONOMY ADVENTURES*. Ranger Rick's NatureScope. Washington, DC: National Wildlife Federation, 1986.
Grade(s): K,1,2,3,4,5,6,7
Supplies: Materials available locally.
Guide: $6.00

ASTRONOMY ADVENTURES presents an interdisciplinary study of stars, planets, and astronomical phenomena through the use of experiments, games, simulations, and demonstrations. Students investigate the behavior of gases and the principles of motion, construct models, and engage in creative writing and arts activities that relate to the universe and to the place of humans in it. There are 29 lessons, ranging in appeal from kindergarten through intermediate grades, enhanced by extensive background information, student activity sheets, and an exhaustive list of resources.

*THE BEST LITTLE PLANET MONEY CAN BUY*. Hansen Planetarium. Salt Lake City, UT: Hansen Planetarium, 1983, 1988.
Grade(s): 5,6,7,8
Supplies: Materials available locally.
Guide: $4.00

THE BEST LITTLE PLANET MONEY CAN BUY is part of an educational star theater program produced by Hansen Planetarium, but much of the information and many of the activities may be used independently. The guide includes fact sheets, concepts, suggestions for classroom activities, and a selected bibliography for further reading, with references for teachers and students. Background information is given for each planet, and possible activities are intertwined.

*CONVECTION: A CURRENT EVENT*. Great Explorations in Math and Science (GEMS). Gould, Alan. Berkeley, CA: Lawrence Hall of Science, 1988.
Grade(s): 6,7,8,9,10,11,12
Supplies: Materials available locally, from commercial suppliers, or from Lawrence Hall of Science.
Guide: $6.50

In CONVECTION: A CURRENT EVENT, students use drops of food coloring to trace the convection currents in water, observe convection in air, and apply these experiences to the real-life situations of ocean currents, house heating, and wind patterns. Extension activities focus on the movement of magma in the earth, continental drift, and a pattern of light and dark areas on the surface of the sun. The guide includes detailed lesson plans for each of the activities, background information, and reproducible student worksheets.

DAYTIME ASTRONOMY enables children to approach an understanding of their universe through investigation of such familiar phenomena as shadows, the sun's daily motion, and the phases of the moon. Children keep records of the sun's movement by watching shadows over a period of time, make moon observations, and through analysis and discussion of their data, gradually discover that the changes they have observed fit into predictable patterns. The guide contains a list of useful materials, detailed advice for conducting indoor and outdoor classroom activities, and instructions for making models.

*DAYTIME ASTRONOMY.* Elementary Science Study (ESS). New York, NY: McGraw-Hill, 1971.
Grade(s): 4,5,6,7,8
Supplies: Materials available locally or from commercial suppliers, or homemade.
Out of print. Available from ERIC (see Sources index).

DOWN TO EARTH: SOLUTIONS FOR MATH + SCIENCE contains 15 investigations of such earth science topics as geology, oceanography, and meteorology. The students interpret information and generalize as they study evaporation rates, daily weather changes, mining techniques, and underwater terrain. Each investigation contains a specific lesson plan, including materials and time needed, background information, procedures, discussion questions, and extensions. Several reproducible student pages are provided with each investigation.

*DOWN TO EARTH: SOLUTIONS FOR MATH + SCIENCE.* Activities to Integrate Mathematics and Science (AIMS). Erickson, Sheldon; Gregg, David; Helling, Frank; King, Morris W.; and Starkweather, Jeri. Fresno, CA: AIMS, 1986.
Grade(s): 5,6,7,8
Supplies: Materials available locally.
Guide: $10.95

In the EARTH activity cards, the fundamental aspects of geology are introduced to children through experiences with rocks, soils, and crystals and the examination of earth processes. Children compare buildings and rock samples formed in their local environment, test the properties of a variety of rock samples, then explore the characteristics of soil. Information and activities concerning crystals, types of rocks, oil, gas, metals, and coal extend the investigations. Teacher direction is a must, as much of the information shared in the 24 activity cards may be new to many children. The teacher's guide contains no formal lesson plans but offers useful information.

*EARTH.* Learning Through Science. Kincaid, Doug, and Richards, Roy. London, England: Macdonald, 1983.
ISBN 0-356-07557-5
Grade(s): 3,4,5,6
Supplies: Materials available locally or from commercial suppliers.
Activity Cards and Guide: $27.00 (Available in the U.S. from Teacher's Laboratory.)

In EARTH, MOON, AND STARS, students investigate ancient models of the world, the earth's shape, gravity, the moon and its phases, star clocks, and star maps. As children progress through these activities, they begin to answer such questions as, If the earth is round, why does it look flat? and Why does the moon change its shape? Each of the six activities includes background information, suggested time needed, a list of materials, ideas for preparation, step-by-step directions, and reproducible student worksheets.

*EARTH, MOON, AND STARS.* Great Explorations in Math and Science (GEMS). Sneider, Cary I. Berkeley, CA: Lawrence Hall of Science, 1986.
Grade(s): 5,6,7,8,9,10,11,12
Supplies: Materials available locally, from commercial suppliers, or from Lawrence Hall of Science.
Guide: $9.00

GEOLOGY: THE ACTIVE EARTH is an interdisciplinary investigation of the nature of the earth. Students engage in classroom and playground experiments and simulations that demonstrate what the earth is made of, how old it is, and how it was—and continues to be—formed. Activities focus on rocks and minerals, landforms, fossil records, the structure of the earth, and earth movements, such as quakes and volcanoes. There are 18 detailed lessons, accompanied by student activity sheets, a resource guide, and extensive background information on facts and theories.

*GEOLOGY: THE ACTIVE EARTH.* Ranger Rick's NatureScope. Washington, DC: National Wildlife Federation, 1987.
Grade(s): K,1,2,3,4,5,6,7
Supplies: Materials available locally.
Guide: $6.00

*INTERSTELLAR JONES IN QUESTION THE ANSWERS.* Hansen Planetarium. Jarvis, Seth; Noffsinger, Joe; and Taylor, Glenn. Salt Lake City, UT: Hansen Planetarium, 1986.
Grade(s): 5,6,7,8
Supplies: Materials available locally.
Guide: $4.00

The introduction of this teacher's guide, INTERSTELLAR JONES IN QUESTION THE ANSWERS, defines what science is, how it works, and how to develop positive attitudes towards science. It contains background information about stars, spectroscopes, light, and parallax. Children build simple and advanced spectroscopes and do experiments with them. They determine how hot a star is, why it is the color it is, and its distance from earth, and they observe the relationship between an object and its parallax. Also included are resources for astronomy teachers, a list of periodicals, selected bibliographies on the stars and pedagogy, and a list of science activity books.

*LIGHT AND SHADOWS.* Elementary Science Study (ESS). New York, NY: McGraw-Hill, 1976.
Grade(s): K,1,2,3
Supplies: Materials available locally.
Out of print. Available from ERIC (see Sources index).

LIGHT AND SHADOWS provides an informal introduction to the investigation of light, shadows, and spatial relationships. Through many photographs and sparse text, the guide illustrates ways to engage young children in such indoor and outdoor activities as tracing shadows, catching each other's shadows, and following flashlight beams. Because it contains no detailed instructions, the book functions more as an inspiration than as a lesson plan.

*MAPPING.* Elementary Science Study (ESS). Nashua, NH: Delta, 1985 (1968).
Grade(s): 5,6,7
Supplies: Materials available locally, from commercial suppliers, or kit from Delta.
Guide: $20.70, Kit: $268.00

In MAPPING, children become familiar with the ways in which data can be arranged to communicate location, direction, or sequence to others. Activities include use of classroom materials for creating miniature environments, and exploration of the school and its locale to answer "life-sized" questions. As children explore problems of scale, proportion, point of view, and distance, they learn to see the relationships between the three-dimensional world and its two-dimensional representation on paper. The guide contains detailed information on required materials and suggested supplementary items.

*MEASUREMENT, MOTION AND CHANGE.* Science Curriculum Improvement Study (SCIS II). Paldy, Lester G.; Amburgey, Leonard L.; Collea, Francis; Cooper, Richard; Maxwell, Donald E.; and Riley, Joseph W. Nashua, NH: Delta [no date].
Grade(s): 4
Supplies: Kit from Delta.
Guide: $15.00, Kit: $343.80, Activity Cards: $17.40

In MEASUREMENT, MOTION AND CHANGE, students participate in activities that help them develop concepts of relative position and motion, and reference objects. Students learn mapping skills by measuring distances, using coordinates, and working with rectangular grids. Strengths of this unit include a section devoted to concepts necessary for students to work with new materials, and a culminating activity that uses the study of weather to incorporate all the concepts involved. This unit is a revision of the original SCIS, RELATIVE POSITION AND MOTION.

*METEOROLOGY.* Franklin Institute Museum-To-Go. Philadelphia, PA: Franklin Institute, 1987.
Grade(s): 4,5,6
Supplies: Materials available locally or kit from Science Kit, Inc.
Kit: $175.00

In the METEOROLOGY unit, children investigate the fundamental concepts of weather: the uneven heating of the earth, changing air pressure, water recycling, and cloud formation. In many of the eight activities, students construct a variety of instruments and use them to increase their understanding of weather prediction. The teacher's guide includes a motivating question, a list of materials, a step-by-step procedure, reproducible student worksheets, and possible extension activities for each lesson.

In the OUT OF DOORS activity cards, children examine the composition of soil, make measurements concerning some everyday weather phenomena, and hone their observation skills by looking for shapes and patterns in the local environment. Information-gathering skills are emphasized, as children learn to recognize the variations in soil types and record changes in wind, rain, and temperature. The ability to discriminate between and define such common terms as thick or thin, short or long, big or small, many or few is tested as children observe outside the classroom. The 24 activity cards can be used independently but are more appropriate for teacher-directed lessons. The teacher's guide contains no formal lesson plans but offers useful information.

*OUT OF DOORS.* Learning Through Science. Collis, Margaret; and Kincaid, Doug. London, England: Macdonald, 1982. ISBN 0-356-07554-0
Grade(s): 3,4,5,6
Supplies: Materials available locally or from commercial suppliers.
Activity Cards and Guide: $27.00 (Available in the U.S. from Teacher's Laboratory.)

In OUT OF THIS WORLD, children learn about the earth and its neighbors by reading facts about the planets and using this information to make Venn diagrams and graphs. Students construct a model solar system, compute travel time to the moon and other planets, predict communication time among the planets, determine their own weight on the moon and other planetary bodies, and play a variety of galactic games. Each of the 15 investigations has a specific lesson plan, including materials, background information, procedures, discussion questions, reproducible student worksheets, and extensions.

*OUT OF THIS WORLD.* Activities to Integrate Mathematics and Science (AIMS). Lind, Mary; Williams, Ana; and Knecht, Pam. Fresno, CA: AIMS, 1987.
Grade(s): 5,6,7,8,9
Supplies: Materials available locally.
Guide: $10.95

OVERHEAD AND UNDERFOOT includes 15 investigations related to the natural environment. Topics covered are weather, plants, soil, geology, and conservation. The students are involved in such activities as making peanut butter-and-jelly "rock" layers, observing cloud formations to predict weather, and comparing soil mixtures for effects on plant growth. Each investigation contains a specific lesson plan, including materials and time needed, background information, procedures, discussion questions, and extensions. Several reproducible student pages are provided with each investigation.

*OVERHEAD AND UNDERFOOT.* Activities to Integrate Mathematics and Science (AIMS). Courtney, Barry; Wiebe, Ann; Dixon, Susan; Hill, Loretta; Rayfield, Helen; Rudig, Anne; Bland, Carol; Wiens, Gina; Williams, Nancy; and House, Kathleen. Fresno, CA: AIMS, 1986.
Grade(s): 3,4
Supplies: Materials available locally.
Guide: $10.95

REASONS FOR SEASONS consists of three volumes: Fall, Winter, and Spring. Each volume contains activities that encourage young children to notice the world around them and to observe its changes throughout the passing year. The guides contain ideas for integrating study of the seasons and the solar system with the arts, language arts, and mathematics. Background information is also supplied, as is a complete materials list. Although these guides are written to accompany Suitcase Science Kits, they can be used independently, with locally obtained materials.

*REASONS FOR SEASONS.* Missouri Botanical Garden. St. Louis, MO: Missouri Botanical Garden [no date].
Grade(s): P,K,1,2
Supplies: Materials available locally or kit from Missouri Botanical Garden.
Kit: free local loan with $25.00 deposit, Consumable materials: $.50/student

ROCKS AND CHARTS invites children to look closely at the characteristics of rocks in order to establish ways of comparing and differentiating them. Excellent introductory chartmaking activities are used to help classify and identify rocks. Children use their own criteria for sorting, then learn more standard tests for streak, hardness, magnetism, and mineral content. The guide contains many activities and games, as well as facts about how rocks are named and how they are used.

*ROCKS AND CHARTS.* Elementary Science Study (ESS). Nashua, NH: Delta, 1986 (1969).
Grade(s): 3,4,5,6
Supplies: Specimens from commercial suppliers or kit from Delta.
Guide: $5.40, Kit: $143.00, Readers (6): $9.50, Activity Cards (23): $5.10

*ROCKS, SAND, AND SOIL (Windows on Science series).* Westly, Joan. Sunnyvale, CA: Creative Publications, 1988. ISBN 0-88488-707-3
Grade(s): K,1,2
Supplies: Materials available locally, from commercial suppliers, or kit from Creative Publications.
Guide: $8.25, Complete Kit for Windows on Science series: $250.00

In ROCKS, SAND, AND SOIL, children sort and classify rocks by texture, weight, color, and hardness; examine soil to determine its components; make sand from rocks; create sand paintings; construct sand timers; and compare soil samples, soil drainage, and plant growth in different soils. Each of the 28 activities includes a learning objective, process skills, a list of materials, suggested questions, directions for the exploration, and extensions.

*SAND.* Elementary Science Study (ESS). New York, NY: McGraw-Hill, 1970.
Grade(s): K,1,2,3
Supplies: Materials available locally. Out of print. Available from ERIC (see Sources index).

In the SAND unit, children investigate the physical properties of sand. They observe the color, shape, and texture of different grades of sand; they investigate how it behaves when wet or dry; and they compare it with other materials, such as dirt, sugar, or salt. Activities in sifting and sorting, timing, weighing, and measuring are suggested, with ideas for additional projects such as jewelry-making and creative writing. The guide contains instructions for coloring sand and for making sandpaper and sand pendulums, and useful hints about classroom management.

*THE SECRET OF THE CARDBOARD ROCKET.* Hansen Planetarium. Salt Lake City, UT: Hansen Planetarium, 1985.
Grade(s): 2,3,4,5,6
Supplies: Materials available locally.
Guide: $4.00

THE SECRET OF THE CARDBOARD ROCKET integrates science, language, and art skills and helps develop creativity. Emphasis is placed on reasoning and imagination as children invent a planet, an alien, and a rocket ship. Directions are given for construction of a balloon rocket, as well as various models of the solar system. Background information, a bibliography, and additional resources are included in this teacher's guide.

*SKY AND SPACE.* Learning Through Science. Kincaid, Doug, and Richards, Roy. London, England: Macdonald, 1982. ISBN 0-356-07552-4
Grade(s): 2,3,4,5
Supplies: Materials available locally or from commercial suppliers.
Activity Cards and Guide: $27.00 (Available in the U.S. from Teacher's Laboratory.)

In the SKY AND SPACE activity cards, investigations emphasize the empirical measurements that children can make through the observation of objects moving through the sky. Children record the movement of the sun and moon, the length of shadows, the time and distance the earth travels, and how the constellations change throughout the night and seasons. Observations of the more immediate atmosphere include activities that demonstrate the importance of water in the formation of clouds and rainbows. The 24 activity cards can be used independently but are more appropriate for a teacher-directed lesson. The teacher's guide contains no formal lesson plans but offers useful information.

*SKY PIRATES.* Hansen Planetarium. Salt Lake City, UT: Hansen Planetarium, 1986.
Grade(s): 2,3,4,5,6
Supplies: Materials available locally.
Guide: $4.00

The major focuses of SKY PIRATES are that stars differ in their distances from Earth and that a constellation is an imaginary construct. This guide includes general background information about stars; the specific constellations, Leo, the Big Dipper, and Orion; and the seasons. Children make a model of Orion and create their own constellations. A bibliography, a list of resources, and suggested periodicals are provided.

With STREAM TABLES, children investigate the action and effects of water circulating in currents, streams, and waves. A waterproof box equipped with a pump and plastic tubing provides an environment to which children add sand, gravel, and water. As the water courses through the box, children can observe how it moves and how its motion affects the land. The guide contains suggestions for building landscapes to erode, creating wind currents, and other activities. There are detailed instructions for using materials and for classroom management. A set of photo cards illustrates various uses of the table, but the quality and composition of the pictures reduce their effectiveness.

*STREAM TABLES.* Elementary Science Study (ESS). Nashua, NH: Delta, 1985 (1971).
Grade(s): 4,5,6
Supplies: Materials available locally, from commercial suppliers, or kit from Delta.
Guide: $7.70, Kit: $89.00

Each USMES unit is based on a challenge that presents a school or community problem to be solved by the children. The WEATHER PREDICTIONS challenge: What do you think the weather will be this afternoon?...tomorrow? Find out what information helps you most in accurately predicting the weather. Children make their own weather instruments as they try to discover the factors that influence weather. Predictions are correlated with observations. The teacher's guide contains no specific lesson plans but does include teachers' logs describing the use of this challenge.

*WEATHER PREDICTIONS.* Unified Science and Mathematics for Elementary Schools (USMES). Newton, MA: Education Development Center, Inc., 1973.
Grade(s): 2,3,4,5,6,7,8
Supplies: Materials available locally. Out of print. Available on SCIENCE HELPER K-8 or from ERIC (see Sources index).

WHERE IS THE MOON? presents an informal introduction to observational astronomy. Through the use of written "reminders," teachers encourage their students to keep an eye on the after-school sky, observing the position and appearance of the moon and prominent planets, such as Venus or Jupiter. Children record their observations in journals and on charts and discuss them in class. Over time they notice patterns of movement and change and begin to make more accurate predictions. The guide contains a calendar with useful information about finding and describing the moon, and hints on preparation of reminders. A student guide, WHERE WAS THE MOON?, accompanies this unit.

*WHERE IS THE MOON?* Elementary Science Study (ESS). New York, NY: McGraw-Hill, 1968.
Grade(s): 3,4,5,6,7
Supplies: Materials available locally. Out of print. Available from ERIC (see Sources index).

WILD ABOUT WEATHER is an interdisciplinary guide to the causes, kinds, and impact of weather. Students from kindergarten to intermediate grades engage in classroom or playground experiments, games, and simulations, as they investigate how weather happens and how it affects the earth and its inhabitants. The 30 well-organized lesson plans are supplemented by student activity sheets and detailed background information. An appendix contains suggestions for evaluation and many useful resources.

*WILD ABOUT WEATHER.* Ranger Rick's NatureScope. Washington, DC: National Wildlife Federation, 1985.
Grade(s): K,1,2,3,4,5,6,7
Supplies: Materials available locally.
Guide: $6.00

## Physical Science

Included in the Physical Science section are curriculum materials relating to the physical properties of matter. Units on such topics as light and color, sound, electricity, chemistry, heat, energy, magnetism, density, forces and motions, and equilibrium may be found here.

*BALLOONS AND GASES*. Elementary Science Study (ESS). Nashua, NH: Delta, 1985 (1971).
Grade(s): 5,6,7,8
Supplies: Materials available locally, from commercial suppliers, or kits from Delta.
Guide: $14.00, Kit: $254.00, Consumable Kit: $150.00

BALLOONS AND GASES enables children to investigate the properties of various gases and to demonstrate that although they may be invisible, gases do exist and can be identified and differentiated. Students begin by experimenting with acids, bases, and indicators, observing chemical reactions, and learning ways of distinguishing similar fluids. They then generate gases and, by measuring weight and observing reactions and effects, begin to recognize the unique properties of each. The guide contains explicit safety recommendations, instructions for conducting lab experiments, and supplementary suggestions for preparing solutions and equipment.

*BATTERIES AND BULBS*. Elementary Science Study (ESS). Nashua, NH: Delta, 1985 (1968).
Grade(s): 4,5,6
Supplies: Materials available locally or kit from Delta.
Guide: $10.10, Kit: $209.00, Activity Cards (40): $19.20, Readers (6): $9.50

BATTERIES AND BULBS introduces children to the study of electricity and magnetism. Using common objects, such as flashlights, batteries, small bulbs, wires, and magnets, children are challenged to predict and trace the path of electricity in a circuit, to find out what's inside a battery, and to make and use their own light bulbs and electromagnets. The guide contains detailed lists of materials for each activity, as well as complete instructions for the experiments and suggestions for classroom discussions.

*BEGINNINGS*. Science Curriculum Improvement Study (SCIS). Herrera, Sharon, and Thier, Herbert D. Nashua, NH: Delta, 1974.
Grade(s): K,1
Supplies: Materials from Delta.
Out of Print. Available on SCIENCE HELPER K-8 (see Sources index).

BEGINNINGS offers a wide variety of activities and experiences in life and physical sciences. Students compare and group objects by color and shape, and describe objects by texture, size, odor, and sounds. They string beads, trace shapes, grow plants, sort leaves, observe animals, and pour liquids. The lessons can be used in any order and offer a comfortable hands-on introduction to science for young children.

*BEGINNINGS*. Science Curriculum Improvement Study (SCIIS/85). Thier, Herbert D.; Karplus, Robert; Lawson, Chester A.; Knott, Robert; and Montgomery, Marshall. Nashua, NH: Delta, 1986 (1979).
ISBN 0-87504-400-X
Grade(s): K,1
Supplies: Kit from Delta.
Guide: $21.95, Kit: $355.00

The SCIIS/85 BEGINNINGS guide is the same as the original SCIS guide with one exception: the SCIIS/85 kit contains an aquarium and an order form to send away for living organisms. Students will be able to observe freshwater crabs, goldfish, newts, snails, and water plants.

In BUBBLE-OLOGY, students use bubbles to investigate light and color, aerodynamics, chemical composition, surface tension, and technology. Children create various bubblemakers, test different bubble solutions, try to make bubbles of varying sizes, discuss Bernoulli's principle, experiment with surface tension, and determine how to make the longest-lasting bubble. For each of the six activities, information is given concerning time needed, preparation, materials, step-by-step directions, and extensions. Useful summary outlines and reproducible student worksheets are included in the guide.

*BUBBLE-OLOGY.* Great Explorations in Math and Science (GEMS). Barber, Jacqueline. Berkeley, CA: Lawrence Hall of Science, 1986.
Grade(s): 5,6,7,8
Supplies: Materials available locally, from commercial suppliers, or from Lawrence Hall of Science.
Guide: $7.50

In CHEMICAL REACTIONS, students investigate chemical reactions and experiment with heat. They observe chemicals in a ziplock bag bubble, change colors, produce gas, generate heat, and produce odors. The guide contains information about assembling materials, safety considerations, specific lesson plans, and possible extension activities.

*CHEMICAL REACTIONS.* Great Explorations in Math and Science (GEMS). Barber, Jacqueline. Berkeley, CA: Lawrence Hall of Science, 1986.
Grade(s): 6,7,8,9,10,11,12
Supplies: Materials available locally, from commercial suppliers, or from Lawrence Hall of Science.
Guide: $6.50

CLAY BOATS is an investigation of buoyancy. Children discover how an object, such as a lump of clay, which might ordinarily sink in water, can be made to float. By shaping the clay in various ways, the children discover that some designs float better than others. They then load their boats with common classroom objects or small uniform weights to find out how much "cargo" the boats can carry and which designs support the most weight. The children go on to experiment with plastic cups, aluminum foil, and other materials to test their ideas about buoyancy. Younger students may have less patience than older ones in conducting the more formal experiments, a factor that should be considered in lesson planning.

*CLAY BOATS.* Elementary Science Study (ESS). Nashua, NH: Delta, 1985 (1969).
Grade(s): 3,4,5,6
Supplies: Materials available locally or kit from Delta.
Guide: $3.70, Kit: $69.00, Activity Cards (42): $5.10, Readers (6): $9.50

COLORED SOLUTIONS is an introduction to density and the layering of liquids. Children observe the patterns created by food coloring as it spreads in plain water. They test for the effects of temperature and color concentration on the behavior of liquids, and then investigate what happens when salt water and fresh water are combined. They experiment with various concentrations of salt water, each dyed a different color. The liquids are layered in transparent straws according to their density. Eventually the children develop a scheme for ordering liquids according to "weight for the same amount." Sample prediction sheets are included, as are suggestions for evaluation.

*COLORED SOLUTIONS.* Elementary Science Study (ESS). Nashua, NH: Delta, 1985 (1974).
Grade(s): 3,4,5,6,7,8
Supplies: Materials available locally or kit from Delta.
Guide: $7.20, Kit (for 6 students): $12.00, Teacher's Kit: $150.00, Activity Cards (38): $5.10

The COMMUNICATION module consists of four activities on sound: Dropping In; Small Sounds, Big Ears; What's Your Pitch?; and Vibration = Sound. Students learn to identify dropped objects by their sounds. Then, assigning a different letter to each sound, they send each other messages by dropping objects in sequence to form words. They experiment with megaphones to find out about amplification, use kalimbas and xylophones to explore the concept of pitch, and experiment with the effects of vibration rate on pitch. The instructions contain scientific information as well as techniques for facilitating successful experiences among all learners.

*COMMUNICATION.* Science Activities for the Visually Impaired/Science Enrichment for Learners with Physical Handicaps (SAVI/SELPH). Berkeley, CA: Lawrence Hall of Science Center for Multisensory Learning, 1982.
Grade(s): 4,5,6,7
Supplies: Kit from Lawrence Hall of Science.
Folio Guide: $5.00, Complete Kit: $81.00, Economy Kit: $70.00

*CRIME LAB CHEMISTRY.* Great Explorations in Math and Science (GEMS). Barber, Jacqueline. Berkeley, CA: Lawrence Hall of Science, 1985.
Grade(s): 4,5,6,7
Supplies: Materials available locally, from commercial suppliers, or from Lawrence Hall of Science.
Guide: $4.50

In CRIME LAB CHEMISTRY, children role-play crime-lab chemists and solve a mystery. Students employ the techniques of chromatography to decide which pen was used to write a ransom note, and they discuss their conclusions and the variables that caused different results. The two lesson plans contain information about time needed, classroom management, materials, activity directions, and extensions.

*DISCOVERING DENSITY.* Great Explorations in Math and Science (GEMS). Buegler, Marion E. Berkeley, CA: Lawrence Hall of Science, 1988.
Grade(s): 4,5,6,7,8
Supplies: Materials available locally, from commercial suppliers, or from Lawrence Hall of Science.
Guide: $7.50

In DISCOVERING DENSITY, children begin to understand density as a property of liquids. Students experiment with layering different liquids, such as oil, water, and colored water with various salt contents. They then create mixtures of different densities, using secret formulas. This guide includes lesson plans for each activity, background information, extension activities, and reproducible student pages.

*DROPS, STREAMS, AND CONTAINERS.* Elementary Science Study (ESS). Nashua, NH: Delta, 1971.
Grade(s): 3,4,5
Supplies: Materials available locally or kit from Delta.
Guide and Activity Cards: $10.30, Kit: $46.00

DROPS, STREAMS, AND CONTAINERS introduces children to some of the physical properties of fluids. Students experiment with water and various other liquids, determining the characteristics of individual drops, observing fluids in containers, and testing the properties of flowing liquids. The guide offers questions for exploration and is accompanied by activity cards with additional challenges.

*ELECTRIC CIRCUITS.* Franklin Institute Museum-To-Go. Philadelphia, PA: Franklin Institute, 1986.
Grade(s): 4,5,6
Supplies: Materials available locally or kit from Science Kit, Inc.
Kit: $195.00

ELECTRIC CIRCUITS contains eight challenging activities related to the properties and uses of electricity. Children observe, measure, and predict as they investigate fuses, diodes, and wiring patterns. The teacher's guide includes a motivating question, a list of materials, a step-by-step procedure, reproducible student worksheets, and possible extension activities for each lesson.

*ELECTRICITY.* Learning Through Science. Kincaid, Doug, and Richards, Roy. London, England: Macdonald, 1983. ISBN 0-356-07558-3
Grade(s): 4,5,6
Supplies: Materials available locally or from commercial suppliers.
Activity Cards and Guide: $27.00 (Available in the U.S. from Teacher's Laboratory.)

In the ELECTRICITY activity cards, basic experiences with circuitry and electromagnetism prepare children to tackle more difficult electrical projects. Hands-on manipulation of wires, bulbs, and batteries leads children to develop rules that help them determine whether a circuit is open or closed. Various activities introduce switches, dimmers, and the relationship between electricity and magnetism. The unit culminates with a series of projects based on the concepts learned in previous activities. The 24 activity cards can be used independently but should be teacher directed if children have limited experience with batteries and bulbs. The teacher's guide contains no formal lesson plans but offers useful information.

The ENERGY unit consists of four activities that provide children with the opportunity to explore the relationship between stored energy and work. Students learn about thermodynamics and the efficiency of machines. The teacher's guide includes a motivating question, a list of materials, a step-by-step procedure, reproducible student worksheets, and possible extension activities for each lesson.

*ENERGY*. Franklin Institute Museum-To-Go. Philadelphia, PA: Franklin Institute, 1988 (1983).
Grade(s): 4,5,6
Supplies: Materials available locally or kit from Science Kit, Inc.
Kit: $95.00

The Franklin Institute ENERGY SOURCES unit consists of six activities that provide children with the opportunity to explore energy in its various forms. They also study the variety of sources from which energy originates. The teacher's guide includes a motivating question, a list of materials, a step-by-step procedure, reproducible student worksheets, and possible extension activities for each lesson.

*ENERGY SOURCES*. Franklin Institute Museum-To-Go. Philadelphia, PA: Franklin Institute, 1988.
Grade(s): 4,5,6
Supplies: Materials available locally or kit from Science Kit, Inc.
Kit: $195.00

In ENERGY SOURCES, students engage in activities that help them understand the major concepts of variables, energy transfer, energy sources, and energy receivers. The pupils use rolling and colliding spheres, paper airplanes, thermometers, warm and cold water, ice, and rubber-stopper shooters to help them discover that motion and changes in temperature are evidence of energy transfer. The final section of the guide offers projects for individuals or groups.

*ENERGY SOURCES*. Science Curriculum Improvement Study (SCIS). Berger, Carl F.; Karplus, Robert; Randle, Joan Coffman; Thier, Herbert D.; and Webb, Sylvester. Chicago, IL: Rand McNally, 1971.
Grade(s): 5
Supplies: Materials from Delta.
Out of print. Available on SCIENCE HELPER K-8 (see Sources index).

SCIS II ENERGY SOURCES is essentially the same as the original version but has been expanded to include 51 lessons.

*ENERGY SOURCES*. Science Curriculum Improvement Study (SCIS II). Paldy, Lester G.; Amburgey, Leonard L.; Collea, Francis; Cooper, Richard; Maxwell, Donald E.; and Riley, Joseph W. Nashua, NH: Delta, 1978 (1970).
ISBN 0-8339-2502-4
Grade(s): 5
Supplies: Kit from Delta.
Guide: $15.00, Kit: $376.50, Activity Cards: $17.40

The ENERGY SOURCES (SCIIS/85) guide has a new section of activities involving solar energy transfer. The pupils use black or white trays filled with water, thermometers, and a variety of insulating materials to experiment with transfer of the sun's light and heat energy. Five new evaluation activities are included in an appendix, and a supplement has been added to the guide to simplify the lesson overview.

*ENERGY SOURCES*. Science Curriculum Improvement Study (SCIIS/85). Thier, Herbert D.; Karplus, Robert; Knott, Robert; Lawson, Chester A.; and Montgomery, Marshall. Nashua, NH: Delta, 1985 (1970). ISBN 0-87504-409-3
Grade(s): 5
Supplies: Kit from Delta.
Guide: $28.95, Kit: $525.00

*ENERGY TRANSFER.* Franklin Institute Museum-To-Go. Philadelphia, PA: Franklin Institute, 1987.
Grade(s): 4,5,6
Supplies: Materials available locally or kit from Science Kit, Inc.
Kit: $180.00

The ENERGY TRANSFER unit consists of eight activities that focus on energy conversion and the relationship between potential energy and kinetic energy. Children explore the principles underlying temperature change, energy conservation, and the workings of simple machines. The teacher's guide includes a motivating question, a list of materials, a step-by-step procedure, reproducible student worksheets, and possible extension activities for each lesson.

*FLOATERS AND SINKERS: SOLUTIONS FOR MATH AND SCIENCE.* Activities to Integrate Mathematics and Science (AIMS). McKibban, Mike; Laidlaw, Walt; Landon, Kathleen; and Lile, David. Fresno, CA: AIMS, 1982.
Grade(s): 5,6,7,8
Supplies: Materials available locally.
Guide: $10.95

FLOATERS AND SINKERS: SOLUTIONS FOR MATH AND SCIENCE contains 26 investigations that demonstrate the concept of density. Volume is calculated, and division is the basic math skill used. Students learn different methods of calculating the volume of spheres. They explore the density of water, salt water, and rectangular wooden prisms. They also compare the volumes of cylinders and generalize about surface area and cargo capacity. Each investigation contains a specific lesson plan, including materials and time needed, background information, procedures, discussion questions, and extensions. Several reproducible student pages are provided with each investigation.

*GASES AND "AIRS."* Elementary Science Study (ESS). Nashua, NH: Delta, 1987 (1967).
Grade(s): 5,6,7,8
Supplies: Commercial suppliers or kit from Delta.
Guide: $21.50, Kit (for 6 students): $63.00, Teacher's Kit: $145.00, Activity Cards (70): $10.40

In GASES AND "AIRS," children investigate the nature of air and how it behaves under certain conditions. Suggested experiments demonstrate the existence of air and show how the gases in air can change and be changed by interactions with materials such as candles, steel wool, germinating seeds, and water. The activities contribute to content knowledge, while fostering development of problem-solving skills, such as collection and analysis of data, prediction, and conclusion. The guide contains detailed instructions for organizing the students' investigations. There are also student worksheets keyed to specific laboratory experiments.

*HEAT.* Franklin Institute Museum-To-Go. Philadelphia, PA: Franklin Institute, 1988 (1983).
Grade(s): 4,5,6
Supplies: Materials available locally or kit from Science Kit, Inc.
Kit: $140.00

The four activities in the HEAT unit feature principles of heat. Heat transfer and insulation are included to help children understand the nature of heat and how it affects their lives. The teacher's guide includes a motivating question, a list of materials, a step-by-step procedure, reproducible student worksheets, and possible extension activities for each lesson.

*HEATING AND COOLING.* Elementary Science Study (ESS). Nashua, NH: Delta, 1985 (1971).
Grade(s): 6,7,8
Supplies: Materials available locally, from commercial suppliers, or kit from Delta.
Guide: $16.10, Kit: $198.00

HEATING AND COOLING enables children to experiment with a variety of materials and to discover similarities and differences in their rates of heat conduction. Using an assortment of mesh screens, wire, candles, metal or glass rods, and sheets of aluminum, lead, or copper, children conduct tests to determine which materials heat fastest and which take longest to cool. They observe that heat goes into materials, that it can be transferred from hot areas to cool ones, and that heating an object can cause measurable expansion. The guide offers safety instructions and brief background information for each activity.

ICE CUBES presents a number of activities and questions about the effects of heat, surface area, and conductivity on melting rates of ice. Children measure the time it takes for an ice cube to melt in air and in different amounts of water; they compare the melting rates of unusually shaped ice cubes to develop ideas about surface-volume relationships; and they compare the melting rates of ice in contact with metal, wood, and other materials. Children collect data from their observations and experiments, learn to use a thermometer, and construct tables and graphs to report their findings. The guide includes three worksheets to give children experience in measuring elapsed time, six problem cards to stimulate independent investigations as free-time projects or homework, and a reproducible article "Can You Make a Better Ice Cube Keeper?" that encourages children to continue their investigation of insulators.

*ICE CUBES.* Elementary Science Study (ESS). Nashua, NH: Delta, 1986 (1974). Grade(s): 3,4,5
Supplies: Materials available locally or kit from Delta.
Guide: $8.00, Kit $105.00

In INTERACTION AND SYSTEMS, children observe and interpret evidence of interaction through the use of magnets, batteries, wires, various chemicals, photographic paper, pulleys, ammonia, bells, and their own senses. Students begin to develop record-keeping skills by drawing picture records of what they observe. Several teacher demonstrations help students observe and describe change.

*INTERACTION AND SYSTEMS.* Science Curriculum Improvement Study (SCIS). Karplus, Robert, and Randle, Joan Coffman. Nashua, NH: Delta, 1970. Grade(s): 2
Supplies: Materials from Delta.
Out of print. Available on SCIENCE HELPER K-8 (see Sources index).

INTERACTION AND SYSTEMS, SCIS II, is similar to the original version, with the addition of 12 lessons.

*INTERACTION AND SYSTEMS.* Science Curriculum Improvement Study (SCIS II). Paldy, Lester G.; Amburgey, Leonard L.; Collea, Francis; Cooper, Richard; Maxwell, Donald E.; and Riley, Joseph W. Cambridge, MA: American Science and Engineering, 1978 (1970).
ISBN 0-8339-2202-5
Grade(s): 2
Supplies: Kit from Delta.
Guide: $15.00, Kit: $360.20, Activity Cards: $17.40

The SCIIS/85 version of INTERACTION AND SYSTEMS is expanded to include a section on evaluation and a simplified lesson plan in the supplement.

*INTERACTION AND SYSTEMS.* Science Curriculum Improvement Study (SCIIS/85). Thier, Herbert D.; Karplus, Robert; Lawson, Chester A.; Knott, Robert; and Montgomery, Marshall. Nashua, NH: Delta, 1985 (1970).
ISBN 0-87504-403-4
Grade(s): 2
Supplies: Kit from Delta.
Guide: $24.95, Kit: $435.00

*KITCHEN INTERACTIONS.* Science Activities for the Visually Impaired/Science Enrichment for Learners with Physical Handicaps (SAVI/SELPH). Berkeley, CA: Lawrence Hall of Science Center for Multisensory Learning, 1981.
Grade(s): 4,5,6,7
Supplies: Kit from Lawrence Hall of Science.
Folio Guide: $5.00, Complete Kit: $107.00, Economy Kit: $61.00

KITCHEN INTERACTIONS contains four sequential activities in chemistry and physics: The Acid Test, How Dense?, The Cookie Monster, and The Sugar Test. Students experiment with acids in foods, using baking soda as an indicator of the presence and strength of these acids. Investigations of the properties of liquids demonstrate that adding salt to water increases its density and alters the floating/sinking behavior of objects immersed. Experimenting with yeast growth, students test for the presence and concentration of sugar in foods. The instructions are well organized and provide science information as well as techniques for enhancing the learning experiences of students of varied physical capabilities.

*KITCHEN PHYSICS.* Elementary Science Study (ESS). Nashua, NH: Delta, 1986 (1967).
Grade(s): 5,6,7,8
Supplies: Materials available locally or kit from Delta.
Guide: $10.75, Kit (for 6 students): $62.00, Teacher's Kit: $50.00

KITCHEN PHYSICS is an investigation of the physical properties of liquids, using familiar household tools and materials to introduce the scientific pro-cess-es of observation, prediction, experimentation, data collection, and analysis. Students compare the surface tensions of various liquids and conduct experiments on viscosity, density, and absorption rates. A section on constructing and using balances enables students to create equipment for some of their experiments. The guide contains student worksheets and a detailed list of materials and provides helpful background information for each set of activities.

*LIGHT AND COLOR.* Franklin Institute Museum-To-Go. Philadelphia, PA: Franklin Institute, 1988 (1983).
Grade(s): 6,7,8,9
Supplies: Materials available locally or kit from Science Kit, Inc.
Kit: $140.00

In the LIGHT AND COLOR unit, children explore the properties of light and learn how color is produced. Students experiment with light and lenses to produce magnified images. The teacher's guide includes a motivating question, a list of materials, a step-by-step procedure, reproducible student worksheets, and possible extension activities for each of the four lessons.

*LIGHT, COLOR, AND SHADOWS (Windows on Science series).* Westly, Joan. Sunnyvale, CA: Creative Publications, 1988. ISBN 0-88488-709-X
Grade(s): K,1,2
Supplies: Materials available locally or from commercial suppliers, or kit from Creative Publications.
Guide: $8.25, Complete Kit for Windows on Science series: $250.00

In the unit LIGHT, COLOR, AND SHADOWS, children use mirrors, prisms, colored cellophane, and stained glass, and play shadow tag to investigate light and shadows. Students observe how much light passes through objects, order colors from lightest to darkest, make rainbows, see how a mirror reflects light, play shadow games, and more. Each of the 28 activities includes a learning objective, process skills, a list of materials, suggested questions, directions for the exploration, and extensions.

*LIQUID EXPLORATIONS.* Great Explorations in Math and Science (GEMS). Agler, Leigh. Berkeley, CA: Lawrence Hall of Science, 1987.
Grade(s): 1,2,3
Supplies: Materials available locally, from commercial suppliers, or from Lawrence Hall of Science.
Guide: $7.50

In LIQUID EXPLORATIONS, children play a liquid-classification game, experiment with swirling colors, explore raindrops and oil drops, and create secret salad dressing and an "ocean in a bottle." Through these activities, students identify the properties of liquids and note changes that occur when other substances are added to liquids. Included in this guide are lesson plans for each activity, helpful hints for hands-on science in the classroom, a letter to parents, and reproducible student worksheets.

The MAGIC OF ELECTRICITY is an hour-long assembly program in which the "Wizard of Electricity" carries out experiments and demonstrates electrical phenomena. Students help create electricity by immersing strips of metal in lemon juice, move a giant magnet inside a coil of wire, use a light to spin a propeller, and more. This program may be adapted for a variety of age levels and group sizes. The guide includes a sample script, a program outline, suggestions for the presentation, and specific directions and background information for each of the activities. This unit may be used as an introduction to a classroom unit on electricity or as a single presentation.

*THE MAGIC OF ELECTRICITY: A SCHOOL ASSEMBLY PROGRAM PRESENTER'S GUIDE.* Great Explorations in Math and Science (GEMS). Sneider, Cary I.; Gould, Alan; and Wentz, Budd. Berkeley, CA: Lawrence Hall of Science, 1985.
Grade(s): 3,4,5,6
Supplies: Materials available locally, from commercial suppliers, or from Lawrence Hall of Science.
Guide: $10.00

MAGNETISM AND ELECTRICITY consists of four sequential activities: The Force, Making Connections, Current Attractions, and Click It. Students investigate the properties of magnets, then conduct experiments with electrical circuits, electromagnets, small motors, and telegraphs, proceeding to explore the relationship between magnetism and electricity. Instructions for each lesson contain science background information, as well as advice for helping learners enjoy a successful experience.

*MAGNETISM AND ELECTRICITY.* Science Activities for the Visually Impaired/Science Enrichment for Learners with Physical Handicaps (SAVI/SELPH). Berkeley, CA: Lawrence Hall of Science Center for Multisensory Learning, 1979.
Grade(s): 4,5,6,7
Supplies: Kit from Lawrence Hall of Science.
Folio Guide: $5.00, Complete Kit: $118.00, Economy Kit: $87.00

The MAGNETISM/ELECTRIC MODELS unit introduces the topic of magnetic force through eight activities focusing on the size, shape, strength, and use of magnets. The relationship between electricity and magnetism is explored as children construct a telegraph and a simple electric motor. The teacher's guide includes a motivating question, a list of materials, a step-by-step procedure, reproducible student worksheets, and possible extension activities for each lesson.

*MAGNETISM/ELECTRIC MODELS.* Franklin Institute Museum-To-Go. Philadelphia, PA: Franklin Institute, 1986.
Grade(s): 4,5,6
Supplies: Materials available locally or kit from Science Kit, Inc.
Kit: $195.00

MATERIAL OBJECTS offers students the opportunity to observe, manipulate, compare, and change the form of common objects. Students learn that an object is a form of matter and that its color, shape, texture, hardness, and weight are called "properties." Comparing properties leads to "serial ordering," or reclassifying, to show finer differences. Students compare sugar cubes and rock candy and contrast objects that sink or float.

*MATERIAL OBJECTS.* Science Curriculum Improvement Study (SCIS). Randle, Joan Coffman, and Thier, Herbert D. Chicago, IL: Rand McNally, 1970.
Grade(s): 1
Supplies: Materials from Delta.
Out of print. Available on SCIENCE HELPER K-8 (see Sources index).

*MATERIAL OBJECTS.* Science Curriculum Improvement Study (SCIS II). Paldy, Lester G.; Amburgey, Leonard L.; Collea, Francis; Cooper, Richard; Maxwell, Donald E.; and Riley, Joseph W. Nashua, NH: Delta, 1985 (1970).
Grade(s): 1
Supplies: Kit from Delta.
Guide: $15.00, Kit: $488.30, Activity Cards: $17.40

The SCIS II version of MATERIAL OBJECTS differs from the original in that the number of lessons has been reduced.

*MATERIAL OBJECTS.* Science Curriculum Improvement Study (SCIIS/85). Thier, Herbert D.; Karplus, Robert; Lawson, Chester A.; Knott, Robert; and Montgomery, Marshall. Nashua, NH: Delta, 1985 (1970). ISBN 0-87504-401-8
Grade(s): 1
Supplies: Kit from Delta.
Guide: $24.95, Kit: $495.00

The teacher's guide for MATERIAL OBJECTS has been revised and a supplement section added. The supplement organizes the lessons in a format that eases the teacher's task and offers optional activities. One new lesson looks at the properties of plastics; students investigate the differences between natural and synthetic objects. In the second new lesson, students compare balloons inflated with air and with helium.

*MEASUREMENT, MOTION AND CHANGE.* Science Curriculum Improvement Study (SCIS II). Paldy, Lester G.; Amburgey, Leonard L.; Collea, Francis; Cooper, Richard; Maxwell, Donald E.; and Riley, Joseph W. Nashua, NH: Delta [no date].
Grade(s): 4
Supplies: Kit from Delta.
Guide: $15.00, Kit: $343.80, Activity Cards: $17.40

In MEASUREMENT, MOTION AND CHANGE, students participate in activities that help them develop concepts of relative position and motion, and reference objects. Students learn mapping skills by measuring distances, using coordinates, and working with rectangular grids. Strengths of this unit include a section devoted to concepts necessary for students to work with new materials and a culminating activity that uses the study of weather to incorporate all the concepts involved. This unit is a revision of the original SCIS, RELATIVE POSITION AND MOTION.

*MIRROR CARDS.* Elementary Science Study (ESS). New York, NY: McGraw-Hill, 1968.
Grade(s): K,1,2,3,4,5,6
Out of print. Available on SCIENCE HELPER K-8 or from ERIC (see Sources index).

The MIRROR CARDS unit offers direct experience in the mathematical and physical concepts of bilateral symmetry. Children juxtapose small mirrors and picture cards to experiment with reflection patterns. Through investigating the effects of angle and distance, they learn what a mirror can and cannot do or where in relation to a design it must be placed in order to create a particular reflection. The guide encourages informal experimentation among small groups of children and provides supplemental information on the mathematical basis for the activities.

In MIXTURES AND SOLUTIONS, children are introduced to basic chemistry through four sequential activities: Separating Mixtures, Concentration, Reaching Saturation, and The Fizz Quiz. After making mixtures of water and various solids, students attempt to separate them with screens or filters or by evaporation. The weights of salt solutions of different concentrations are compared, and students attempt to determine the amount of solid required to saturate a solution. In the final activity, students observe that a combination of two solutions creates a reaction quite different from what might have been expected from either solution alone. The module contains instructions for conducting enjoyable, successful lessons for students of varying physical capabilities, and science background information.

*MIXTURES AND SOLUTIONS.* Science Activities for the Visually Impaired/Science Enrichment for Learners with Physical Handicaps (SAVI/SELPH). Berkeley, CA: Lawrence Hall of Science Center for Multisensory Learning, 1981.
Grade(s): 4,5,6,7
Supplies: Kit from Lawrence Hall of Science.
Folio Guide: $5.00, Complete Kit: $114.00, Economy Kit: $70.00

In MOBILES, children investigate principles of balance, experimenting with the effects of symmetry and weight on a balanced system. Using oaktag or cardboard, they design and construct the shapes for their mobiles. The children then explore the various ways of hanging and balancing their shapes with yarn and reeds or sticks.

*MOBILES.* Elementary Science Study (ESS). Nashua, NH: Delta, 1985 (1969).
Grade(s): K,1,2,3,4
Supplies: Materials available locally or kit from Delta.
Guide: $4.10, Kit: $32.00, Activity Cards: $5.10

In MODELS: ELECTRIC AND MAGNETIC INTERACTIONS, electricity and magnetism are investigated. Students begin by reviewing circuit concepts with the use of light bulbs, batteries, magnets, and compasses, then test themselves with circuit puzzles and mystery boxes. They use compasses and iron filings to explore magnetic fields and learn to interpret and draw electric circuits. A final section helps individuals or teams design their own projects and experiments.

*MODELS: ELECTRIC AND MAGNETIC INTERACTIONS.* Science Curriculum Improvement Study (SCIS). Berger, Carl F.; Bunshoft, Sylvia; Karplus, Robert; and Randle, Joan Coffman. Chicago, IL: Rand McNally, 1971.
Grade(s): 6
Supplies: Materials from Delta.
Out of print. Available on SCIENCE HELPER K-8 (see Sources index).

In MODELING SYSTEMS SCIS II, there are two changes from the original version of the teacher's guide (MODELS: ELECTRIC AND MAGNETIC INTERACTIONS). First, the section on projects has been deleted, and second, a unit on modeling the atmospheric system has been added. Students determine properties of air, experiment with evaporation and condensation, and model the weather system. The teacher's notes are very helpful in understanding the difficult concepts of electricity, magnetism, and atmosphere.

*MODELING SYSTEMS.* Science Curriculum Improvement Study (SCIS II). Paldy, Lester G.; Amburgey, Leonard L.; Collea, Francis; Cooper, Richard; Maxwell, Donald E.; and Riley, Joseph W. Nashua, NH: Delta, 1974 (1970). ISBN 0-8339-2602-0
Grade(s): 6
Supplies: Kit from Delta.
Guide: $15.00, Kit: $387.40, Activity Cards: $17.40

In MORE THAN MAGNIFIERS, children discover how lenses are used in magnifiers, cameras, projectors, and telescopes. They examine the properties of lenses and come to realize that some lenses are better suited for specific purposes than others are. The guide includes detailed lesson plans for each activity, background information, reproducible student worksheets, and extension activities.

*MORE THAN MAGNIFIERS.* Great Explorations in Math and Science (GEMS). Sneider, Cary I. Berkeley, CA: Lawrence Hall of Science, 1988.
Grade(s): 6,7,8
Supplies: Materials available locally, from commercial suppliers, or from Lawrence Hall of Science.
Guide: $6.50

*MOVING AROUND.* Learning Through Science. Kincaid, Doug, and Richards, Roy. London, England: Macdonald, 1983. ISBN 0-356-07556-7
Grade(s): 2,3,4
Supplies: Materials available locally or from commercial suppliers.
Activity Cards and Guide: $27.00 (Available in the U.S. from Teacher's Laboratory.)

In the MOVING AROUND activity cards, investigations form an introduction to the concepts and characteristics of energy. The movement of vehicles on ramps is used to illustrate the relationship between speed and distance. Activities provide children with experience manipulating simple machines, such as levers, wheels, gears, screws, and pulleys. Additionally, children become familiar with the basic behavior of simple magnets. Many opportunities are available for the introduction of such terms as friction, force, gravity, and energy. Teacher-directed lessons are more appropriate than independent use of the 24 activity cards. The teacher's guide contains no formal lesson plans but offers useful information.

*THE MUSICAL INSTRUMENT RECIPE BOOK.* Elementary Science Study (ESS). Newton, MA: Education Development Center, Inc., 1968.
Grade(s): K,1,2,3,4,5
Supplies: Materials available locally or homemade.
Out of print. Available from ERIC (see Sources index).

Use of the MUSICAL INSTRUMENT RECIPE BOOK provides an opportunity to explore the acoustic properties of various materials and to combine these materials in the construction of sound-producing devices. The guide contains a list of useful materials, with instructions for building and playing 20 different instruments.

*MYSTERY POWDERS.* Elementary Science Study (ESS). Nashua, NH: Delta, 1986 (1966).
Grade(s): 3,4
Supplies: Materials available locally or kit from Delta.
Guide: $3.80, Kit: $62.00, Activity Cards (16): $5.10, Readers (6): $9.50

MYSTERY POWDERS introduces children to the detailed examination of chemical and physical properties of familiar substances and to the use of indicators as a means of identifying these substances. At the start, students receive four unnamed white powders: sugar, salt, baking soda, and starch. They try to identify these by tasting smelling, feeling, and comparing their powders with identified substances. Next, the children use magnifying lenses to observe size and shape of individual particles. They mix the powders with water and perform tests with heat, iodine, and vinegar in order to gain additional information about the powders' properties. Each powder reacts in a specific way. By using what they've learned, children apply their tests to determine the presence of individual powders in new mystery mixtures. Careful observation and discussion of results are encouraged, as is the use of charts for organizing data.

*OOBLECK: WHAT SCIENTISTS DO.* Great Explorations in Math and Science (GEMS). Sneider, Cary I. Berkeley, CA: Lawrence Hall of Science, 1985.
Grade(s): 5,6,7
Supplies: Materials available locally, from commercial suppliers, or from Lawrence Hall of Science.
Guide: $6.50

In the OOBLECK unit, students investigate an unknown substance called Oobleck, describe its physical properties, experiment to identify its unique characteristics, and discuss the similarities and differences among their findings. In successive activities, children design a spacecraft that would be able to land on an ocean of Oobleck and compare the scientific methods they employed with those of real scientists. The format for the four lessons includes a list of materials, suggestions for preparation, and directions for the activity.

*OPTICS.* Elementary Science Study (ESS). Nashua, NH: Delta, 1985 (1968).
Grade(s): 4,5,6
Supplies: Materials available locally or kit from Delta.
Guide: $13.60, Kit: $159.00

In OPTICS, children analyze the properties of light, observing its interaction with various transparent, opaque, or reflective objects. They explore mirrors, shadows, and colored light, comparing their observations to what they already know about reflections and color. They experiment with refraction, trying different ways of bending light. The guide contains detailed information on materials and their use in the unit.

PENDULUMS offers an opportunity to investigate swinging things. Children use fishline to suspend various objects from a crossbar, then conduct experiments to compare the effects of the length of line, the weight and shape of the suspended object, and the distance and rate of swing. There are additional activities suggested for hand-held pendulums, coupled swings, and salt pendulums, as well as hints for constructing classroom equipment.

*PENDULUMS.* Elementary Science Study (ESS). Nashua, NH: Delta, 1985 (1969).
Grade(s): 4,5,6
Supplies: Materials available locally or kit from Delta.
Guide: $12.00, Kit: $456.00

POPPING WITH POWER includes 21 investigations relating to physical science. The students engage in such activities as operating machines to simplify work, swinging and timing pendulums and bouncing balls, and observing color effects on temperature. Each investigation contains a specific lesson plan, including materials and time needed, background information, procedures, discussion questions, and extensions. Several reproducible student pages are provided with each investigation.

*POPPING WITH POWER.* Activities to Integrate Mathematics and Science (AIMS). Greene, Sean; Crossley, Helen; Dixon, Susan; Hill, Loretta; Rayfield, Helen; Rudig, Anne; Bland, Carol; Wiens, Gina; and Williams, Nancy. Fresno, CA: AIMS, 1985.
Grade(s): 3,4
Supplies: Materials available locally.
Guide: $10.95

In PRIMARY BALANCING, children experiment with balance boards and double-pan balances, as they investigate the concepts of symmetry and equilibrium. Students discover that different objects, though they take up similar amounts of space, may not balance because they weigh different amounts. They are encouraged to develop their own questions and carry out experiments in search of solutions. The guide contains helpful information, with descriptions of children's experiments.

*PRIMARY BALANCING.* Elementary Science Study (ESS). Nashua, NH: Delta, 1985 (1969).
Grade(s): K,1,2,3,4
Supplies: Materials available locally or homemade or kit from Delta.
Guide: $21.50, Kit: $309.00

In RELATIVE POSITION AND MOTION, students learn new concepts through such activities as playing games to locate objects, solving puzzles that use relative position, drawing and interpreting flip-books, surveying the school grounds with a transit, and investigating the motion of colliding steel spheres.

*RELATIVE POSITION AND MOTION.* Science Curriculum Improvement Study (SCIS). Berger, Carl F.; Karplus, Robert; Montgomery, Marshall A.; Randle, Joan Coffman; and Thier, Herbert D. Chicago, IL: Rand McNally, 1972.
Grade(s): 4
Supplies: Materials from Delta.
Out of print. Available on SCIENCE HELPER K-8 (see Sources index).

RELATIVE POSITION AND MOTION, SCIIS/85, is very similar to the previous guides, RELATIVE POSITION AND MOTION (SCIS) and MEASUREMENT, MOTION AND CHANGE (SCIS II), with a few exceptions. An initial lesson uses paper airplanes to review the terms, object, property, interaction, system, and variable. The appendices "Process Evaluation" and "Attitudes in Science" offer new dimensions to the science program. Last, a supplement simplifies the lesson plans, but because it does not contain background information, it should be used along with the basic materials.

*RELATIVE POSITION AND MOTION.* Science Curriculum Improvement Study (SCIIS/85). Karplus, Robert; Thier, Herbert D.; Lawson, Chester A.; Knott, Robert; and Montgomery, Marshall. Nashua, NH: Delta, 1985 (1970).
ISBN 0-87504-407-7
Grade(s): 4
Supplies: Kit from Delta.
Guide: $26.95, Kit: $465.00

*SCIENCE, MODELS AND TOYS: STAGE 3.* Science 5/13. Radford, Don. London, England: Macdonald, 1974. ISBN 0-356-04351-7
Grade(s): 7,8,9
Supplies: Materials available locally or from commercial suppliers.
Guide: $9.00 (Available in the U.S. from Teacher's Laboratory.)

In SCIENCE, MODELS AND TOYS: STAGE 3, toys are used at an advanced level to stimulate interest in a variety of scientific concepts. Through the use of toy boats and bouncing balls, children begin to experience the concepts of force, velocity, energy conversion, and simple ideas of momentum. Each experiment lends itself to numerous investigations, all of which involve children in the manipulation of variables, measurement, record keeping, and problem solving. By including activities on cameras, motors, flight, and mechanical systems, the guide offers a potpourri of activities that a teacher could use in a variety of ways.

*SCIENTIFIC THEORIES.* Science Curriculum Improvement Study (SCIIS/85). Karplus, Robert; Thier, Herbert D.; Knott, Robert; Lawson, Chester A.; and Montgomery, Marshall. Nashua, NH: Delta, 1985 (1970). ISBN 0-87504-411-5
Grade(s): 6
Supplies: Kit from Delta.
Guide: $26.95, Kit: $525.00

Two sections have been added to the SCIIS/85 guide, and the topic/title has been changed from MODELING SYSTEMS to SCIENTIFIC THEORIES. In one new section, students study the properties of colored light by working with prisms, colored plastic, and light sources. In the other new section, the children use light sources, mirrors, and lenses to explore images. A supplement is added to simplify each lesson plan.

*SENIOR BALANCING.* Elementary Science Study (ESS). Nashua, NH: Delta, 1985 (1968).
Grade(s): 4,5,6,7,8
Supplies: Materials homemade or kit from Delta.
Guide: $12.50, Kit (for 6 students): $70.00, Teacher's Kit: $62.00

In SENIOR BALANCING, students investigate the concepts of equilibrium, symmetry, force, and gravity. They use pegboard balance beams and steel washers, attempting to determine how one weight balances another and how balance is affected by changing the position of the fulcrum. The guide contains a list of useful materials, examples of children's experiments, and suggestions for further investigations.

*SINK OR FLOAT.* Elementary Science Study (ESS). Nashua, NH: Delta, 1986 (1971).
Grade(s): 1,2,3,4,5,6,7
Supplies: Materials available locally or kit from Delta.
Guide: $6.10, Kit: $97.00, Activity Cards (48): $5.10

In SINK OR FLOAT, children explore the concept of density of materials by experimenting with displacement and buoyancy. The objects used are cylinders, cubes, and spheres in various sizes and densities (wood, acrylic, aluminum, and polyethylene). As they work with these items, the children find objects that sink in oil but float in water, some that float high and others that barely float. Children sort the objects by weight and buoyancy, measuring and comparing amounts of water displaced by various objects. They find ways to change a "sinker" into a "floater," or vice versa and discover that by adding salt to water, they may be able to affect buoyancy.

*SOLIDS, LIQUIDS, AND GASES: A SCHOOL ASSEMBLY PROGRAM PRESENTER'S GUIDE.* Great Explorations in Math and Science (GEMS). Barber, Jacqueline. Berkeley, CA: Lawrence Hall of Science, 1986.
Grade(s): 3,4,5,6,7
Supplies: Materials available locally, from commercial suppliers, or from Lawrence Hall of Science.
Guide: $10.00

SOLIDS, LIQUIDS, AND GASES may be used as an introduction to a classroom unit on matter or as an assembly program for a large group of students. Experiments and demonstrations are done with giant test tubes, strawberry gas, dry ice, iodine gas, BB models, balloons, and nitinol wire. Children attempt to predict results and participate in the activities. This program may be adapted for a variety of age levels and group sizes. The guide includes a sample script, a program outline, suggestions for the presentation, and specific directions and background information for each of the activities.

The four activities in the SOUND unit explore the invisible vibrations that we hear as sound. Children apply the basic rules of sound production to construct simple musical instruments. The teacher's guide includes a motivating question, a list of materials, a step-by-step procedure, reproducible student worksheets, and possible extension activities for each lesson.

*SOUND*. Franklin Institute Museum-To-Go. Philadelphia, PA: Franklin Institute, 1988 (1983).
Grade(s): 4,5,6
Supplies: Materials available locally or kit from Science Kit, Inc.
Kit: $95.00

SPINNING TABLES provides an opportunity to investigate circular motion, to make predictions, and to observe how various materials behave when placed on a revolving surface. Chalkboard or pegboard disks are set into motion by students turning the crank on an adjacent drive wheel. Children predict how chalkline drawn on the disk will appear when it is set into a spin, and whether it will change as the disk's speed is changed. They can experiment with the paths of marbles or cubes on the spinning table or observe the effects of revolution on closed containers of liquid or powder. The guide suggests small-group work and offers ideas for classroom management and related activities.

*SPINNING TABLES*. Elementary Science Study (ESS). Nashua, NH: Delta, 1985 (1968).
Grade(s): 1,2,3
Supplies: Homemade or kit from Delta.
Guide: $9.80, Kit $216.00

In STRUCTURES, children explore the physical properties of materials and experiment with various design configurations. By working with such materials as clay, straws, paper, wood, dry spaghetti, or cardboard, children learn the possibilities for building towers, bridges, and other structures. They experiment with height, stability, and strength, designing strategies for testing their constructions. Opportunities are offered for small-group work, as well as whole class activities. The guide also provides ideas for additional building projects and suggestions for supplemental classroom tools and supplies.

*STRUCTURES*. Elementary Science Study (ESS). Nashua, NH: Delta, 1985 (1970).
Grade(s): 2,3,4,5,6
Supplies: Materials available locally or kit from Delta.
Guide: $10.60, Kit: $89.00

In STRUCTURES AND FORCES: STAGES 1 AND 2, ideas and activities build upon the natural interest that children have in buildings, bridges, tunnels, and dams. After beginning with observation and discussion about structures in their own environment, children then use a variety of materials to build structures. They test their creations for strength and flexibility, then look for relationships between people-made structures and the structures of animals and plants. Diagrams and photographs are included.

*STRUCTURES AND FORCES: STAGES 1 AND 2*. Science 5/13. James, Albert. London, England: Macdonald, 1972.
ISBN 0-356-04007-0
Grade(s): 3,4,5,6
Supplies: Materials available locally or from commercial suppliers.
Guide: $9.00 (Available in the U.S. from Teacher's Laboratory.)

In STRUCTURES AND FORCES: STAGE 3, the concepts of power, force, acceleration, inertia, and tensile strength are explored through concrete models and materials. Activities that demonstrate energy changes are illustrated with rotating objects, rolling objects, and thrown objects. Methods are provided for measuring various changes, and children are asked to hypothesize about the effects of gravity and velocity on these changes. Additional experiences are included in which children test liquids, springs, paper, and metals with regard to their strength and elasticity. Teacher's using this guide will benefit from some physics background, and children should have prior science experience.

*STRUCTURES AND FORCES: STAGE 3*. Science 5/13. James, Albert. London, England: Macdonald, 1973.
ISBN 0-356-04107-7
Grade(s): 6,7,8
Supplies: Materials available locally or from commercial suppliers.
Guide: $9.00 (Available in the U.S. from Teacher's Laboratory.)

*SUBSYSTEMS AND VARIABLES.*
Science Curriculum Improvement Study
(SCIS). Berger, Carl F.; Bunshoft, Sylvia; Karplus, Robert; and Montgomery, Marshall A. Chicago, IL: Rand McNally, 1970.
Grade(s): 3
Supplies: Materials from Delta.
Out of print. Available on SCIENCE HELPER K-8 (see Sources index).

In SUBSYSTEMS AND VARIABLES, students investigate and identify subsystems by separating sand, salt, and baking soda from a mixture. They classify liquid mixtures as solutions or nonsolutions and use evaporation or filtering to separate the mixtures into subsystems. They compare liquid freon and water in order to determine the properties of each. In the final section, the children experiment with a whirlybird system to explore variables.

*SUBSYSTEMS AND VARIABLES.*
Science Curriculum Improvement Study
(SCIS II). Paldy, Lester G.; Amburgey, Leonard L.; Collea, Francis; Cooper, Richard; Maxwell, Donald E.; and Riley, Joseph W. Nashua, NH: Delta, 1986 (1970).
Grade(s): 3
Supplies: Kit from Delta.
Guide: $15.00, Kit: $392.90, Activity Cards: $17.40

Activities and format for SUBSYSTEMS AND VARIABLES are similar to those in SCIS, with the exception that liquid butyl stearate replaces liquid freon. This was implemented for safety reasons.

*SUBSYSTEMS AND VARIABLES.*
Science Curriculum Improvement Study
(SCIIS/85). Thier, Herbert D.; Karplus, Robert; Knott, Robert; Lawson, Chester A.; and Montgomery, Marshall. Nashua, NH: Delta, 1985 (1970).
ISBN 0-87504-405-0
Grade(s): 3
Supplies: Kit from Delta.
Guide: $26.95, Kit: $525.00

The lessons and organization of SUBSYSTEMS AND VARIABLES in SCIIS/85 are similar to those in SCIS and SCIS II. In this version, however, a section about evaluation has been added and a supplement that simplifies each lesson plan is provided.

*VITAMIN C TESTING.* Great Explorations in Math and Science (GEMS). Barber, Jacqueline. Berkeley, CA: Lawrence Hall of Science, 1988.
Grade(s): 4,5,6,7
Supplies: Materials available locally, from commercial suppliers, or from Lawrence Hall of Science.
Guide: $6.50

In VITAMIN C TESTING, students learn to use the chemistry lab technique titration in a test for vitamin C. They make graphs of test results, measure the amount of vitamin C in familiar fruit juices, and investigate how the treatment of foods affects nutritional value. The guide includes specific lesson plans for each activity, reproducible student data sheets, extension activities, background information, and a list of annotated resources.

In WATER AND ICE, children experiment with bubbles, paper boats, and rainbows in order to explore melting, dissolving, absorbing, evaporating, and freezing. Students make bubbles, construct boats, create marbled paintings, and more. Each of the 28 activities includes a learning objective, process skills, a list of materials, suggested questions, directions for the exploration, and extensions.

*WATER AND ICE (Windows on Science series).* Westly, Joan. Sunnyvale, CA: Creative Publications, 1988. ISBN 0-88488-708-1
Grade(s): K,1,2
Supplies: Materials available locally, from commercial suppliers, or kit from Creative Publications.
Guide: $8.25, Complete Kit for Windows on Science series: $250.00

In WATER FLOW, children observe the circulation of water in closed systems. The students combine clear plastic tubing with other common materials to construct pathways for water flow. They make predictions, then use various tubing configurations to conduct experiments on rate of flow, water levels, and effects of air pressure. Children are encouraged to devise their own problems and to create strategies for solving them. The guide contains many helpful suggestions for activities and classroom management.

*WATER FLOW.* Elementary Science Study (ESS). Nashua, NH: Delta, 1985 (1971).
Grade(s): 5,6
Supplies: Materials available locally or from commercial suppliers, or kit from Delta.
Guide: $15.60, Kit: $152.00

WHISTLES AND STRINGS offers children the opportunity to investigate the acoustic properties of common materials and to construct and play their own musical instruments. Students experiment with plastic tubing, straws, string, paper cups, and other familiar materials, manipulating them in various ways to discover amplitude, pitch, and tone quality, and to discern the relationships between a material and the sound it produces. The guide provides a materials list, instructions for the activities, and examples of how some children have worked with the unit.

*WHISTLES AND STRINGS.* Elementary Science Study (ESS). Nashua, NH: Delta, 1968, 1985.
Grade(s): 3,4,5,6
Supplies: Materials available locally or kit from Delta.
Guide: $19.80, Kit: $143.00

# Multidisciplinary and Applied Science

The Multidisciplinary and Applied Science section contains curriculum materials that integrate several scientific disciplines or math and science, or that focus on the application of scientific processes.

*ADVERTISING.* Unified Science and Mathematics for Elementary Schools (USMES). Newton, MA: Education Development Center, Inc., 1974.
Grade(s): 4,5,6,7,8
Supplies: Materials available locally.
Out of print. Available on SCIENCE HELPER K-8 or from ERIC (see Sources index).

Each USMES unit is based on a challenge that presents a school or community problem to be solved by the children. The ADVERTISING challenge: Find the best way to advertise a product or idea that you want to promote. Children are involved in all aspects of developing an advertising campaign. After the advertising is in progress, data are collected to assess the campaign's effectiveness, and improvements can be made. The teacher's guide has examples of possible campaign strategies; however, no specific lesson plans are provided. A list of questions is included to stimulate further investigation or analysis.

*ARCHI-TEACHER: A GUIDE FOR ARCHITECTURE IN THE SCHOOLS.*
Olsen, Gary L., and Olsen, Michelle J. Chicago, IL: Museum of Science and Industry [no date].
Grade(s): 4,5,6,7
Supplies: Materials available locally.
Guide: free

ARCHI-TEACHER introduces elementary students to design for the human environment through the integration of art, science, math, and history. Children investigate the shape, texture, history, and settings of buildings, experiment with soils and structural supports, make measurements, and create building designs to satisfy a variety of living and working needs. There are eight lessons accompanied by background information and a bibliography.

*ATTRIBUTE GAMES AND PROBLEMS.* Elementary Science Study (ESS). Nashua, NH: Delta, 1984 (1968).
Grade(s): K,1,2,3,4,5,6,7,8,9
Supplies: Kit from Delta.
Guide: $16.90, Kit: $29.00, Activity Cards (70): $25.00, Readers (6): $9.50

In ATTRIBUTE GAMES AND PROBLEMS, children apply processes of observation and classification as they manipulate wooden or plastic objects of various shapes, sizes, and colors. Using their own or suggested criteria, children order the objects by attribute and value, defining sets and subsets, such as yellow squares, large red circles, blue adult females, and so on. Problem cards encourage children to develop strategies for identifying or constructing patterns that meet specific criteria; for example, determining how many unique two-color combinations and presentations can be made using six different colors of cubes, or how many ways there are of putting four cubes of different color in a row. Activities can be used to foster cooperative learning in small groups, as children work together to establish classification criteria and to collect and share data for problem solving, either during scheduled class time, or during free time at classroom learning centers. The guide's inventory of activity materials is not detailed enough to facilitate local purchase or production of supplies.

*BATTERIES AND BULBS II.* Elementary Science Study (ESS). New York, NY: McGraw-Hill [no date].
Grade(s): 4,5,6,7,8
Supplies: Materials available locally or from commercial suppliers.
Out of print. Available from ERIC (see Sources index).

BATTERIES AND BULBS II is a resource book that enhances the study of electricity by offering lists of materials, suggested projects, a trouble-shooting guide, and recommended reading. There are illustrated instructions for making switches, battery testers, electronic games, flashlights, radios, and much more. A list of suppliers is appended, but owing to the age of this publication, it is somewhat outdated.

Each USMES unit is based on a challenge that presents a school or community problem to be solved by the children. The BICYCLE TRANSPORTATION challenge: Find ways to make bicycle riding a safe and convenient way to travel. In the unit, the children investigate safety problems associated with cycling in their community. Discussions lead to the planning of bike paths, requiring cost analyses of labor and materials, investigations of community laws, and submission of organized data and plans to proper authorities. The teacher's guide includes examples of methods used for data collection; however, no specific lesson plans are provided. A list of questions is included to stimulate further investigation or analysis.

*BICYCLE TRANSPORTATION.* Unified Science and Mathematics for Elementary Schools (USMES). Newton, MA: Education Development Center, Inc., 1973. Grade(s): 4,5,6,7,8 Supplies: Materials available locally. Out of print. Available on SCIENCE HELPER K-8 or from ERIC (see Sources index).

Each USMES unit is based on a challenge that presents a school or community problem to be solved by the children. The BURGLAR ALARM DESIGN challenge: Build a burglar alarm that will give adequate warning. Children proceed from simple alarms with warning lights and buzzers to more complex alarms with mechanical improvements. The teacher's guide contains no specific lesson plans but does include teachers' logs describing the use of this challenge.

*BURGLAR ALARM DESIGN.* Unified Science and Mathematics for Elementary Schools (USMES). Newton, MA: Education Development Center, Inc., 1973. Grade(s): 3,4,5,6,7,8 Supplies: Materials available locally. Out of print. Available on SCIENCE HELPER K-8 or from ERIC (see Sources index).

In CHANGE: STAGES 1 AND 2 AND BACKGROUND, a variety of natural phenomena and physical happenings are examined as illustrations of the concept of change. Children look at weather, plants, and toys, and monitor changes in their environment. In the kitchen area, children wash objects, cool and heat things, then mix and measure materials to understand simple changes that occur daily. The guide supports the teacher's understanding of change with background information and examples of the work of other teachers.

*CHANGE: STAGES 1 AND 2 AND BACKGROUND.* Science 5/13. Radford, Don. London, England: Macdonald, 1973. ISBN 0-356-04105-0 Grade(s): 3,4,5,6,7 Supplies: Materials available locally or from commercial suppliers. Guide: $9.00 (Available in the U.S. from Teacher's Laboratory.)

In CHANGE: STAGE 3, activities give children experience with a variety of chemical, electrical, and physical changes and also provide specific knowledge about these processes. Children see the importance of energy changes and how these changes are ultimately related to the sun's energy. Numerous experiments illustrate the properties of chemical and electrical change and how energy produced from these changes can be used. The guide is comprehensive, but the teacher will need a solid understanding of these topics to engage the children successfully.

*CHANGE: STAGE 3.* Science 5/13. Radford, Don. London, England: Macdonald, 1973. ISBN 0-356-04346-0 Grade(s): 7,8,9,10,11,12 Supplies: Materials available locally or from commercial suppliers. Guide: $9.00 (Available in the U.S. from Teacher's Laboratory.)

CHANGES provides children with the opportunity to observe, discuss, record, and predict natural changes brought about by both living and nonliving processes. Children place common materials, such as bread, seeds, ice cubes, nails, rocks, candles, and oranges into separate glass jars and leave them in a safe place. As time passes, children compare their observations and attempt to determine what changes, if any, have occurred, and why. They investigate the effects of moisture, light, temperature, or preservatives. They are encouraged to apply their findings to changes occurring outside the classroom; for example, in rusty bicycles, trash cans, or neighborhood ponds.

*CHANGES.* Elementary Science Study (ESS). New York, NY: McGraw-Hill, 1968. Grade(s): 1,2,3,4 Supplies: Materials available locally. Out of print. Available on SCIENCE HELPER K-8 or from ERIC (see Sources index).

*CHILDREN AND PLASTICS: STAGES 1 AND 2 AND BACKGROUND.* Science 5/13. Horn, Mary. London, England: Macdonald, 1974. ISBN 0-356-04352-5
Grade(s): 4,5,6,7
Supplies: Materials available locally or from commercial suppliers.
Guide: $9.00 (Available in the U.S. from Teacher's Laboratory.)

In CHILDREN AND PLASTICS, a common, everyday material is used as the stimulus to involve children in a variety of scientific processes. The teacher raises questions about the properties of plastic. Then children propose inquiries, design experiments, communicate, measure, and solve problems as they investigate the strength, bendability, and stretchability of plastic bags, bottles, and threads. The uses of plastic are explored, and children set up tests to compare how different plastic clothes repel water, stay warm, or get clean. The background information provides enough support so that the teacher can successfully direct the learning experiences.

*CLASSIFICATION FUN.* Missouri Botanical Garden (Suitcase Science). St. Louis, MO: Missouri Botanical Garden [no date].
Grade(s): P,K,1,2,3
Supplies: Materials available locally or kit from Missouri Botanical Garden.
Kit: free local loan with $25.00 deposit

In CLASSIFICATION FUN, children learn to distinguish between living and nonliving objects, use careful observation to establish criteria for sorting, and investigate adaptations that influence formal classification of plants and animals. The guide contains a complete materials list and many ideas for extension. Although written to accompany a Suitcase Science kit, this guide can be used very effectively alone.

*CLASSROOM DESIGN.* Unified Science and Mathematics for Elementary Schools (USMES). Newton, MA: Education Development Center, Inc., 1974.
Grade(s): 1,2,3,4,5,6,7,8
Supplies: Materials available locally.
Out of print. Available on SCIENCE HELPER K-8 or from ERIC (see Sources index).

Each USMES unit is based on a challenge that presents a school or community problem to be solved by the children. The CLASSROOM DESIGN challenge: Find ways to make the classroom a better place. Children help to establish priorities among areas needing change. They assess the suitability of the proposed changes to their room and also consider costs and availability of materials before changes can be implemented. The teacher's guide includes examples of student-drawn class designs and preference surveys; however, no specific lesson plans are provided. A list of questions is included to stimulate further investigation or analysis.

*CLASSROOM MANAGEMENT.* Unified Science and Mathematics for Elementary Schools (USMES). Newton, MA: Education Development Center, Inc., 1975.
Grade(s): 1,2,3,4,5,6
Supplies: Materials available locally.
Out of print. Available from ERIC (see Sources index).

Each USMES unit is based on a challenge that presents a school or community problem to be solved by the children. The CLASSROOM MANAGEMENT challenge: Find ways of developing and maintaining a well-run classroom. This challenge can be introduced easily at the beginning of the school year before class routines have been established. It can also be used effectively to solve problems of management that occur during the course of the year. The teacher's guide includes a range of possible activities; however, no specific lesson plans are provided. A list of questions is included to stimulate further investigation or analysis.

*COLOUR.* Learning Through Science. Kincaid, Doug, and Richards, Roy. London, England: Macdonald, 1981.
ISBN 0-356-07550-8
Grade(s): K,1,2,3,4
Supplies: Materials available locally or from commercial suppliers.
Activity Cards and Guide: $27.00 (Available in the U.S. from Teacher's Laboratory.)

In the COLOUR activity cards, observation skills are heightened as children study the world of color. Each activity raises questions then proposes inquiries that will lead children to a better understanding of colors in relation to the local environment. Children collect items of various colors, experiment with the mixing of colors, assess the usefulness of color in certain items, investigate color perception, and learn about the importance of color to the success of plants and animals. The 24 activity cards can be used independently by children or as a guide for a total class lesson. The teacher's guide contains no formal lesson plans but offers useful information.

In COLOURED THINGS: STAGES 1 AND 2, observation skills are emphasized as children look at the world around them to the spectrum and diversity of color. Activities encourage collecting, listing, and comparing, and then communicating about what was seen and learned. Plants and animals are eyed for their unique colors, and children examine the environment to find the essence of color in everyday, familiar objects. The guide provides lead-in questions that will stimulate thought and direct discussion.

*COLOURED THINGS: STAGES 1 AND 2.* Science 5/13. Parker, Sheila. London, England: Macdonald, 1973.
ISBN 0-356-04348-7
Grade(s): K,1,2,3,4,5
Supplies: Materials available locally or from commercial suppliers.
Guide: $9.00 (Available in the U.S. from Teacher's Laboratory.)

In the CONSTRUCTIONS unit, children classify and compare building materials, explore how materials may be made weaker or stronger, investigate support in structures and what affects stability and balance, experiment with a variety of simple machines, and create different constructions. Each of the 28 activities includes a learning objective, process skills, list of materials, suggested questions, directions for the exploration, and extensions.

*CONSTRUCTIONS (Windows on Science series).* Westly, Joan. Sunnyvale, CA: Creative Publications, 1988.
ISBN 0-88488-711-1
Grade(s): K,1,2
Supplies: Materials available locally, from commercial suppliers, or kit from Creative Publications.
Guide: $8.25, Complete Kit for Windows on Science series: $250.00

Each USMES unit is based on a challenge that presents a school or community problem to be solved by the children. The CONSUMER RESEARCH—PRODUCT TESTING challenge: Determine which brand is the best buy for a certain purpose. The children are involved in all phases of testing several brands of a product for quality. They formulate test procedures, predict outcomes, record data, graph information, and reach conclusions based on results. The teacher's guide contains no specific lesson plans but does include teachers' logs of previously tested products.

*CONSUMER RESEARCH—PRODUCT TESTING.* Unified Science and Mathematics for Elementary Schools (USMES). Newton, MA: Education Development Center, Inc., 1973.
Grade(s): 1,2,3,4,5,6,7,8
Supplies: Materials available locally.
Out of print. Available from ERIC (see Sources index).

The COPES TEACHER'S GUIDE FOR KINDERGARTEN/GRADE ONE sequence introduces learning skills that are considered basic to the study of key science concepts in later grades. Kindergarten children learn to observe carefully; to describe and record the properties of objects; to classify objects according to their properties; to make comparisons in number, dimensions, weight, and group characteristics; and to note the processes of change and the results of interactions between objects. In first grade, students continue to sharpen these skills and add to them, engaging in activities in measurement, conservation of matter, and variability of populations. There are 19 lessons in the kindergarten sequence and 24 for first grade. Student activity sheets are included, as are materials lists and science background information. Advice on classroom management and suggestions for extensions are also provided.

*COPES TEACHER'S GUIDE FOR KINDERGARTEN/GRADE ONE.* Conceptually Oriented Program in Elementary Science (COPES). New York, NY: New York University, Center for Educational Research and Field Services, 1971.
Grade(s): K,1,2
Supplies: Materials available locally.
Out of print. Available on SCIENCE HELPER K-8 (see Sources index).

*COPES TEACHER'S GUIDE FOR GRADE TWO*. Conceptually Oriented Program in Elementary Science (COPES). New York, NY: New York University, Center for Educational Research and Field Services, 1971.
Grade(s): 2,3
Supplies: Materials available locally.
Out of print. Available on SCIENCE HELPER K-8 (see Sources index).

The COPES TEACHER'S GUIDE FOR GRADE TWO encourages second grade students to draw on the skills taught in earlier sequences, as they look for patterns of relationships among objects and phenomena. Children begin by sorting familiar articles, then investigate relationships between vibrating objects and the sounds they produce, iron filings and magnets, and inks and their color components. They create and calibrate their own measurement devices, produce bar graphs, make predictions based on what they know from their measurements and their recognition of patterns, and learn that they can impose order on seemingly chaotic groupings. The guide contains instructions for 15 activities, with materials lists and evaluation instruments. Background information, classroom management techniques, and extension ideas are provided.

*COPES TEACHER'S GUIDE FOR GRADE THREE*. Conceptually Oriented Program in Elementary Science (COPES). New York, NY: New York University, Center for Educational Research and Field Services, 1972.
Grade(s): 3,4
Supplies: Materials available locally.
Out of print. Available on SCIENCE HELPER K-8 (see Sources index).

The COPES TEACHER'S GUIDE FOR GRADE THREE builds on prior learning in science and introduces skills needed for later grades. Students work with mixtures and solutions, identifying characteristics of constituent components and how they interact. They experiment with balanced forces, investigate the variability of populations, and calculate averages. Then, in explorations of interaction and change, they build electrical circuits and conduct heat- transfer experiments with water. There are 26 sequential lessons with assessments and suggested equipment lists. Science background information, classroom management techniques, and ideas for extension are provided.

*COPES TEACHER'S GUIDE FOR GRADE FOUR*. Conceptually Oriented Program in Elementary Science (COPES). New York, NY: New York University, Center for Educational Research and Field Services, 1972.
Grade(s): 4,5,6
Supplies: Materials available locally.
Out of print. Available on SCIENCE HELPER K-8 (see Sources index).

The COPES TEACHER'S GUIDE FOR GRADE FOUR focuses on conservation of matter and energy. Children investigate the effects of change or interaction on states of matter in closed or open systems, observing weight of solid and melted ice cubes, the dry weight of peeled and unpeeled apples, and mold growth on bread in a plastic bag. They conduct experiments with heat transfer in water and investigate transport of molecules through membranes, using red cabbage pigment, starch, vinegar, food coloring, and ammonia. The students continue to study and graph variability and frequency of distribution, as they calculate averages for peas in a pod and ages of students, and try to predict spins of a game wheel. There are 33 lessons with suggested assessments and lists of supplies. Advice on classroom management, science background information, and extension ideas are provided as well.

*COPES TEACHER'S GUIDE FOR GRADE FIVE*. Conceptually Oriented Program in Elementary Science (COPES). New York, NY: New York University, Center for Educational Research and Field Services, 1973.
Grade(s): 5,6,7
Supplies: Materials available locally.
Out of print. Available on SCIENCE HELPER K-8 (see Sources index).

The COPES TEACHER'S GUIDE FOR GRADE FIVE applies previously learned science process skills to new activities with microscopes, mechanical energy, energy transformation, and statistical sampling. Students examine the structure of plant and animal cells; investigate potential and kinetic energy as they experiment with weights and forces; explore the role of temperature variation in solutions and the precipitation of salts in water; convert light energy to heat energy; and apply statistical methods to experiments with marbles, dice, and seeds. The 21 lessons are accompanied by assessment tools and supply lists. Tips on classroom management, explanations of science content, and suggestions for further exploration are provided, as is a detailed discussion of microscopes and their use.

The COPES TEACHER'S GUIDE FOR GRADE SIX presents activities culminating the conceptual schemes of the entire series. Students investigate the interactions between plants and their soil or water environment; observe the role of heat in chemical bonding of salts; examine the crystalline structure of copper; test the transfer of heat energy in liquids and solids; apply statistical methods to random diffusion of molecules in water or gelatin, or to children's movements in the classroom; and use pendulums to explore the possibility of "perpetual" conservation of mechanical energy. There are 32 lessons, accompanied by assessment tools, supply lists, advice on classroom management, and science background information.

*COPES TEACHER'S GUIDE FOR GRADE SIX.* Conceptually Oriented Program in Elementary Science (COPES). New York, NY: New York University, Center for Educational Research and Field Services, 1973.
Grade(s): 6,7,8
Supplies: Materials available locally.
Out of print. Available on SCIENCE HELPER K-8 (see Sources index).

Each USMES unit is based on a challenge that presents a school or community problem to be solved by the children. The DESCRIBING PEOPLE challenge: Find out what is the best information to put in a description so that a person can be quickly and easily identified. Children look for a systematic way to identify a person in real situations by specifying certain physical characteristics. They test their hypotheses by a Sit-Down game or Venn diagrams. They also investigate different identification problems. The teacher's guide contains no specific lesson plans but does include teachers' logs describing the use of this challenge.

*DESCRIBING PEOPLE.* Unified Science and Mathematics for Elementary Schools (USMES). Newton, MA: Education Development Center, Inc., 1973.
Grade(s): 1,2,3,4,5,6,7,8
Supplies: Materials available locally.
Out of print. Available from ERIC (see Sources index).

Each USMES unit is based on a challenge that presents a school or community problem to be solved by the children. The DESIGNING FOR HUMAN PROPORTIONS challenge: Find a way to design or make changes in things that you use or wear so that they will be a good fit. After discussing and assessing what needs to be changed, children determine the sizes of items needed for a varied population. Measurement skills are called for throughout. The teacher's guide contains no specific lesson plans but does include teachers' logs describing the use of this challenge.

*DESIGNING FOR HUMAN PROPORTIONS.* Unified Science and Mathematics for Elementary Schools (USMES). Newton, MA: Education Development Center, Inc., 1974.
Grade(s): 3,4,5,6,7,8
Supplies: Materials available locally.
Out of print. Available from ERIC (see Sources index).

Each USMES unit is based on a challenge that presents a school or community problem to be solved by the children. The DICE DESIGN challenge: Construct practical shapes that can be used as dice to make fair decisions between two or among three or four or more choices. The children explore regular and non-regular solids, construct polyhedra, collect and record data, play dice games, and bet on games. The teacher's guide includes logs from several teachers who have used this challenge. No specific lesson plans are provided.

*DICE DESIGN.* Unified Science and Mathematics for Elementary Schools (USMES). Newton, MA: Education Development Center, Inc., 1973.
Grade(s): 1,2,3,4,5,6,7,8
Supplies: Materials available locally.
Out of print. Available from ERIC (see Sources index).

In EARLY EXPERIENCES, children are encouraged to use their senses to find out the true meaning of science. Activities involve looking at things close at hand or in the sky, listening to sounds and trying to create sound, growing things, and then talking about change. The guide provides many helpful suggestions for how to use everyday classroom and household items to stimulate scientific thought, and to encourage communication and hands-on involvement. A healthy sprinkling of children's drawings and charts provides ideas on appropriate record keeping for the early science explorer.

*EARLY EXPERIENCES.* Science 5/13. Richards, Roy. London, England: Macdonald, 1972. ISBN 0-356-04005-4
Grade(s): K,1,2
Supplies: Materials available locally or from commercial suppliers.
Guide: $9.00 (Available in the U.S. from Teacher's Laboratory.)

*ELECTROMAGNET DEVICE DESIGN.* Unified Science and Mathematics for Elementary Schools (USMES). Newton, MA: Education Development Center, Inc., 1973.
Grade(s): 3,4,5,6,7,8
Supplies: Materials available locally.
Out of print. Available from ERIC (see Sources index).

Each USMES unit is based on a challenge that presents a school or community problem to be solved by the children. The ELECTROMAGNET DEVICE DESIGN challenge: Design a good electromagnet for a specific purpose. The activities suggested for this unit generally focus on the problem of building either strong or lightweight electromagnets that won't quickly wear down batteries. The children identify and test variables. The teacher's guide contains no specific lesson plans but does include teachers' logs describing the use of this challenge.

*ENVIRONMENTAL ENERGY.* Science Activities for the Visually Impaired/Science Enrichment for Learners with Physical Handicaps (SAVI/SELPH). Berkeley, CA: Lawrence Hall of Science Center for Multisensory Learning, 1983.
Grade(s): 4,5,6,7
Supplies: Kit from Lawrence Hall of Science.
Folio Guide: $5.00, Complete Kit: $107.00, Economy Kit: $61.00

The ENVIRONMENTAL ENERGY module contains four activities focusing on energy sources: Solar Water Heater, Sun Power, Blowin' in the Wind, and Wind Power. Students investigate the concepts of active and stored energy and experiment with energy transfer, as they set up simple solar water heaters in the schoolyard, then test the effects of varying size, covering, or color on water temperature. Pinwheels are used to study the availability of wind power in various locations and to compare the amount of work that can be done by pinwheels of various sizes. The instructions are well organized and supported by science information, as well as by techniques for offering successful experiences to learners of varied physical capabilities.

*FALL INTO MATH AND SCIENCE.* Activities to Integrate Mathematics and Science (AIMS). Adair, Robin; Ewing, Jill; Faircloth, Shirley; Nikoghosian, Janice; Peterson, Cynthia; Smith, Darlene; and Wiebe, Sheila. Fresno, CA: AIMS, 1987.
Grade(s): K,1
Supplies: Materials available locally.
Guide: $10.95

FALL INTO MATH AND SCIENCE contains 15 investigations that emphasize a variety of graphing activities related to the beginning of the school year. Topics include weather, food, human growth, plant life, fall holidays, and leaves. Each investigation has a specific lesson plan, including materials and time needed, background information, procedures, discussion questions, and extensions. Several reproducible student pages can be found after each lesson plan. The students practice making three types of graphs—real, representational, and abstract.

*FINGERPRINTING.* Great Explorations in Math and Science (GEMS). Ahouse, Jeremy John. Berkeley, CA: Lawrence Hall of Science, 1987.
Grade(s): 4,5,6
Supplies: Materials available locally, from commercial suppliers, or from Lawrence Hall of Science.
Guide: $6.50

In FINGERPRINTING, students make and classify fingerprints and use fingerprints to help solve a "crime." The guide includes suggestions for extensions and information that will help children answer such questions as, Who keeps track of fingerprints? Can a person change or remove his/her fingerprints? How do police officers obtain fingerprints from the scene of a crime? Lesson plans for the specific activities are well written and include reproducible student worksheets.

FUN WITH FOODS contains 25 investigations that use food and equipment found in kitchens, supermarkets, or school classrooms to teach and reinforce process skills in math and science. The students determine the edible part of an orange by volume, analyze cafeteria lunches, discover that mayonnaise is an emulsion, and find fractions in fondue. Each investigation contains a specific lesson plan, including materials and time needed, background information, procedures, discussion questions, and extensions. Several reproducible student pages are provided with each investigation.

*FUN WITH FOODS: A RECIPE FOR MATH + SCIENCE.* Activities to Integrate Mathematics and Science (AIMS). Alfving, Alberta M.; Eitzen, C. Lloyd; Hyman, Joanne; Patron, Rose Lee; Holve, Helen; and Nelson, Philip. Fresno, CA: AIMS, 1987.
Grade(s): 5,6,7,8
Supplies: Materials available locally.
Guide: $10.95

GEO BLOCKS is a unit that enables young children to become familiar with surface area and volume relationships. As children create designs and constructions with the blocks, either in free play or during more directed activity, they learn to recognize geometric shapes and to see how the shapes relate to one another. The guide contains complete details as to the number and dimensions of blocks appropriate for the activities.

*GEO BLOCKS.* Elementary Science Study (ESS). Nashua, NH: Delta, 1985 (1969).
Grade(s): K,1,2,3,4
Supplies: Materials available locally or homemade, or kit from Delta.
Guide: $4.80, Kit: $84.00, Activity Cards (42): $16.00

GLIDE INTO WINTER WITH MATH AND SCIENCE contains 16 investigations that employ graphing skills, as children observe, interpret, and record data provided by the happenings of the winter season. Topics include weather, static electricity, growing crystals, nutrition, and the human body. Each investigation has a specific lesson plan, including materials and time needed, background information, procedures, discussion questions, and extensions. Several reproducible student pages can be found after each lesson plan.

*GLIDE INTO WINTER WITH MATH AND SCIENCE.* Activities to Integrate Mathematics and Science (AIMS). Adair, Robin; Ewing, Jill; Faircloth, Shirley; Nikoghosian, Janice; Peterson, Cynthia; Smith, Darlene; and Wiebe, Sheila. Fresno, CA: AIMS, 1985.
Grade(s): K,1
Supplies: Materials available locally.
Guide: $10.95

In the Learning Through Science GUIDE AND INDEX, the educational premises upon which the series is based are detailed and organized. Charts provide an excellent reference to identify the scope and sequence of learning objectives. Elementary science concepts and processes are elucidated. A section on evaluation identifies criteria through which the teacher may determine when children have attained proficiency in certain science education objectives.

*GUIDE AND INDEX.* Learning Through Science. Richards, Roy; Collis, Margaret; and Kincaid, Doug. London, England: Macdonald, 1985.
ISBN 0-356-11258-6
Guide: $27.00 (Available in the U.S. from Teacher's Laboratory.)

HARD HATTING IN A GEO-WORLD includes 25 investigations relating to geometry, structures, and measurement. The students carry out many activities involving measurement, as they build and test structures and joints, observe and classify geometric shapes, and discover the mysteries surrounding skyscrapers and bridges. Each investigation contains a specific lesson plan, including materials and time needed, background information, procedures, discussion questions, and extensions. Several reproducible student pages accompany each investigation.

*HARD HATTING IN A GEO-WORLD.* Activities to Integrate Mathematics and Science (AIMS). Courtney, Barry; Haracz, Geraldine; Crossley, Helen; Hill, Loretta; Dixon, Susan; Wiebe, Ann; and Williams, Nancy. Fresno, CA: AIMS, 1986.
Grade(s): 3,4
Supplies: Materials available locally.
Guide: $10.95

*HOLES, GAPS AND CAVITIES: STAGES 1 AND 2*. Science 5/13. Richards, Roy. London, England: Macdonald, 1973. ISBN 0-356-04108-5
Grade(s): 2,3,4,5,5
Supplies: Materials available locally or from commercial suppliers.
Guide: $9.00 (Available in the U.S. from Teacher's Laboratory.)

In HOLES, GAPS AND CAVITIES: STAGES 1 AND 2, activities focus on the inquisitive nature of children as the unusual topic of holes is investigated. Collecting, observing, measuring, creating, and communicating about holes set the stage for in-depth explorations. By filling holes with air, liquids, and light, children gain an appreciation for the uniqueness of holes, based on their size and shape. The eye and other cranial openings are examined as unique holes that have very specialized and important functions. This is a particularly well organized and thorough guide.

*HOT WATER AND WARM HOMES FROM SUNLIGHT*. Great Explorations in Math and Science (GEMS). Gould, Alan. Berkeley, CA: Lawrence Hall of Science, 1986.
Grade(s): 5,6,7,8
Supplies: Materials available locally, from commercial suppliers, or from Lawrence Hall of Science.
Guide: $7.50

In HOT WATER AND WARM HOMES FROM SUNLIGHT, children conduct simple experiments to find out how sunlight can be used to heat houses and water. Students build paper model houses; conduct a solar house experiment; investigate solar water heaters; and discuss controlled experiments, variables, and results. Each of the four lesson plans includes an overview, duration, a list of materials, suggestions for preparation, directions for the activity, and extensions.

*LIKE AND UNLIKE: STAGES 1, 2, AND 3*. Science 5/13. James, Albert. London, England: Macdonald, 1973.
ISBN 0-356-04350-9
Grade(s): K,1,2,3,4,5,6,7
Supplies: Materials available locally or from commercial suppliers.
Guide: $9.00 (Available in the U.S. from Teacher's Laboratory.)

In LIKE AND UNLIKE: STAGES 1, 2, AND 3, children are involved in numerous activities that teach and reinforce science process skills. After looking for similarities and differences among familiar household and classroom objects, children use their senses, measure, and sort to arrive at easily defined classification schemes. Objects such as shells and leaves, with patterns based on sequences, are presented, as are activities that give children hands-on experience with the separation of such materials as soil or salt water into component parts. This guide concludes with a discussion of the uses and overall importance of sorting to the development of scientific thinking.

*LUNCH LINES*. Unified Science and Mathematics for Elementary Schools (USMES). Newton, MA: Education Development Center, Inc., 1973.
Grade(s): 1,2,3,4,5,6,7,8
Supplies: Materials available locally.
Out of print. Available from ERIC (see Sources index).

Each USMES unit is based on a challenge that presents a school or community problem to be solved by the children. The LUNCH LINES challenge: Recommend and try to have changes made which would improve the service in your lunchroom. Children observe the present cafeteria situation, collect relevant data, draw conclusions, and recommend improvements. The teacher's guide contains no specific lesson plans but does include teachers' logs describing the use of this challenge.

*MANAGEMENT GUIDE (Windows on Science series)*. Brummett, Micaelia R. Sunnyvale, CA: Creative Publications, 1988. ISBN 0-88488-712-X
Supplies: Materials available locally, from commercial suppliers, or kit from Creative Publications.
Guide: $8.25, Complete Kit for Windows on Science series: $250.00

The MANAGEMENT GUIDE for Windows on Science explains the philosophy and organization and describes the individual components of this early childhood program. The authors include information about safety guidelines and about developing thinking skills. Science process skills are delineated for each unit, and reproducible student data sheets, sorting mat labels, templates, and word cards are contained in this guide.

Each USMES unit is based on a challenge that presents a school or community problem to be solved by the children. The MANUFACTURING challenge: Find the best way to produce in quantity an item that is needed. Children are involved in all aspects of making and distributing a product. Some of these include creating product designs, testing materials, raising money to purchase materials, and surveying customers' preferences. Children determine work style, i.e., individually, in groups, or on an assembly line. The teacher's guide includes several examples of class production plans; however, no specific lesson plans are provided. A list of questions is included to stimulate further investigation or analysis.

*MANUFACTURING.* Unified Science and Mathematics for Elementary Schools (USMES). Newton, MA: Education Development Center, Inc., 1974.
Grade(s): 4,5,6,7,8
Supplies: Materials available locally.
Out of print. Available on SCIENCE HELPER K-8 or from ERIC (see Sources index).

MATCH AND MEASURE suggests contexts across the curriculum in which young children can match and compare objects, gradually approaching an understanding of formal measurement. While engaged in classroom activities, such as building with blocks, growing plants, or listening to stories, children are encouraged to find out how big, how far, how small things are, and how they compare with other things, such as lengths of string or widths of hands. Activities for measuring area and volume are suggested as well, and the guide contains a list of useful classroom measuring materials.

*MATCH AND MEASURE.* Elementary Science Study (ESS). Nashua, NH: Delta, 1985 (1969).
Grade(s): K,1,2
Supplies: Materials available locally or kit from Delta.
Guide: $18.70, Kit: $198.00

In the MATERIALS activity cards, a careful look around the house or classroom provides numerous items that can be investigated. Containers of various sorts, tools, fabrics, and paper are all used as the bases of experiments that emphasize classification, observation, and recording results. Once questions are raised, activities are illustrated that will lead the children to answers or to further investigations. The 24 activity cards can be used independently by children or as a guide for a total class lesson. The teacher's guide contains no formal lesson plans but offers useful information.

*MATERIALS.* Learning Through Science. Kincaid, Doug, and Richards, Roy. London, England: Macdonald, 1982.
ISBN 0-356-07551-6
Grade(s): K,1,2,3,4
Supplies: Materials available locally or from commercial suppliers.
Activity Cards and Guide: $27.00 (Available in the U.S. from Teacher's Laboratory.)

MATH + SCIENCE, A SOLUTION presents 25 introductory investigations, sequenced from the simple to the complex according to these science processes: observing and classifying, measuring, estimating, predicting and hypothesizing, controlling variables, gathering and recording data, interpreting data, and applying and generalizing. The students observe and predict minting dates of pennies, compare the amount of bounce in different balls, and predict patterns in the occurrence of certain colors of candies in bags of M&M's. Each investigation contains a specific lesson plan, including materials and time needed, background information, procedures, discussion questions, and extensions. Several reproducible student pages are provided with each investigation.

*MATH + SCIENCE, A SOLUTION.* Activities to Integrate Mathematics and Science (AIMS). Campopiano, John; Hillen, Judith; Kinnear, John; Laidlaw, Walt; Rice, Nancy; and Zahlis, Karen. Fresno, CA: AIMS, 1986.
Grade(s): 5,6,7,8
Supplies: Materials available locally.
Guide: $10.95

*MEASUREMENT.* Science Activities for the Visually Impaired/Science Enrichment for Learners with Physical Handicaps (SAVI/SELPH). Berkeley, CA: Lawrence Hall of Science Center for Multisensory Learning, 1982.
Grade(s): 4,5,6,7
Supplies: Kit from Lawrence Hall of Science.
Folio Guide: $5.00, Complete Kit: $174.00, Economy Kit: $157.00

The MEASUREMENT module introduces the metric system through four activities: The First Straw, Take Me to Your Liter, Weight Watching, and The Third Degree. Students learn the importance of standard units of measure as they investigate length, volume, weight, and temperature of familiar items, using tools that are adapted to the needs of children with visual impairments or other physical handicaps. The instructions provide science background information, and although originally written for children with special needs, they contain many helpful suggestions for facilitating successful learning experiences among all learners. The kit includes student worksheets in either print or braille.

*METALS: BACKGROUND INFORMATION.* Science 5/13. Radford, Don. London, England: Macdonald, 1973. ISBN 0-356-04104-2
Supplies: Materials available locally or from commercial suppliers.
Guide: $9.00 (Available in the U.S. from Teacher's Laboratory.)

In METALS: BACKGROUND INFORMATION, information on the composition, extraction, physical and chemical properties, and shaping of metals is provided to aid the teacher using METALS, STAGES 1 AND 2. All aspects of the study of metals are covered in this examination of some of the most important elements. There are detailed sections on the most common metals (aluminum, copper, lead, magnesium, nickel, tin, and zinc). The guide is illustrated with helpful charts and diagrams.

*METALS: STAGES 1 AND 2.* Science 5/13. Radford, Don. London, England: Macdonald, 1973. ISBN 0-356-04103-2
Grade(s): 6,7,8
Supplies: Materials available locally or from commercial suppliers.
Guide: $9.00 (Available in the U.S. from Teacher's Laboratory.)

In METALS: STAGES 1 AND 2, difficult activities concerning the nature of metals demand careful and accurate investigations. By examining the hardness, shininess, and bendability of various metals, children come to appreciate how properties of materials influence their use. Additional challenges focus on the chemical changes that affect metals and what this means when one is choosing a specific metal for a particular job. This unit is especially suited to scientifically motivated students.

*MYSTERY BOXES.* Missouri Botanical Garden (Suitcase Science). St. Louis: Missouri Botanical Garden [no date].
Grade(s): P,K,1,2,3
Supplies: Materials available locally or kit from Missouri Botanical Garden.
Kit: free local loan with $25.00 deposit

MYSTERY BOXES invites young children to sharpen their sensory perception skills. Students try to determine the contents of closed boxes by using only their sense of touch or their sense of smell. The guide contains ideas for extensions, as well as background information on the kinds of mystery materials that may be used.

*ON THE MOVE.* Learning Through Science. Kincaid, Doug, and Richards, Roy. London, England: Macdonald, 1983. ISBN 0-356-07555-9
Grade(s): K,1,2,3
Supplies: Materials available locally or from commercial suppliers.
Activity Cards and Guide: $27.00 (Available in the U.S. from Teacher's Laboratory.)

In the ON THE MOVE activity cards, children engage in observations about, and investigations into, the nature of movement. They compare the movement of mammals, birds, fish, and various invertebrates to get a sense of the variety of forms of locomotion seen in the animal kingdom. The principles of flight are illustrated through the examination of paper airplanes, boomerangs, parachutes, and autogyros. Movement on water and land is explored as children build clay boats, tops, wheeled vehicles, and thread spools. The teacher's guide contains no formal lesson plans but offers useful information. The 24 activity cards can be used independently or in teacher-directed lessons.

Each USMES unit is based on a challenge that presents a school or community problem to be solved by the children. The ORIENTATION challenge: Find ways to help yourselves and/or others adapt to new situations. Children determine where orientation problems exist for themselves or for others in the school and then decide on possible solutions. Surveys of students' opinions, tallying and graphing of data, making maps, directories, information packets, or slide-tape shows are only some of the possibilities for this unit. The teacher's guide includes a range of possible activities; however, no specific lesson plans are provided. A list of questions is included to stimulate further investigation or analysis.

*ORIENTATION.* Unified Science and Mathematics for Elementary Schools (USMES). Newton, MA: Education Development Center, Inc., 1975.
Grade(s): 2,3,4,5,6,7,8
Supplies: Materials available locally.
Out of print. Available on SCIENCE HELPER K-8 or from ERIC (see Sources index).

In PAPER TOWEL TESTING, students examine the wet strength and absorbency of four brands of paper towels, consider the results and the cost of each product, and then determine the best buy. This unit not only reinforces science and math concepts but also helps prepare students to make informed consumer decisions. The teacher's guide contains well-written lesson plans for each activity and reproducible student data sheets.

*PAPER TOWEL TESTING.* Great Explorations in Math and Science (GEMS). Sneider, Cary I., and Barber, Jacqueline. Berkeley, CA: Lawrence Hall of Science, 1988.
Grade(s): 4,5,6,7
Supplies: Materials available locally, from commercial suppliers, or from Lawrence Hall of Science.
Guide: $6.50

PATTERN BLOCKS may be used to encourage children in experimenting with shapes and patterns. Using colored wooden blocks of six different geometric shapes, children invent their own designs or attempt to solve puzzles and problems, filling in outlines, investigating perimeter and area, or experimenting with symmetry. Mirrors may also be added to the activities. The guide suggests informal, small group work or learning stations. The guide also contains detailed description of materials to facilitate easy local production, and it provides supplemental information on some of the mathematical principles involved.

*PATTERN BLOCKS.* Elementary Science Study (ESS). Nashua, NH: Delta, 1986 (1970).
Grade(s): K,1,2,3,4,5,6
Supplies: Materials available locally or homemade, or kit from Delta.
Guide: $5.70, Kit: $30.00, Activity Cards (44):$20.55

PEAS AND PARTICLES is a unit concerned with large numbers, approximation, and estimation. Using real-life situations, common objects, or photographs, children learn various methods for estimating area, volume, weight, quantity, and distance. They discover when precision is necessary and when approximations are appropriate. The guide contains many photos for use in the activities and includes some entertaining examples from literature that illustrate the value of estimation.

*PEAS AND PARTICLES.* Elementary Science Study (ESS). Nashua, NH: Delta, 1974, 1986.
Grade(s): 4,5,6
Supplies: Materials available locally or kit from Delta.
Guide: $13.10, Kit: $49.00, Activity Cards (58): $9.30

Each USMES unit is based on a challenge that presents a school or community problem to be solved by the children. The PEDESTRIAN CROSSINGS challenge: Recommend and try to have a change made that would improve the safety and convenience of a pedestrian crossing near your school. Children observe, collect data, draw conclusions, and make recommendations for certain improvements. They also see the need for more data or different data; a single solution may not necessarily be sought. Groups of students may work together to document and make their own recommendations. The teacher's guide includes a range of possible activities; however, no specific lesson plans are provided. A list of questions is included to stimulate further investigation or analysis.

*PEDESTRIAN CROSSINGS.* Unified Science and Mathematics for Elementary Schools (USMES). Newton, MA: Education Development Center, Inc., 1974.
Grade(s): 2,3,4,5,6
Supplies: Materials available locally.
Out of print. Available from ERIC (see Sources index).

*PIECES AND PATTERNS: A PATCHWORK IN MATH AND SCIENCE.* Activities to Integrate Mathematics and Science (AIMS). Hillen, Judith A. Fresno, CA: AIMS, 1986.
Grade(s): 5,6,7,8,9
Supplies: Materials available locally.
Guide: $10.95

PIECES AND PATTERNS: A PATCHWORK IN MATH AND SCIENCE contains 19 sequenced investigations on a variety of topics, such as probability and statistics, turtle graphics, and geometry. The students participate in a range of activities from classifying jelly beans and recording data to using Hot Wheels to generalize about kinetic energy, inclined planes, and friction. Each investigation contains a specific lesson plan, including materials and time needed, background information, procedures, discussion questions, and extensions. Several reproducible student pages are provided with each investigation.

*PLAY AREA DESIGN AND USE.* Unified Science and Mathematics for Elementary Schools (USMES). Newton, MA: Education Development Center, Inc., 1973.
Grade(s): 1,2,3,4,5,6,7,8
Supplies: Materials available locally.
Out of print. Available from ERIC (see Sources index).

Each USMES unit is based on a challenge that presents a school or community problem to be solved by the children. The PLAY AREA DESIGN AND USE challenge: Recommend and try to have changes made that would improve the design or use of your school's play area. Children establish priorities of areas needing improvement. They assess the suitability of the proposed improvements and also consider costs and availability of materials. They make models, graph survey results, and plan an improved play area. The teacher's guide contains no specific lesson plans but does include teachers' logs describing the use of this challenge.

*PRIMARILY BEARS, BOOK 1: A COLLECTION OF ELEMENTARY ACTIVITIES.* Activities to Integrate Mathematics and Science (AIMS). Berdugo, Aviva; Allen, Maureen; Glasser, Daneen; McConnell, Pat; and Jones, Susan. Fresno, CA: AIMS, 1987.
Grade(s): K,1,2,3
Supplies: Materials available locally.
Guide: $10.95

PRIMARILY BEARS, BOOK 1 contains 16 investigations that include problems in logic, permutations and arrangements, probability and statistics, and measurement and graphing. Using teddy bears, paper cut-outs, Gummy Bears, M&Ms, and jelly beans, children find solutions to situational math and science problems using methods similar to those encountered by the scientist. Each investigation has a specific lesson plan, listing materials, background information, management suggestions, procedures, discussion questions, and extensions. Many reproducible student pages accompany each lesson.

*PRINTING.* Elementary Science Study (ESS). Newton, MA: Education Development Center, Inc., 1969.
Grade(s): K,1,2,3,4,5,6
Supplies: Materials available from commercial suppliers.
Out of print. Available on SCIENCE HELPER K-8 or from ERIC (see Sources index).

PRINTING is an informal guide to the kinds of work that children do with printing materials. Illustrated with photos and examples of student projects, the accompanying booklet, CHILDREN PRINTING, provides a pictorial representation of what the classroom teacher might expect from writing and art activities involving a small press.

*QUADICE.* Great Explorations in Math and Science (GEMS). Stage, Elizabeth; Thier, Herbert; Cossey, Ruth; and Karplus, Robert. Berkeley, CA: Lawrence Hall of Science, 1987.
Grade(s): 3,4,5,6,7,8
Supplies: Materials available locally, from commercial suppliers, or from Lawrence Hall of Science.
Guide: $6.50

QUADICE is a challenging game that encourages children to work cooperatively, discuss mathematical relationships, and perform computations more confidently. The level of difficulty of the game may be adjusted to meet the needs of specific children. To be successful students need to decide strategies as well as do mathematical calculations. The guide includes specific game rules, a list of materials, and alternative student groupings and directions.

SCIENCE—A PROCESS APPROACH, PART A introduces kindergarten children to basic process skills of observation, description, measurement, classification, and communication. Children sort sets of objects by color, texture, odor, sound, shape, and size. They make measurements of length, time, and temperature, and engage in other activities that enhance their abilities to observe and describe differences or similarities among objects and experiences. There are 22 detailed lessons that indicate precisely what the teacher should do and say to achieve stated objectives. Science content and background information are minimal. Evaluation questions are included.

*SCIENCE—A PROCESS APPROACH, PART A* . American Association for the Advancement of Science (AAAS). New York: Xerox Education Division, 1967. Grade(s): K,1,2
Supplies: Materials available locally or from commercial suppliers.
Out of print. Available on SCIENCE HELPER K-8 (see Sources index).

SCIENCE—A PROCESS APPROACH, PART B builds on children's kindergarten experience to acquaint first grade students with more detailed observation and measurement. Children develop criteria for determining whether something is living or nonliving. They learn the principles of symmetry; explore similarities and differences among objects; observe and record changes in weather, plants, or characteristics of objects; and experiment with magnets and balances. There are 26 lessons, each containing explicit instructions for classroom management, and evaluation activities are included. The unit provides little science content or background information.

*SCIENCE—A PROCESS APPROACH, PART B*. American Association for the Advancement of Science (AAAS). New York: Xerox Education Division, 1967. Grade(s): 1,2,3
Supplies: Materials available locally or from commercial suppliers.
Out of print. Available on SCIENCE HELPER K-8 (see Sources index).

In SCIENCE—A PROCESS APPROACH, PART C, second grade students continue to develop their skills of observation, classification, and description, and proceed to additional activities on inference and prediction. Children observe plants and animals, graph measurements, estimate distances, and use sundials to mark shadow changes. They learn the difference between observation and inference and collect evidence as the basis for inference about objects or predictions about survey samples. The 23 lessons in the unit contain explicit instructions for the teacher, as well as evaluation questions. There is a minimal amount of background information to support the activities.

*SCIENCE—A PROCESS APPROACH, PART C*. American Association for the Advancement of Science (AAAS). New York: Xerox Education Division, 1967. Grade(s): 2,3,4
Supplies: Materials available locally or from commercial suppliers.
Out of print. Available on SCIENCE HELPER K-8 (see Sources index).

SCIENCE—A PROCESS APPROACH, PART D introduces third grade students to the use of variables. Children learn to describe relative position and motion, evaporation, mapping, forces, plant growth, and other phenomena, all in terms of variables. Inference and prediction continue in this unit, as well. There are 22 activities with detailed instructions for teacher behavior and evaluation. Science background information is sparse.

*SCIENCE—A PROCESS APPROACH, PART D*. American Association for the Advancement of Science (AAAS). New York: Xerox Education Division, 1967. Grade(s): 3,4,5
Supplies: Materials available locally or from commercial suppliers.
Out of print. Available on SCIENCE HELPER K-8 (see Sources index).

In SCIENCE—A PROCESS APPROACH, PART E, fourth grade students learn to formulate and test hypotheses, to interpret data, and to make operational definitions. Using observation and inference skills and building on prior experience working with variables, children investigate forces and motions, electrical circuits, cells, sensory perception, chemical reactions, the behavior of guinea pigs, and mold growth and moisture loss in plants. There are 23 lessons, each of which contains explicit information as to what the teacher should do and say to facilitate classroom activities. Evaluation questions are included.

*SCIENCE—A PROCESS APPROACH, PART E*. American Association for the Advancement of Science (AAAS). New York: Xerox Education Division, 1967. Grade(s): 4,5,6
Supplies: Materials available locally or from commercial suppliers.
Out of print. Available on SCIENCE HELPER K-8 (see Sources index).

*SCIENCE—A PROCESS APPROACH, PART F.* American Association for the Advancement of Science (AAAS). New York: Xerox Education Division, 1967.
Grade(s): 5,6,7
Supplies: Materials available locally or from commercial suppliers.
Out of print. Available on SCIENCE HELPER K-8 (see Sources index).

In SCIENCE—A PROCESS APPROACH, PART F, fifth grade students hone the science process skills that have been introduced through earlier SAPA experiences. They apply their skills to study of the earth, its physical features and magnetic properties; to investigation of life cycles and behavior; and to experimentation with chemical reactions, ratios, and mathematical probabilities. There are 24 exercises, accompanied by detailed instructions for the teacher. Evaluation questions are included.

*SCIENCE—A PROCESS APPROACH, PART G.* American Association for the Advancement of Science (AAAS). New York: Xerox Education Division, 1967.
Grade(s): 6,7,8
Supplies: Materials available locally or from commercial suppliers.
Out of print. Available on SCIENCE HELPER K-8 (see Sources index).

SCIENCE—A PROCESS APPROACH, PART G focuses on experimentation, incorporating all the science process skills taught in earlier units. Sixth grade students formulate hypotheses, carry out experiments, and interpret data resulting from investigations of sensory perception, plant growth, chemical reactions, forces and motions, mass, and density. There are instructions for 22 lessons, accompanied by suggestions for evaluation.

*SCIENCE...A PROCESS APPROACH II, LEVEL K.* American Association for the Advancement of Science (AAAS). Nashua, NH: Delta, 1974.
Grade(s): K,1,2
Supplies: Kit from Delta.
Guide: $21.95, Kit: $264.20

SCIENCE...A PROCESS APPROACH II, LEVEL K introduces rudimentary science process skills at the kindergarten level, through a series of 15 modules adapted from the 22 original SAPA, PART A exercises. Instructions for the teacher's behavior and language are still explicitly stated, and evaluation activities are included, as in the original.

*SCIENCE...A PROCESS APPROACH II, LEVEL 1.* American Association for the Advancement of Science (AAAS). Nashua, NH: Delta, 1974.
Grade(s): K,1,2,3
Supplies: Kit from Delta.
Guide: $21.95, Kit: $462.05

SCIENCE...A PROCESS APPROACH II, LEVEL 1 extends the kindergarten experiences of observing and classifying to first grade. Using activities adapted from the original SAPA, PART B materials, as well as new lessons, children investigate living and nonliving things, begin to make simple measurements, and report their findings. There are 15 modules at this level, as compared with the original 26. Teacher instructions and evaluation questions continue to be explicitly stated.

*SCIENCE...A PROCESS APPROACH II, LEVEL 2.* American Association for the Advancement of Science (AAAS). Nashua, NH: Delta, 1974.
Grade(s): 1,2,3
Supplies: Kit from Delta.
Guide: $21.95, Kit: $462.05

SCIENCE...A PROCESS APPROACH II, LEVEL 2 introduces the process of inference to skills already learned. Second grade students begin to make inferences and predictions based on their observations of plants, animals, and physical phenomena. They engage in simple collection of data and estimation activities derived from the original SAPA, PART C exercises. Detailed instructions for teaching and evaluating the 15 modules are supported by inadequate scientific information.

*SCIENCE...A PROCESS APPROACH II, LEVEL 3.* American Association for the Advancement of Science (AAAS). Nashua, NH: Delta, 1974.
Grade(s): 2,3,4
Supplies: Kit from Delta.
Guide: $21.95, Kit: $462.05

In SCIENCE...A PROCESS APPROACH II, LEVEL 3, third grade students continue investigations that incorporate observation, classification, measurement, inference, prediction, and learning how to control variables in their activities. The 15 modules are derived from 22 original SAPA, PART D exercises involving plants and animals, physical forces, and geometry. Teacher instructions are explicit, but there is little science background information to support or extend the SAPA II experiences.

SCIENCE...A PROCESS APPROACH II, LEVEL 4 introduces fourth grade students to operational definition, hypothesis, and data analysis. Adapted from 23 original SAPA, PART E exercises, the 15 modules in this sequence engage students in life, earth, and physical science investigations. There is more biology and health study than in the original and less math. Teacher instructions and evaluation questions are explicit, but scientific background information is absent.

*SCIENCE...A PROCESS APPROACH II, LEVEL 4*. American Association for the Advancement of Science (AAAS). Nashua, NH: Delta, 1974.
Grade(s): 3,4,5
Supplies: Kit from Delta.
Guide: $21.95, Kit: $577.30

SCIENCE...A PROCESS APPROACH II, LEVEL 5 reinforces the skills taught at level 4, investigating phenomena in the life, earth, and physical sciences in somewhat more detail. There are 15 lessons, derived from the original 24 in SAPA, PART F, that are slightly more oriented toward environmental topics than the original lessons were. Each module contains detailed instructions and questions for evaluation, but science background information is inadequate to support further investigations.

*SCIENCE...A PROCESS APPROACH II, LEVEL 5*. American Association for the Advancement of Science (AAAS). Nashua, NH: Delta, 1974.
Grade(s): 4,5,6
Supplies: Kit from Delta.
Guide: $21.95, Kit: $617.00

SCIENCE...A PROCESS APPROACH II, LEVEL 6 uses all the science process skills that have been taught through the entire sequence as a basis for extensive experimenting at the sixth grade level. In 15 modules derived from the original 22 SAPA, PART G exercises, students conduct investigations in the three major topic areas of life, earth, and physical sciences. Instructions for teaching and evaluating the modules are explicit. Science background information to support the experiments is lacking.

*SCIENCE...A PROCESS APPROACH II, LEVEL 6*. American Association for the Advancement of Science (AAAS). Nashua, NH: Delta, 1974.
Grade(s): 5,6,7
Supplies: Kit from Delta.
Guide: $21.95, Kit: $577.30

In SCIENCE FROM TOYS: STAGES 1 AND 2 AND BACKGROUND, a variety of homemade and commercial toys are used to demonstrate basic scientific concepts. Using springs, tops, music makers, pumps, and cars, teachers can introduce the ideas of pressure, gravity, vibration, and inertia, as well as concepts on time, distance, and speed. From dolls and boats to bouncing balls and trains, numerous activities are provided that pique scientific interest, demand critical thinking, and create an atmosphere where learning and playing are one and the same. The guide emphasizes the not-so-subtle link between toys and science that educators often overlook.

*SCIENCE FROM TOYS: STAGES 1 AND 2 AND BACKGROUND*. Science 5/13. Radford, Don. London, England: Macdonald, 1972. ISBN 0-356-04006-2
Grade(s): K,1,2,3,4,5,6,7
Supplies: Materials available locally or from commercial suppliers.
Guide: $9.00 (Available in the U.S. from Teacher's Laboratory.)

The SCIENTIFIC REASONING module encourages development of analytic reasoning skills through the use of controlled experimentation. In five modules, Jump It, Howdy Heart, Swingers, Plane Sense, and Rafts, students hypothesize and manipulate variables as they test their jumping ability, the effects of exercise on heart rate, the behavior of pendulums, rubber-band powered airplanes, and buoyancy. Instructions offer science background information, as well as techniques for adapting the lessons to children with varying physical abilities.

*SCIENTIFIC REASONING*. Science Activities for the Visually Impaired/Science Enrichment for Learners with Physical Handicaps (SAVI/SELPH). Berkeley, CA: Lawrence Hall of Science Center for Multisensory Learning, 1981.
Grade(s): 4,5,6,7
Supplies: Kit from Lawrence Hall of Science.
Folio Guide: $5.00, Complete Kit: $80.00, Economy Kit: $65.00

*SEASONING MATH AND SCIENCE: FALL & WINTER.* Activities to Integrate Mathematics and Science (AIMS). Ginocchio, Cherie; Haggard, Ruth; Jenkins, Sherry; Newton, Nancy; Olson, Betsy; and Roberts-Worley, Wendy. Fresno, CA: AIMS, 1984.
Grade(s): 2
Supplies: Materials available locally.
Guide: $10.95

SEASONING MATH AND SCIENCE: FALL & WINTER is most appropriate for the first half of the school year. This volume includes such topics as holidays, plants, weather, color, and light. After gathering and recording data, the children participate in a variety of graphing activities. The teacher's guide contains 22 investigations, each with a specific lesson plan that includes a list of materials, time needed, background information, procedures, discussion questions, and extensions. Several reproducible student pages accompany each investigation.

*SEASONING MATH & SCIENCE: SPRING & SUMMER.* Activities to Integrate Mathematics and Science (AIMS). Ginocchio, Cherie; Haggard, Ruth; Jenkins, Sherry; Newton, Nancy; Olson, Betsy; and Roberts-Worley, Wendy. Fresno, CA: AIMS, 1986.
Grade(s): 2
Supplies: Materials available locally.
Guide: $10.95

SEASONING MATH & SCIENCE: SPRING & SUMMER is most appropriate for the second half of the school year. It includes three main units: Life Sciences, Earth-Space Sciences, and Physical Sciences. The children use estimation, graphing, and problem solving in investigations that relate to February through April holidays. The teacher's guide contains 22 investigations, each with specific lesson plans that include materials and time needed, background information, procedures, discussion questions, and extensions. Several reproducible student pages accompany each investigation.

*THE SKY'S THE LIMIT! WITH MATH AND SCIENCE.* Activities to Integrate Mathematics and Science (AIMS). Adair, Stan; Barker, Bill; Ivans, Dennis; Shennan, Bill; Sconiers, Zachary; and Welmers, Marney. Fresno, CA: AIMS, 1982.
Grade(s): 4,5,6,7,8
Supplies: Materials available locally.
Guide: $10.95

THE SKY'S THE LIMIT! WITH MATH AND SCIENCE contains 24 investigations related to the science of aerodynamics. The lessons also provide practice with, and application of, basic math and science skills in problem-solving situations. The students use clinometers to determine heights, explore flight properties of various shapes, and construct parachutes and calculate their rates of descent. Each investigation contains a specific lesson plan, including materials and time needed, background information, procedures, discussion questions, and extensions. Several reproducible student pages are provided with each investigation.

*SOFT DRINK DESIGN.* Unified Science and Mathematics for Elementary Schools (USMES). Newton, MA: Education Development Center, Inc., 1974.
Grade(s): 1,2,3,4,5,6,7,8
Supplies: Materials available locally.
Out of print. Available on SCIENCE HELPER K-8 or from ERIC (see Sources index).

Each USMES unit is based on a challenge that presents a school or community problem to be solved by the children. The SOFT DRINK DESIGN challenge: Invent a new soft drink that would be popular and that could be produced at low cost. Children conduct preference surveys and record the data in graph form. They determine factors that make a soft drink popular. The teacher's guide contains no specific lesson plans but includes teachers' logs describing the use of this challenge.

*SPRING INTO MATH AND SCIENCE.* Activities to Integrate Mathematics and Science (AIMS). Adair, Robin; Ewing, Jill; Faircloth, Shirley; Nikoghosian, Janice; Peterson, Cynthia; Smith, Darlene; and Wiebe, Sheila. Fresno, CA: AIMS, 1984.
Grade(s): K,1
Supplies: Materials available locally.
Guide: $10.95

SPRING INTO MATH AND SCIENCE contains 15 investigations that draw on the events of the spring season to provide practice in observing, measuring, and recording data. Each investigation has a specific lesson plan, including materials and time needed, background information, procedures, discussion questions, and extensions. Several reproducible student pages can be found after each lesson plan. The children make graphs related to such topics as water, solar energy, rainbows, holiday cooking, and chemical reactions.

With TANGRAMS, children manipulate geometric shapes to develop skills in pattern recognition, design, and problem solving. There are seven geometric pieces, all of which can be fit together to form a square. Problem cards challenge students to combine the pieces in other ways, matching designs or creating their own. The children are encouraged to discover multiple solutions to each challenge. There are 28 problem cards and four plastic tangram sets to accompany the teacher's guide.

*TANGRAMS.* Elementary Science Study (ESS). Nashua, NH: Delta, 1987 (1968). Grade(s): K,1,2,3,4,5,6,7,8
Supplies: Kit from Delta.
Guide: $3.20, Kit: $4.00, Activity Cards (28): $10.50

In the TIME, GROWTH AND CHANGE activity cards, initial investigations provide opportunities for children to build and work with primitive timers, using water, sand, candles, and springs. Ways of measuring time are detailed, with an emphasis on swinging, ticking, and electronic methods. Investigations with seeds, trout, tadpoles, and chicks serve to illustrate the processes of growth and change. Experiments with kitchen powders, bread, sugar, and dairy products demonstrate changes in form over time. Much teacher direction is needed to insure success in these investigations. The teacher's guide contains no formal lesson plans but offers useful information. There are 12 activity cards included in the unit.

*TIME, GROWTH AND CHANGE.* Learning Through Science. Collis, Margaret; Kincaid, Doug; and Richards, Roy. London, England: Macdonald, 1984.
ISBN 0-356-07560-5
Grade(s): 3,4,5,6
Supplies: Materials available locally or from commercial suppliers.
Activity Cards and Guide: $27.00 (Available in the U.S. from Teacher's Laboratory.)

In TIME: STAGE 1 AND 2 AND BACKGROUND, children are presented with numerous activities that help them understand the concept of time. Initial activities involve sequencing and the passage of time. Children build and operate timers and clocks of all sorts. Using the sun, water, sand, candles, and pendulums, they investigate the passage of time. Detailed information about humankind's understanding of time through the ages is included in a valuable appendix.

*TIME: STAGES 1 AND 2 AND BACKGROUND.* Science 5/13. Richards, Roy. London, England: Macdonald, 1972.
ISBN 0-356-04008-9
Grade(s): K,1,2,3,4,5,6
Supplies: Materials available locally or from commercial suppliers.
Guide: $9.00 (Available in the U.S. from Teacher's Laboratory.)

Each USMES unit is based on a challenge that presents a school or community problem to be solved by the children. The TRAFFIC FLOW challenge: Recommend and try to have a new road design or a system for rerouting traffic accepted so that cars and trucks can move safely at a reasonable speed through a busy intersection near your school. The children assess community traffic patterns and make firsthand observations to obtain data. They predict the feasibility of new designs in terms of safety, cost, and minimum use of land. The teacher's guide contains no specific lesson plans but does include teachers' logs describing the use of this challenge.

*TRAFFIC FLOW.* Unified Science and Mathematics for Elementary Schools (USMES). Newton, MA: Education Development Center, Inc., 1973.
Grade(s): 1,2,3,4,5,6,7,8
Supplies: Materials available locally. Out of print. Available on SCIENCE HELPER K-8 or from ERIC (see Sources index).

In USING THE ENVIRONMENT 2: INVESTIGATIONS, PART 1, children look for and compare plants and animals, use their senses to investigate their environment, and observe the movements of small creatures. The students work with balances and other tools to learn about mass, weight, force, and density. Further experimentation involves testing a variety of materials for flexibility, elasticity, and changeability. The guide offers suggestions for projects and further investigations.

*USING THE ENVIRONMENT 2: INVESTIGATIONS, PART 1.* Science 5/13. Collis, Margaret. London, England: Macdonald, 1979 (1974).
ISBN 0-356-04354-1
Grade(s): 3,4,5,6,7
Supplies: Materials available locally or from commercial suppliers.
Guide: $9.00 (Available in the U.S. from Teacher's Laboratory.)

*USMES DESIGN LAB MANUAL.*
Unified Science and Mathematics for
Elementary Schools (USMES). Newton,
MA: Education Development Center,
Inc., 1974.
Out of print. Available from ERIC (see
Sources index).

The DESIGN LAB MANUAL is a major focus of the USMES philosophy, combining a range of physical resources and expertise in solving problems. The Design Lab provides a central location for tools and materials and a work space where apparatus may be constructed and tested without disrupting ongoing classroom activities. The USMES DESIGN LAB MANUAL includes chapters on the aspects of space, cost, scheduling and use, safety, staffing, staff training, and teacher orientation, as well as an inventory of Design Lab tools and supplies.

*THE USMES GUIDE.* Unified Science
and Mathematics for Elementary Schools
(USMES). Newton, MA: Education
Development Center, Inc., 1974.
Out of print. Available from ERIC (see
Sources index).

THE USMES GUIDE is a compilation of materials that may be used for long-range planning of a curriculum that includes the USMES program. In addition to the basic information about the project and the units, it contains charts assessing the strengths of the various units in terms of their possible math, science, social science, and language content.

*WATER PRECIOUS WATER, BOOK A.*
Activities to Integrate Mathematics and
Science (AIMS). Allen, Maureen; Deal,
Debby; Terman, Dorothy; Kahn, Gale;
and Sipkovich, Vincent. Fresno, CA:
AIMS, 1988.
Grade(s): 2,3,4,5,6
Supplies: Materials available locally.
Guide: $10.95

WATER PRECIOUS WATER, BOOK A contains 27 investigations related to water. Children learn about the water cycle, water conservation, water treatment, water quality, absorption, erosion, water distribution, and the properties of water. Each investigation has a specific lesson plan, including materials, background information, procedures, discussion questions, extensions, and suggested activities for integrating these activities with the rest of the curriculum. Reproducible student pages accompany each lesson. The majority of the activities seem appropriate for upper elementary students.

*WAYS TO LEARN/TEACH.* Unified
Science and Mathematics for Elementary
Schools (USMES). Newton, MA: Education Development Center, Inc., 1975.
Grade(s): 2,3,4,5,6,7,8
Supplies: Materials available locally.
Out of print. Available from ERIC (see
Sources index).

Each USMES unit is based on a challenge that presents a school or community problem to be solved by the children. The WAYS TO LEARN/TEACH challenge: Find the best way to learn or teach someone else certain things. This challenge may be introduced as the class prepares to study some new topic. Children carry out class discussions and list possible ways to learn the same thing. As they investigate the various alternatives, they collect and interpret data to support the overall effectiveness of each method. The teacher's guide includes a range of possible activities; however, no specific lesson plans are provided. A list of questions is included to stimulate further investigation or analysis.

*WHICH AND WHAT?* Learning Through
Science. Allen, Gwen, and Richards,
Roy. London, England: Macdonald,
1984. ISBN 0-356-07559-1
Grade(s): 3,4,5,6
Supplies: Materials available locally or
from commercial suppliers.
Activity Cards and Guide: $27.00 (Available in the U.S. from Teacher's
Laboratory.)

In WHICH AND WHAT?, 12 activity cards provide an excellent field guide and identification scheme to help children become familiar with the flowers, trees, birds, and land and water invertebrates of Great Britain. Detailed color illustrations highlight the visual characteristics of the flowers and animals. Two color drawings of the leaf, fruit, and reproductive parts are presented for 24 of the most common English trees. The teacher's guide contains no formal lesson plans but offers useful information. The 12 activity cards can be used easily and independently by children in their field studies.

In WITH OBJECTIVES IN MIND, the authors of the Science 5/13 series describe the philosophical basis of their program. They relate their beliefs about the value of science education for elementary education and discuss the relationship of Piagetian stages of development to science instruction. They detail the learning objectives of the program and show how these objectives were derived. The appendix includes an annotation for each unit in the program, as well as a comprehensive chart that relates each learning objective to a more general educational aim.

*WITH OBJECTIVES IN MIND.* Science 5/13. Ennever, Len, and Harlen, Wynne. London, England: Macdonald, 1972. ISBN 0-356-04009-7
Guide: $9.00 (Available in the U.S. from Teacher's Laboratory.)

WORKING WITH WOOD: BACKGROUND INFORMATION provides teachers with factual information about the nature of wood to complement the classroom activities suggested in WORKING WITH WOOD, STAGES 1 AND 2. Information is included about the structure of wood cells, how a tree makes wood, the differences between hardwood and softwood, and the mechanical, thermal, and electrical properties of wood. The durability of timber is discussed with regard to natural defects and defects caused by living organisms and improper seasoning. This guide is a valuable resource for the teacher who plans extensive use of wood products in the classroom.

*WORKING WITH WOOD: BACK-GROUND INFORMATION.* Science 5/13. Parker, Sheila. London, England: Macdonald, 1972. ISBN 0-356-04010-0
Grade(s): 3,4,5,6
Supplies: Materials available locally or from commercial suppliers.
Guide: $9.00 (Available in the U.S. from Teacher's Laboratory.)

In WORKING WITH WOOD: STAGES 1 AND 2, children work with a familiar material to gain scientific understanding and confidence in working with tools. Instructions are provided for the safe use of equipment and the proper selection of materials. Investigations with rotting wood, driftwood, wood and water, and wood strength present many opportunities for scientific insight through experimentation. The activities encourage children to research certain aspects of the use of wood, its sources, and its relationship to trees. The guide includes many suggestions for student-designed projects that use wood.

*WORKING WITH WOOD: STAGES 1 AND 2.* Science 5/13. Parker, Sheila. London, England: Macdonald, 1972. ISBN 0-356-04011-9
Grade(s): 3,4,5,6
Supplies: Materials available locally or from commercial suppliers.
Guide: $9.00 (Available in the U.S. from Teacher's Laboratory.)

# II. SUPPLEMENTARY RESOURCES

Many outstanding printed materials have been published to support hands-on science programs. There are books of activities that can be integrated with a core curriculum; books offering philosophy and practical strategies for teaching science; and books about the resources available to teachers and children. There are also some excellent periodicals that provide science background information or classroom activities. These supplementary items can be found in the four sections that follow.

## Science Activity Books

Many books offer excellent hands-on science activities for children. Such guides provide practical ideas for facilitating science learning but are often either too broad in scope or too specific in focus to serve as the foundation of an elementary science program. These materials can be used, however, as supplements to existing curriculum or as independent investigations to enhance children's experience of science. We have included some noteworthy activity books in this section, and we encourage readers to advise us of others they have found helpful. Consult the Sources index to locate publishers' addresses.

ACTIVITIES IN THE LIFE SCIENCES presents a variety of experiments involving living organisms. Children grow bacteria, calculate the rate of seed germination, measure the height of trees, feed a stinging hydra, set up a food chain, make prints of human fingers and feet, and participate in many other hands-on, intercurricular activities. Each chapter focuses on a specific topic and includes motivating questions, several activities, and new science words and their definitions. The appendix contains background information for each chapter.

*ACTIVITIES IN THE LIFE SCIENCES.* Challand, Helen J. Chicago, IL: Children's Press, 1982. ISBN 0-516-00507-3 Grade(s): 4,5,6,7 $13.00

ADVENTURES WITH ATOMS AND MOLECULES presents a variety of experiments involving physical science and chemistry. The authors ask questions, give answers, and ask children to initiate their own questions through observation and experimentation. Students learn about the properties of molecules, how temperature affects the behavior of molecules, and how the molecules in different liquids act. They engage in many activities to discover more about themselves and the world around them. Each activity includes a list of materials, procedure, focus questions, background information, and other things to try.

*ADVENTURES WITH ATOMS AND MOLECULES: CHEMISTRY EXPERIMENTS FOR YOUNG PEOPLE.* Mebane, Robert C., and Rybolt, Thomas R. Hillside, NJ: Enslow, 1985. ISBN 0-89490-120-6 Grade(s): 4,5,6,7,8,9 $13.95

ADVENTURES WITH ATOMS AND MOLECULES, BOOK II presents more experiments involving physical science and chemistry. The authors maintain the original format and ask questions, give answers, and ask children to initiate their own questions through observation and experimentation. Students learn how water acts like glue, how baking soda traps odor molecules, and how certain molecules in the air spoil food, and they continue to engage in activities to discover more about themselves and the world around them. Each activity includes a list of materials, procedure, focus questions, background information, and other things to try.

*ADVENTURES WITH ATOMS AND MOLECULES: CHEMISTRY EXPERIMENTS FOR YOUNG PEOPLE, BOOK II.* Mebane, Robert C., and Rybolt, Thomas R. Hillside, NJ: Enslow, 1987. ISBN 0-89490-164-8 Grade(s): 4,5,6,7,8,9 $13.95

*BEASTLY NEIGHBORS: ALL ABOUT WILD THINGS IN THE CITY, OR WHY EARWIGS MAKE GOOD MOTHERS.* Rights, Mollie. Boston, MA: Little, Brown, 1981. ISBN 0-316-74577-4
Grade(s): 3,4,5,6,7
$7.95

BEASTLY NEIGHBORS gives children the opportunity to explore the world around them. All environments contain a wide variety of plant and animal life, and this book guides students on their search for inhabitants. The activities include gathering seeds for a windowsill garden, feeding birds, growing wildflowers, making a nest box for squirrels, and other exciting adventures. Using the children's own environment as the study site enhances the learning experience and encourages real problem solving.

*BLOOD AND GUTS: A WORKING GUIDE TO YOUR OWN INSIDES.* Allison, Linda. Boston, MA: Little, Brown, 1976. ISBN 0-316-03443-6
Grade(s): 5,6,7,8
$7.95

BLOOD AND GUTS is a guidebook to finding out about the human body. There are about 70 experiments that allow children to stop, look, listen, thump, poke, and test in order to become acquainted with their own anatomy. Background information, ideas for investigations, and amazing facts are given for each subtopic.

*THE BOOK OF WHERE: OR HOW TO BE NATURALLY GEOGRAPHIC.* Bell, Neill. Boston, MA: Little, Brown, 1982. ISBN 0-316-08831-5
Grade(s): 3,4,5,6,7,8
$7.95

THE BOOK OF WHERE: OR HOW TO BE NATURALLY GEOGRAPHIC presents children with an enjoyable way to learn about the world and its places. Pencils, paper, some maps, and things that can easily be found around the house are what children need to explore the Andes, Philippines, Africa, or the neighborhood in which they live. Children make things, do puzzles, read stories, examine history, and become navigators.

*BUBBLES.* Zubrowski, Bernie. Boston, MA: Little, Brown, 1979.
ISBN 0-316-98881-2
Grade(s): K,1,2,3,4,5
$6.95

BUBBLES presents an ideal combination of play and discovery. Activities suggested in this book challenge children to create bubbles of different sizes, using original tools and techniques. They design bubble sculptures, geometric shapes, bubble houses, domes, and building blocks, and measure and change bubble size. This book offers the perfect opportunity for fun and learning.

*CANDLES.* Bird, John, and Diamond, Dorothy. London, England: Macdonald, 1975. ISBN 0-356-05070-X
Grade(s): P,K,1,2,3,4,5,6
$8.95 (Available in the U.S. from Teacher's Laboratory.)

CANDLES presents many investigations that use the candle as a starting point, both as the object of experimentation and as the material used to illustrate scientific processes. The authors make a special effort to stress how to use the candle safely within the classroom environment. The activities allow children to explore energy, burning, evaporation, convection, solubility, the candle as a clock, and more. Suggestions are given for extensions and further resources.

*COMETS PROFILES. Career Oriented Modules to Explore Topics in Science, Volume I.* Noyce, Ruth (editor). Washington, DC: National Science Teachers Association, 1982, 1984.
Grade(s): 5,6,7,8,9
Volume I: $12.50 Set, Volumes I & II: $24.00

COMETS PROFILES contains biographical sketches of 24 women with science careers. Through reading interviews or biographies and carrying out language arts activities related to their reading, adolescent students, especially girls, are encouraged to recognize the applications of science and mathematics skills to their future careers, and to consider occupations in the sciences. The profiles are keyed to science activities contained in the second volume of this series (see below).

COMETS SCIENCE offers activities that correlate with the career profiles contained in Volume I of this series, COMETS PROFILES (see above). The guide lists materials and procedures, provides brief biographies and background information on the activities and the professions to which they relate, and suggests ideas for extension. There are also hints on finding resource people in the local community, and inviting them to visit the classroom to enhance activities and discussions of science-related careers.

*COMETS SCIENCE. Career Oriented Modules to Explore Topics in Science, Volume II*. Smith, Walter L.; Molitor, Loretta L.; Nelson, Bess J.; and Matthews, Catherine L. Washington, DC: National Science Teachers Association, 1982, 1984.
Grade(s): 5,6,7,8,9
Volume II: $12.50 Set, Volumes I & II: $24.00

THE CURIOUS NATURALIST offers tidbits of information, both fact and folklore, about common plants and animals from a humane perspective on the natural world. The book has four sections, each devoted to subjects that would be of interest during a particular season of the year. The author takes all participants on a field trip through the various habitats and conveys the notion that what is seen and learned at a specific moment and place will foster a desire to learn more. (Compiled from Massachusetts Audubon Society publications.)

*THE CURIOUS NATURALIST*. The Massachusetts Audubon Society. Mitchell, John. Englewood Cliffs, NJ: Prentice Hall, 1980. ISBN 0-13-195404-0
Grade(s): K,1,2,3,4,5,6
$12.95

DINOSAURS: A JOURNEY THROUGH TIME is a children's activity book with an adult teaching guide. Through such activities as identifying the characteristics of a variety of dinosaurs, making a geological time scale, interpreting dinosaur tracks, and constructing dinosaurs, children learn what we know about dinosaurs, the major dinosaur groups, what fossils tell us about dinosaurs, and why dinosaurs may have become extinct. The teaching guide includes directions for each activity and sources of information about dinosaurs.

*DINOSAURS: A JOURNEY THROUGH TIME*. Schatz, Dennis. Seattle, WA: Pacific Science Center, 1987.
ISBN 0-935-05101-5
Grade(s): 3,4,5,6
$9.95

ELABORATIONS is a collection of 20 activities focusing on physical science and life science. Each activity includes motivating questions or narratives, background information, specific learning objectives, a list of materials, and step-by-step instructions. The authors include suggestions for asking good questions, maintaining safety standards, collecting data, follow-up discussions, and sources for materials. The content and organization of this book indicate a clear understanding of the needs and interests of upper elementary grade students and teachers.

*ELABORATIONS: SCIENCE LABS FOR INTERMEDIATE STUDENTS*. Blackmer, Marilyn, and Schlichting, Sandi. Riverview, FL: Idea Factory, 1988.
Grade(s): 4,5,6
$16.99

THE EVERYDAY SCIENCE SOURCEBOOK includes more than 1000 science activities designed to supplement the science program and to help reinforce student knowledge and skills. The book is divided into six major categories: Inorganic Matter; Organic Matter; Energy; Inference Models; Technology; and Instructional Apparatus, Materials, and Systems. Within each section are lessons appropriate for children in grades K-8. Background information and directions are given for specific activities within the topics. Investigations require simple, readily available materials.

*THE EVERYDAY SCIENCE SOURCEBOOK: IDEAS FOR TEACHING IN THE ELEMENTARY AND MIDDLE SCHOOL*. Lowery, Lawrence. Palo Alto, CA: Dale Seymour, 1985.
ISBN 0-205-05782-9
Grade(s): K,1,2,3,4,5,6,7,8
$18.95

*EXPANDING CHILDREN'S THINKING THROUGH SCIENCE: CESI SOURCE-BOOK II.* Council for Elementary Science, International (CESI). Columbus, OH: ERIC Clearinghouse for Science, Mathematics, and Environmental Education.
Grade(s): 1,2,3,4,5,6,7,8
$6.50 for CESI members, $6.50 for non-members

EXPANDING CHILDREN'S THINKING THROUGH SCIENCE offers ideas to improve instruction and suggests ways to increase the ability of students and teachers to simplify a seemingly difficult task. This sourcebook contains activities that enhance creativity, problem-solving skills, values development, self-esteem, and visual thinking. Students make temperature meters, design and build a fish, and invent a civilization. Each activity includes a title, focus, challenge(s), background information, a list of materials and equipment, step-by-step directions, further challenges, a list of additional references for teachers and students, and safety precautions. For these activities to be effective, the teacher must pay attention to the cultural, ethnic, gender, and religious sensitivities of the children in the classroom.

*EXPLORATIONS & INVESTIGATIONS: SCIENCE FOR PRIMARY STUDENTS.* Green, Bea, and Schlichting, Sandi. Riverview, FL: Idea Factory, 1985.
Grade(s): K,1,2,3
$15.99

EXPLORATIONS & INVESTIGATIONS includes eight one-day investigations and six long-term investigations of topics in physical science and biology. Each activity contains a behavioral objective, a list of materials, teacher directions, possible extensions, and reproducible pages for student use. The lessons are organized to allow children to become active participants, questioners, and problem solvers. The authors present the pedagogy of effective elementary science teaching, ideas for science language development, methods for collecting data, and suggestions for the implementation of science process skills and graphing.

*FOODWORKS: OVER 100 SCIENCE ACTIVITIES AND FASCINATING FACTS THAT EXPLORE THE MAGIC OF FOOD.* Ontario Science Centre. Donev, Mary; Donev, Stef; and Gold, Carol. Reading, MA: Addison-Wesley, 1987. ISBN 0-201-16780-8
Grade(s): 4,5,6
$7.95

FOODWORKS is a collection of activities, games, and fascinating facts about food. Children read about the history of food, cultural aspects of food, and the inside story of hot dogs, soda pop, and other popular foods. They make their own ice cream, create a hydroponic garden, grow mold, and recycle food. Each topic has background information, suggested projects with step-by-step instructions, and a list of easy-to-acquire materials. The authors pay special attention to health and encourage children to become aware of what they eat and determine what is good for them and what is not.

*FUN WITH PHYSICS.* McGrath, Susan. Washington, DC: National Geographic Society, 1986. ISBN 0-87044-581-2
Grade(s): 5,6,7,8,9,10,11,12
$8.50

FUN WITH PHYSICS relates physics to everyday occurrences in the world around us. Physics is the study of energy and matter, and that covers just about everything. Children investigate sound, color, jumping, speed and acceleration, light, ice cream, and other common things in a new way. The book is divided into four sections that investigate physics of fun, physics of the natural world, physics at home, and physics of sports. Each section is filled with exceptional color photographs, background information, and activities. A glossary lists important terms.

*GEE WIZ!* Allison, Linda, and Katz, David. Boston, MA: Little, Brown, 1983. ISBN 0-316-03445-2
Grade(s): 4,5,6,7,8
$7.95

GEE WIZ! brings science to a comfortable level by describing it as a way of thinking about the world. It defines the requirements to be a scientist—to have questions and the curiosity to search for answers. Children explore exploding colors, fantastic elastics, capillary action, surface tension, unmixable liquids, vision, magnification, symmetry, balancing, and forces. Through the reading of factual information, experimenting with objects, and figuring out puzzles, children begin to develop an understanding of basic science concepts. This book presents aspects of the world to investigate; all the children need is imagination.

HANDS-ON NATURE invites children and teachers to investigate the natural world. This book combines factual information, creative approaches, and hands-on experiences as the format for learning. Children discover the wonder of animal and plant adaptations, habitats, life cycles, and designs of nature. The author presents background information, ideas for activities, lists of materials, science and other curriculum area extensions, and suggested readings on a wide variety of topics. Appendices dealing with equipment, vocabulary, and additional reading are included.

*HANDS-ON NATURE: INFORMATION AND ACTIVITIES FOR EXPLORING THE ENVIRONMENT WITH CHILDREN.* Lingelbach, Jenepher. Woodstock, VT: Vermont Institute of Natural Science, 1986.
ISBN 0-9617627-0-5
Grade(s): K,1,2,3,4,5,6
$16.95

The IDEA FACTORY'S SUPER SCIENCE SOURCEBOOK is filled with student-centered, hands-on activities dealing with life science, physical science, and earth science. Each activity includes an objective, background information, needed materials, and step-by-step procedures. There are more than 100 lessons that are intriguing, require inexpensive materials, and help to create a comfortable learning environment for the children and the science-shy teacher. Also included are cooking activities; instructions for making equipment; "magic" activities; trivia questions; biographical sketches of, and quotations from, scientists; suggestions for integrating reading, language arts, math, social studies, art, music, and physical education; and other useful ideas for the classroom teacher.

*IDEA FACTORY'S SUPER SCIENCE SOURCEBOOK.* Smith, Ellyn; Blackmer, Marilyn; and Schlichting, Sandi. Riverview, FL: Idea Factory, 1987.
Grade(s): K,1,2,3,4,5,6
$19.95

INVENTION BOOK is divided into two main sections: The Inventor's Handbook and Great Invention Stories. The first part of the book guides children from the planning stages of an invention to marketing strategies. In the second section, the author relates stories about specific inventors and their inventions. Narratives about the invention of earmuffs, Levis, basketball, Kleenex, ballpoint pens, zippers, and so on are intriguing and motivational. Children begin to think like inventors and realize that most new ideas and inventions come from old ones and that the only thing that needs to be done is to ask how this existing knowledge may be used to solve a problem or create something new.

*INVENTION BOOK.* Caney, Steven. New York, NY: Workman, 1985.
ISBN 0-89480-076-0
Grade(s): 4,5,6,7,8
$7.95

INVESTIGATE AND DISCOVER has approximately 150 activities for elementary school children. There is a balance of investigations among the physical sciences, biological sciences, and earth sciences. For each activity, the author provides teacher's notes, materials needed, recommended grade level, discussion questions, concepts, objectives, and possible extensions.

*INVESTIGATE AND DISCOVER: ELEMENTARY SCIENCE LESSONS.* Sund, Robert B.; Tillery, Bill W.; and Trowbridge, Leslie W. Boston, MA: Allyn and Bacon, 1975.
Grade(s): K,1,2,3,4,5,6,7,8
(Out of print. Available in libraries.)

In MESSING AROUND WITH BAKING CHEMISTRY, children start with the familiar activity of baking a cake and uncover a mystery. Cooking offers many opportunities for learning basic physics and chemistry, and this book describes how to investigate changing cake recipes, identifying the special properties of baking soda, capturing the gas from baking powder, assembling a gas generator, and learning how dough rises. Adult supervision is necessary for these activities.

*MESSING AROUND WITH BAKING CHEMISTRY.* Zubrowski, Bernie. Boston, MA: Little, Brown, 1981.
ISBN 0-316-98879-0
Grade(s): 3,4,5,6
$6.95

*MESSING AROUND WITH WATER PUMPS AND SIPHONS.* Zubrowski, Bernie. Boston, MA: Little, Brown, 1981. ISBN 0-316-98877-4
Grade(s): 3,4,5,6
$6.95

MESSING AROUND WITH WATER PUMPS AND SIPHONS is designed to help children learn that pumps that perform different tasks operate on similar principles. Children start with simple investigations of pumps and siphons, then relate their findings to the human heart, auto fuel pumps, and other complex, but familiar, systems. The author describes many water devices, offers instructions, motivating questions, explanations, and challenges. Many of these activities need adult supervision.

*MORE SCIENCE EXPERIMENTS YOU CAN EAT.* Cobb, Vicki. New York, NY: Lippincott, 1979. ISBN 0-06-446003-7
Grade(s): 4,5,6,7
$4.95

MORE SCIENCE EXPERIMENTS YOU CAN EAT gives children the opportunity to look at familiar food items in new ways. Children investigate the composition of foods, how they came to be, how they change, and how to recognize these changes. Using the senses of sight, smell, and taste, they measure and compare foodstuffs. Background information and guiding questions are given for each investigation. Often, experiments will turn out to be the motivation for further student-initiated activities. (Sequel to SCIENCE EXPERIMENTS YOU CAN EAT—see entry.)

*NATURE ACTIVITIES FOR EARLY CHILDHOOD.* Nickelsburg, Janet. Menlo Park, CA: Addison-Wesley, 1976. ISBN 0-201-05097-8
Grade(s): P,K,1,2,3
$11.40

The purpose of NATURE ACTIVITIES FOR EARLY CHILDHOOD is to assist teachers in providing young children with experiences in observing nature and encouraging them to explore the unknown. The author describes 44 projects that may, in turn, extend to a number of other activities. The activities need not be presented in any set order nor is it necessary to complete them all. They deal with animals, plants, or nonliving things common to almost all areas. Each hands-on investigation gives background information, specific activities in which the children experience nature directly, ideas for helpful materials, key vocabulary words, and a bibliography for children and adults.

*NATURE WITH CHILDREN OF ALL AGES.* The Massachusetts Audubon Society. Sisson, Edith A. Englewood Cliffs, NJ: Prentice Hall, 1982. ISBN 0-13-610436-3
Grade(s): K,1,2,3,4,5
$10.95

NATURE WITH CHILDREN OF ALL AGES fosters attitudes of appreciation, care, and concern for our natural environment. The author suggests many activities that adults may do with children. The ideas offered are diverse in subject, interest, and age appropriateness. The activities relate directly to natural history and are integrated with other disciplines. The author has taken special care to select experiences that call for simple, easy-to-obtain materials, require little or no technical equipment or laboratory supplies, and most of all, are easy to do. Each chapter includes a bibliography of children's and adult's resources.

*NUTS AND BOLTS: A MATTER OF FACT GUIDE TO SCIENCE FAIR PROJECTS.* Van Deman, Barry A., and McDonald, Ed. Harwood Heights, IL: Science Man, 1982. ISBN 0-936046-01-5
Grade(s): 5,6,7,8
$6.95

NUTS AND BOLTS will help elementary and middle school teachers guide their students through the process of selecting, organizing, implementing, and presenting a creative and scientific project. Excellent suggestions are given for carrying out research, taking notes, and writing a report. Appendices supply information about award-winning projects, sources of information, a glossary, and a bibliography.

In OUTDOOR AREAS AS LEARNING LABORATORIES, students investigate playground puddles, melting snow, common plants and animals, weeds, lawn grass, and many other "real" things found in the outdoors. Chapter one of this sourcebook presents ideas for using the outdoors for learning. The subsequent chapters contain activities about animals, plants, ecology, physical science, and a variety of other topics. The format for each activity includes an objective, challenges, a list of materials and equipment, step-by-step directions, extensions, and suggestions for articles and books to give both teachers and students useful information related to the activity. Background information is given in the beginning chapter, as well as within each activity.

*OUTDOOR AREAS AS LEARNING LABORATORIES: CESI SOURCE-BOOK*. Council for Elementary Science, International (CESI). Columbus, OH: ERIC Clearinghouse for Science, Mathematics, and Environmental Education, 1979.
Grade(s): K,1,2,3,4,5,6,7,8,9,10,11,12
$5.50 for CESI members, $6.50 for non-members

Working with PAINTS AND MATERIALS is an enjoyable way for children to learn how to record data on paper, discuss concepts, and examine scientific skills. Each chapter of this book contains an activity and a list of materials for a hands-on experience. A bibliography includes additional sources for activity and pedagogy books.

*PAINTS AND MATERIALS*. Brady, Charles. Milwaukee, WI: Macdonald-Raintree, 1981. ISBN 0-356-05075-0
Grade(s): P,K,1,2,3,4,5,6
$8.95 (Available from Teacher's Laboratory.)

PROJECTS is one of a 25-volume encyclopedia of scientific subjects. This book focuses on activities that encourage discovery learning through experimentation. It is divided into four sections: Puzzles, Codes, and Computers; Looking at Earth and Space; Experiments and Inventions; and Looking at Nature.

*PROJECTS: THE WORLD OF SCIENCE*. Taylor, Ron. New York, NY: Facts on File, 1986.
ISBN 0-8160-1076-5
Grade(s): 3,4,5,6,7
$9.95

RACEWAYS illustrates several types of games you can construct with balls and tracks. Little equipment is necessary, and children play some popular games, some new ones, and some they can create on their own. Children learn how to make a ball go up and down hills, travel in a circle, and jump from track to track without falling off. By questioning their methods and experimenting with the different models that are made, children develop an understanding of energy, acceleration, and momentum. The author presents a variety of challenges that will provide hours of fun and learning for children.

*RACEWAYS: HAVING FUN WITH BALLS AND TRACKS*. Zubrowski, Bernie. New York, NY: Morrow, 1985.
ISBN 0-688-04160-4
Grade(s): 4,5,6,
$5.95

THE REASONS FOR SEASONS includes activities that can be done by children of all ages, with easily accessible materials. The investigations are not sequential, but some of the projects are best suited for certain times of the year. Children make solar collectors, garbage gardens, worm farms, ginger beer, crystals, and many other things. Directions are given, but children are encouraged to find their own way too. This book is about the earth—things to make, ideas to ponder, stories to read, and things to collect, explore, and change.

*THE REASONS FOR SEASONS*. Allison, Linda. Boston, MA: Little, Brown, 1975.
ISBN 0-316-03440-1
Grade(s): 3,4,5,6
$7.70

The most effective way to gain an understanding of electricity is to do hands-on experiments. SAFE AND SIMPLE ELECTRICAL EXPERIMENTS contains 101 investigations that require easily accessible and inexpensive materials. Children explore static electricity, magnetism, electrical current, and electromagnetism. They do tricks with a comb, make dancing soap bubbles and magnetic boats, get electricity from a lemon, test series and parallel circuits, and participate in a variety of other activities. The author includes a limited chronological history of great discoveries in electricity.

*SAFE AND SIMPLE ELECTRICAL EXPERIMENTS*. Graf, Rudolph F. New York, NY: Dover, 1973.
ISBN 0-486-22950-5
Grade(s): 3,4,5,6,7
$14.00

*SCIENCE AROUND THE HOUSE.*
Gardner, Robert. New York, NY: Julian
Messner, 1985. ISBN 0-671-54663-5
Grade(s): 3,4,5,6
$9.29

SCIENCE AROUND THE HOUSE presents the home as a natural place to conduct experiments. Materials are readily available, and equipment is often built in. Family permission and involvement are encouraged. Many of these experiments may be initiated or duplicated in a school environment. Children explore gravity, density, weighing liquids and solids, evaporation, speed and acceleration, forces, matter, motion, and light. The author provides background information, motivating questions, and hands-on activities.

*THE SCIENCE BOOK.* Stein, Sara. New
York, NY: Workman, 1980.
ISBN 0-89480-120-1
Grade(s): 2,3,4,5,6,7,8
$7.95

THE SCIENCE BOOK answers many questions and encourages even more. Activities center on materials, specimens, and apparatus that are available in the home, school, and outdoor environment. Children look at pests, animals, people, protists, and plants, and investigate touches, noises, sights, tastes, smells, charges, and thoughts, while working on puzzles, observing specimens, experimenting, building habitats, or reading information. Discussion of human sexuality is accompanied by diagrams. This book has a potpourri of activities that may be done in any order, using as much or as little time as the user desires.

*SCIENCE EXPERIENCES FOR PRE-
SCHOOLERS: CESI SOURCEBOOK IV.*
Council for Elementary Science, International (CESI). Columbus, OH: ERIC
Clearinghouse for Science, Mathematics
and Environmental Education, 1986.
Grade(s): P,K
$5.50 for CESI members, $6.50 for non-members

SCIENCE EXPERIENCES FOR PRESCHOOLERS suggests many opportunities for involving children in the world around them. Young children will investigate sounds, fallen branches, seeds, animal habitats, mixing colors, colored light, magnetism, and many other topics in life science and physical science. The format for each activity includes the title, focus, challenge(s), a list of materials and equipment, directions, extensions, and additional references. This book also contains three articles: "Integrating Science into the Early Childhood Curriculum," "Science Is Being There," and "Description of the Cognitive Development of the Preschooler."

*SCIENCE EXPERIENCES FOR THE
EARLY CHILDHOOD YEARS.* Harlan,
Jean. Columbus, OH: Merrill, 1984.
ISBN 0-675-20118-7
Grade(s): P,K,1,2,3,4
$16.95

Teachers must encourage the natural curiosity and interest of young children in learning about and understanding the world around them. Teachers also have to guide children to use knowledge to solve problems and make decisions in a rational and systematic way. The author of SCIENCE EXPERIENCES FOR THE EARLY CHILDHOOD YEARS promotes these ideas and others as the rationale for the activities presented. Children have the opportunity to investigate, observe, discuss, record, and experiment within a variety of science topics. The activities are a balanced assortment of physical, earth, and life sciences. Background information, concepts, lists of materials, step-by-step instructions, ways to integrate activities for primary and secondary students, extensions, ideas for parent involvement, and additional references are given for each section.

*SCIENCE EXPERIMENTS.* Webster,
Vera R. Chicago, IL: Children's Press,
1982. ISBN 0-516-01646-6
Grade(s): 2,3
$11.68

SCIENCE EXPERIMENTS presents background information and activities that deal with force and motion, gravity, magnets, energy, pulleys, gears, and wheels. Children are engaged in investigations that answer such questions as, How much force is needed? Can magnets pick up objects made of different materials? How are pulleys, wheels, and gears used to simplify jobs? The author provides a list of vocabulary words applicable to these experiments.

SCIENCE EXPERIMENTS YOU CAN EAT presents 39 science experiments that use everyday items and foodstuffs that would be found in a kitchen. Children investigate the composition of foods, how foods are processed, and how cooking changes food. They design experiments to assess changes, they record data, and often, they eat the results. The author suggests guiding questions and ideas for follow-up experiments. (A sequel to this book is MORE SCIENCE EXPERIMENTS YOU CAN EAT—see entry.)

*SCIENCE EXPERIMENTS YOU CAN EAT.* Cobb, Vicki. New York, NY: Harper & Row, 1972. ISBN 0-06-446002-9
Grade(s): 4,5,6,7
$4.95

SCIENCE FROM WATER PLAY offers activities for water play and opportunities for scientific investigations. Children explore floating and sinking and capacity and volume. The activities suggested in this book may be used with children of all ages, and teachers are encouraged to introduce them to older students. Each chapter gives specific directions for organizing and implementing the investigations. A bibliography supplies additional information about children's and teacher's resource books, and suppliers.

*SCIENCE FROM WATER PLAY.* Bird, John. London, England: Macdonald, 1983. ISBN 0-356-05071-8
Grade(s): P,K,1,2,3,4,5,6
$8.95 (Available in the U.S. from Teacher's Laboratory.)

In SCIENCE FUN WITH MUD AND DIRT, children learn about different types of soil, insects and animals that live underground, the kinds of homes the animals have, and more. The author suggests many hands-on activities, such as building a nest, making and testing mudpies, and building mud houses, and relates these activities to the real world. This book makes getting "down and dirty" a truly educational experience.

*SCIENCE FUN WITH MUD AND DIRT.* Wyler, Rose. New York, NY: Julian Messner, 1986. ISBN 0-671-62904-2
Grade(s): 4,5,6
$4.95

SCIENCE MAGIC TRICKS provides ways for children to discover and begin to understand science concepts— through magic. It includes more than 50 tricks that depend upon the laws of science and may be explained in scientific terms. Children investigate mathematical puzzles, secret writing, energetic coins, monster dolls, magic rings, the impossible fork, a flying ping-pong ball, Jacob's Ladder, and many other "tricks." The author suggests sources for the chemicals and other ingredients used in these tricks and tells how to make some of the ingredients, too.

*SCIENCE MAGIC TRICKS.* Shalit, Nathan. New York, NY: Henry Holt, 1981. ISBN 0-8050-0234-0
Grade(s): 5,6,7,8
$4.95

SCIENCE ON A SHOESTRING includes 50 investigations about scientific methods; change; and energy, fields, and forces. These activities may be used as the basic science program for a class or in conjunction with other hands-on units or texts. The lesson format includes suggested level, materials (all inexpensive and easily obtainable), new vocabulary, ideas for advanced preparation, step-by-step procedures for implementation of the activity, extensions for home investigations, and questions for discussion and/or evaluation. The author includes a list of materials with sources and approximate prices.

*SCIENCE ON A SHOESTRING.* Strongin, Herb. Menlo Park, CA: Addison-Wesley, 1976. ISBN 0-201-07329-3
Grade(s): K,1,2,3,4,5,6,7
$11.60

SCIENCEWORKS includes 65 experiments that introduce the fun and wonder of science to children. Children develop an understanding of science principles as they engage in such activities as testing body strength, ice fishing, making moebius strips, making low-energy breakfasts, flying airplanes, and many other topics. Children also make butter, invisible ink, magnetic images, and various structures. Clear, step-by-step directions are given for each project. Some activities may be done independently, but most need adult supervision.

*SCIENCEWORKS.* Ontario Science Centre. Toronto, Canada: Kids Can Press, 1984. ISBN 0-919964-61-3
Grade(s): 3,4,5,6,7
$7.95

*SEEDS AND SEEDLINGS*. Diamond, Dorothy. London, England: Macdonald, 1983. ISBN 0-356-05072-6
Grade(s): P,K,1,2,3,4,5,6
$8.95 (Available in the U.S. from Teacher's Laboratory.)

SEEDS AND SEEDLINGS looks at this traditional classroom topic in many new ways. These activities may be used with children of all ages. Children observe, classify, experiment, measure, make and test hypotheses, control variables, and share information while working with seeds and seedlings. The author suggests many ideas for organization and implementation of investigations. A bibliography includes children's books and teacher's resources.

*SUPER SCIENCE ACTIVITIES: FAVORITE LESSONS FROM MASTER TEACHERS*. Beattie, Rob; Bredt, Diane; Lyford, Jean; Wight, Tom; Oshita, Steven; Martinez, Jacinta; Scotchmoor, Judith; and Graeber, Janet. Palo Alto, CA: Dale Seymour, 1988.
ISBN 0-86651-445-7
Grade(s): 5,6,7,8,9
$15.95

SUPER SCIENCE ACTIVITIES includes physical, earth, and life science activities for students in middle and junior high schools. Students invent a seismograph, use chromatography to identify the author of a mystery note, build a working battery, and create a balanced ecosystem in an aquarium. The book contains six units, each with three to five lessons and an appropriate bibliography. Each lesson has background information, new vocabulary, a list of materials, classroom management suggestions, step-by-step procedures, and enrichment activities. All these activities are classroom-proven lessons from the repertoires of eight teachers.

*TEACHING SCIENCE WITH EVERYDAY THINGS*. Schmidt, Victor E., and Rockcastle, Verne N. New York, NY: McGraw-Hill, 1982.
ISBN 0-07-055355-6
Grade(s): K,1,2,3,4,5,6
$18.95

TEACHING SCIENCE WITH EVERYDAY THINGS is a practical guide for elementary school teachers who are not as comfortable with science as they would like to be; all the teacher has to do is to be willing to try new things. Teachers are given the opportunity to explore, observe, investigate, and experiment with their students. The author presents ideas about science and how it should be taught. The main part of the book details activities that engage children in developing positive attitudes and science skills, and in learning specific content. Chapters are organized by topics, such as counting and measuring; air and weather; plants and animals; water and other liquids; powders and solutions; rocks and the land environment and conservation; forces and motions; vibrations and sounds; magnetism and electricity; heat and energy; and sun, moon, and stars. Background information, suggestions for investigations, and references are given for each subject area.

*THINK ABOUT IT! SCIENCE PROBLEMS OF THE DAY*. Fredericks, Anthony D. Oak Lawn, IL: Creative Publications, 1988. ISBN 0-88488-705-7
Grade(s): 5,6,7
$14.95

THINK ABOUT IT! SCIENCE PROBLEMS OF THE DAY contains 180 daily problems and 36 weekly challenges focusing on the life sciences, earth and space sciences, and physical sciences. Children explore real-life situations and apply scientific knowledge to solve problems. The Weekly Challenges encourage students to do independent or group investigations, use reference materials to gather data, and then interpret the information and organize their thoughts.

*TREEmendous ACTIVITIES FOR YOUNG LEARNERS*. Rose, Mary. Riverview, FL: Idea Factory, 1987.
Grade(s): K,1,2,3,4
$8.95

TREEmendous ACTIVITIES FOR YOUNG LEARNERS is filled with many enjoyable activities for studying the outdoors, and trees in particular. The lessons, written by an elementary school teacher, are well organized and easy to follow, and include objectives, background information, a list of needed materials, specific directions, suggestions for discussion questions, and extensions. The children investigate a variety of trees, identify how people and animals benefit from trees, become aware of the parts of a tree, observe animals that use trees as shelter, and learn about some plants that live in or on trees. Also included are an informal evaluation, interesting facts about trees, and a list of resources.

THE UNCONVENTIONAL INVENTION BOOK encourages student inventiveness and originality. This book may be used in conjunction with the regular curriculum, or as strategies to accommodate student creativity. The author describes the whys, wherefores, and how-tos in the first section of the book. In subsequent parts, the author includes student activity pages, teacher directions, hands-on activities, and teaching suggestions that motivate students to think inventively. Children are offered many opportunities to produce original products and learn firsthand what invention feels like.

*THE UNCONVENTIONAL INVENTION BOOK.* Stanish, Bob. Carthage, IL: Good Apple, 1981. ISBN 0-86653-035-5
Grade(s): 4,5,6,7,8,9,10,11,12
$8.95

UNDERSTANDING THE HEALTHY BODY contains 54 activities about the functions, systems, health, and growth and development of the human body. The activities are varied in content and level of difficulty so as to meet the needs of each classroom teacher. Chapter one defines health education and explains the need for it in the elementary school. The following six chapters describe activities about body organs and systems: the five senses, human growth and development, nutrition and foods, pollution and diseases, and drugs, poison, and safety. Each activity includes an objective, background information, challenges, a list of materials and equipment, how-to-do-it, extensions, and additional references.

*UNDERSTANDING THE HEALTHY BODY: CESI SOURCEBOOK III.* Council for Elementary Science, International (CESI). Columbus, OH: SMEAC Information Reference Center, 1983.
Grade(s): K,1,2,3,4,5,6
$5.50 for CESI members, $6.50 for non-members

WHEELS AT WORK describes wheels that have enabled people to do work that would otherwise have been nearly impossible. The author demonstrates that wheels are not only fun to make but also fascinating to watch. Using easily available materials and equipment, children follow directions to build pulleys, windlasses, gears, waterwheels, bubble-blowing devices, windmills, and paddle wheels. Additionally, in the section about each different machine, the author provides historical information, experiments to try, explanations of what is happening, and in some instances, extra challenges. The activities in this book give children the opportunity to learn how machines work and to experience the feeling of being an inventor.

*WHEELS AT WORK: BUILDING AND EXPERIMENTING WITH MODELS OF MACHINES.* Zubrowski, Bernie. New York, NY: Morrow, 1986.
ISBN 0-688-06349-7
Grade(s): 3,4,5,6
$5.95

## Books on Teaching Science

Good teaching can become even better when provided with adequate support. The books listed in this section offer guidance, through reviews of learning theory and discussion of pedagogical techniques. These titles represent only a sampling of the books we have found to be most helpful and accessible. Readers are encouraged to inform us of other outstanding publications they have used. Consult the Sources index to locate publishers.

*4MAT AND SCIENCE—TOWARDS WHOLENESS IN SCIENCE EDUCATION.* Samples, Bob; Hammond, Bill; and McCarthy, Bernice. Barrington, IL: Excel, 1985. ISBN 0-9608992-2-7 $12.95

Many learning styles are effective in the acquisition of skills and knowledge. In 4MAT AND SCIENCE, the authors examine four different learning styles (concrete experience, reflective observation, abstract concepts, and active experimentation) and methods that educators may use to teach the variety of children encountered in an elementary classroom. Included are concrete examples of how to apply these teaching skills. Specific science lessons about rocks, plants, galaxies, and mapping are excellent models for writing appropriate science units. The original text, THE 4MAT SYSTEM (Samples, Hammond, and McCarthy, Barrington, IL: Excel, Inc., 1985), offers more philosophical detail and additional sample lessons in science and other curriculum areas.

*EARLY CHILDHOOD AND SCIENCE.* McIntyre, Margaret. Washington, DC: National Science Teachers Association, 1984. ISBN 0-87355-029-3 $7.50

EARLY CHILDHOOD AND SCIENCE is a collection of articles reprinted from SCIENCE AND CHILDREN that focus on philosophy, teaching ideas, and topics of special interest to early childhood educators. The articles emphasize practical experience, incorporating a knowledge of child development and learning styles. The authors of the articles describe appropriate science for young children; suggest a variety of activities in life science, physical science, and earth science; and offer ideas for involving parents in science, conducting a science fair, developing curriculum, and identifying and working with children with special needs.

*ELEMENTARY SCHOOL SCIENCE AND HOW TO TEACH IT.* Blough, Glenn O., and Schwartz, Julius. New York, NY: Holt, Rinehart & Winston, 1984. ISBN 0-03-062866-0 $30.95

ELEMENTARY SCHOOL SCIENCE AND HOW TO TEACH IT is divided into two sections. The first five chapters give a comprehensive look at the role of science in elementary education—what needs to be taught and how to teach it most effectively and enjoyably. The remaining 15 chapters focus on activities in specific subject areas. Background information is given for each topic and is followed by age-appropriate teaching ideas, resources to investigate, and suggestions for teacher preparation. The bibliography includes professional publications, subject-matter background books for teachers, and magazines for science teaching.

The authors of ELEMENTARY SCIENCE METHODS assert that any approach to the teaching of science should begin with children's interests and ideas. The first part of the text is devoted to issues that a teacher needs to consider when designing an elementary science program, such as child development, topic choices, aims, goals, objectives, evaluation, skills, activities, resources, and integration with other curriculum areas. Part two, focused on implementation, describes concepts, activities, related children's literature, field trips, and more, as they complement topics in life science, earth science, and physical science. Suggestions are given for primary grades and intermediate grades, and each chapter ends with sources of assistance, free and inexpensive materials, ways to strengthen teacher background, teacher and student resource books, and ideas for planning.

*ELEMENTARY SCIENCE METHODS.* Henson, Kenneth T., and Janke, Delmar. New York, NY: McGraw-Hill, 1984. ISBN 0-07-028265-X $30.95

To allow learners the opportunity to have wonderful ideas and consequently feel good about themselves is the essence of pedagogy, according to Duckworth. "THE HAVING OF WONDERFUL IDEAS" is a collection of essays that trace the evolution of the author's thoughts about children's thinking and teacher education from her early work with Jean Piaget through her experiences as an associate professor at the Harvard Graduate School of Education. The major themes of the book are these: the learner's role in constructing new knowledge, the development of broad views of curriculum and the application of these views to evaluation, the importance of teacher research, the investigation of ways in which children think about war and peace and interpersonal conflict, and the identification of approaches to teacher education that focus upon the learner's point of view—both the child's and the teacher's. Anyone interested in curriculum development, educational and developmental psychology, teacher education, and science education will come away from this publication with a richer understanding of children, teaching, and learning.

*"THE HAVING OF WONDERFUL IDEAS" AND OTHER ESSAYS ON TEACHING AND LEARNING.* Duckworth, Eleanor. New York, NY: Teachers College Press, 1987. ISBN 0-8077-2876-4 $13.95

INTRODUCTION AND GUIDE TO TEACHING PRIMARY SCIENCE is the first volume in a series jointly sponsored by the Nuffield Foundation and the Social Science Research Council. This book is specifically designed to provide helpful suggestions, models, and activities for the classroom teacher who lacks a science orientation. Ideas about topic choices and student and teacher attitudes and preconceptions are discussed in the first section. The major portion of the book is devoted to science topics that are appropriate for the elementary child, and ways to organize and implement lessons based on them. Easy-to-follow directions accompany each activity. There are nine other books in the series and each is each designed around a single science topic, such as seeds, mirrors, and magnifiers.

*INTRODUCTION AND GUIDE TO TEACHING PRIMARY SCIENCE.* Diamond, Dorothy. London, England: Macdonald, 1983. ISBN 0-356-05082-3 $8.75 (Available in the U.S. from Teacher's Laboratory.)

LEARNING BY DOING offers a rationale for hands-on assessment of performance in science and provides 11 sample tasks that test students' ability to employ higher-order thinking skills in solving problems. Pilot testing, based on Britain's Assessment of Performance Unit, was carried out in 12 school districts in a variety of settings across the United States. Students in third, seventh, and eleventh grades participated in group activities and individual experiments. The results of the pilot project demonstrate the effectiveness of practical testing and hold implications for teacher training, school science curriculum, and administrative support. (This manual is adapted from A PILOT STUDY OF HIGHER-ORDER THINKING SKILLS ASSESSMENT TECHNIQUES IN SCIENCE AND MATHEMATICS, FINAL REPORT, published by the National Assessment of Educational Progress, Princeton, NJ.)

*LEARNING BY DOING: A MANUAL FOR TEACHING AND ASSESSING HIGHER-ORDER THINKING IN SCIENCE AND MATHEMATICS.* National Assessment of Educational Progress (NAEP). Princeton, NJ: Educational Testing Service, 1987. Manual: $5.00

*THE LEARNING CYCLE AND ELEMENTARY SCHOOL SCIENCE TEACHING.* Renner, John W., and Marek, Edmund A. Portsmouth, NH: Heinemann, 1988. ISBN 0-435-08300-7 $25.00

THE LEARNING CYCLE AND ELEMENTARY SCHOOL SCIENCE TEACHING offers teachers the opportunity to explore what children think about, how children learn, what children learn, and how this information may be used to create a dynamic science program in a classroom. Content and implementation ideas are discussed and specifics are given for the development of learning cycles for biological, earth, and physical sciences. This information is arranged within each topic by grade appropriateness. Each section includes background information, questions, ideas for experimentation, teaching suggestions, extensions, and ideas for evaluative tasks. A separate chapter is devoted to learning cycles for kindergarten children. Each chapter about philosophy and/or research has a reference section at the end.

*LEARNING IN SCIENCE: THE IMPLICATIONS OF CHILDREN'S SCIENCE.* Osborne, Roger, and Freyberg, Peter. Portsmouth, NH: Heinemann, 1985. ISBN 0-86863-275-9 $15.00

LEARNING IN SCIENCE describes the ways in which children learn science. The authors discuss the ideas that children bring with them to the science experience, how these ideas are communicated and received, and how these conceptions can be used as building blocks for new learning. The role assigned by the authors to the science teacher is broad yet comfortable and an entire section of the book delineates the teacher as a guide, motivator, diagnostician, innovator, experimenter, and researcher. The appendices provide additional information about children, educators, and science. A list of related resources is included.

*MATHEMATICS AND SCIENCE: CRITICAL FILTERS FOR THE FUTURE OF MINORITY STUDENTS.* Beane, DeAnna Banks. Washington, DC: The Mid-Atlantic Center for Race Equity, 1985. Resource Manual: free

MATHEMATICS AND SCIENCE: CRITICAL FILTERS FOR THE FUTURE OF MINORITY STUDENTS is a resource manual for improving learning opportunities for children in the early grades. This guide reviews data concerning the underrepresentation of females and blacks in science and mathematics, identifies components of programs that successfully engage all learners, examines the role of administrators and teachers in effecting change, and offers materials and resources to support intervention. There are detailed discussions of social and academic factors affecting students' attitudes and performance, and their implications for educational practice.

*MUSEUMS, MAGIC & CHILDREN: YOUTH EDUCATION IN MUSEUMS.* Pitman-Gelles, Bonnie. Washington, DC: Association of Science-Technology Centers, 1981. $17.00 for ASTC members, $21.00 for nonmembers

MUSEUMS, MAGIC & CHILDREN describes exhibitions, museum programs, and approaches to teaching that are effective with young people. The book is divided into three sections. The first part offers methods for developing museum programs and exhibits. The second describes more than 200 children's programs, including hands-on science activities. The third lists organizations, distributors, and books that will prove useful for children, parents, and educators. This text illustrates how museums and schools may work together to improve the education of elementary school children.

*THE NATURE OF SCIENCE.* Aicken, Frederick. Portsmouth, NH: Heinemann, 1984. ISBN 0-435-54020-3 $15.00

THE NATURE OF SCIENCE offers a personal look at science and how it affects the way we think and behave. The author discusses how the readers' views of science may be expanded to include art, history, and the world around us. Educators can use this book as a methods text, to employ the suggested strategies in classrooms. The goal is to demystify science, put it into the context of the everyday world, and present a more balanced approach to the study of this broad subject. A section on suggestions for further reading is valuable for references and ideas.

The Assessment of Performance Unit offers a unique and much-needed approach to the evaluation of learning in hands-on science. PLANNING SCIENTIFIC INVESTIGATIONS AT AGE 11, the eighth in a series of science reports for teachers, proposes a rationale for assessing students' skills in planning investigations, analyzes the results of practical tests of planning abilities, and discusses implications of these results for science teaching. Experience in planning enhances children's abilities to think through the steps required for an investigation, to choose among various courses of action, to obtain accurate information, to apply previous knowledge, and to acquire new understanding. Test results suggest that engaging in planning and carrying out investigations enhances children's thinking skills, as well as their level of knowledge.

*PLANNING SCIENTIFIC INVESTIGATIONS AT AGE 11 (Science Report for Teachers: 8).* Assessment of Performance Unit. Harlen, Wynne. London, England: Department of Education and Science, 1986.
£1.00 (Available from the Department of Education and Science, London.)

The Assessment of Performance Unit offers a unique and much needed approach to the evaluation of learning in hands-on science. PRACTICAL TESTING AT AGES 11, 13, AND 15, the sixth in a series of science reports for teachers, offers a framework for assessing skills in observating, using apparatus and measuring instruments, using graphs and other symbolic representations, interpreting information, applying concepts, and planning and performing investigations. The report offers guidelines for developing and administering practical examinations, recruiting and training testers, and providing equipment and apparatus.

*PRACTICAL TESTING AT AGES 11, 13, AND 15 (Science Report for Teachers: 6).* Assessment of Performance Unit. Harlen, Wynne; Welford, Geoff; and Schofield, Beta. London, England: Department of Education and Science, 1985.
£1.00 (Available from the Department of Education and Science, London.)

PRIMARY SCIENCE...TAKING THE PLUNGE is a collection of articles that may be read in sequence or as the subject of each relates to the reader's own priorities and concerns. The authors recognize that science is an important vehicle through which children can develop mental and manipulative skills concurrently with attitudes about the world around them. Particular emphasis is placed on the teacher's role in this learning process, for how an activity is carried out is often more important than its content. This book presents well-researched ideas that will benefit any educator interested in encouraging children to build on their own experiences as they learn science.

*PRIMARY SCIENCE...TAKING THE PLUNGE.* Elstgeest, Jos; Harlen, Wynne; Jelly, Sheila; Osborne, Roger; and Symington, David. Portsmouth, NH: Heinemann, 1985. ISBN 0-435-57350-0
$15.00

THE PUPIL AS SCIENTIST? presents evidence that children use many preconceived ideas to make sense of new experiences. This book explores an approach to teaching science that encompasses the acquisition of knowledge and the use of children's own inquiries to achieve further knowledge. Classroom teachers are encouraged to recognize children's preconceptions, to respect them and see their worth in a historical sense, and to use them to promote discussion and further experimentation. Though much of the author's focus is secondary school science, the theory and practice discussed are applicable to all learners.

*THE PUPIL AS SCIENTIST?* Driver, Rosalind. Philadelphia, PA: Open University Press, Taylor and Francis, 1983. ISBN 0-335-10178-X
$15.00

SCIENCE 5-16: A STATEMENT OF POLICY concisely defines a framework within which improvement in science education can occur. The document sets priorities for science programs that are both broad and deep, that are equitable, and that engage students of all ages and abilities in challenging experiences relevant to their lives in and out of school. Evaluation criteria are discussed, as are the issues of teacher supply and training. The document places responsibility for implementation in the hands of schools, local education authorities, curriculum developers, teacher training institutions, and test developers.

*SCIENCE 5-16: A STATEMENT OF POLICY.* Department of Education and Science, and Welsh Office. London, England: Her Majesty's Stationery Office, 1985.
Free (Available from the Department of Education and Science, London.)

*SCIENCE AT AGE 11 (Science Report for Teachers: 1).* Assessment of Performance Unit. Harlen, Wynne. London, England: Department of Education and Science, 1983.
£1.00 (Available from the Department of Education and Science, London.)

The Assessment of Performance Unit offers a unique and much-needed approach to the evaluation of learning in hands-on science. SCIENCE AT AGE 11, the first in a series of reports for teachers, reviews the results of surveys of student performance on written and practical examinations. Most students at this age were shown to recognize similarities and differences among objects, to use measurement instruments correctly, to read and understand various charts and diagrams, and to use relevant methods in their practical investigations. Although many students also demonstrated the ability to make predictions, use controls, propose hypotheses, and apply science concepts to solve problems, few carried these processes further to detailed observation of objects and events, planning investigations, checking measurements for accuracy, or explaining their predictions.

*SCIENCE IN SCHOOLS: AGE 11 (Research Report: 4).* Assessment of Performance Unit. Harlen, Wynne; Khaligh, Nasrin; Palacio, David; Russell, Terry; and Black, Paul. London, England: Department of Education and Science, [no date]
£1.00 (Available from the Department of Education and Science, London.)

SCIENCE IN SCHOOLS is one of a series of research reports from the Assessment of Performance Unit, which has developed techniques for evaluating learning in hands-on science. This volume presents detailed results from the 1983 survey of 11-year-old children. Students were required to demonstrate their skills in observing phenomena, interpreting events and information, planning investigations, and applying knowledge to new situations. Test items involved either written or demonstrated solutions. Analysis of survey results indicated strong correlation between school resources and student achievement, and showed that although children enjoyed planning and carrying out their experiments and were able to make careful observations and accurate predictions, they needed more practice in explaining their reasoning and in transferring school learning to everyday situations.

*I. SCIENCE TEACHES BASIC SKILLS; II. THE PRINCIPAL'S ROLE IN ELEMENTARY SCHOOL SCIENCE; III. CHARACTERISTICS OF A GOOD ELEMENTARY SCIENCE PROGRAM (PARTS A and B); IV. WHAT RESEARCH SAYS ABOUT ELEMENTARY SCHOOL SCIENCE.* Mechling, Kenneth R., and Oliver, Donna L. Washington, DC: National Science Teachers Association, 1982, 1983.
$15.25 per set

The Project for Promoting Science Among Elementary School Principals has published a set of five useful handbooks: SCIENCE TEACHES BASIC SKILLS, THE PRINCIPAL'S ROLE IN ELEMENTARY SCHOOL SCIENCE, CHARACTERISTICS OF A GOOD ELEMENTARY SCIENCE PROGRAM (PARTS A and B), and WHAT RESEARCH SAYS ABOUT ELEMENTARY SCHOOL SCIENCE. The information in this series encourages elementary school principals to think about science as a vital part of their school's curriculum, to improve and maintain science education while strengthening their role as science curriculum leaders, to assess their science programs, and to investigate research studies that provide direction for the improvement of elementary school science programs.

*SCIENCE WITH CHILDREN.* Trojcak, Doris A. New York, NY: McGraw-Hill, 1979. ISBN 0-07-065217-1
$39.95

What do educators need in order to help children learn, and enjoy learning, science? SCIENCE WITH CHILDREN tries to answer this question. Teachers need to understand the basic ideas of science and how children learn science. They need to help children see science as a way of understanding the world around them and acquire instructional strategies for accomplishing these goals. The author presents choices; it is the reader's responsibility to assess, assimilate, and act upon what will best foster professional growth and student learning.

To provide the teacher with insight into the teaching and learning of science, SCIENCING devotes its first section to identifying the nature of science, the nature of learning, and the nature of the child. The second section of the book describes the science curricula available to the elementary school teacher, including kits, textbooks, a text-kit combination, use of trade books, and specific elementary science projects. The remainder of this volume presents ideas for implementing an effective science program, where children are actively involved and the best of microcomputer software and math curricula are integrated with science. Each chapter within the sections has a summary and a bibliography.

*SCIENCING.* Cain, Sandra E., and Evans, Jack M. Columbus, OH: Merrill, 1984. ISBN 0-675-20055-5
$21.95

SOURCEBOOK: SCIENCE EDUCATION AND THE PHYSICALLY HANDICAPPED includes papers and articles that help students, teachers, counselors, scientists, parents, and administrators make science a vital part of the environment and lives of all people, regardless of physical handicaps. The book is divided into ten sections: an overview of science education for the handicapped; implications for mainstreaming handicapped students into science classes; teacher education programs; bibliographies and lists of agencies, organizations, associations, and journals; science for the deaf; science and support systems for the orthopedically handicapped; an overview and specific techniques for science for the visually impaired; extending science beyond the school setting; science careers for the handicapped; and implications for the future of science education and the handicapped. This publication offers philosophy, practical strategies, and much food for thought.

*SOURCEBOOK: SCIENCE EDUCATION AND THE PHYSICALLY HANDICAPPED.* Hofman, Helenmarie H., and Ricker, Kenneth S. Washington, DC: National Science Teachers Association, 1979.
$5.00

TEACHING ELEMENTARY SCHOOL SCIENCE is designed to provide information, research, activities, and strategies to implement a laboratory-centered approach to teaching science. In the opening chapters the author explains the function of the laboratory in an elementary school and the conceptual and quantitative approaches to life science and physical science. Subsequent chapters discuss the intellectual development of the learner and the teaching strategies applicable to the various stages of a child's development. Each chapter has a summary, exercises, and further readings. The final section of the book is devoted to laboratory experiments in life and physical sciences. The experiments are grouped according to subtopics, with a materials list, suggested procedure, and background information for each. General questions and additional experiments are listed for each subtopic.

*TEACHING ELEMENTARY SCHOOL SCIENCE: A LABORATORY APPROACH.* Thier, Herbert D. Lexington, MA: D.C. Heath and Company, 1970. ISBN 0-669-51805-0
$15.95

TEACHING MODERN SCIENCE suggests that the learning of science is ideally suited for the student's active participation in the education process. This book will help a teacher to explore many topics in science, decide which to teach and why, and devise practical methods for planning and implementing a guided discovery approach to teaching science. The ideas presented in this book are applicable to all grade levels and to children of varying abilities. There are extensive and useful appendices containing the following information: historical summary of science education, elementary science curriculum projects, community sources for supplies and equipment, commercial suppliers, ways to plan a learning center, professional books, science education periodicals, professional societies, noncommercial sources for organisms, ways to care for various animals, free and inexpensive materials, research studies of the relationship between science and language/reading development, and more.

*TEACHING MODERN SCIENCE.* Carin, Arthur A., and Sund, Robert B. Columbus, OH: Merrill, 1985. ISBN 0-675-20221-3
$21.95

*TEACHING SCIENCE AS CON-
TINUOUS INQUIRY: A BASIC.* Rowe,
Mary Budd. New York, NY: McGraw-
Hill, 1978. ISBN 0-07-054116-7

In TEACHING SCIENCE AS CONTINUOUS INQUIRY, the author con-
cludes that an activity-based science program leads to greater language and logic
development, improved problem-solving strategies, and a more positive attitude
towards science. This book is divided into four sections. In part one, the basic
concepts and processes applicable to all science programs are explained. The
second section includes inquiry-based activities that are experimental or inves-
tigative in nature. Section three focuses on implementation strategies, and the
last section discusses evaluation. Many chapters have bibliographies that include books for children as well as adults. The publication offers the classroom
teacher philosophy, practical activities, teaching strategies, and room to grow.

*TEACHING SCIENCE THROUGH DIS-
COVERY.* Carin, Arthur A., and Sund,
Robert B. Columbus, OH: Merrill, 1985.
ISBN 0-675-20387-2
$29.95

TEACHING SCIENCE THROUGH DISCOVERY will enrich science instruction for the teacher and the children, through guided discovery. It capitalizes on
students' natural curiosity about the world around them and solicits their active
involvement in the learning process. The beginning chapters discuss the what
and why of science—what topics ought to be taught and the authors' rationale.
Subsequent chapters explain how to make the classroom an exciting place by
using enjoyable methods of scientific investigation. The ideas suggested in this
text are applicable to children of all grade levels and abilities. Activities for life
science and physical science are included. The authors seem to display a real
understanding of the role of elementary school teachers and the challenges they
face each day. Excellent information is supplied in the appendices.

*TOWARDS A SCIENCE OF SCIENCE
TEACHING: COGNITIVE DEVELOP-
MENT AND CURRICULUM DEMAND.*
Shayer, Michael, and Adey, Philip.
Portsmouth, NH: Heinemann, 1987.
ISBN 0-435-57825-1
$12.95

Science for all students is the underlying theme of TOWARDS A SCIENCE
OF SCIENCE TEACHING. The authors' purpose, therefore, is to explore what
needs to be done to accomplish this great task. What changes are necessary in
the traditional teaching of secondary school science, how teachers choose activities appropriate for their students, how these choices are evaluated, and how
curriculum is modified based on the evaluations are the focal issues. The results
of substantial research support the ideas offered within the text.

# Science Book Lists and Other References

Hands-on science experiences are enriched, not only by the use of good materials, but also by access to ideas and information. The directories contained in this section provide such access. They include bibliographies of trade books that serve successfully, either as reading matter for children or as background material for teachers. Also listed here are directories of human and material resources that can support good science teaching. (Readers are referred to the Magazines section of this book for *Appraisal, Science Books and Films*, and *Science and Children*, all of which offer reviews of outstanding science books for children. *Scientific American*, available at newsstands, also publishes a list of exceptional science books for children each December.)

The AAAS SCIENCE BOOK LIST, 1978-1986 is a useful guide to recommended books in all of the sciences and mathematics for junior and senior high school students. Many of the books may be used by elementary school teachers as sources of background information. This book is organized by topic and within each topic by the last name of the author. Entries are indexed by author and title and subject.

*AAAS SCIENCE BOOK LIST, 1978-1986*. Washington, DC: American Association for the Advancement of Science, 1986. ISBN 0-87168-313-6 $25.00

The third edition of THE AAAS SCIENCE BOOK LIST FOR CHILDREN contains 1530 annotated bibliographies. The titles are organized by subject according to Dewey Decimal Classification, and entries are indexed by author, title, and subject. This book also supplies a directory of publishers.

*THE AAAS SCIENCE BOOK LIST FOR CHILDREN, 3rd Edition*. Washington, DC: American Association for the Advancement of Science, 1972. ISBN 0-87168-202-8 $8.95

The AAAS SCIENCE EDUCATION DIRECTORY 1988 lists key persons in the nation who are responsible for science, mathematics, and technology education. Each entry for museums, associations, scientific academies, educational research centers, educational laboratories, and state and federal agencies includes the principal executive, other key personnel, address, and telephone number. The directory also provides information about the projects and educational activities of these organizations. The index includes separate listings of names, organizations and programs, geographical locations, and publications.

*AAAS SCIENCE EDUCATION DIRECTORY 1988*. Washington, DC: American Association for the Advancement of Science, 1988. Free

THE ASTC MEMBER STAFF DIRECTORY is published annually. The directory lists the name of the museum, the address, telephone number, museum director, and key personnel. The book is organized by country and within the U.S. section, by state.

*THE 1988 ASTC MEMBER STAFF DIRECTORY*. Washington, DC: Association of Science-Technology Centers, 1988. $10.00 for ASTC members, $20.00 for nonmembers

BEST BOOKS FOR CHILDREN offers a list of highly recommended books and annotations gathered from a number of review sources to satisfy the interests and academic needs of children. Although this book includes entries on a broad range of topics, it contains an extensive section on the sciences. The book is organized by subject area, and entries are indexed by author/illustrator, title, and subject.

*BEST BOOKS FOR CHILDREN: PRESCHOOL THROUGH THE MIDDLE GRADES*. New York, NY: Bowker, 1985. ISBN 0-8352-2131-8 $34.50

*THE BEST SCIENCE BOOKS FOR CHILDREN*. Washington, DC: American Association for the Advancement of Science, 1983. ISBN 0-87168-307-5 $14.35

THE BEST SCIENCE BOOKS FOR CHILDREN presents citations and annotations for more than 1200 children's science and math books. The editors include trade books written to help students increase their understanding of the real world. This book is organized by subject area, and entries are indexed by author and subject and title.

*EDUCATORS GUIDE TO FREE SCIENCE MATERIALS*. Randolph, WI: Educators Progress Service, Inc., 1987. ISBN 0-87708-183-2 $24.75

The EDUCATORS GUIDE TO FREE SCIENCE MATERIALS is published annually. It is designed to provide a continuing means of identifying materials that are currently available. This edition offers full information, arranged in alphabetical order by title, about free films, filmstrips, slides, printed materials, tapes, scripts, and transcriptions. Included are indexes of titles, subjects, sources and availability, Canadian availability, and industry sources.

*THE MUSEUM OF SCIENCE AND INDUSTRY BASIC LIST OF CHILDREN'S SCIENCE BOOKS 1973-1984*. Richter, Bernice, and Wenzel, Duane. Chicago, IL: American Library Association, 1985. ISBN 0-8389-3294-0 $9.75

THE MUSEUM OF SCIENCE AND INDUSTRY BASIC LIST OF CHILDREN'S SCIENCE BOOKS 1973-1984 includes short reviews of children's trade books, an annotated listing of adult resource books, a list of children's magazines, a list of review journals, and a directory of publishers' names and addresses. This book is divided into 17 main subject areas, and entries are indexed by author and title.

*THE MUSEUM OF SCIENCE AND INDUSTRY BASIC LIST OF CHILDREN'S SCIENCE BOOKS 1986 and 1987*. Richter, Bernice, and Wenzel, Duane. Chicago, IL: American Library Association, 1986, 1987. ISBN 0-8389-0465-3; 0-8389-0484-X $6.95/1986, $8.95/1987

The MUSEUM OF SCIENCE AND INDUSTRY BASIC LIST OF CHILDREN'S SCIENCE BOOKS 1986 and 1987 includes short reviews of science trade books for students in grades K-12. A directory of publishers, an annotated listing of sourcebooks for adults, children's magazines, and review journals are listed in appendices. Trade-book entries are organized according to subject and are indexed by title and author.

*NSTA SUPPLEMENT OF SCIENCE EDUCATION SUPPLIERS 1988*. Washington, DC: National Science Teachers Association, 1988. $3.00

The NSTA SUPPLEMENT OF SCIENCE EDUCATION SUPPLIERS 1988 was originally published in the January 1988 issues of SCIENCE AND CHILDREN and THE SCIENCE TEACHER, and in the February 1988 issues of SCIENCE SCOPE and the JOURNAL OF COLLEGE SCIENCE TEACHING. This yearly publication includes lists of suppliers of school science laboratory equipment; lists of firms producing computer hardware and software; manufacturers and distributors of audiovisual materials and other media; and textbook, resource materials, and trade-book publishers.

OUTSTANDING SCIENCE TRADE BOOKS FOR CHILDREN IN 1987 is an annotated bibliography of children's science trade books published in 1987. The books included are appropriate for students in grades K-8 and were evaluated by a special book review committee sponsored by the National Science Teachers Association (NSTA) and the Children's Book Council (CBC). Selection for this publication was based on the accuracy of information presented in a book, its readability, and its format and illustrations. The books are grouped by subject and, within each section, alphabetically by title. The books are categorized according to these subject areas: animals; biography; space science and astronomy; earth science, environment, and conservation; life sciences; medical and health sciences; physics, technology, and engineering; and other.

*OUTSTANDING SCIENCE TRADE BOOKS FOR CHILDREN IN 1987.* National Science Teachers Association (NSTA), and Children's Book Council (CBC). Washington, DC: National Science Teachers Association, 1987. Free

RESOURCES FOR EDUCATIONAL EQUITY 1988 provides annotated bibliographies for a variety of tools that help to create equitable education for females and males. The sections on curricula, career development and guidance, educational administration, teacher training/inservice, and women's centers contain descriptions of books, workshops, units, videocassettes, filmstrips, textbooks, and other materials designed to expand the expectations and options of women and girls.

*RESOURCES FOR EDUCATIONAL EQUITY 1988.* Women's Educational Equity Act Publishing Center. Newton, MA: Education Development Center, Inc., 1988. Free

SCIENCE BOOKS FOR CHILDREN includes brief, but useful, reviews of science trade books for children, chosen primarily from books reviewed by BOOKLIST magazine. The reviews are organized by topic and, within each topic, by the last name of the author. Entries are indexed by author, title, and subject.

*SCIENCE BOOKS FOR CHILDREN: SELECTIONS FROM BOOKLIST, 1976-1983.* Chicago, IL: American Library Association, 1985. ISBN 0-8389-3312-2 $15.00

SCIENCE EDUCATION is volume 6 of the ORYX SCIENCE BIBLIOGRAPHIES series. It provides over 200 annotated references and a research review covering the history and current issues in science education. The topics detailed in this book are elementary school science, secondary school science, teacher and teacher education, teaching methods and attitudes, educational reform and the science curriculum, achievement test scores, science education for special populations, and science and society.

*SCIENCE EDUCATION (ORYX SCIENCE BIBLIOGRAPHIES, VOLUME 6)* Schroeder, Eileen E. Phoenix, AZ: Oryx Press, 1986. ISBN 0-89774-227-3 $15.00

SCIENCE FARE presents many ideas for the teacher who is ready to capitalize on the natural curiosity and interest of children. The author suggests approaches to science education that are positive and enjoyable; recommends toys, books, and equipment that enhance any curriculum already in place; and in general, helps adults provide children with resources that will assist them to understand, explain, and question their world. Practical advice is offered for purchasing science kits, tools, and written materials. This guide and catalog is an excellent sourcebook for everything children should know about science.

*SCIENCE FARE.* Saul, Wendy, and Newman, Alan R. New York, NY: Harper & Row, 1986. ISBN 0-06-091218-9 $14.95

*SCIENCE HELPER K-8*. Knowledge Utilization Project in Science (KUPS) Sunnyvale, CA: PC-SIG/IASC CD-ROM Publishing Group, 1987.
$195.00 (One CD-ROM disk, two 5.25" disks for IBM PC)

SCIENCE HELPER K-8 provides access to some of the materials developed by the major National Science Foundation curriculum projects of the sixties and seventies. Information is indexed by grade, subject, skill, keyword, and content. The CD-ROM disk includes actual lesson plans from these projects included in this guide: Conceptually Oriented Program in Elementary Science (COPES), Elementary Science Study (ESS), Science...A Process Approach (SAPA), Science Curriculum Improvement Study (SCIS), and Unified Science and Mathematics for Elementary Schools (USMES). The SCIENCE HELPER undertaking was directed by Mary Budd Rowe at the University of Florida.

*TEACHING SCIENCE TO CHILDREN: A RESOURCEBOOK*. Iatridis, Mary D. New York, NY: Garland Publishing, Inc., 1986. ISBN 0-8240-8747-X
$30.00

In Part I of TEACHING SCIENCE TO CHILDREN, the author presents a multiplicity of approaches on how to teach science to young children. Part II of the book offers annotated bibliographies of science activity books. Part III lists and reviews science books for children, a contribution of Phylis Morrison. This latter part includes books about anthropology, biology, ecology, geology, mathematics, observation, poetry, technology, and other topics that will encourage teachers to integrate science across curriculum areas.

*TESS (THE EDUCATIONAL SOFTWARE SELECTOR)*. Educational Products Information Exchange (EPIE). Water Mill, NY: Educational Products Information Exchange, 1987, 1988.
$66.95

TESS, a comprehensive directory of computer software, lists over 12,000 programs for preschool through college by subject. It also includes EPIE recommendations, citations of other reviews, publishers, ordering policies, and a guide to software selection and use. The present purchase price includes the 1986-1987 directory, plus the 1988 supplement. Separate subject directories will be available quarterly, beginning in the fall of 1988.

# Magazines for Children and Teachers

Periodicals can provide a timely flow of current information in the sciences, ideas and activities for science teaching, or engaging reading matter for children. The magazines listed here have been selected for their excellence as instructional tools, their high quality coverage of scientific topics, their appeal to children, and their adaptability to classroom use.

## 3-2-1 CONTACT

Grade(s): 3,4,5,6,7,8,9
10 per year, $11.95 per year
Children's Television Workshop
One Lincoln Plaza
New York, NY 10023

Puzzles, projects, experiments, questions, and answers about the world around us, including computer programming and technology, make up the content of this magazine.

## AMERICAN BIOLOGY TEACHER

Grade(s): Teacher Resource
9 per year, $32.00 for NABT members, $38.00 for nonmembers
Membership Director
National Association of Biology Teachers
11250 Roger Bacon Drive
Reston, VA 22090

This publication is designed for junior and senior high school teachers but may serve as an excellent source of background information for the elementary teacher. Articles cover a wide range of biological topics including simplified explanations of current research.

## APPRAISAL: SCIENCE BOOKS FOR YOUNG PEOPLE

Grade(s): Teacher Resource
4 per year, $24 per year/$6.00 per single copy
Boston University
School of Education
605 Commonwealth Avenue
Boston, MA 02215

APPRAISAL contains reviews, written by librarians and subject specialists, of science trade books and series. Within each issue, single-book reviews are arranged alphabetically by author; series reviews, grouped at the end of the issue, are arranged alphabetically by series title.

## ART-TO-ZOO

Grade(s): Teacher Resource
4 per year, free
Office of Elementary and Secondary Education
Smithsonian Institution
Arts and Industries Building
Washington, DC 20560

ART-TO-ZOO brings news from the Smithsonian Institution to teachers of grades three through eight. Each issue focuses on one topic, such as animal size, using the yellow pages, nineteenth-century family portraits, or wolves as communicators. Included in an issue is a lesson plan, a pull-out page, and ideas for using museums, parks, libraries, zoos, trade books, and community resources.

## ASTRONOMY

Grade(s): Teacher Resource
monthly, $21.00 per year
Kalmbach Publishing Company
1027 North Seventh Street
Milwaukee, WI 53233

ASTRONOMY is the largest circulating journal in popular astronomy.

## AUDUBON ADVENTURE

Grade(s): 4,5,6
6 per year, $25.00 per year
National Audubon Society
613 Riversville Road
Greenwich, CT 06830

AUDUBON ADVENTURE is a nature newspaper for elementary school children. It focuses on animals, plants, and current environmental issues.

## CHEM MATTERS

Grade(s): Teacher Resource
4 per year, $5.50 per year
American Chemical Society
Room 805L
P.O. Box 57136
West End Station
Washington, DC 20037

A popular chemistry magazine that explains real-world chemistry.

## CHICKADEE

Grade(s): K,1,2,3,4
10 per year, $12.95 per year
Young Naturalist Foundation
P.O. Box 11314
Des Moines, IA 50340

This magazine includes information, activities, and children's contributions about nature-related topics.

## CLASSROOM COMPUTER LEARNING

Grade(s): Teacher Resource
8 per year, $22.50 per year
Peter Li, Inc.
2451 E. River Road
Dayton, OH 45439

Articles about how the computer can be used in a practical way to improve the educational process are the focus of this magazine. Useful advice about software and hardware is included.

## THE COMPUTING TEACHER

Grade(s): Teacher Resource
9 per year, $21.50 per year with membership in ICCE
International Council for Computers in Education (ICCE)
University of Oregon
1787 Agate Street
Eugene, OR 97403-1923

This journal emphasizes teaching about computers, teacher education, teaching with computers, and the impact of computers on curricula. Useful reviews of software are included.

## CONNECT

Grade(s): Teacher Resource
10 per year, $35.00 per year
Teacher's Laboratory, Inc.
P.O. Box 6480
Brattleboro, VT 05301-6480

CONNECT is a newsletter of practical science and math for K-8 teachers. Each newsletter focuses upon a single math and/or science topic and presents information about current research, history, and activities. Articles from teachers are welcomed.

## ELECTRIC COMPANY

Grade(s): 1,2,3,4
10 per year, $10.95 per year
Children's Television Workshop
One Lincoln Plaza
New York, NY 10023

Each issue of this magazine focuses upon one theme. Colorful visuals and intriguing content invite young readers to explore a variety of subjects.

## ELECTRONIC LEARNING

Grade(s): Teacher Resource
8 per year, $23.95
Scholastic, Inc.
730 Broadway
New York, NY 10003-9538

Educational technology, industry news, conference reports, college and university news, videodisk technology, and research reports are all standard features of this magazine. In-depth reviews of hardware and software are also included.

## EXPLORATORIUM QUARTERLY

Grade(s): HS,Teacher Resource
quarterly, $12.00 per year
The Exploratorium
3601 Lyon Street
San Francisco, CA 94123

The purpose of this magazine is to extend the museum beyond its walls and communicate ideas that exhibits alone are not able to convey. Each issue focuses on a single topic and offers background information and suggestions for activities.

## FACES

Grade(s): 3,4,5,6,7,8
10 per year, $17.95 per year
Cobblestone Publishing, Inc.
20 Grove Street
Peterborough, NH 03458

This magazine is produced in cooperation with the American Museum of Natural History. It offers a well organized and lively introduction to cultural anthropology.

## INTERNATIONAL WILDLIFE

Grade(s): 6,7,8,9,10,11,12,Teacher Resource
bimonthly, $15 per year
National Wildlife Federation
1412 16th Street, NW
Washington, DC 20036-2266

Wildlife and natural wonders from Antarctica to a London park, and virtually everywhere in-between, are explored, with excellent photographs and text.

## NATIONAL GEOGRAPHIC WORLD

Grade(s): 3,4,5,6,7,8
monthly, $10.95 per year
National Geographic Society
17th and M Streets, NW
Washington, DC 20036

Excellent photographs, art, and narratives offer children a friendly and motivating source of information.

## NATIONAL WILDLIFE

Grade(s): 6,7,8,9,10,11,12,Teacher Resource
bimonthly, $15 per year
National Wildlife Federation
1412 16th Street, NW
Washington, DC 20036-2266

Articles about nature, outdoor activities, and camping, and wildlife photography make the magazine an excellent addition to a classroom library.

## OCEANUS

Grade(s): 9,10,11,12,Teacher Resource
quarterly, $22 per year
The Allen Press, Inc.
104 New Hampshire Street, Box 368
Lawrence, KS 66044

An excellent resource for the study of the oceans and the questions facing scientists working with marine life.

## ODYSSEY

Grade(s): 3,4,5,6
monthly, $12 per year
Kalmbach Publishing Company
1027 North Seventh Street
Milwaukee, WI 53233

This magazine describes the basic concepts and principles of astronomy, through excellent photographs and illustrations.

## OWL

Grade(s): 2,3,4,5,6,7,8,9
10 per year, $12.95 per year
Young Naturalist Foundation
P.O. Box 11314
Des Moines, IA 50304

A magazine that answers children's questions about nature and science and generates greater interest and more questions.

## RANGER RICK

Grade(s): 1,2,3,4,5,6
monthly, $14 per year
National Wildlife Federation
1412 16th Street, NW
Washington, DC 20036-2266

This magazine helps children enjoy nature and appreciate the need for conservation through highly motivating indoor and outdoor activities.

## SCIENCE AND CHILDREN

Grade(s): Teacher Resource
8 per year, $34 per year including membership
National Science Teachers Association
1742 Connecticut Avenue, NW
Washington, DC 20009

Ideas are given to elementary and junior high school teachers for hands-on activities that will arouse and maintain children's interest in science.

## SCIENCE BOOKS & FILMS

Grade(s): Teacher Resource
five per year, $28 per year/$6.00 single issue
American Association for the Advancement of Science
1333 H Street, NW
Washington, DC 20005

SCIENCE BOOKS & FILMS reviews trade books, textbooks, 16mm films, filmstrips, and videos in all areas of science and mathematics that are appropriate for each level.

## SCIENCE NEWS

Grade(s): 6,7,8,9,10,11,12,Teacher Resource
weekly, $34.50 per year
Science Service, Inc.
1719 N Street, NW
Washington, DC 20036

Each issue contains articles and commentary describing new developments in science.

## SCIENCE SCOPE

Grade(s): Teacher Resource
6 per year, $42 per year (includes membership and one additional NSTA journal)
National Science Teachers Association
1742 Connecticut Avenue, NW
Washington, DC 20009

This publication includes ideas for activities, posters, teaching tips, and reviews of materials geared towards the middle school and junior high school teacher.

## THE SCIENCE TEACHER

Grade(s): Teacher Resource
9 per year, $34 including membership
National Science Teachers Association
1742 Connecticut Avenue, NW
Washington, DC 20009

This publication is designed for junior and senior high school teachers but may serve as an excellent source of background information for the elementary school teacher. Articles cover a wide range of science topics and include current research.

## SCIENCE WEEKLY

Grade(s): K,1,2,3,4,5,6,7,8
18 per year, $8.00 per year for 1-20 subscriptions; $3.95 per year for 20 or more subscriptions
Subscription Department
SCIENCE WEEKLY
P.O. Box 70154
Washington, DC 20088-0154

SCIENCE WEEKLY focuses on topics in science, math, and technology. Each issue introduces one subject and contains written materials for each grade level, K-8, and teaching notes for all levels. The teaching notes include background information, a bibliography, initiating questions, follow-up questions, suggestions for hands-on activities, directions for using the student booklets, and ideas for curriculum integration.

## SCIENCELAND

Grade(s): K,1,2,3
8 per year, $26.00 per year (deluxe edition)/$4.00 per single copy; $12.95 per year (lighter stock)/$3.00 per single copy
SCIENCELAND, Inc.
501 Fifth Avenue
New York, NY 10017-6165

Each volume of SCIENCELAND focuses on one scientific topic, such as pill bugs, space adventures, hands, or rubber bands. The written material, detailed and lifelike illustrations, and color photographs pique a child's curiosity and encourage scientific thinking. An accompanying teacher's manual includes background information, suggestions for activities, discussion questions, and ideas for projects.

## TEACHING AND COMPUTERS

Grade(s): Teacher Resource
8 per year, $19.95 per year
Scholastic, Inc.
730 Broadway
New York, NY 10003-9538

A practical computer magazine for elementary teachers, TEACHING AND COMPUTERS contains activities, task cards, blackline masters, suggested ideas from other teachers, and a teacher-reviewed software section.

## THE UNIVERSE IN THE CLASSROOM

Grade(s): Teacher Resource
quarterly, free
Teacher's Newsletter Department
Astronomical Society of the Pacific
1290 24th Street
San Francisco, CA 94122

THE UNIVERSE IN THE CLASSROOM is a newsletter on teaching astronomy. Up-to-date information and activities are given for a variety of astronomy-related topics.

## WONDERSCIENCE

Grade(s): 4,5,6
4 per year, $4.00 each
American Chemical Society
P.O. Box 57136 West End Station
Washington, DC 20037

WONDERSCIENCE relates science concepts to technology through physical science investigations for children and adults to do together. Each issue contains background information, hands-on activities, and ideas for integrating science with other curriculum areas.

## YOUR BIG BACKYARD

Grade(s): P,K,1
monthly, $10 per year
National Wildlife Federation
1412 16th Street, NW
Washington, DC 20036-2266

Young children learn about animals and nature through photographs and simple text.

## ZOOBOOKS

Grade(s): K,1,2,3,4,5
10 per year, $14.95 per year/$1.95 per issue
Wildlife Education, Ltd.
930 West Washington St.
San Diego, CA 92103

Each issue contains numerous color photographs with brief factual text, and focuses on a specific animal or group of animals. This series can be purchased by subscription or single copy. Back issues are available.

# III. SOURCES OF INFORMATION AND ASSISTANCE

There are many organizations that serve as resources for teachers, offering information and assistance to support hands-on science. Museums, associations, publishers, and suppliers provide programs and materials for classroom use, both regionally and nationally. In addition to these organizations, there are funded projects whose activities can either be implemented directly or serve as models for hands-on school science. Such organizations and projects are included in Section III.

## Museums and Science-Technology Centers

Museums and science-technology centers can do much to enrich hands-on science programs. Listed here are museums that, in response to a national survey by the NSRC, indicated that they provide local outreach, kits, publications, teacher training, or other services that extend beyond museum walls to teachers and learners at school sites. They are organized alphabetically by institution, with a regional list at the end. We encourage readers to look outside their immediate geographical areas for programs and materials of outstanding quality.

**THE ACADEMY OF NATURAL SCIENCES OF PHILADELPHIA**
19th and The Benjamin Franklin Parkway
Philadelphia, PA 19103
(215) 299-1100
Keith S. Thomson, President
Russell S. Daws, Director of Education

The Academy of Natural Sciences of Philadelphia offers classes and museum safaris among its field-trip options, and also provides programs to encourage girls and underserved students in science. School outreach includes the Eco-Show-on-the-Road, and ideas and materials for teaching science are offered through teacher workshops.

**ALLEY POND ENVIRONMENTAL CENTER, INC.**
228-06 Northern Boulevard
Douglaston, NY 11363
(718) 229-4000
George O. Pratt, Executive Director
Aline Euler, Youth Education Director

The Alley Pond Environmental Center offers school and adult outreach programs, educational programs for grades P-HS, and environmental exhibits.

**AMERICAN MUSEUM OF NATURAL HISTORY HAYDEN PLANETARIUM**
Central Park West at 79th Street
New York, NY 10024
(212) 769-5000
Thomas D. Nicholson, Director
Malcolm Arth, Chairman of the Department of Education
William A. Gutsch, Chairman of the Hayden Planetarium

In addition to numerous classes, workshops, and exhibits on natural science and anthropology, the museum offers pre-visit materials, and courses and workshops for teachers. Curriculum packets on dinosaurs and Eastern Woodland Indians are under development.

**AMERICAN MUSEUM OF SCIENCE & ENERGY**
300 South Tulane Avenue
Oak Ridge, TN 37830
(615) 576-3200
Marion Marsee, Director of Museum Operations

Sponsored by the U.S. Department of Energy, the museum offers displays, traveling exhibits, programs, and curriculum materials for pre-college energy studies.

**ANNISTON MUSEUM OF NATURAL HISTORY**
P.O. Box 1587
Anniston, AL 36202
(205) 237-6766
Christopher J. Reich, Director
W. Peter Conroy, Curator of Natural History

Exhibits, field studies, camps, and educational programs relating to the environment and the place of human beings in it.

## AQUARIUM OF NIAGARA FALLS

701 Whirlpool Street
Niagara Falls, NY 14301
(716) 285-3575
Albert Y. Clifton, Jr., Director
Helen Domske, Curator of Education

The Aquarium of Niagara Falls provides presentations and publishes field-trip guides and booklets on aquatic organisms.

## ARIZONA MUSEUM OF SCIENCE AND TECHNOLOGY

80 North Second Street
Phoenix, AZ 85004
(602) 256-9388
Dan Zirpoli, Executive Director
Ann Silver, Education Coordinator

This is a new museum, expanding its offerings of teacher inservice and school-site programs for children.

## ARIZONA-SONORA DESERT MUSEUM

2021 North Kinney Road
Tucson, AZ 85743
(602) 883-1380
Dan Davis, Director
Carol Cochran, Curator of Education

Exhibits and programs featuring live animals and plants in their natural habitats, and community outreach for school children and adults.

## ARKANSAS MUSEUM OF SCIENCE AND HISTORY

MacArthur Park
Little Rock, AR 72202
(501) 371-3521
Alison Sanchez, Executive Director
Joyce Godfrey, Director of Natural Science Education
Berna Love, Director of Social Science Education and Media Production

The Arkansas Museum of Science and History provides field-trip programs, school outreach, statewide teacher inservice, and lending boxes on topics relating to the natural and social history of the region, as well as more distant cultures. The museum sponsors public television series on ecology and on topics in regional history and loans audiovisual materials to schools.

## AUDUBON PARK AND ZOOLOGICAL GARDEN

6500 Magazine Street
Audubon Park
New Orleans, LA 70178
(504) 861-2537
L. Ronald Forman, Executive Director
Ann Weber, Director of Education

The Audubon Park and Zoological Garden publishes six activity books and sponsors a Junior Keeper Program, an Audubon Zoomobile, and a Read-the-Zoo Reading Certificate Program.

## BADLANDS NATIONAL PARK

Box 6
Cedar Pass
SH240
Interior, SD 57750
(605) 433-5361
Donald Falvey, Superintendent

Badlands National Park offers field study experiences and publishes three nature trail guides, CLIFF SHELF, THE DOOR TRAIL, and FOSSIL EXHIBIT TRAIL.

## THE BISHOP MUSEUM

1525 Bernice Street
Honolulu, HI 96817
(808) 847-3511
W. Donald Duckworth, Director

Planetarium, observatory, and exhibits.

## BOWERS MUSEUM

2002 North Main Street
Santa Ana, CA 92706
(714) 972-1900
Paul Piazza, Director
James B. Malesky, Curator of Education

Exhibits and educational programs relating to natural science, technology, art, and anthropology.

## BROOKHAVEN NATIONAL LABORATORY EXHIBIT CENTER—SCIENCE MUSEUM

Brookhaven National Laboratory
Upton, NY 11973
(516) 282-4049
Janet Tempel, Exhibit Coordinator
Eloise Gmur, Education Director

The Exhibit Center's field trips and tours are supported by written brochures and workshops for teachers. The Center also sponsors a regional science fair and an annual balsa wood bridge-building contest.

## BROOKLYN BOTANIC GARDEN

1000 Washington Avenue
Brooklyn, NY 11225
(718) 622-4433/4544
Donald Moore, President
Lucy Jones, Vice President of Education and Information Services
Betsy Jacobs, Director of Children's Education

In addition to field trips, tours, and youth gardening projects at the site, the Brooklyn Botanic Garden offers hands-on school outreach, a video kit and several books about gardening or visiting the botanic garden with children, and 25-cent seed packets for school groups. The Garden collaborates with local school districts on teacher workshops and will join a consortium of Brooklyn cultural institutions to offer inservice programs beginning in spring 1989.

## BUFFALO MUSEUM OF SCIENCE

Humboldt Parkway
Buffalo, NY 14211
(716) 896-5200
Ernst E. Both, Director
Marilou Debak, Chairman of Education

Exhibits, educational programs, and publications relating to natural science and anthropology.

## BUHL SCIENCE CENTER

Allegheny Square
Pittsburgh, PA 15212
(412) 321-4302
Alphonse T. DeSena, Director
Ron J. Baillie, Director of Exhibits and Science Programs

The Buhl Planetarium and its Institute of Popular Science provide exhibits and educational programs.

## CABRILLO MARINE MUSEUM

3720 Stephen White Drive
San Pedro, CA 90731
(213) 548-7563
John M. Olguin, Associate Director

The Cabrillo Marine Museum offers educational programs, whale-watching trips, and exhibits about grunion and whales.

## CALIFORNIA ACADEMY OF SCIENCE

Golden Gate Park
San Francisco, CA 94118
(415) 221-5100
Frank H. Talbot, Executive Director
Susan Douglas, Education Chairperson

The California Academy of Science hosts classes in natural history and houses a hands-on Discovery Room for use by school groups. Outreach lectures and inservice programs are also available.

## CALIFORNIA MUSEUM OF SCIENCE AND INDUSTRY

700 State Drive
Los Angeles, CA 90037
(213) 744-7400
Jeffrey Rudolph, Managing Director
Sarah Galloway, Assistant Director for Education

Exhibits, workshops, and educational programs relating to technology and health.

## CALVERT MARINE MUSEUM

P.O. Box 97
Solomons, MD 20688
(301) 326-2042
Paul Berry, Chairman
Ralph E. Eshelman, Director

Exhibits, programs, and publications relating to marine ecology and history.

## CAPITAL CHILDREN'S MUSEUM

800 Third Street, NE
Washington, DC 20002
(202) 543-8600
Ann W. Lewin, Director
Ed Lee, Coordinator of Lab IV

Participatory exhibits and educational programs integrating science, technology, arts, and humanities.

## THE CARNEGIE MUSEUM OF NATURAL HISTORY

4400 Forbes Avenue
Pittsburgh, PA 15213
(412) 622-3131
Robert C. Wilburn, President

Exhibits, research, workshops, field study, and loan and educational programs for children and adults. Includes Buhl Planetarium.

## CENTER FOR AMERICAN ARCHEOLOGY KAMPSVILLE ARCHEOLOGICAL CENTER

P.O. Box 366
Kampsville, IL 62053
(618) 653-4316
Anthony Schwinghamer, Director of Education

The Center for American Archeology sponsors field-school experiences for middle, junior high, and high school students. They also offer a five-week workshop for teachers during July and August.

## CENTER FOR METEORITE STUDIES

Arizona State University
Tempe, AZ 85287
(602) 965-6511
Carleton B. Moore, Director

The Center for Meteorite Studies publishes two informative booklets HAVE YOU SEEN A METEORITE? and IDENTIFICATION OF METEORITES.

## THE CHARLESTON MUSEUM

360 Meeting Street
Charleston, SC 29403
(803) 722-2996
Dr. John Brumgardt, Director
Karen King, Education Coordinator

Exhibits and educational programs relating to natural science, anthropology, history, and the arts.

## CHICAGO ZOOLOGICAL PARK (BROOKFIELD ZOO)

8400 West 31st Street
Brookfield, IL 60513
(312) 485-0263
George B. Rabb, Director
Sandford Friedman, Assistant Director of Education and Planning

Live animal exhibits, educational programs, and publications.

## CHILDREN'S MUSEUM DETROIT PUBLIC SCHOOLS

67 East Kirby
Detroit, MI 48202
(313) 494-1210
Beatrice Parsons, Director

The Children's Museum/Detroit Public Schools presents classes for children in grades K-12 that integrate all curriculum areas. They also sponsor a Museum-to-the-Schools Program, a lending department, classes for teachers, and after-school activities.

## THE CHILDREN'S MUSEUM (BOSTON)

Museum Wharf
300 Congress Avenue
Boston, MA 02210
(617) 426-6500
Kenneth Brecher, Director

In addition to its interactive exhibits and field trips, the Children's Museum offers teacher workshops on science and culture, curriculum kits for local loan, outreach in collaboration with local school systems, and publications on a variety of topics. The Museum also houses a resource center for teachers and parents, and a recycling center with inexpensive materials for classroom or home activities.

## THE CHILDREN'S MUSEUM, INDIANAPOLIS

30th and Meridian Streets
P.O. Box 3000
Indianapolis, IN 46206
(317) 924-5431
Peter Sterling, Director
David Cassady, Education Director

Participatory exhibits and educational programs relating to science, technology, and culture.

## CHILDREN'S MUSEUM OF UTAH

840 North 300 West
Salt Lake City, UT 84103
(801) 328-3383
Celeste Bowers-Irons Schow, Executive Director
Mary L. Kenny, Programming Administrator

The Children's Museum of Utah, in addition to providing exhibits and field-trip programs for students and teachers in the western United States, is one of 12 host sites for National Science and Technology Week. The Museum offers packets of materials, teacher training through the University of Utah, and a bimonthly calendar (free to residents of Utah, $5.00 for out-of-state subscription).

## CINCINNATI MUSEUM OF NATURAL HISTORY

1720 Gilbert Avenue
Cincinnati, OH 45202
(513) 621-3889
DeVere Burt, Director
David M. Imbrogno, Director of Programs

Planetarium, exhibits, inservice programs, research, field studies, educational programs, and school outreach relating to natural history, culture, and conservation.

## CLEVELAND CHILDREN'S MUSEUM

10730 Euclid Avenue
Cleveland, OH 44106
(216) 791-7114
Gerald T. Johnson, Director
Nancy King Smith, Director of Education
Fleka Andersen, Traveling Exhibits and Programs

The Cleveland Children's Museum offers student programs, teacher workshops, and traveling exhibits and materials, and has produced a videotape BUILDING PARTNERSHIPS: MUSEUMS, SCHOOLS, AND COMMUNITIES to encourage bridges between formal and informal learning. The tape is available for purchase ($10.00) or may be viewed on public television in autumn 1988.

## CLEVELAND HEALTH EDUCATION MUSEUM

8911 Euclid Avenue
Cleveland, OH 44106
(216) 231-5010
Lowell F. Bernard, Director
Carolyn Beears, Administrator of Youth Programs

Exhibits, educational programs, research, and community outreach for adults and children. Affiliated with Case Western Reserve University.

## THE COMPUTER MUSEUM (BOSTON)

Museum Wharf
300 Congress Street
Boston, MA 02210
(617) 426-2800
Joseph Cashen, Executive Director
Adeline Naiman, Director of Education
Michael Chertok, Education Coordinator

The Computer Museum (Boston) is the world's only museum exclusively devoted to computers. It has historical collections, more than 50 hands-on exhibits, tours, teacher workshops, a Kids' Computer Fair, and classroom materials for teachers to use with their students.

## CRANBROOK INSTITUTE OF SCIENCE

500 Lone Pine Road
Bloomfield Hills, MI 48013
(313) 645-3261
Dr. Robert M. West, Director
Janet Johnson, Curator of Educational Programs

Planetarium, exhibits, and educational programs on natural history and physical science.

## CUMBERLAND SCIENCE MUSEUM

800 Ridley Road
Nashville, TN 37203
(615) 259-6099
William Bradshaw, Science Museum Director
William Malone, Physical Science Educator
Carol Norton, Health Educator
Carolyn Okoomian, Life and Social Science Educator

The Cumberland Science Museum has developed programs in physical, earth, and life science for students in all grades. They produce teacher "sheets" that supply a list of goals, background information, a list of new vocabulary words, suggestions for pre- and post-visit activities, and a description of related museum exhibits.

## DALLAS MUSEUM OF NATURAL HISTORY/ DALLAS AQUARIUM

P.O. Box 26193
Fair Park Station
Dallas, TX 75226
(214) 670-8460
Richard W. Fullington, Director
Marilyn Stidham, Assistant Director for Public Programs

The Dallas Museum, in addition to hosting hands-on science classes and puppet shows, offers outreach and free loan of materials kits to local schools. Teacher workshops support investigations of the urban environment, and curriculum materials on a variety of topics are available.

## DENVER MUSEUM OF NATURAL HISTORY THE HALL OF LIFE

2001 Colorado Boulevard
Denver, CO 80206
(719) 376-6423
James Goddard, Director
Patty Cook, Teaching Coordinator

Participatory exhibits, workshops, and educational programs relating to health.

## DEPARTMENT OF MARINE RESOURCES

State House Station #21
Augusta, ME 04333
(207) 289-2099
Lorraine L. Shabbs, Director

The Department of Marine Resources publishes three booklets HARVESTERS OF THE SEA, THE AMERICAN LOBSTER, and BIOGRAPHY OF FOOD FROM THE SEA.

## DETROIT SCIENCE CENTER

5020 John R. Street
Detroit, MI 48202
(313) 577-8400
Corey Van Fleet, President/Executive Director
Barbara Pepper, Education Coordinator

The Detroit Science Center has hands-on exhibits, sponsors Saturday workshops for grades K-6, provides outreach for home experimenting, and publishes activity sheets and a bimonthly newsletter.

## DIABLO VALLEY COLLEGE MUSEUM

Golf Club Road
Pleasant Hill, CA 94523
(415) 685-1230
J.S. Byrne, Acting Director

The Diablo Valley College Museum publishes teacher guides for the study of common insects, fish, exotic arthropods, California Indians, rocks and minerals, amphibians, and reptiles. These guides include questions and other activities to be done as follow-up to a museum visit.

## THE DISCOVERY CENTER

1944 North Winery Avenue
Fresno, CA 93703
(209) 251-5533
Jeanne Larson, Director
Susan Shaver, Coordinator of School Visits

Participatory exhibits and educational programs relating to natural history and anthropology of the San Joaquin Valley.

## THE DISCOVERY CENTER

231 Southwest 2nd Avenue
Ft. Lauderdale, FL 33301
(305) 462-4116
Kim L. Maher, Executive Director
Barbara L. Berry, Director of Education

In addition to its on-site exhibits and educational programs relating to art, science, and history, the Discovery Center serves three counties through its eight school outreach programs. A STEAM grant (see ASTC) provides support for the Center's teacher training collaborative with Florida Atlantic University.

## DISCOVERY CENTER OF SCIENCE & TECHNOLOGY

321 South Clinton Street
Syracuse, NY 13202
(315) 425-9068
Dr. Stephen A. Karon, Executive Director
Rachel Nettleton, Education Coordinator

Exhibits, educational programs, and outreach.

## THE DISCOVERY PLACE

1320 22nd Street South
Birmingham, AL 35205
(205) 939-1176
Barbara Royal, Director
Diane D. Presley, Director of Education

The Discovery Place provides a summer science program for students in grades K-6; workshops for teachers; written materials that consist of activities, suggestions to improve teaching techniques, and ideas to extend museum visits; and kits that may be borrowed for use in classrooms.

## DISCOVERY WORLD MUSEUM OF SCIENCE, ECONOMICS AND TECHNOLOGY

818 West Wisconsin Avenue
Milwaukee, WI 53233
(414) 765-9966
William P. Chapman, Executive Director
Julie LaPorte, Community Relations Executive

Offers interactive hands-on exhibits on magnetism, electricity, light, health, and simple machines, with educational programs for children and for teachers on such topics as chemistry, electricity, and lasers.

## DON HARRINGTON DISCOVERY CENTER

1200 Streit Drive
Amarillo, TX 79106
(806) 355-9547
Jack N. McKinney, Director
Robert W. Bauman, Jr., Director of Education

The Don Harrington Discovery Center supplements its planetarium, health, and hands-on physical science programs, with distribution of printed curriculum materials and loan of equipment to schools.

## EVANSVILLE MUSEUM OF ARTS AND SCIENCES

411 S.E. Riverside Drive
Evansville, IN 47713
(812) 425-2406
John W. Streetman III, Director
Chairman Meyer, Public Program Coordinator

Participatory exhibits, research facilities, and educational programs.

## THE EXPLORATORIUM

3601 Lyon Street
San Francisco, CA 94123
(415) 563-7337
Robert White, Director
Karen Mendelow, Administrative Assistant
Linda Dackman, Public Information Director

A totally interactive museum, the Exploratorium publishes Pathways packets to enhance field trips, activity idea sheets, and many other materials for hands-on science in any setting. They also offer teacher workshops and other special programs.

## EXPLORERS HALL

17th and M Streets, NW
Washington, DC 20036
(202) 857-7000
Nancy W. Beers, Administrative Coordinator

Exhibits and programs relating to research supported by the National Geographic Society.

## FAIRBANKS MUSEUM AND PLANETARIUM

Main and Prospect Streets
St. Johnsbury, VT 05819
(802) 748-2372
Howard B. Reed, Jr., Director
Charles C. Browne, Director
Peggy Daniels, Education Coordinator

Displays, participatory exhibits, field studies, research facilities, educational programs, nature center, and community outreach for schoolchildren and adults.

## FERNBANK SCIENCE CENTER

156 Heaton Park Drive, NE
Atlanta, GA 30307
(404) 378-4311
Mary A. Hiers, Director
Robert A. Haywood, Director of Education

Planetarium, observatory, displays, educational programs, and traveling exhibits, all created for use by regional schools.

## FIELD MUSEUM OF NATURAL HISTORY

Roosevelt Road at Lake Shore Drive
Chicago, IL 60605
(312) 922-9410
Michael J. Spock, Vice President of Public Programs
Carolyn Blackmon, Chairman of Department of Education

The Field Museum has 19,000,000 items in its collection of zoological, botanical, anthropological, and geological specimens. It offers courses, workshops, film and lecture series for children and adults, a loan program for area schools, and publications, including TEACH THE MIND, TOUCH THE SPIRIT, a guide for effective use of museum learning opportunities.

## FONTENELLE FOREST NATURE CENTER

1111 Bellevue Boulevard North
Bellevue, NE 68005
(402) 731-3140
Bruce Lund, Executive Director
Kay Young, Chief Naturalist

This center provides, in addition to tours of its site, pre-visit curriculum packets and loan kits relating to natural and social history. Teacher workshops are offered at beginning and advanced levels.

## FORT WORTH MUSEUM OF SCIENCE AND HISTORY

1501 Montgomery Street
Fort Worth, TX 76107
(817) 732-1631
Donald R. Otto, Director
Polly Renfro, Museum School Director

Exhibits, educational programs, and materials-loan service. Founded by teachers.

## FRANKLIN INSTITUTE SCIENCE MUSEUM AND PLANETARIUM AND THE MUSEUM-TO-GO RESOURCE CENTER

20th and The Benjamin Franklin Parkway
Philadelphia, PA 19103
(215) 448-1200
Joel N. Bloom, Director
Wayne Ransom, Vice President and Director of Education and Programs
Roree Iris-Williams, Director, Educational Services, Museum-To-Go Resource Center

Exhibits, workshops, hands-on science activity kits, teacher inservice, and educational programs relating to science and technology in America.

## GULF COAST RESEARCH LABORATORY J. L. SCOTT MARINE EDUCATION CENTER

P.O. Box 7000
Ocean Springs, MS 39564-7000
(601) 374-5550
Gerald C. Corcoran, Curator

The Marine Education Center publishes a series of 15 leaflets about the north central Gulf of Mexico's living marine and coastal resources.

## HANFORD SCIENCE CENTER

825 Jadwin Avenue
Box 1970, Mail Stop A1-60
Richland, WA 99352
(509) 376-6374
Jay Haney, Manager
Ann Cowan, Education Specialist
Jeff Estes, Specialist, Outreach Education Programs

The Hanford Science Center enhances energy/science curriculum by providing kits, books, films, magazines, statewide teacher inservice, summer workshops, and suggested museum field trips through their outreach program. Affiliated with the U.S. Department of Energy, the facility offers regional outreach for National Science-Technology month; provides instruction and materials, programs, and software; and is a distribution point for Westinghouse Energy Source in the Northwest.

## HANSEN PLANETARIUM

15 South State Street
Salt Lake City, UT 84111
(801) 538-2104
VonDel Chamberlain, Director
Seth Jarvis, Education Director

The Hansen Planetarium publishes five teacher's guides to go along with its planetarium star program for grades K-6. The guides contain background information and bibliographies that would be useful to any classroom teacher.

## THE HARVARD UNIVERSITY MUSEUMS

24 Oxford Street
Cambridge, MA 02138
(617) 495-1000
(617) 495-2248
C. C. Lambert-Karlovski, Director, Peabody Museum

The Harvard University Museums feature exhibits, educational programs, and outreach relating to natural history and human culture.

## THE HEALTH ADVENTURE

501 Biltmore Avenue
Asheville, NC 28801
(704) 254-6373
Connie McConnell, CEO
Myra Lynch, Health Educator
Jasmine Gentling, Health Educator
Mary Sue Corn, Health Educator

The Health Adventure offers programs about all aspects of human biology, for class and family groups. Each program is accompanied by a list of pre- and post-visit activity suggestions.

## HOUSTON MUSEUM OF MEDICAL SCIENCE

1 Herman Circle Drive, 2nd Floor
P.O. Box 88087
Houston, TX 77030
(713) 529-3766
Dora Redman, President
Diana Lewis, Director

The Houston Museum of Medical Science provides health education programs and special hands-on events for grades 3-12, sponsors workshops for teachers and administrators involved in the "Just Say Yes" program (see National Urban Coalition), and offers local-school loans of lesson plans, models, and materials.

## HOWARD B. OWENS SCIENCE CENTER
## PRINCE GEORGE'S COUNTY PUBLIC SCHOOLS

9601 Greenbelt Road
Lanham, MD 20706
(301) 577-8718
Winney S. Wooley, Education Coordinator

Planetarium, hands-on exhibits, and educational programs for regional school children.

## HUNT INSTITUTE FOR BOTANICAL DOCUMENTATION

Carnegie Mellon University
Pittsburgh, PA 15213
(412) 268-2434
Michael T. Stieber, Archivist

Research and publications relating to botanical classification.

## IMPRESSION 5 SCIENCE MUSEUM

200 Museum Drive
Lansing, MI 48933
(517) 485-8116
Robert L. Russell, Director
Dennis Drobeck, Chemistry Lab Director
Marcianna Wade, Science Workshop Coordinator

In addition to providing field-trip opportunities, the Impression 5 Science Museum offers Camp-Ins, school outreach, gifted and talented programs, kits for local loan, weekend and summer workshops for children, and a minorities science program. As part of the Michigan Science Museum Collaborative, the museum also provides outreach to teachers and students in regions throughout the state.

## INSIGHTS—EL PASO SCIENCE MUSEUM

303 North Oregon Street
El Paso, TX 79901
(915) 542-2990
Charles H. Dodson, Jr., President
Buena T. Milson, Executive Director

Insights supplements its on-site activities with curriculum packets and a "Suitcase Science" loan program of interdisciplinary kits, as well as workshops on materials and techniques for teaching science.

## JAMES FORD BELL MUSEUM OF NATURAL HISTORY

University of Minnesota
10 Church Street, SE
Minneapolis, MN 55455
(612) 624-1852
Donald E. Gilbertson, Director
Gordon Murdock, Public Education Director

Exhibits and research related to evolution, ecology, and behavior. Affiliated with the University of Minnesota.

## JOHN G. SHEDD AQUARIUM

1200 South Lake Shore Drive
Chicago, IL 60605
(312) 939-2426
William P. Braker, Director
Linda Wilson, Curator of Education

In its classrooms, labs, and exhibit areas, the Shedd Aquarium offers educational programs that are linked to local science curriculum for grades K-12. The Aquarium also sponsors teacher workshops and a program for gifted children, and publishes a schedule of educational events.

## JOHN YOUNG MUSEUM AND PLANETARIUM ORLANDO SCIENCE CENTER

810 East Rollins Street
Orlando, FL 32803
(305) 896-7151
Janet McMillan, Acting Director
Anne Hartman, Director of Education

Planetarium, exhibits, and educational programs relating to natural history, physical science, and anthropology.

## THE KANSAS CITY MUSEUM

3218 Gladstone Boulevard
Kansas City, MO 64123
(816) 483-8300
Jean H. Svadlenak, President
Tim Shickles, Director of Education and Interpretation

The Kansas City Museum provides teacher workshops, a portable planetarium, and hands-on outreach activities in addition to field-trip opportunities.

## KANSAS LEARNING CENTER FOR HEALTH

309 Main Street
Halstead, KS 67056
(316) 835-2662
Maxwell E. Sloop, Director

The Learning Center offers on-site programs in health and human growth and development. Although there are no outreach projects at present, the center does provide teacher training in local districts.

## KIRKPATRICK CENTER MUSEUM COMPLEX

2100 Northeast 52nd
Oklahoma City, OK 73111
(405) 427-5461
Mary Ann Haliburton, Executive Director
Mary Jo Watson, Educational Coordinator

The Kirkpatrick Center Museum Complex consists of the Air Space Museum, the International Photography Hall of Fame and Museum, the Kirkpatrick Greenhouse and Garden, the Omniplex Science Museum, the Center of the American Indian, and the Kirkpatrick Planetarium. Classes for children in grades K-12 and inservice workshops for teachers are available at each section of the Complex.

## LAKEVIEW MUSEUM OF THE ARTS AND SCIENCES

1125 West Lake Avenue
Peoria, IL 61614
(309) 686-7000
William Landwehr, Director
George Ann Danehower, Curator of Education

Planetarium, exhibits, on-site preschool, materials loan service, and educational programs. Serves the regional Arts and Sciences Council.

## LAWRENCE HALL OF SCIENCE

University of California
Centennial Drive
Berkeley, CA 94720
(415) 642-5133
Marjorie Gardner, Director
Glenn T. Seaborg, Chairman

In addition to providing field-trip opportunities, the Lawrence Hall of Science sponsors major curriculum development projects for hands-on science, offers teacher training and leadership institutes, and publishes a wide variety of curriculum materials.

## LINCOLN PARK ZOOLOGICAL GARDEN

2200 North Cannon Drive
Chicago, IL 60614
(312) 294-4660
Lester B. Fisher, Director
Judith R. Kolar, Curator of Education

The Lincoln Park Zoo offers classes, tours, workshops, and opportunities to explore two new hands-on discovery areas at its facility, and it also provides curriculum packets and outreach to the Chicago Public Schools. Professional development services include environmental workshops for teachers, and faculty inservice days. Hands-on Zoo kits, designed for use with special needs students, are available for loan anywhere in the U.S.

## THE LIVING ARTS AND SCIENCE CENTER, INC.

362 Walnut Street
Lexington, KY 40508
(606) 252-5222
Susan B. Thompson, Co-Director
Marty Henton, Co-Director

The Living Arts and Science Center offers natural science and technology education programs and exhibits. It also provides media dissemination and teacher inservice programs.

## LOUISIANA NATURE AND SCIENCE CENTER

11000 Lake Forest Boulevard
New Orleans, LA 70127
(504) 241-9606
Robert A. Thomas, Director
Margaret Daly, Educational Coordinator
Woodrum Person, Educational Director

Nature trails, indoor exhibits, educational programs, and school outreach.

## LSU MUSEUM OF GEOSCIENCE

Howe-Russell Geoscience Complex
Room 135, Louisiana State University
Baton Rouge, LA 70803
(504) 388-2296
Judith A. Schiebout, Director

Exhibits, research, and educational programs relating to geology, paleontology, and archaeology.

## LUTZ CHILDREN'S MUSEUM

247 South Main Street
Manchester, CT 06040
(203) 643-0949
Loretta Rivers, Curator of Education

The Lutz Children's Museum offers kits, display cases, and mounts for classroom use on topics across all the curriculum areas. The Museum programs include outreach resource lessons, parent/child workshops, and summer classes. The museum also publishes three teacher newsletters per year.

## THE MAGIC HOUSE
## ST. LOUIS'S CHILDREN MUSEUM

516 South Kirkwood Road
St. Louis, MO 63122
(314) 822-8900
Elizabeth Fitzgerald, Director
Andrea Lapins, Education Coordinator

A children's museum featuring participatory science exhibits and programs.

## MARINE WORLD AFRICA USA

Marine World Parkway
Vallejo, CA 94589
(707) 644-4000
Anne Monk, Director of Education

Marine World Africa USA publishes teacher's guides: RAINFORESTS and HABITATS. Both booklets contain background information and activities suitable for grades K-12.

## MARYLAND ACADEMY OF SCIENCES/
## MARYLAND SCIENCE CENTER

601 Light Street
Baltimore, MD 21230
(301) 685-2370 and 685-5225
Paul Hanle, Executive Director
Mary Hyman, Director of Education

In addition to hosting field trips, Camp-Ins, teacher training, gifted and talented programs, and minority career workshops, the Maryland Science Center sponsors Science on the Move, a model outreach program in the Baltimore City Schools. The Center also has developed preschool pupil and teacher programs under NSF funding and is training teachers to work in home and hospital environments.

## THE MAYO MEDICAL MUSEUM

Mayo Clinic
200 First Street SW
Rochester, MN 55901
(507) 284-3280
Linda Romme, Director
Rebecca Schulz, Director of Education

Exhibits and educational programs relating to health and medical technology. Affiliated with the Mayo Clinic.

## MEMPHIS PINK PALACE MUSEUM AND
## PLANETARIUM

3050 Central Avenue
Memphis, TN 38111
(901) 454-5603
Douglas R. Noble, Director of Museums
Roger E. Van Cleef, Curator of Education

The largest museum in Tennessee, this municipal museum serves students and teachers from the south central United States, offering laboratory experiences, school outreach programs, and a free bimonthly newsletter for teachers. A Christa MacAuliffe grant supports the museum's inservice project for teachers in the region.

## METROZOO

12400 SW 152nd Street
Miami, FL 33177
(305) 251-0401
Robert Yokel, Director
Gordon Hubbell, Education Director

Metrozoo offers pre- and post-visit curriculum packages to enhance field trips, and publishes a regular newsletter and schedule of events. Its docent manual is available for $15.00.

## MIAMI SEAQUARIUM

4400 Rickenbacker Causeway
Miami, FL 33149
(305) 361-5705
Eric A. Eimstad, Education Coordinator

Background information for teachers, and student worksheets to enhance field trips and the study of marine mammals.

## MICHIGAN SPACE CENTER

Jackson Community College
2111 Emmons Road
Jackson, MI 49201
(517) 787-4425
James Satterelli, Director

Exhibits, workshops, and educational programs relating to astronomy and the history of space exploration.

## THE MICHIGAN STATE UNIVERSITY MUSEUM

West Circle Drive
East Lansing, MI 48824
(517) 355-2370
Martin Hetherington, Curator of Education

The Michigan State University Museum produces kits and worksheets to be used in conjunction with museum visits. They also offer a Junior Explorers Club and present summer classes for preschool to grade 4 students. Six newsletters per year are printed and disseminated for the Michigan Science Teachers Association.

## MILWAUKEE PUBLIC MUSEUM

800 W. Wells Street
Milwaukee, WI 53233
(414) 278-2700
Arthur Saltzman, Acting Director
Marion Davison, Chair of Education

Exhibits and educational programs relating to science and culture, Wizard Wing hands-on discovery center.

## MISSISSIPPI MUSEUM OF NATURAL SCIENCE

Mississippi Department of Wildlife Conservation
111 North Jefferson Street
Jackson, MS 39202-2897
(601) 354-7303
Elizabeth Hartfield, Director

Informative pamphlets and fact sheets on plants and animals of the region.

## MISSOURI BOTANICAL GARDEN

P.O. Box 299
St. Louis, MO 63166
(314) 577-5100
Peter H. Raven, Director
Kenneth D. Laser, Chairman of the Education Department
Stephanie Finke, Instructional Coordinator, Youth Programs

In addition to field trips, tours, and classes, the Missouri Botanical Garden sponsors teacher workshops and school outreach, a resource center, and Suitcase Science kits for local loan. The ECO-ACT leadership program trains high school students to teach elementary children's nature programs, and the Master Gardener program prepares volunteers for school and community outreach.

## MONMOUTH MUSEUM

Newman Springs Road
P.O. Box 359
Lincroft, NJ 07738
(201) 747-2266
Dorothy V. Morehouse, CEO and President
Marian Kanaga, Curator of Education

History, art, and technology exhibits and outreach programs.

## MUSEUM OF ART, SCIENCE, AND INDUSTRY

4450 Park Avenue
Bridgeport, CT 06604
(203) 372-3521
Mark J. Meister, Director

Exhibits and educational programs in natural science and technology.

## MUSEUM OF ARTS AND SCIENCE

1040 Museum Boulevard
Daytona Beach, FL 32014
(904) 255-0285
Judith Zollinger, Curator of Education

The Museum of Arts and Sciences offers educational programs at its planetarium and science building.

## MUSEUM OF ARTS AND SCIENCES

4182 Forsyth Road
Macon, GA 31210
(912) 477-3232
Nancy Anderson, Executive Director
Mary Ann Ellis, Director of Education

Life science, physical science, and earth science programs and exhibits.

## MUSEUM OF HISTORY AND SCIENCE

727 West Main Street
Louisville, KY 40202
(502) 589-4584
William M. Sudduth, President
Theresa Mattei, Vice President, Education and Programs

In addition to the classes and workshops held at the Museum of History and Science, this institution offers a Museum-To-Go program; field experiences in rafting, caving, and fossil exploration; Camp-Ins; and teacher inservice that includes both training and mentor components. Curriculum materials are available to accompany some of these programs.

## MUSEUM OF HOLOGRAPHY

11 Mercer Street
New York, NY 10013
(212) 925-0581
Laura J. Plybon, Administrative Assistant

The Museum of Holography designs special lectures and hands-on workshops tailored to the needs and understanding of specific audiences, provides outreach, and offers a quarterly publication: HOLOSPLORE.

## MUSEUM OF NEW MEXICO

113 Lincoln Avenue
Santa Fe, NM 87503
(505) 827-6450
Thomas A. Livesay, Director
Elizabeth Dean, Chief of Public Programs and Education

Offers folk history, southwestern history, and cultural and fine arts exhibits at five museums. Includes a research library, traveling exhibits, and teacher resources on Southwest history.

## MUSEUM OF SCIENCE AND INDUSTRY

4801 East Fowler Avenue
Tampa, FL 33617
(813) 985-5531
Wit Ostrenko, Executive Director
Eldon Grimm, Education Director

Science and technology exhibits, programs, outreach kits, and publications.

## MUSEUM OF SCIENCE AND INDUSTRY

57th and Lake Shore Drive
Chicago, IL 60637
(312) 684-1414
James S. Kahn, President and Director
Barry Van Deman, Acting Director of Education

The Museum of Science and Industry produces science kits, sponsors the Outstanding Young Scientist Award and an annual science book fair, publishes teacher's guides and student activity sheets for use with hands-on exhibits, and offers science classes for children and their families.

## MUSEUM OF SCIENCE AND SPACE TRANSIT PLANETARIUM

3280 South Miami Avenue
Miami, FL 33129
(305) 854-4247
Margot Johnson, Education Director

Planetarium, exhibits, educational programs, field study, and school outreach.

## MUSEUM OF SCIENCE, BOSTON

Science Park
Boston, MA 02114
(617) 589-0100
Bradford I. Towle, Interim Director
Peter Ames, Director, Visitor Services Division

Boston's Museum of Science includes a planetarium, an Omnimax theater, the Computer Place, and interactive exhibits. The museum offers teacher workshops, educational programs, school kits, Science-by-Mail, publications, and outreach, and it also houses the Museum Institute for Teaching Science, a seven-museum collaborative that provides materials and programs to support regional teachers.

## MUSEUM OF THE CHICAGO ACADEMY OF SCIENCES

2001 North Clark Street
Chicago, IL 60614
(312) 549-0606
Paul G. Heltne, Director
Mary Lamb, Education Coordinator

Natural science exhibits and classes for grades P-HS.

## MYSTIC MARINELIFE AQUARIUM

55 Coogan Boulevard
Mystic, CT 06355
(203) 536-9631
Howard Stirn, President
Stephen Spotte, Executive Director

The Mystic Marinelife Aquarium offers field trips, camps, and school outreach, and sponsors maritime educational programs jointly with the Mystic Seaport Museum. Teachers on Tour represents a consortium of regional institutions enhancing teacher access to local resources.

## NATIONAL AIR AND SPACE MUSEUM
## SMITHSONIAN INSTITUTION

Independence Avenue and 7th Street
Washington, DC 20560
(202) 357-1504/782-2106
Martin O. Harwit, Director
Kasse Andrews-Weller, Chief of Education

Collections of aircraft and spacecraft representing the history of flight, tours, films, planetarium, and a Resource Center that provides teachers with materials from such agencies as the Federal Aviation Administration, NASA, National Geographic Society, and Franklin Institute.

## THE NATIONAL AQUARIUM

U.S. Department of Commerce Building
14th Street and Constitution Avenue, NW
Washington, DC 20230
(202) 377-2825
Julie Onie, Director of Programs/Docents

The National Aquarium offers tours relative to the adaptations of animals and their environments; a multisensory tour for visually impaired students; a preschool tour, entitled "How to Read a Fish"; and an "Adopt a Fish" program.

## NATIONAL AQUARIUM IN BALTIMORE

501 East Pratt Street
Pier 3
Baltimore, MD 21202
(301) 576-3800
Nicholas Brown, Executive Director

The National Aquarium in Baltimore has marine life exhibits and produces aquatic science curriculum units for upper elementary school children.

## NATIONAL MARINE FISHERIES SERVICE
## AQUARIUM

United States Department of Commerce
National Oceanic and Atmospheric Administration
(NOAA)
Woods Hole, MA 02543
(617) 548-7684
Fred E. Nichy, Chief, Aquarium Program

The National Marine Fisheries Service Aquarium has hands-on exhibits and publishes six educational program guides and student booklets for grades P-12.

## NATIONAL MUSEUM OF AMERICAN HISTORY
## SMITHSONIAN INSTITUTION

12th Street and Constitution Avenue, NW
Washington, DC 20560
(202) 357-1300
Roger G. Kennedy, Director

Exhibits, research facilities, and programs on the history of American technology.

## NATIONAL MUSEUM OF NATURAL HISTORY
## SMITHSONIAN INSTITUTION

10th Street and Constitution Avenue, NW
Washington, DC 20560
(202) 357-2700
James C. Tyler, Acting Director

Exhibits; research facilities for students, teachers, and scientists; and programs on natural history.

## NATIONAL MUSEUM OF SCIENCE AND
## TECHNOLOGY

1867 St. Laurent Boulevard
P.O. Box 9724
Ottawa Terminal
Ottawa, Ontario K1G-5A3
(613) 991-3044/991-3073
David M. Baird, Acting Director
Gordon Bruce and James Cutting, Chiefs of Outreach

Participatory exhibits and demonstrations on science and technology.

## NATIONAL ZOOLOGICAL PARK
## SMITHSONIAN INSTITUTION

3001 Connecticut Avenue, NW
Washington, DC 20008
(202) 673-4800
Michael Robinson, Director
Judith White, Director, Office of Education

Offers free pre-visit materials and educational programs, school visits to Zoolab, and opportunities to observe 500 species of mammals, amphibians, and reptiles.

## NATURE SCIENCE CENTER

Museum Drive
Winston-Salem, NC 27105
(919) 767-6730
David D. Bonney II, Executive Director
Edward Falco. Director of Education

Exhibits, live-animal and health demonstrations, workshops, education programs, and school outreach.

## NEW ENGLAND AQUARIUM

Central Wharf
Boston, MA 02110
(617) 973-5200
John H. Prescott, Executive Director

Live sea-life exhibits, educational programs, publications, and school outreach.

## NEW MEXICO MUSEUM OF NATURAL HISTORY

P.O. Box 7010
Albuquerque, NM 87194
(505) 841-8837
Jonathan Callender, Director

This museum supplements its field-trip opportunities with statewide teacher inservice. The New Mexico Rural Education Project, cosponsored by New Mexico State University, takes museum staff to rural sites to train teachers to use local resources for science teaching. The Summer Elementary Science Teachers Institute (SESTI) invites teachers on week-long field trips to explore natural resources and enhance skills.

## NEW YORK AQUARIUM

Boardwalk and West 8th Street
Brooklyn, NY 11224
(718) 265-3400
Louis Garibaldi, Director
Ellie Fries, Curator of Education

Live sea-life exhibits and educational programs.

## NEW YORK HALL OF SCIENCE

P.O. Box 1032
47-01 111th Street
Corona, NY 11368
(718) 699-0005
Alan Friedman, Director
Peggy Cole, Director of Museum Programming

Planetarium, exhibits, educational programs for children and adults, and school outreach that includes a traveling planetarium.

## NEW YORK ZOOLOGICAL SOCIETY—BRONX ZOO

Bronx, NY 10460
(212) 220-5131
William G. Conway, General Director
Annette Berkovitz, Curator of Education

The New York Zoological Society operates the Bronx Zoo and the New York Aquarium, and will soon take charge of the Central Park Zoo, Prospect Park, and Flushing Meadow Zoo. Its educational programs include courses at the Zoo's facilities, development and dissemination of the Project

WIZE curriculum, and intensive teacher inservice programs that include ZEST: Zoos for Effective Science Teaching.

## NORTH CAROLINA AQUARIUM, FORT FISHER

P.O. Box 130
Kure Beach, NC 28449
(919) 458-8257
James A. Lanier III, Director
Bill Martin, Education Curator

The North Carolina Aquarium at Fort Fisher serves as a center for public information, marine education, and research.

## NORTH CAROLINA DEPARTMENT OF AGRICULTURE—NORTH CAROLINA MARITIME MUSEUM

315 Front Street
Beaufort, NC 28516-2125
(919) 728-7317
Rodney Barfield, Director
Joanne Powell, Educator

The North Carolina Maritime Museum provides written educational materials about coastal and marine habitats, plants, birds, snakes, seashells, and local geology.

## NORTH CAROLINA MUSEUM OF LIFE AND SCIENCE

433 Murray Avenue
Durham, NC 27704
(919) 477-0431
Thomas Krakauer, Director
Georgie Searles, Director of Education

This museum's services include teacher workshops emphasizing use of the natural environment, school outreach that includes pre- and post-visit materials, and a portable planetarium, a 6th grade space-education project, and science kits for purchase or local loan.

## OHIO'S CENTER OF SCIENCE AND INDUSTRY (COSI)

280 East Broad Street
Columbus, OH 43215
(614) 228-5619
Roy L. Shafer, President
Michael Stanley, Vice President of Education

In addition to field trips, COSI offers Camp-Ins, summer workshops; a nationwide outreach program, called COSI on Wheels; and the Young Experimental Scientists (YES) program, which unites teachers and children from Ohio in joint workshops. Curriculum packets on a variety of topics are free to any teacher.

## OMNIPLEX SCIENCE MUSEUM

2100 N.E. 52nd Street
Oklahoma City, OK 73111
(405) 424-5545
Sherman Kent, Director
Beth Bussey, Education Director

Planetarium, participatory exhibits, and educational programs.

## ONTARIO SCIENCE CENTRE

770 Don Mills Road
Don Mills, Ontario, Canada M3C 1T3
(416) 429-4100
Gerry Gillman, Associate Director General
George Vanderkuur, Associate Director General
John Fowles, Chief of Education

The Ontario Science Centre offers workshops and summer courses for teachers, a science circus that travels throughout the province, as well as school outreach in the local Toronto area. Science kits are free to Ontario schools or available for purchase by schools outside Ontario.

## OREGON MUSEUM OF SCIENCE AND INDUSTRY

4015 S.W. Canyon Road
Portland, OR 97221
(503) 222-2828
Marilynne Eichinger, Executive Director
Robert Larson, Manager of Adult and Teacher Education
Jeffrey Gottfried, Director of Outreach Programs and Services

The Oregon Museum provides outreach on a variety of science topics, offers field experiences and camp programs with teacher components, and collaborates with schools, universities, and colleges to provide professional-development workshops for teachers.

## PACIFIC SCIENCE CENTER

200 Second Avenue N
Seattle, WA 98109
(206) 443-2001
George Moynihan, Executive Director
William Schmitt, Director of Education

The Pacific Science Center offers several innovative programs for children, including the Science Champions program, in which students grades 3-5 attend museum workshops, then return to their schools to share their experiences with others. The Center also sponsors regional outreach developed and staffed by teachers, provides field-study programs at camps and at sea, and hosts Camp-Ins, in-service workshops, and teacher award programs.

## PLANET OCEAN

The International Oceanographic Foundation (IOF)
3979 Rickenbacker Causeway
Miami, FL 33149
(305) 361-5786
Jim Kay, Comptroller
Pat Ryan, Education Director

Planet Ocean presents marine education programs and provides a field-trip kit for classroom use. The IOF also publishes a bimonthly magazine: SEA FRONTIERS.

## READING PUBLIC MUSEUM AND ART GALLERY

500 Museum Road
Reading, PA 19611
(215) 371-5850
Bruce L. Dietrich, Director
Jefferson Gore, Curator of Fine Arts
George R. Miller, Administrative Director

As part of the Reading School District, the Reading Public Museum offers field-trip opportunities and summer science/art programs for children, provides pre- and post-visit materials, and sponsors museum exhibits at schools.

## RED MOUNTAIN MUSEUM

1421 22nd Street South
Birmingham, AL 35205
(205) 933-4152
Whitman Cross II, Director
Barbara Williams, Education Director

The Red Mountain Museum provides field trips and statewide school outreach. A series of intensive teacher workshops is offered in collaboration with the University of Alabama and supported by the National Science Foundation.

## REUBEN H. FLEET SPACE THEATER AND SCIENCE CENTER

1875 El Prado
Balboa Park
P.O. Box 33303
San Diego, CA 92103
(619) 238-1233
Jeffrey Kirsch, Director
Lynn Kennedy, Director of Education

In addition to field trips and after-school programs for children, this institution offers outreach exhibits for schools, teacher workshops for materials development and investigation of current issues in science, and a curriculum guide to enhance visits to the planetarium.

## ROBERSON CENTER FOR THE ARTS AND SCIENCES

30 Front Street
Binghamton, NY 13905
(607) 772-0660
Robert W. Aber, Executive Director
Michele Morrisson, Director of Education

Student workshops and exhibits about astronomy and light.

## ROPER MOUNTAIN SCIENCE CENTER

504 Roper Mountain Road
Greenville, SC 29615
(803) 297-0232
Darrell Harrison, Director
Greg Cornwell, Curator of Education

The Roper Mountain Science Center provides in-house and outreach student programs for its exhibitions in life science, astronomy, and history. Teachers guides to student programs are available along with pre-visit materials for classroom use. Roper Mountain Science Center also maintains a hands-on Discovery Room.

## SACRAMENTO SCIENCE CENTER AND JUNIOR MUSEUM

3615 Auburn Boulevard
Sacramento, CA 95821
(916) 449-8255
William B. Pond, Executive Director
Bruce Forman, Education Coordinator
Pat McVicar, Science Delta Coordinator (STEAM and SMART curriculum)

In addition to field-trip programs, the Sacramento Science Museum offers outreach, a traveling planetarium, and teacher workshops supported by STEAM funding (see ASTC). The museum's publications include a regular newsletter and two series of curriculum packets, each consisting of four volumes (one book per grade, K-3): THE SCIENTIFIC METHOD series ($7.50/volume) and ASTRONOMY AND SPACE ($10.00/volume).

## SANTA BARBARA MUSEUM OF NATURAL HISTORY

2559 Puesta Del Sol Road
Santa Barbara, CA 93105
(805) 682-4711
Dr. Dennis M. Power, Director
Catherine Woolsey, Curator of Education

Exhibits, research, and educational programs in regional natural history and anthropology.

## SCHENECTADY MUSEUM

2500 West Broad Street
Schenectady, NY 12308
(804) 367-1013
William K. Verner, Director
Al Hulstrunk, Education Director

Planetarium, nature preserve, exhibits, and educational programs.

## THE SCIENCE CENTER OF IOWA

4500 Grand Avenue
Des Moines, IA 50312
(515) 274-4138
Kirk Brocker, Executive Director
Judy Miller, Program Coordinator

The Science Center offers field trips, summer programs, and midwestern regional school outreach consisting of assemblies, demonstrations, and small group workshops. Teacher training provides materials and techniques for teaching hands-on science.

## SCIENCE MUSEUM OF CONNECTICUT

950 Trout Brook Drive
West Hartford, CT 06119
(203) 236-2961
Robert Content, Director
Jacob Mendelssohn, Director, New Technology Projects

The Science Museum of Connecticut provides outreach and teacher inservice, and sponsors the Connecticut Pre-Engineering Program (CPEP) to foster urban students' interest in science and engineering. The museum staff will custom-design classes and activities to suit a school's specific needs.

## SCIENCE MUSEUM OF LONG ISLAND

1526 N. Plandome Road
Manhasset, NY 11030
(516) 627-9400
John Loret, Director
Thomas Hurtubise, Associate Director for Education

Exhibits and education programs on natural science.

## SCIENCE MUSEUM OF MINNESOTA

30 East 10th Street
St. Paul, MN 55101
(612) 221-9410
(612) 221-9488
James Peterson, President
Phillip Taylor, Director
David Chittenden, Director of Education
Kathleen Lundgren, Director of School Services

Participatory displays, educational programs, traveling exhibits, Omnimax theater, and nature center.

## SCIENCE MUSEUM OF VIRGINIA

2500 West Broad Avenue
Richmond, VA 23220
(804) 257-1013
Paul H. Knappenberger, Jr., Director
Rose Dean, Education Director

Planetarium, traveling exhibits, hands-on displays, and educational programs.

## SCIENCE MUSEUM OF WESTERN VIRGINIA

1 Market Square
Roanoke, VA 24011
(703) 343-7876/342-7876
Christine Houmes, Executive Director
Bernice Smith, Collections Curator, Education Department

In addition to its traveling exhibits and school outreach, the Science Museum of Western Virginia offers one-day activity workshops for teachers on such topics as science magic, electricity, marine biology, and successful schoolyard field trips.

## SCIENCE MUSEUMS OF CHARLOTTE, INC. NATURE MUSEUM/DISCOVERY PLACE

301 North Tryon Street
Charlotte, NC 28202
(704) 372-6262
Freda H. Nicholson, CEO and Executive Director
Beverly Sanford, Director of Education and Programs

The Science Museums of Charlotte offer learning activities for children of all ages, including an aquarium, an aviary, exhibits, workshops, and educational programs. A teacher's guide is available to aid field-trip planning.

## THE SCIENCE PLACE

P.O. Box 11158
Fair Park
Dallas, TX 75223
(214) 428-7200
Richard F. Coyne, Chief Executive Officer
Patrick Miller, Education Director

Planetarium, exhibits, and educational programs relating to health, natural, physical, and earth science.

## SCRIPPS AQUARIUM—MUSEUM SCRIPPS INSTITUTION OF OCEANOGRAPHY

8602 La Jolla Shores Drive
La Jolla, CA 92093
(619) 534-6804
Donald W. Wilkie, Director
Diane Baxter, Aquarium Curator

Live animal exhibits and educational programs.

## SEA WORLD, INC.

1720 South Shores Road
San Diego, CA 92109
(619) 222-6363
Jan Schultz, President

Live sea-life exhibits, performances, educational programs, and publications.

## THE SEATTLE AQUARIUM

Pier 59
Waterfront Park
Seattle, WA 98101
(206) 625-5015
Cindi Shiota, Interim Director
John McMahon, Manager of Programs and Exhibits

The Seattle Aquarium offers numerous educational programs for all ages at its facilities, and also provides regional outreach in the form of a speakers' bureau and Puget Sound on Wheels, a traveling aquarium that visits schools. In addition to hosting teacher inservice and summer workshops on marine topics, the Aquarium offers curriculum packets free to field-trip visitors, for a fee to others.

## SMITHSONIAN INSTITUTION OFFICE OF ELEMENTARY AND SECONDARY EDUCATION

Arts and Industries Building, Room 1163
Washington, DC 20560
(202) 357-2425
Ann I. Bay, Director

The Office of Elementary and Secondary Education (OESE) is the Smithsonian Institution's central education office. OESE serves elementary and secondary teachers and students throughout the country directly through internships, workshops, and teaching materials.

## SMITHSONIAN INSTITUTION

See: National Air and Space Museum
National Museum of American History
National Museum of Natural History
National Zoological Park
Office of Elementary and Secondary Education

## THE SOUTH FLORIDA SCIENCE MUSEUM

4801 Dreher Trail N.
West Palm Beach, FL 33405
(305) 832-2026
Mary T. O'Connor, Acting Director
Maribil S. Walsh, Director of Education

Educational programs, exhibits, and courses for all grade levels in physical science, life science, and earth science.

## SPACE STUDIES INSTITUTE

P.O. Box 82
Princeton, NJ 08540
(609) 921-0377
Gregg E. Maryniak, Executive Vice President

The Space Studies Institute produces a bibliography of space books for young children.

## SPRINGFIELD SCIENCE MUSEUM

236 State Street
Springfield, MA 01103
(413) 733-1194
Glen P. Ives, Director
Gloria Keeney, Curator of Education

Planetarium, aquarium, exhibits, and educational programs.

## ST. LOUIS SCIENCE CENTER AND SCIENCE PARK

Forest Park
5050 Oakland Avenue
St. Louis, MO 63110
(314) 289-4400/4444
Dwight Crandell, Executive Director
Dennis M. Wint, President
David Wilson, Director of Education

The St. Louis Science Center offers school outreach through its Discovery Van portable planetarium, speaker programs, science shows, and the Pulsar Curriculum Kit, which is available for local loan ($15.00 for six weeks). The institution also sponsors workshops for teachers and assists teachers with mini-grants for development of energy-related curriculum.

## STATE OF MAINE MARINE RESOURCES LABORATORY

McKown Point
West Boothbay Harbor, ME 04575
(207) 633-5572
Brian Marcotte, Director

Exhibits of marine life native to the Maine shore.

## STRECKER MUSEUM

South 4th Street
Baylor University
Waco, TX 76798
(817) 755-1110
Calvin B. Smith, Director
Rene Harris, Director of Education

Publishes cultural and historical materials and offers exhibits and educational programs about ornithology, mammalogy, and geology for grades P-HS.

## THAMES SCIENCE CENTER

Gallows Lane
New London, CT 06320
(203) 442-0391
Jane A. Holdsworth, Director and Chief Executive Officer
JoEllen Sefton, Education Services Coordinator
Linda Tugurian, Adult and Teacher Programs Coordinator

The Thames Science Center offers teacher inservice and summer institutes focusing on the land, life, and technology of Eastern Connecticut and the Thames River watershed. A workbook for grades 4-7 enhances museum field trips, and can be adapted for other areas, particularly those in New England.

## TUCSON CHILDREN'S MUSEUM

300 East University Boulevard
Tucson, AZ 85705
(602) 884-7511
Sheila Hoban, Director

Tucson Children's Museum is a health/science learning center that provides hands-on experience and traveling exhibits.

## UNIVERSITY OF KANSAS MUSEUM OF NATURAL HISTORY

University of Kansas
Lawrence, KS 66045
(913) 864-4541
Philip S. Humphrey, Director
Ruth Gennrich, Director for Public Education

The University of Kansas Museum of Natural History is one of a consortium of six museums, featuring exhibits, research, educational programs, and school outreach on the topics of natural history, anthropology, paleontology, entomology, and botany.

## UNIVERSITY OF NEBRASKA STATE MUSEUM OF NATURAL SCIENCE

212 Morrill Hall
14th and U Streets
Lincoln, NE 68588-0338
(402) 472-2637
Hugh H. Genoways, Director

Planetarium, participatory exhibits, and educational programs on natural and cultural history.

## VIRGINIA LIVING MUSEUM

524 J. Clyde Morris Boulevard
Newport News, VA 23601
(804) 595-1900
Robert Sullivan, Executive Director
Peter Money, Director of Education

Aquarium, observatory, planetarium, outdoor exhibits of animals in their natural habitats, and educational programs in natural science and technology.

## VIRGINIA MARINE SCIENCE MUSEUM

717 General Booth Boulevard
Virginia Beach, VA 23451
(804) 425-3474
C. Mac Rawls, Director
Lynn Clements, Education Director

The Virginia Marine Science Museum has exhibits and educational programs, and publishes curriculum materials.

## WASHINGTON PARK ARBORETUM/ CENTER FOR URBAN HORTICULTURE

University of Washington, XD-10
Seattle, WA 98195
(206) 325-4510
Harold B. Tukey, Director
Timothy Hohn, Curator
John Wott, Director of Continuing Education

Outdoor trails and educational programs.

## WILLAMETTE SCIENCE AND TECHNOLOGY CENTER

2300 Centennial Boulevard
P.O. Box 1518
Eugene, OR 97440
(503) 687-3619
Lucy Lynch, Interim Director

Participatory exhibits and educational programs relating to health, physical science, and natural history.

## ZOOLOGICAL SOCIETY OF SAN DIEGO SAN DIEGO ZOO AND WILD ANIMAL PARK

Post Office Box 551
San Diego, CA 92112
(619) 231-1515
Douglas Myers, Executive Director
Pegi Harvey, Education Director
Sara Hanscom, School and Community Relations Coordinator

In addition to a variety of tours and educational programs provided at these sites, the San Diego Zoo and Wild Animal Park offer outreach in the form of assemblies and hands-on classroom programs for schools in San Diego County. In-service workshops that feature distinguished speakers or train teachers to use Conservation Safari Kits during their class field trips.

# Museums—Regional Listing

## DISTRICT OF COLUMBIA

Capital Children's Museum
Explorers Hall
National Air and Space Museum
The National Aquarium
National Museum of American History
National Museum of Natural History
National Zoological Park
Smithsonian Institution
Smithsonian Institution, Office of Elementary and
    Secondary Education

## MIDWEST (Illinois, Indiana, Michigan, Ohio, Wisconsin)

Center for American Archeology
    Kampsville Archeological Center
Chicago Zoological Park (Brookfield Zoo)
Children's Museum, Detroit Public Schools
The Children's Museum, Indianapolis
Cincinnati Museum of Natural History
Cleveland Children's Museum
Cleveland Health Education Museum
Cranbrook Institute of Science
Detroit Science Center
Discovery World Museum of Science, Economics and
    Technology
Evansville Museum of Arts and Sciences
Field Museum of Natural History
Impression 5 Science Museum
John G. Shedd Aquarium
Lakeview Museum of the Arts and Sciences
Lincoln Park Zoological Garden
Michigan Space Center
The Michigan State University Museum
Milwaukee Public Museum
Museum of Science and Industry
Museum of the Chicago Academy of Sciences
Ohio's Center of Science and Industry (COSI)

## NORTH CENTRAL (Iowa, Kansas, Minnesota, Missouri, Nebraska, North Dakota, South Dakota)

Badlands National Park
Fontenelle Forest Nature Center
James Ford Bell Museum of Natural History
The Kansas City Museum
Kansas Learning Center for Health
The Magic House, St. Louis's Children Museum
The Mayo Medical Museum
Missouri Botanical Garden

St. Louis Science Center and Science Park
The Science Center of Iowa
Science Museum of Minnesota
University of Kansas Museum of Natural History
University of Nebraska State Museum of Natural Science

## NORTHEAST (Connecticut, Delaware, Maine, Maryland, Massachusetts, New Hampshire, New Jersey, New York, Pennsylvania, Rhode Island, Vermont, West Virginia)

The Academy of Natural Sciences of Philadelphia
Alley Pond Environmental Center Inc.
American Museum of Natural History/Hayden
    Planetarium
Aquarium of Niagara Falls
Brookhaven National Laboratory, Exhibit
    Center—Science Museum
Brooklyn Botanic Garden
Buffalo Museum of Science
Buhl Science Center
Calvert Marine Museum
The Carnegie Museum of Natural History,
The Children's Museum (Boston)
The Computer Museum (Boston)
Department of Marine Resources
Discovery Center of Science & Technology
Fairbanks Museum and Planetarium
Franklin Institute Science Museum and Planetarium and
    the Museum-To-Go
The Harvard University Museums
Howard B. Owens Science Center
    Prince Georges County Public Schools
Hunt Institute for Botanical Documentation
Lutz Children's Museum
Maryland Academy of Sciences/Maryland Science Center
Monmouth Museum
Museum of Art, Science, and Industry
Museum of Holography
Museum of Science, Boston
Mystic Marinelife Aquarium
National Aquarium in Baltimore
National Marine Fisheries Service Aquarium
New England Aquarium
New York Aquarium
New York Hall of Science
New York Zoological Society—Bronx Zoo
Reading Public Museum and Art Gallery
Roberson Center for the Arts and Sciences
Schenectady Museum
Science Museum of Connecticut

Science Museum of Long Island
Space Studies Institute
Springfield Science Museum
State of Maine Marine Resources Laboratory
Thames Science Center

## NORTHWEST (Alaska, Idaho, Montana, Oregon, Washington, Wyoming)

Hanford Science Center
Oregon Museum of Science and Industry
Pacific Science Center
The Seattle Aquarium
Washington Park Arboretum/Center for Urban
    Horticulture
Willamette Science and Technology Center

## SOUTH CENTRAL (Arkansas, Louisiana, Oklahoma, Texas)

Arkansas Museum of Science and History
Audubon Park and Zoological Garden
Dallas Museum of Natural History/Dallas Aquarium
Don Harrington Discovery Center
Fort Worth Museum of Science and History
Houston Museum of Medical Science
Insights—El Paso Science Museum
Kirkpatrick Center Museum Complex
Louisiana Nature and Science Center
LSU Museum of Geoscience
Omniplex Science Museum
The Science Place
Strecker Museum

## SOUTHEAST (Alabama, Florida, Georgia, Kentucky, Mississippi, North Carolina, South Carolina, Tennessee, Virginia)

American Museum of Science & Energy
Anniston Museum of Natural History
The Charleston Museum
Cumberland Science Museum
The Discovery Center
The Discovery Place
Fernbank Science Center
Gulf Coast Research Laboratory
    J.L. Scott Marine Education Center
The Health Adventure
John Young Museum and Planetarium
    Orlando Science Center
The Living Arts and Science Center, Inc.
Memphis Pink Palace Museum and Planetarium
Metrozoo
Miami Seaquarium
Mississippi Museum of Natural Science
Museum of Arts and Science (Florida)
Museum of Arts and Sciences (Georgia)

Museum of History and Science
Museum of Science and Industry
Museum of Science and Space Transit Planetarium
Nature Science Center
North Carolina Aquarium, Fort Fisher
North Carolina Department of Agriculture—North
    Carolina Maritime Museum
North Carolina Museum of Life and Science
Planet Ocean
Red Mountain Museum
Roper Mountain Science Center
Science Museum of Virginia
Science Museum of Western Virginia
Science Museums of Charlotte, Inc.
    Nature Museum/Discovery Place
The South Florida Science Museum
Virginia Living Museum
Virginia Marine Science Museum

## SOUTHWEST (Arizona, California, Colorado, Hawaii, Nevada, New Mexico, Utah)

Arizona Museum of Science and Technology
Arizona-Sonora Desert Museum
The Bishop Museum
Bowers Museum
Cabrillo Marine Museum
California Academy of Science
California Museum of Science and Industry
Center for Meteorite Studies
Children's Museum of Utah
Denver Museum of Natural History
    The Hall of Life
Diablo Valley College Museum
The Discovery Center
The Exploratorium
Hansen Planetarium
Lawrence Hall of Science
Marine World Africa USA
Museum of New Mexico
New Mexico Museum of Natural History
Reuben H. Fleet Space Theater and Science Center
Sacramento Science Center and Junior Museum
Santa Barbara Museum of Natural History
Scripps Aquarium—Museum
    Scripps Institution of Oceanography
Sea World, Inc.
Tucson Children's Museum
Zoological Society of San Diego
    San Diego Zoo and Wild Animal Park

## CANADA

National Museum of Science and Technology
Ontario Science Centre

# Professional Associations and Organizations

Listed in this section are professional associations and organizations that, in a national survey conducted by the NSRC, indicated active efforts to provide information, services, or materials for enhancement of elementary science teaching. It is not a long list; we are anxious to hear about other groups who are working effectively to support hands-on science in the schools.

### AMATEUR ASTRONOMERS ASSOCIATION OF NEW YORK CITY

John Pazmino, President
Sidney Scheuer, Vice President
1010 Park Avenue
New York, NY 10028
(212) 337-2618

EYEPIECE newsletter, materials, and regional speakers bureau.

### AMERICAN ASSOCIATION FOR THE ADVANCEMENT OF SCIENCE (AAAS)

F. James Rutherford, Chief Education Officer
Shirley M. Malcom, Office of Opportunities in Science
1333 H Street, NW
Washington, DC 20005
(202) 326-6620

Furthers work of scientists; facilitates cooperation among them; fosters scientific freedom and responsibility; works to improve the effectiveness of science education; furthers public understanding of sciences; and sponsors the Minority Women in Science (MWIS) network that facilitates the entrance of minority women into science careers.

### AMERICAN ASSOCIATION OF PHYSICS TEACHERS (AAPT)

Jack Wilson, Executive Officer
5112 Berwyn Road
College Park, MD 20740
(301) 345-4200

Workshops, speakers, and an extensive collection of materials for the physicist or teacher: publications, reprint books, slides, and videotapes.

### AMERICAN ASTRONAUTICAL SOCIETY

Peter Bainum, Vice President
Department of Mechanical Engineering
Howard University
Washington, DC 20059
(202) 636-6612

Sponsors activities to interest students in astronomy.

### AMERICAN ASTRONOMICAL SOCIETY

Charles R. Tolbert, Education Officer
Box 3818, University Station
Charlottesville, VA 22903
(804) 924-7955

Newsletters for students and teachers, activities for teachers, primarily college level.

### AMERICAN BRYOLOGICAL AND LICHENOLOGICAL SOCIETY

Lucy Davis, Chairman, Education Program
213C West Duke Building
Duke University
Durham, NC 27706
(919) 684-3924

Activities for students.

### AMERICAN CHEMICAL SOCIETY (ACS)

Sylvia A. Ware, Division Director, Education
1155 16th Street, NW
Washington, DC 20036
(202) 872-6179

Publication for high school teachers, CHEM MATTERS, newsletter for students and teachers, and WONDER-SCIENCE, a magazine for elementary school children and parents.

### AMERICAN GEOLOGICAL INSTITUTE (AGI)

Andrew J. Verdon, Director of Education
National Center for Earth Science Education
4220 King Street
Alexandria, VA 22302
(703) 379-2480

Activities for students and teachers, and curriculum development.

## AMERICAN GEOPHYSICAL UNION

Cynthia Bravo, Director of Meetings and Member
Programs
2000 Florida Avenue, NW
Washington, DC 20009
(202) 462-6903

Fosters research, disseminates information through its publications, and enhances educational opportunities in science.

## AMERICAN INSTITUTE OF AERONAUTICS AND ASTRONAUTICS

Nelson W. Friedman, Administrator
Educational Programs
370 L'Enfant Promenade, SW
Washington, DC 20024
(202) 646-7400

Activities for students and career information.

## AMERICAN INSTITUTE OF BIOLOGICAL SCIENCES (AIBS)

Roy H. Saigo, Chairman, Education Committee
College of Natural Sciences
University of Northern Iowa
Cedar Falls, IA 50614-0181
(319) 273-2585

Activities for students and teachers, and career information.

## AMERICAN INSTITUTE OF CHEMICAL ENGINEERS

Harold I. Abramson, Manager
Educational Services-Operations
345 East 47th Street
New York, NY 10017
(212) 705-7370

Provides career information and sponsors programs for students.

## AMERICAN INSTITUTE OF CHEMISTS

Roger R. Festa, Educational Consultant
Northeast Missouri State University
Kirksville, MO 63501
(816) 785-4620

Activities for teachers and professional publications.

## AMERICAN INSTITUTE OF PHYSICS

Donald Kirwan, Education Division Chairman
335 East 45th Street
New York, NY 10017
(212) 661-9404

Newsletters and activities for students and teachers.

## AMERICAN METEOROLOGICAL SOCIETY

David Houghton, Commissioner, Education and
Manpower
Department of Meteorology
University of Wisconsin
Madison, WI 53706
(608) 262-0776

Professional publications, newsletters, and career information.

## AMERICAN NATURE STUDY SOCIETY

John J. Padalino, Director
Pocono Environmental Education Center
R.D. 1, Box 268
Dingman's Ferry, PA 18328
(717) 828-2319

Newsletter and activities for students and teachers.

## AMERICAN PHYSICAL SOCIETY (APS)

Brian Schwartz, Program Officer
335 East 45th Street
New York, NY 10017
(212) 682-7341

Supports professional research, sponsors programs for physics teachers, provides career information and activities for students and teachers, and publishes a newsletter.

## AMERICAN SOCIETY FOR MICROBIOLOGY

Helen L. Bishop, Director of Education
1913 Eye Street, NW
Washington, DC 20006
(202) 833-9680

Newsletters and activities for students and teachers.

## ASSOCIATION FOR SUPERVISION AND CURRICULUM DEVELOPMENT (ASCD)

Gordon Cawelti, Executive Director
125 North West Street
Alexandria, VA 22314-2798
(703) 549-9110

ASCD identifies, studies, and evaluates issues in supervision, curriculum, and instruction. Also offers conferences, newsletters, and opportunities for professional exchanges.

## ASSOCIATION FOR WOMEN IN SCIENCE (AWIS)

Valerie Strauss, Executive Director
2401 Virginia Avenue, NW, No. 303
Washington, DC 20037
(202) 833)2998

Publishes a professional newsletter and provides career information.

## ASSOCIATION OF SCIENCE-TECHNOLOGY CENTERS (ASTC)

Bonnie VanDorn, Executive Director
1413 K Street, NW, Tenth Floor
Washington, DC 20005-3405
(202) 371-1171

Conducts surveys on science museum programs, encourages and arranges cooperative projects among science museums, and, with General Electric, sponsors Project STEAM. Its programs and services include traveling exhibitions, consulting with schools, conferences and workshops, and publications.

## ASTRONOMICAL SOCIETY OF THE PACIFIC

Andrew Fraknoi, Executive Officer
390 Ashton Avenue
San Francisco, CA 94112
(415) 337-1100

Newsletter for teachers and activities for students and teachers.

## BIOLOGICAL SCIENCES CURRICULUM STUDY (BSCS)

Joseph McInerney, Director
830 N. Tejom Street
Suite 405
Colorado Springs, CO 80903
(719) 578-1136

Develops curriculum materials for science and technology education for grades K-12; publishes newsletter.

## CENTER FOR AMERICAN ARCHAEOLOGY

Jane E. Buikstra, Director and President
P.O. Box 366
Kampsville, IL 62053
(618) 653-4316

Newsletter and materials on archaeology and anthropology.

## CENTER FOR EXCELLENCE IN EDUCATION

Medi K. Hoover, Director of Programs
7710 Old Springhouse Road, Suite 100
McLean, VA 22102
(703) 448-9062

The Center provides a forum for outstanding students and teachers to explore the world of science and technology through lectures, science mentor programs, laboratory experiences, and other field experiences.

## THE CENTER FOR TEACHING AND LEARNING

Mary Harris, Dean
University of North Dakota
Box 8158, University Station
Grand Forks, ND 58202
(701) 777-2674

Publishes research monographs on educational topics.

## CITY COLLEGE WORKSHOP CENTER

Hubert Dyasi, Director
136th and Convent Avenue
Room 4-220, North Academic Complex
City College School of Education
New York, NY 10031
(212) 690-4162

Provides teaching resources, encourages a practical inquiry approach to education, conducts classes and workshops at the preservice and inservice levels, publishes monographs based on annual lectures by scientists, such as Philip Morrison and Lynn Margulis, about topical issues in primary science and investigations and inquiry projects done by teachers. The staff also provides workshops in other states and internationally.

## COUNCIL FOR ELEMENTARY SCIENCE INTERNATIONAL (CESI)

Betty Burchett
Department of Curriculum and Instruction
212 Townsend Hall
University of Missouri
Columbia, MO 65211
(314) 882-7247

Fosters elementary science teaching and publishes source books.

## COUNCIL OF STATE SCIENCE SUPERVISORS (CSSS)

David Kennedy, President
Department of Public Instruction
Science Department
Old Capitol Building
Mail Stop FG-11
Olympia, WA 98504
(206) 753-6738/6757

Strengthens science by sponsoring programs for science supervisors, disseminating information, and engaging in cooperative activities with NSTA.

## THE COUNCIL ON INTERRACIAL BOOKS FOR CHILDREN

Melba Kgositsile, Director
1841 Broadway
New York, NY 10023
(212) 757-5339

Pamphlets to assist in selection of sexually and racially unbiased textbooks and storybooks for children.

## DEPARTMENT OF EDUCATION AND SCIENCE

Wynne Harlen
Elizabeth House
York Road
London SE1 7PH, England
01-934-9323

Materials relating to implementation and evaluation of hands-on science programs in England.

## EDUCATIONAL PRODUCTS INFORMATION EXCHANGE (EPIE)

Kenneth Komoski, Executive Director
EPIE Institute
P.O. Box 839
Water Mill, NY 11976
(516) 283-4922

Publishes THE EDUCATIONAL SOFTWARE SELECTOR (TESS), and newsletters (EPIEGRAM and MICROGRAM) and sponsors the CASE program involved with curriculum alignment in schools nationwide.

## EDUCATIONAL RESOURCES INFORMATION CENTER (ERIC)
## Clearinghouse for Science, Mathematics, and Environmental Education

Robert W. Howe, Director
Ohio State University
1200 Chambers Road, Third Floor
Columbus, OH 43212
(614) 292-6717

Clearinghouse for published and unpublished materials relating to science, mathematics, and environmental education. The Elementary Science Study (ESS) and Unified Science and Mathematics for Elementary Schools (USMES) curriculum materials are accessible on-line, or supplied on microfiche or photocopy for a fee.

## EQUALS

Elizabeth Stage
Lawrence Hall of Science
University of California
Berkeley, CA 94720
(415) 642-1823

Programs and publications promoting equity in math and science for students and teachers at 15 sites nationwide.

## FOUNDATION FOR SCIENCE AND THE HANDICAPPED

E. C. Keller, Jr., Newsletter Editor/Publisher
West Virginia University
Morgantown, WV 26506-6057
(304) 293-5201

Produces professional publications and newsletters related to science and the handicapped.

## GIRLS CLUBS OF AMERICA, INC.
## Operation SMART

Margaret Gates, Executive Director
Jane Quinn, Director of Program Services
Ellen Wahl, Director, Operation SMART
30 East 33rd Street
New York, NY 10016
(212) 689-3700

Activities and mentor programs to encourage students, especially girls and minorities, to persist in science, math and math studies and consider careers in these fields.

## GOVERNMENT PRINTING OFFICE (GPO)

Donald E. Fossedal, Assistant Public Printer
Superintendent of Documents
Washington, DC 20402
(202) 783-3238

Publishes a free catalog of current federal agency publications and responds to requests for specific-subject bibliographies.

## HARVARD-SMITHSONIAN CENTER FOR ASTROPHYSICS

Irwin Shapiro, Director
Philip Sadler, Director, Project STAR
60 Garden Street
Cambridge, MA 02138
(617) 495-9798

Conducts basic research in astronomy. Project STAR is an astronomy education project, which helps students understand the role of science. Curriculum units, computer software, videotapes, films, and teacher-support materials are available.

## THE MID-ATLANTIC EQUITY CENTER

Sheryl Denbo, Executive Director
Warren Simmons, Director of Race Programming
Susan Shaffer, Director of Sex Equity Programming
Lorraine Valdez-Pierce, Director of National Origin
Programming
The American University
School of Education
5010 Wisconsin Avenue, NW, #310
Washington, DC 20016
(202) 885-8517

Administrative consultations, staff development programs, training of trainers workshops, needs assessment, and dissemination of information and materials emphasizing race, sex, and national origin desegregation.

## NATIONAL ACADEMY OF SCIENCES (NAS)
**National Research Council**

Robert Caplan, Executive Director, Commission on
Behavioral and Social Sciences and Education
2101 Constitution Avenue, NW
Washington, DC 20148
(202) 334-2300

Conducts studies related to science and technical education and learning psychology. Also assesses the overall effectiveness of the educational system and studies issues of equity for women and minorities. In addition, the National Academy of Sciences sponsors the National Science Resources Center with the Smithsonian Institution.

## NATIONAL AERONAUTICS AND SPACE ADMINISTRATION (NASA)
**Teacher Resource Centers**

Eddie Anderson, Chief, Elementary and Secondary
Programs Branch
NASA Headquarters
Code XEE
Washington, DC 20546
(202) 453-8396

Provides specialists for school visits and educational materials for teachers through the CORE project. Also disseminates materials at each of the nine NASA centers and at more than 20 regional centers.

## NATIONAL ASSOCIATION FOR RESEARCH IN SCIENCE TEACHING (NARST)

Glenn Markle, Secretary
College of Education
University of Cincinnati
Cincinnati, OH 45221-0002
(513) 475-2335

Research monographs for science education.

## THE NATIONAL ASSOCIATION FOR SCIENCE, TECHNOLOGY AND SOCIETY (NASTS)

Rustum Roy, Director
The Pennsylvania State University
128 Willard Building
University Park, PA 16802
(814) 865-9951

Publishes the NASTS newsletter, a journal, BULLETIN OF SCIENCE, TECHNOLOGY AND SOCIETY, and other publications, and conducts an annual meeting.

## NATIONAL ASSOCIATION OF BIOLOGY TEACHERS (NABT)

Rosalina Hairston, Education Director
11250 Roger Bacon Drive, #19
Reston, VA 22090
(703) 471-1134

Activities for students and teachers.

## NATIONAL ASSOCIATION OF ELEMENTARY SCHOOL PRINCIPALS (NAESP)

Samuel G. Sava, Executive Director
Mary Hahn, Program Coordinator
June Million, Director of Public Information
1615 Duke Street
Alexandria, VA 22314
(703) 684-3345

Publishes papers for elementary and middle school educators that are research based but practical, a magazine, PRINCIPAL, and a monthly newsletter called COMMUNICATOR.

## NATIONAL ASSOCIATION OF GEOLOGY TEACHERS

Arlan Alan, Executive Director
1041 New Hampshire Street
P.O. Box 368
Lawrence, KS 66044
(913) 843-1234

Newsletters and activities for teachers.

## NATIONAL AUDUBON SOCIETY

Peter A. A. Berle, President
Susan Randolph, Registrar, AUDUBON ADVENTURES
613 Riversville Road
Greenwich, CT 06830
(203) 869-5272

Publishes a nature newspaper for children, AUDUBON ADVENTURES, produces software and television specials and conducts workshops and a summer ecology camp for teachers.

## NATIONAL CENTER FOR THE IMPROVEMENT OF SCIENCE TEACHING AND LEARNING

David Crandall, Director
Senta Raizen, Project Director
The NETWORK, Inc.
290 South Main Street
Andover, MA 01810
(617) 470-1080

The Center develops recommendations for changes in science education and promotes changes in state and local policies to improve science assessment, curriculum, and instruction.

## NATIONAL DIFFUSION NETWORK (NDN)

Shirley Curry, Director of Recognition Division
Lee Wickline, Team Leader
Office of Educational Research and Improvement
U.S. Department of Education
555 New Jersey Avenue, NW
Washington, DC 20208-1525
(202) 357-6134

Federally funded system providing access to exemplary educational programs nationwide.

## NATIONAL SCIENCE FOUNDATION (NSF)

Bassam Z. Shakhashiri, Assistant Director for Science and Engineering Education
1800 G Street, NW, Room 516
Washington, DC 20550
(202) 357-7078

Federal agency responsible for developing and funding programs in science, mathematics, and technology education. The NSF also publishes the DIRECTORY OF FEDERAL R&D AGENCIES PROGRAMS TO ATTRACT WOMEN, MINORITIES, AND THE PHYSICALLY HANDICAPPED TO CAREERS IN SCIENCE AND ENGINEERING. This directory lists more than 40 federally sponsored programs located at various government agencies.

## NATIONAL SCIENCE RESOURCES CENTER (NSRC)

Douglas M. Lapp, Executive Director
Arts and Industries Building, Room 1201
Smithsonian Institution
Washington, DC 20560
(202) 357-2555

The National Science Resources Center was established in 1985 as a joint undertaking of the National Academy of Sciences and the Smithsonian Institution. The NSRC's mission is to contribute to the improvement of science and mathematics teaching in the nation's schools by establishing a science and mathematics curriculum resources center and information database, developing and disseminating resource materials for science and mathematics teachers, and offering a program of outreach and leadership-development activities. Because there is a pressing need to start in the early years to improve the scientific and technological literacy of young people, the NSRC has placed a high priority on the development of programs to reform the teaching of science in the nation's elementary schools. The NSRC has several projects under way in this area, including Science and Technology for Children (described under Elementary Science Curriculum Projects).

## NATIONAL SCIENCE SUPERVISORS ASSOCIATION (NSSA)

Emma Walton, President
Anchorage School District
4600 DeBarr Avenue
P.O. Box 196614
Anchorage, AK 99519-6614
(907) 269-2274

Promotes support services for science supervisors.

## NATIONAL SCIENCE TEACHERS ASSOCIATION (NSTA)

Bill G. Aldridge, Executive Director
1742 Connecticut Avenue, NW
Washington, DC 20009
(202) 328-5800

Numerous professional publications, newsletters, and resource materials for science teachers, including SCIENCE AND CHILDREN, a magazine for elementary school teachers. This magazine highlights science suppliers in its January issue, and science trade books for children in its March issue. NSTA also sponsors the Beers School collaboration and a computer network.

## THE NATIONAL URBAN COALITION

DeAnna Banks Beane, Director of Education
1120 G Street, NW, Suite 900
Washington, DC 20005
(202) 628-2990

Publishes documents on equal opportunity in education, such as CRITICAL FILTERS and sponsors the Say Yes program aimed at improving the mathematics and science proficiency of minority students in elementary grades through hands-on lessons, mentors, career information, and other activities.

## NATIONAL WILDLIFE FEDERATION

Sue Sandmeyer, Director of Education Programs
1400 16th Street, NW
Washington, DC 20036
(703) 790-4360

Publishes science magazines and curriculum materials, including RANGER RICK magazine and the NatureScope series of activity guides for teachers.

## NATIVE AMERICAN SCIENCE EDUCATION ASSOCIATION (NASEA)

Roberta Lewis, Acting Executive Director
1333 H Street, NW, Room 750
Washington, DC 20005
(202) 371-8100

Newsletters and curriculum materials for teachers.

## SCIENCE RESOURCE CENTRE

Irwin Talesnick, Chairman
Science, Technical Education, and Mathematics
Faculty of Education
Duncan McArthur Hall
Queen's University
Kingston, Ontario, Canada K7L 3N6
(613) 545-6224

Publishes materials for classroom teaching.

## SIGMA XI, THE SCIENTIFIC RESEARCH SOCIETY

Ed J. Poziomek, Executive Director
345 Whitney Avenue
New Haven, CT 06511
(203) 624-9883

Produces professional publications and newsletters; local chapters sponsor science education activities.

## SMITHSONIAN INSTITUTION

Anne Bay, Executive Director, Office of Elementary and Secondary Education
Arts and Industries Building, Room 1163
Smithsonian Institution
Washington, DC 20560
(202) 357-2425

Sponsors teacher-training programs and special events and produces ART-TO-ZOO, a newsletter for teachers.

## THE SOCIETY FOR THE ADVANCEMENT OF CHICANOS AND NATIVE AMERICANS IN SCIENCE

Frank Talamantes, President
Thimann Laboratories
University of California
Santa Cruz, CA 95064
(408) 429-2295

Newsletters and activities for teachers.

## SOIL AND WATER CONSERVATION SOCIETY

Tim Kautza, Program Assistant
7515 Northeast Ankeny Road
Ankeny, IA 50021
(515) 289-2331

Activities for students, curriculum development, computer software for grades 4-12, and career information.

## TRIANGLE COALITION FOR SCIENCE AND TECHNOLOGY EDUCATION

John Fowler, Executive Director
Special Projects
5112 Berwyn Road
College Park, MD 20740
(301) 220-0873

Forum in which curriculum may be discussed, materials for teachers and policy makers, bimonthly newsletter.

## U.S. DEPARTMENT OF EDUCATION

400 Maryland Avenue, SW
Washington, DC 20202
(202) 732-3000

Federal agency responsible for funding a variety of programs related to science education; also publishes statistical studies and state reports.

## THE WILDLIFE SOCIETY

Harry E. Hodgdon, Executive Director
5410 Grosvenor Lane
Bethesda, MD 20814
(301) 897-9770

Produces curriculum materials and professional publications, and sponsors programs related to wildlife conservation.

## YOUNG ASTRONAUT COUNCIL

T. Wendell Butler, Executive Director
Jennifer Rae, Administrative Assistant, Membership
Services
Box 65432
1211 Connecticut Avenue, NW, #800
Washington, DC 20036
(202) 682-1986

Sponsors a program of mathematics and science enrichment activities for elementary school aged children, based in local chapters and headed by a teacher or community leader. Supplies background information, hands-on activities, and posters related to space education.

## Elementary Science Curriculum Projects—Past and Present

Included here are brief descriptions of major funded projects in hands-on elementary science. The National Science Foundation supported several such programs in the late sixties and early seventies, as did other agencies. These notable projects are listed, together with more recent projects and current ones. Some of the earlier materials are still commercially available in their original or revised form. Trial editions of some of the NSF-supported materials have been reproduced and are once again being disseminated by means of CD-ROM. This reissue, called *Science Helper K-8*, was produced by the Knowledge Utilization Project in Science (see listing in this section).

### Activities to Integrate Mathematics and Science (AIMS)
AIMS Education Foundation
P.O. Box 7766
Fresno, CA 93747
(209) 291-1766
Arthur Wiebe, Director

AIMS conducts research, provides national leadership training and local workshops and seminars, and publishes elementary and intermediate integrated curriculum materials (K-9) that have been written and tested by teachers. Publications provide grade-appropriate activities in a flexible format. The AIMS materials are an outgrowth of a National Science Foundation project, under the auspices of Fresno Pacific College.

*Down to Earth*
*Fall into Math & Science*
*Floater and Sinkers*
*From Head to Toe*
*Fun with Foods*
*Glide into Winter with Math & Science*
*Hardhatting in a Geo-World*
*Jawbreakers & Heart Thumpers*
*Math + Science, A Solution*
*Our Wonderful World*
*Out of this World*
*Overhead and Underfoot*
*Pieces and Patterns*
*Popping with Power*
*Primarily Bears*
*Seasoning Math & Science: Spring & Summer*
*Seasoning Math & Science: Fall & Winter*
*The Sky's the Limit!*
*Spring into Math & Science*
*Water Precious Water*

### Chemical Education for Public Understanding (CEPUP)
Lawrence Hall of Science
University of California
Berkeley, CA 94720
(415) 642-8718
Herbert D. Thier, Project Director

CEPUP provides hands-on materials to increase understanding of chemicals and chemical issues among middle/junior high school students and the general public. The project links schools, education organizations, community groups, scientists, and industry, and provides materials, leadership training, community outreach, and a National Fellows program. Financial support has been provided by industry and private foundations.

*Chemical Survey*
*Determining Threshold Limits*
*Risk Comparison*
*Solutions and Pollution*
*Toxic Trouble in Fruitvale*
*Toxic Waste: Treatment and Disposal*

### Conceptually Oriented Program in Elementary Science (COPES)
New York University
Inactive; materials now available on SCIENCE HELPER K-8.

COPES is a general elementary science program (K-6) published in the early seventies that focuses on five major conceptual schemes: structural units of the universe, interaction and change, conservation of energy, degradation of energy, and a statistical view of nature. Relationships between lessons in the units are based on these themes, rather than on familiar subject strands. COPES was funded by the National Science Foundation.

*Teacher's Guide for Kindergarten/Grade One*
*Teacher's Guide for Grade Two*
*Teacher's Guide for Grade Three*
*Teacher's Guide for Grade Four*
*Teacher's Guide for Grade Five*
*Teacher's Guide for Grade Six*
*Teacher's Guide for a Conservation of Energy Sequence*

## Conservation for Children

John Muir Elementary School
6560 Hanover Drive
San Jose, CA 95129
(408) 725-8376
Marilyn Bodourian, Project Director

Conservation for Children provides students in grades 1-6 with basic skills activities designed to teach ecology and conservation concepts through the integration of science with language arts, math, and social studies. Curriculum guides and inservice training are available. Developmental funding was provided through the Elementary and Secondary Education Act (ESEA) Title IV-C, with dissemination support from the National Diffusion Network.

## Elementary Science Study (ESS)

Education Development Center, Inc.
Newton, MA 02160
(617) 969-7100
Inactive; some trial editions are now available on SCIENCE HELPER K-8. Trial and commercial editions are available from ERIC. Some commercial or revised editions are available from Delta Education.

The original ESS curriculum materials consisted of 56 hands-on units that could be used either as the core of, or as a supplement to, a general elementary science program. Trial editions were extensively revised for commercial publication on the basis of large-scale classroom teaching. In both trial and commercial editions, children experiment with objects and concepts, defining their own questions, and setting their own goals. Teachers and children are encouraged to work with materials in their own way. The project was funded by the National Science Foundation, and the commercial editions were originally published by Mc-Graw-Hill. (* Starred titles are currently available in revised edition from Delta.)

| | |
|---|---|
| *Animal Activity* | *Earthworms** |
| *Animals in the Classroom* | *Eggs & Tadpoles** |
| *Attribute Games and Problems** | *Gases and "Airs"** |
| | *Geo Blocks** |
| *Balloons and Gases** | *Growing Seeds** |
| *Behavior of Mealworms** | *Heating and Cooling** |
| *Batteries and Bulbs** | *Ice Cubes** |
| *Batteries and Bulbs II* | *Kitchen Physics** |
| *Bones* | *Life of Beans and Peas* |
| *Brine Shrimp** | *Light and Shadows* |
| *Budding Twigs* | *Mapping** |
| *Butterflies* | *Match and Measure** |
| *Changes* | *Microgardening** |
| *Clay Boats** | *Mirror Cards* |
| *Colored Solutions** | *Mobiles** |
| *Crayfish* | *Mosquitoes* |
| *Daytime Astronomy* | *Musical Instrument Recipe Book* |
| *Drops, Streams, and Containers** | *Mystery Powders** |

| | |
|---|---|
| *Optics** | *Small Things** |
| *Pattern Blocks** | *Spinning Tables** |
| *Peas and Particles** | *Starting from Seeds* |
| *Pendulums** | *Stream Tables** |
| *Pond Water* | *Structures** |
| *Primary Balancing** | *Tangrams** |
| *Printing* | *Tracks* |
| *Rocks and Charts** | *Water Flow** |
| *Sand* | *Where Is the Moon?* |
| *Senior Balancing** | *Whistles and Strings** |
| *Sink or Float** | |

## Foundational Approaches in Science Teaching (FAST)

Curriculum Research and Development Group
University of Hawaii
1776 University Avenue, Room UHS 2-202
Honolulu, HI 96822
(808) 948-7863
Donald B. Young, Project Director

FAST uses laboratory and field activities to engage students in investigations of physical science, ecology, and relational study. Students study the properties of matter and the characteristics of the earth environment, then integrate and apply the skills and knowledge they have acquired to such concepts as resource management, technology, and conservation. This program has been used in grades 6-8. Teacher's guides, student record books, kits, and inservice training are available. Developmental funding was through the University of Hawaii, with dissemination support from the National Diffusion Network.

## Full Option Science System (FOSS)

(In development)
Center for Multisensory Learning
Lawrence Hall of Science
University of California
Berkeley, CA 94720
(415) 642-8941
Lawrence F. Lowery, Project Director

FOSS will build on the SAVI/SELPH units to provide 16 interdisciplinary, laboratory-based modules for grades three through six. Modules will cover biological, physical, and earth sciences, and will be supported by laboratory and tool kits, instructions for building equipment, and correlation tables to aid integration with texts and/or district science guidelines. Developers will collaborate with local school districts. Ohaus Scale Corporation is assisting in production and distribution, and funding is provided in part by the National Science Foundation.

## Great Explorations in Math and Science (GEMS)

Lawrence Hall of Science
University of California
Berkeley, CA 94720
(415) 642-7771
Glenn T. Seaborg, Project Director

GEMS materials consist of teacher's guides, assembly presenter's guides, and exhibit guides, and range in appeal from preschool through high school. These 24 publications integrate math with life, earth, and physical science, fostering a "guided discovery" approach to learning. Materials are easily accessible, and lessons are written for teachers with little training in math or science. Funding for the program has been provided by the A.W. Mellon Foundation and the Carnegie Corporation of New York.

| | |
|---|---|
| *Animal Defenses* | *Liquid Explorations* |
| *Animals in Action* | *The "Magic" of Electricity* |
| *Bubble-ology* | *Mapping Animal Movements* |
| *Buzzing a Hive* | *Mapping Fish Habitats* |
| *Chemical Reactions* | *More Than Magnifiers* |
| *Convection: A Current Event* | *Oobleck: What Do Scientists Do?* |
| *Crime Lab Chemistry* | *Paper Towel Testing* |
| *Discovering Density* | *QUADICE* |
| *Earth, Moon, and Stars* | *Shapes, Loops, and Images* |
| *Fingerprinting* | *Solids, Liquids, and Gases* |
| *Hide a Butterfly* | *Vitamin C Testing* |
| *Hot Water and Warm Homes from Sunlight* | *The Wizard's Lab* |

## Hands-On Elementary Science

Education Department
Hood College
Frederick, MD 21701
(301) 663-3131, ext. 205 or 350
Dean A. Wood, Project Director

Hands-On Elementary Science focuses on development of science process skills in students in grades 1-5. At each successive level, student activities emphasize one skill practiced across the content areas: observation in grade one, classification in grade two, and so on. There are curriculum guides and materials kits for each level, and inservice is available. Development funding was provided by federal, state, and local sources; dissemination is supported by the National Diffusion Network.

## Health Activities Project (HAP)

Lawrence Hall of Science
University of California
Berkeley, CA 94702
(415) 642-4193
Robert Knott, Principal Investigator

The Health Activities Project provides elementary students with activities and information relevant to health and safety in their daily lives. The first phase of the project, for grades 4-8, was funded by the Robert Wood Johnson Foundation, the Lyndhurst Foundation, and the Atlantic Richfield Company. Materials are available from Hubbard. A second phase, for grades K-3, is now in development.

### HAP 4-8:

| | |
|---|---|
| *Action/Reaction* | *Growth Trends* |
| *Balance in Movement* | *Heart Fitness* |
| *Breathing Fitness* | *Nutritional/Dental Health* |
| *Consumer Health Decisions* | *Personal Health Decisions* |
| *Environmental Health and Safety* | *Sight and Sound* |
| *Flexibility and Strength* | *Skin Temperature* |

## Improving Urban Elementary Science (IUES)
(In development)

Education Development Center, Inc.
55 Chapel Street
Newton, MA 02160
(617) 969-7100
Karen Worth, Judith Sandler, Principal Investigators

The IUES project will produce 24-36 activity-based modules for life, earth, and physical science, grades K-6. The units, developed by teachers and tested in urban schools, will integrate experimental studies of the natural world with language arts and mathematics, enhancing critical thinking, communication, and problem-solving skills. Funding is provided by the National Science Foundation. Sunburst Publications will collaborate in production and distribution.

## Informal Science Study (ISS)

University of Houston
Room 450 Farish Hall
Houston, TX 77004
(713) 749-1692, 1685
Howard Jones, Project Director

In ISS, students investigate physical science concepts demonstrated in such familiar contexts as amusement park rides, sports, and playground activities. Designed for children in grades 5-12, the ISS mini-units consist of materials, equipment, and inservice training. Developmental funding has been provided through the National Science Foundation, with dissemination support from the National Diffusion Network.

## Knowledge Utilization Project in Science (KUPS)

Room 302 Norman Hall
University of Florida
Gainesville, FL 32607
(904) 392-0761
Mary Budd Rowe, Project Director

KUPS has produced a CD-ROM (Compact Disk-Read Only Memory) database entitled SCIENCE HELPER K-8, which provides access to materials developed by the major NSF curriculum projects of the sixties and seventies. Special equipment is required to use the disks. Information is indexed by grade, subject, skill, keyword, and content. A search of the database results in an on-screen image of a page of the original document and this can be printed out. Some documents are reproduced in their commercially published versions. Others, such as ESS, are reproduced from their early trial editions, though the manual does not make this clear. Only a limited selection of ESS and USMES units are included. Screen formatting makes it difficult to see an entire page without scrolling both vertically and horizontally, and print formats are not clearly defined, limiting the readability of an otherwise useful product. Funding was provided by the Carnegie Corporation of New York, with production and distribution by PC-SIG/IASC CD-ROM Publishing Group.

| | |
|---|---|
| COPES | Conceptually Oriented Program for Elementary Science |
| ESS | Elementary Science Study (partial) |
| SAPA | Science—A Process Approach |
| SCIS | Science Curriculum Improvement Study |
| USMES | Unified Science and Mathematics for Elementary Schools (partial) |

## Learning About Plants (LEAP)

(In development)
Cornell Plantations
Cornell University
One Plantations Road
Ithaca, NY 14850
(607) 255-3020
Julie Shattuck, Program Administrator

LEAP is an activity-based life science program for grades K-6. The project integrates classroom and field experiences, emphasizing conceptual development through exploration of biology in general, and plants in particular. The curriculum materials currently under development consist of four units for each grade. Teacher training is offered through workshops, and may be expanded to include a peer coaching model. Developmental funding has been provided by the National Science Foundation.

| | |
|---|---|
| Kindergarten: | Growing |
| | Using Our Senses |
| | Kinds of Plants and Animals |
| | One Life |
| Grade One: | What's Alive? |
| | Seeds |
| | People Use Plants |
| | Life Cycles |
| Grade Two: | Alike or Different |
| | Making It Through the Winter: Plants |
| | Making It Through the Winter: Animals |
| | What Plants Need |
| Grade Three: | Weaving the Web |
| | Communities |
| | From Pieces to Plants |
| | Why Spring Happens |
| Grade Four: | Flower Power |
| | Adaptations |
| | Species and Populations |
| | Plants in Action |
| Grade Five: | Energy for Green Plants |
| | Materials Cycle |
| | Populations and Competition |
| | Ecosystems: Everything Is Connected |
| Grade Six: | Getting Energy (Respiration) |
| | Storing Energy (Photosynthesis) |
| | Species Change |
| | A Green Future |

## Learning Labs

(In development)
The National Learning Center
800 3rd Street, NE
Washington, DC 20002
(202) 675-4153
Ed Lee, Project Director

The National Learning Center, which includes the Capital Children's Museum, is producing three kinds of materials: school kits with teacher's guides and small-scale equipment, associated software, and sets of manipulatives for museum installations. The first school and museum units are available from Delta. Funding for the project has been provided by the National Science Foundation.

Lenses and Mirrors (school unit)
Light and Color (museum unit)
Colortrope (software)

## Learning Through Science

School Curriculum Development Committee
School of Education
University of London Goldsmiths' College
Lewisham Way
New Cross, SE14 6NW, London, England
(01) 692-7171
Roy Richards, Project Director

Learning Through Science is a project jointly sponsored by the Schools Council (Great Britain) and the Scottish Education Department, for the purpose of providing hands-on science experiences for children ages 5-13. There are 13 modules containing activities in life, earth, and physical science. Each module includes a teacher's guide and activity cards emphasizing independent investigation and development of science process skills. (These activities can provide an introduction to the more detailed investigations in Science 5/13.) Learning Through Science materials are published by Macdonald Educational, England, and available in the U.S. from Teacher's Laboratory (see Publishers listing).

| | |
|---|---|
| *All Around* | *On the Move* |
| *Colour* | *Ourselves* |
| *Earth* | *Out of Doors* |
| *Electricity* | *Sky and Space* |
| *Guide and Index* | *Time, Growth and Change* |
| *Materials* | *Which and What?* |
| *Moving Around* | |

## The Life Lab Science Program

(In development)
1156 High Street
Santa Cruz, CA 95064
(408) 476-7140
Roberta M. Jaffe, Lisa Glick, Gary Appel, Project Directors

Life Lab is a garden-based program for grades K-6. It employs familiar, manageable materials as the foundation for activities that integrate life, earth, and physical sciences. Students are encouraged to apply their knowledge and skills to everyday situations, including ecological debates, ethical issues, and problem solving. Funding has been provided by the National Science Foundation and the U.S. Department of Education. Addison-Wesley Publishing Company will collaborate in production and dissemination of Life Lab's current project materials.
*The Growing Classroom*

## The Marine Science Project: FOR SEA

Marine Science Center
17771 Fjord Drive N.E.
Poulsbo, WA 98370
(206) 779-5549
Laurie Dumdie, Project Director

FOR SEA is a marine education project designed to supplement or replace existing science programs in grades 2, 4, 6, 7-8, and 9-12. There is a curriculum guide for each grade, and inservice training is available. Developmental funding has been provided through the Elementary and Secondary Education Act (ESEA) Title IV-C, with dissemination support from the National Diffusion Network.

## National Geographic Kids Network

(In development)
Technical Education Research Centers, Inc. (TERC)
1696 Massachusetts Avenue
Cambridge, MA 02138
(617) 547-0430
Robert F. Tinker, Project Director

The National Geographic Kids Network links children grades 4-6 in a cooperative, nationwide set of experiments on timely and significant science issues. A total of ten science units are to be developed by TERC and the National Geographic Society, offering materials and software for classroom learning and national computer networking. Industry members of the Triangle Coalition for Science and Technology Education will supply technical assistance. Funding has been provided by the National Science Foundation, and the National Geographic Society will publish all materials.
*Acid Rain*
*Hello!*
*Weather*

## Outdoor Biology Instructional Strategies (OBIS)

Lawrence Hall of Science
University of California
Berkeley, CA 94720
(415) 642-4193
Robert Knott, Principal Investigator

OBIS consists of 97 modules for children ages 8-15. Activities take students outdoors to schoolyards, backyards, vacant lots, and wilderness areas, to increase their environmental awareness through games, crafts, and experiments. Materials are readily accessible, and lessons are easily conducted by teachers with little science experience. The project was funded by the National Science Foundation. Curriculum guides are available from the Lawrence Hall of Science; guides and supplies from Delta Education.

*Acorns*
*Animal Anti-Freeze*
*Animal Diversity*
*Animal Movement in Water*
*Animals in a Grassland*
*Ants*
*Attention!*
*Attract a Fish*
*Beach Zonation*
*Beachcombing*
*Bean Bugs*
*A Better Fly Trap*
*Bird Nests*
*Birdfeeder*
*Bugs, Worms, and Others*
*Cactus Wheel*
*Can Fishing*
*Cardiac Hill*
*Clam Hooping*
*Cool It*
*Crawdad Grab*
*Creepers and Climbers*
*Damsels and Dragons*
*Desert Hunt*
*Desert Water Keepers*
*Envirolopes*
*Environmental Sun Prints*
*Flocking to Food*
*Flower Powder*
*Fly a Leaf*
*Follow the Scent*
*Food Chain Game*
*Food Grab*
*For the Birds*
*Gaming in the Outdoors*
*Great Streamboat Race*
*Habitats of the Pond*
*Hold a Hill*
*Hold It*
*Hopper Circus*
*Hopper Herding*
*How Many Organisms Live Here?*
*Invent an Animal*
*Invent a Plant*
*Isopods*
*Jay Play*
*Junk-in-the-Box*
*Leaf Living*
*Leapin' Lizards*
*Lichen Looking*
*Litter Critters*
*Logs to Soil*
*Mapping a Study Site*
*Metric Capers*
*Moisture Makers*
*Mystery Marauders*
*Night Eyes*
*Night Shine*
*OBIS Oil Spill*
*The Old White Sheet Trick*
*Out of Control*
*Pigment Puzzles*
*Plant Hunt*
*Plant Patterns*
*Plants Around a Building*
*Population Game*
*Rock Pioneers*
*Roots and Shoots*
*Salt Water Revival*
*Sawing Away*
*Scent Tracking*
*Scram or Freeze*
*Seas in Motion*
*Seed Dispersal*
*Sensory Hi-Lo Hunt*
*Shake It!*
*Silent Stalking*
*Snug as a Bug*
*Sound Off!*
*Sticklers*
*Super Soil*
*Swell Homes*
*Terrestrial Hi-Lo Hunt*
*Too Many Mosquitoes*
*Trail Construction*
*Trail Impact Study*
*Tree Tally*
*Variation Game*
*Water Breathers*
*Water Holes to Mini Ponds*
*Water Snails*
*Water Striders*
*Web It*
*Web Weavers*
*What Lives Here?*
*Who Goes There?*
*Wintergreen*

## Project STARWALK

Lakeview Museum Planetarium
1125 W. Lake Avenue
Peoria, IL 61614
(309) 686-6682
Bob Riddle, Project Director

STARWALK integrates field trips to a planetarium with sequential classroom lessons about earth and space concepts for grades 3 and 5. Materials include instructional, management, and training materials. Developmental funding has been provided through the Elementary and Secondary Education Act (ESEA) Title IV-C, with dissemination support from the National Diffusion Network.

## Science 5/13

Schools Council
School of Education
University of Bristol
Bristol, England
Len Ennever, Project Director

Science 5/13 is a British project jointly sponsored by the Schools Council, the Nuffield Foundation, and the Scottish Education Department. Consisting of 24 volumes, this general science series for children ages 5 to 13 fosters development of content knowledge and science process skills through independent, hands-on investigations of familiar materials. (These activities extend and intensify those presented in the Learning Through Science Series.) Published in Britain by Macdonald, Science 5/13 is distributed in the U.S. by Teacher's Laboratory (see Publishers listing).

*Change: Stages 1 and 2, and Background*
*Change: Stage 3*
*Children and Plastics: Stages 1 and 2, and Background*
*Coloured Things: Stages 1 and 2*
*Early Experiences*
*Holes, Gaps and Cavities*
*Like and Unlike: Stages 1, 2, and 3*
*Metals: Background Information*
*Metals: Stages 1 and 2*
*Minibeasts: Stages 1 and 2*
*Ourselves: Stages 1 and 2*
*Science From Toys: Stages 1 and 2, and Background*

*Science, Models, and Toys: Stage 3*
*Structures and Forces: Stages 1 and 2*
*Structures and Forces: Stage 3*
*Time: Stages 1 and 2, and Background*
*Trees: Stages 1 and 2*
*Using the Environment:*
   *1: Early Explorations*
   *2: Investigations, Parts 1 and 2*
   *3: Tackling Problems, Parts 1 and 2*
   *4: Ways and Means*
*With Objectives in Mind*
*Working with Wood: Background Information*
*Working with Wood: Stages 1 and 2*

## Science Activities for the Visually Impaired/Science Enrichment for Learners with Physical Handicaps (SAVI/SELPH)

Center for Multisensory Learning
Lawrence Hall of Science
University of California
Berkeley, CA 94720
(415)642-8941
Herbert D. Thier, Director

SAVI/SELPH consists of nine modules designed for special education students, grades 4-7. The activities enable all children to participate successfully in multisensory investigations of life, earth, and physical sciences, increasing their understanding of science concepts and enhancing their science process skills. The modules work well in a variety of settings, and can be directed by teachers with little science background. Funding has been provided by the U.S. Office of Education. Materials are available from the Lawrence Hall of Science.

| | |
|---|---|
| *Communication* | *Measurement* |
| *Environmental Energy* | *Mixtures and Solutions* |
| *Environments* | *Scientific Reasoning* |
| *Kitchen Interactions* | *Structures of Life* |
| *Magnetism and Electricity* | |

## Science and Technology for Children (STC)

(In development)
National Science Resources Center
Arts and Industries Building, Room 1201
Smithsonian Institution
Washington, DC 20560
(202) 357-2555
Joe H. Griffith, Project Director

STC is a four-year NSRC elementary science curriculum-development project that is supported by a grant from the John D. and Catherine T. MacArthur Foundation. The STC project will develop curriculum units for grades 1 through 6 in the areas of physical science, life science, earth science, and technology.

The STC project is developing units that are intrinsically interesting for children and that will encourage further reading and investigations. The STC program will make hands-on science manageable for teachers by making use of simple, inexpensive materials that can be easily maintained in an elementary school setting. The STC units, which together will form a coherent and fundamental set of science experiences, will link science to the broader curriculum through an emphasis on reading, writing, art, and mathematics. The units will be field-tested in classrooms across the country to refine and validate the activities.

## Science—A Process Approach (SAPA/SAPA II)

American Association for the Advancement of Science
Washington, DC 20005
(202) 326-6400
John Mayor, Director
Inactive; Original SAPA materials available on
SCIENCE HELPER K-8. SAPA II revisions available
from Delta.

SAPA and SAPA II are general Science Programs that focus heavily on processes of science, rather than on concepts. In both the first and the second versions, activities form a sequential K-6 modular program in which mastery of specific skills is predicated upon the accumulation of experience. Funded by the National Science Foundation, SAPA was published in the sixties by the Xerox Education Division and consisted of seven parts, each containing activity modules appropriate to a particular grade. The SAPA II folio version was originally published in the seventies by Ginn and Company. Its revised edition contains 105 modules.

| SAPA | SAPA II |
|---|---|
| *Part A* | *Level K: Modules 1-15* |
| *Part B* | *Level 1: Modules 16-30* |
| *Part C* | *Level 2: Modules 31-45* |
| *Part D* | *Level 3: Modules 46-60* |
| *Part E* | *Level 4: Modules 61-75* |
| *Part F* | *Level 5: Modules 76-90* |
| *Part G* | *Level 6: Modules 91-105* |

## The Science Connection
(In development)
Houston Museum of Natural Science
1 Hermann Circle Drive
Houston, TX 88087
(713) 526-1763
Carolyn Sumners, Terry Contant, Principal Investigators

The Science Connection will enhance basal science texts for grades 1-6 by providing a Science Discovery Reader, a Science Shoebox Recipe File with instructions for hands-on activities, and the Science Extension, which suggests techniques for integrating science with other activities in and out of school. Silver Burdett & Ginn will assist in development, dissemination, and teacher training. Funding has been provided by the National Science Foundation.

## Science Curriculum Improvement Study (SCIS/SCIS II/SCIIS)
Lawrence Hall of Science
University of California
Berkeley, CA 94720
(415) 642-8718
Robert Karplus/Lester Paldy/Herbert D. Thier, Directors

In all three stages of its existence, SCIS has focused on the concepts and processes of science for grades K-6. Investigations in life science and physical science build from exploration of materials, through interpretation of information, to application of knowledge and skills to new situations. The project was funded by the National Science Foundation in the late sixties. Both its first and third versions were published by Rand McNally; the second version, SCIS II, was distributed by American Science and Engineering. Original units are now available in reissue on SCIENCE HELPER K-8. Delta Education distributes current editions of all three versions and is revising SCIIS/85.

| SCIS | SCIS II | SCIIS/85 |
|------|---------|----------|
| *Beginnings* | | *Beginnings* |
| *Communities* | *Communities* | *Communities* |
| *Ecosystems* | *Ecosystems* | *Ecosystems* |
| *Energy Sources* | *Energy Sources* | *Energy Sources* |
| *Environments* | *Environments* | *Environments* |
| *Interaction and Systems* | *Interaction and Systems* | *Interaction and Systems* |
| *Life Cycles* | *Life Cycles* | *Life Cycles* |
| *Material Objects* | *Material Objects* | *Material Objects* |
| *Models: Electric and Magnetic Interactions* | *Modeling Systems* | *Scientific Theories* |
| *Organisms* | *Organisms* | *Organisms* |
| *Populations* | *Populations* | *Populations* |
| *Relative Position and Motion* | *Measurement, Motion and Change* | *Relative Position and Motion* |
| *Subsystems & Variables* | *Subsystems & Variables* | *Subsystems & Variables* |

## Science for Life and Living: Integrating Science, Technology, and Health
(In development)
Biological Sciences Curriculum Study (BSCS)
1115 North Cascade Avenue
Colorado Springs, CO 80903
(719) 473-2233
Rodger Bybee, Principal Investigator

In addition to its published projects in high school biology, BSCS has initiated a general elementary science and health program that will foster development of content knowledge and process skills in 28 activity-based modules. Curriculum materials will be supported by program management software, implementation guides, and supplementary activities. The program is funded by the National Science Foundation and will be published by Kendall/Hunt.

## Self Help Elementary Level Science (SHELLS)
(In development)
Florida State University
Gainesville, FL 32611
(904) 392-0761
Mary Budd Rowe, Principal Investigator

SHELLS will integrate audio and video tapes with print materials as a form of inservice for teachers and administrators. The program will provide an inventory of obstacles to elementary science, strategies for dealing with these obstacles, lessons in physical science, and techniques for research-based teaching. The Association for Supervision and Curriculum Development (ASCD) will collaborate with the University of Florida in the development and dissemination of materials. Major funding is provided by the National Science Foundation.

## Super Science: A Mass Media Program
(In development)
Scholastic, Inc.
730 Broadway
New York, NY 10003
(212) 505-3000
Victoria Chapman, Principal Investigator

Super Science will consist of two science magazines, one for grades 1-3 and the other for grades 4-6. Together with supporting science software, these publications will encourage hands-on, inquiry-based activities, integrating science with other disciplines and stressing applications to contemporary life. Funding is provided by the National Science Foundation.

## Unified Science and Mathematics for Elementary Schools (USMES)

Education Development Center, Inc.
Newton, MA 02160
(617) 969-7100
Inactive; some original materials have been reissued on SCIENCE HELPER K-8; all are available from ERIC.

USMES is a series of 23 guides published in the early seventies for use in grades K-8. Each unit consists of an opening challenge, out of which the students create their own investigations, honing their problem-solving skills and acquiring an understanding of major concepts. The USMES project includes activity cards and background papers, as well as the guides. Information provided for teachers and students is useful, but lessons demand careful planning and management to insure that the students' independent activities are fruitful.

*Advertising*
*Bicycle Transportation*
*Burglar Alarm Design*
*Classroom Design*
*Classroom Management*
*Consumer Research—*
  *Product Testing*
*Describing People*
*Designing for Human*
  *Proportions*
*Dice Design*
*Electromagnet Device*
  *Design*

*Growing Plants*
*Lunch Lines*
*Manufacturing*
*Orientation*
*Pedestrian Crossings*
*Play Area Design and Use*
*School Zoo*
*Soft Drink Design*
*Traffic Flow*
*USMES Design Lab Manual*
*The USMES Guide*
*Ways to Learn/Teach*
*Weather Predictions*

## Wisconsin Fast Plants

(In development)
University of Wisconsin–Madison
Department of Plant Pathology–Fast Plants
1630 Linden Drive
Madison, WI 53706
(608) 262-8638
Paul Williams, Principal Investigator
James Stewart, Co-Principal Investigator
Coe Williams and Jane Scharer, Project Coordinators

The Wisconsin Fast Plants project integrates university research with elementary school science by bringing *Brassica campestris*, the rapidly growing product of genetics experimentation, into children's classrooms. Students examine and plant seeds, then study their quick growth and maturation, in a unit that can last as little as 40 days. The program is supported by the National Science Foundation, with materials available from Carolina Biological.

*Wisconsin Fast Plants Manual*

# Publishers

Included in this section are the publishers and distributors of the materials reviewed in the resource guide.

**ADDISON-WESLEY PUBLISHING COMPANY**
1 Jacob Way
Reading, MA 01867
(617) 944-3700
(800) 447-2226

**AIMS EDUCATION FOUNDATION**
P.O. Box 7766
Fresno, CA 93747
(209) 291-1766

**AMERICAN ASSOCIATION FOR THE ADVANCE-MENT OF SCIENCE**
1515 Massachusetts Avenue, NW
Washington, DC 20005
(202) 326-6405

**AMERICAN LIBRARY ASSOCIATION**
50 East Huron Street
Chicago, IL 60611
(800) 545-2433
(312) 944-6780

**AMERICAN SCIENCE & ENGINEERING**
See DELTA EDUCATION

**AQUARIUM OF NIAGARA FALLS**
701 Whirlpool Street
Niagara Falls, NY 14301
(716) 285-3575

**ASSESSMENT OF PERFORMANCE UNIT**
Department of Education and Science
Elizabeth House
Room 4/77a
York Road
London, SE1 7PH, England
01-934-9323

**THE ASSOCIATION FOR SCIENCE EDUCATION**
College Lane Hatfield
Hertfordshire, AL 10 9AA, England

**ASSOCIATION OF SCIENCE-TECHNOLOGY CENTERS (ASTC)**
1413 K Street, NW, Tenth Floor
Washington, DC 20005
(202) 371-1171

**AUDUBON ZOO**
PO Box 4327
New Orleans, LA 70178
(504) 861-2537

**R. R. BOWKER COMPANY**
245 West 17th Street
New York, NY 10011
(800) 521-8110
(800) 537-8416
(212) 645-9700

**CALVERT MARINE MUSEUM**
P.O. Box 97 Solomons
Solomons, MD 20688
(301) 326-2042

**CENTER FOR MULTISENSORY LEARNING**
Lawrence Hall of Science
University of California
Berkeley, CA 94720
(415) 642-8941

**CHICAGO ZOOLOGICAL SOCIETY**
Education Department
Brookfield Zoo
Brookfield, IL 60513
(312) 485-0263

**CHILDREN'S PRESS**
5440 N. Cumberland Avenue
Chicago, IL 60656
(312) 693-0800
(800) 621-1115

**CREATIVE COMPANY**
3623 Hanley Road
Cincinnati, OH 45239
(513) 542-8610

**CREATIVE PUBLICATIONS**
Order Department
5005 West 110th Street
Oak Lawn, IL 60453
(800) 642-0822

**DALE SEYMOUR PUBLICATIONS**
P.O. Box 10888
Palo Alto, CA 94303
(800) 872-1100 (Outside CA)
(800) 222-0766 (CA)

**DELTA EDUCATION, INC.**
PO Box M
Nashua, NH 03061-6012
(800) 258-1302
(603) 889-8899

**DEPARTMENT OF EDUCATION AND SCIENCE**
Elizabeth House
York Road
London, SE1 7PH England
01-934-9323

**DOVER PUBLICATIONS, INC.**
180 Varick Street
New York, NY 10014
(800) 223-3130
(516) 294-7000

**EDUCATION DEVELOPMENT CENTER, INC. (EDC)**
55 Chapel Street
Newton, MA 02160
(617) 969-7100

**EDUCATIONAL PRODUCTS INFORMATION EXCHANGE (EPIE)**
EPIE Institute
P.O. Box 839
Water Mill, NY 11976
(516) 283-4922

**EDUCATIONAL TESTING SERVICE NATIONAL ASSESSMENT OF EDUCATIONAL PROGRESS**
CN 6710
Princeton, NJ 08541-6710
(609) 921-9000

**EDUCATORS PROGRESS SERVICE, INC.**
214 Center Street
Randolph, WI 53956
(414) 326-3126

**ENSLOW PUBLISHERS, INC.**
Bloy Street & Ramsey Avenue
P.O. Box 777
Hillside, NJ 07205
(201) 964-4116

**ERIC CLEARINGHOUSE FOR SCIENCE, MATHEMATICS, AND ENVIRONMENTAL EDUCATION**
Ohio State University
1200 Chambers Road, Third Floor
Columbus, OH 43212
(614) 292-6717

**EXCEL, INC.**
200 West Station Street
Barrington, IL 60010
(312) 382-7272

**FACTS ON FILE**
460 Park Avenue
New York, NY 10016
(800) 322-8755
(212) 683-2244

**FRANKLIN INSTITUTE**
**MUSEUM-TO-GO RESOURCE CENTER**
20th and The Benjamin Franklin Parkway
Philadelphia, PA 19103
(215) 448-1200

**GARLAND PUBLISHING, INC.**
136 Madison Avenue
New York, NY 10016
(212) 686-7492

**GOOD APPLE, INC.**
Box 299
Carthage, IL 62321
(800) 435-7234
(217) 357-3981

**GREAT EXPLORATIONS IN MATH AND SCIENCE**
**(GEMS)**
Lawrence Hall of Science
University of California
Berkeley, CA 94720
(415) 642-7771

**HANSEN PLANETARIUM**
15 South State Street
Salt Lake City, UT 84111
(801) 538-2098

**HARPER & ROW**
10 East 53rd Street
New York, NY 10022
(800) 242-7737
(212) 207-7000

**D. C. HEATH CO.**
125 Spring Street
Lexington, MA 02173
(617) 862-6650
(800) 334-3284

**HEINEMANN EDUCATIONAL BOOKS**
70 Court Street
Portsmouth, NH 03801
(603) 431-7894

**HENRY HOLT AND CO.**
521 Fifth Avenue
New York, NY 10175
(212) 599-7600

**HOLT, RINEHART & WINSTON, INC.**
383 Madison Avenue
New York, NY 10017
(212) 750-1330

**HUBBARD**
P.O. Box 104
Northbrook, IL 60062
(800) 323-8368

**IDEA FACTORY, INC.**
10710 Dixon Drive
Riverview, FL 33569
(813) 677-6727

**KIDS CAN PRESS**
585 1/2 Bloor Street West
Toronto, Ontario, Canada M6G 1K5
(416) 534-6389

**LAWRENCE HALL OF SCIENCE**
University of California
Berkeley, CA 94720
(415) 642-7771
(See also CENTER FOR MULTISENSORY
LEARNING)

**LIFE LAB SCIENCE PROGRAM**
1156 High Street
Santa Cruz, CA 95064
(408) 476-7140

**J. B. LIPPINCOTT CO.**
East Washington Square
Philadelphia, PA 19105
(215) 238-4200
(800) 242-7737

**LITTLE, BROWN AND COMPANY**
34 Beacon Street
Boston, MA 02108
(800) 343-9204
(617) 227-0730

**MACDONALD**
See TEACHER'S LABORATORY

**MANOMET BIRD OBSERVATORY**
P.O. Box 936
Manomet, MA 02345
(617) 224-6521

**MARINE WORLD AFRICA USA**
Marine World Parkway
Vallejo, CA 94589
(707) 644-4000

**MCGRAW-HILL, INC.**
1221 Avenue of the Americas
New York, NY 10020
(212) 512-2000
(609) 426-5254

**CHARLES E. MERRILL PUBLISHING CO.**
1300 Alum Creek Drive
Columbus, OH 43216
(800) 848-1567
(800) 848-6205
(614) 258-8441

**JULIAN MESSNER**
1230 Avenue of the Americas
New York, NY 10020
(800) 223-1360
(212) 698-7000

**MID-ATLANTIC CENTER FOR RACE EQUITY**
The American University
5010 Wisconsin Avenue, NW, #310
Washington, DC 20016
(202) 885-8517

**MISSOURI BOTANICAL GARDEN**
P.O. Box 299
St. Louis, MO 63166
(314) 577-5149

**WILLIAM MORROW AND COMPANY**
105 Madison Avenue
New York, NY 10016
(800) 631-1199
(212) 889-3050

**MUSEUM OF SCIENCE AND INDUSTRY**
57th Street and Lake Shore Drive
Chicago, IL 60637-2093
(312) 684-1414

**NATIONAL AQUARIUM IN BALTIMORE**
Department of Education and Interpretation
Pier 3
501 E. Pratt Street
Baltimore, MD 21202
(301) 576-3810

**NATIONAL GARDENING ASSOCIATION**
180 Flynn Avenue
Burlington, VT 05401
(802) 863-1308

**NATIONAL GEOGRAPHIC SOCIETY**
17th and M Streets, NW
Washington, DC 20036
(202) 857-7000

**NATIONAL SCIENCE TEACHERS ASSOCIATION**
1742 Connecticut Avenue, NW
Washington, DC 20009
(202) 328-5800

**NATIONAL WILDLIFE FEDERATION**
1412 16th Street, NW
Washington, D.C. 20036-2266
(202) 797-6800

**NORTHERN NEW ENGLAND MARINE EDUCA-
TION PROJECT**
206 Shibles Hall
University of Maine
Orono, ME 04669
(207) 581-1495

**OPEN UNIVERSITY PRESS
TAYLOR AND FRANCIS**
242 Cherry Street
Philadelphia, PA 19106
(215) 238-0940

**ORYX PRESS**
2214 North Central at Encanto
Phoenix, AZ 85004-1483
(602) 254-6156

**PACIFIC SCIENCE CENTER**
200 Second Avenue North
Seattle, WA 98109
(206) 443-2001

**PRENTICE HALL**
Route 9W
Englewood Cliffs, NJ 07632
(201) 592-2000

**PROJECT WILD**
California Department of Fish and Game Conservation
Education Branch
1416 9th Street
Sacramento, CA 95814
(916) 445-7613

**RAND MCNALLY**
See DELTA EDUCATION

**SCIENCE HELPER K-8**
**PC-SIG/IASC CD-ROM PUBLISHING GROUP**
1030E East Duane Avenue
Sunnyvale, CA 94086
(408) 730-9291

**SCIENCE KIT, INC.**
777 E. Park Drive
Tonawanda, NY 14150-6781
(800) 828-7777

**SCIENCE MAN**
4738 North Harlem Avenue
Harwood Heights, IL 60656
(312) 867-4441

**SMEAC INFORMATION REFERENCE CENTER**
**THE OHIO STATE UNIVERSITY**
1200 Chambers Road, Third Floor
Columbus, OH 43212
(614) 292-6717

**THE STEWARDSHIP INSTITUTE**
Shelburne Farms
Shelburne, VT 05482
(802) 985-8686

**TEACHERS COLLEGE PRESS**
1234 Amsterdam Avenue
New York, NY 10027
(212) 678-3929

**TEACHER'S LABORATORY**
P.O. Box 6480
214 Main Street
Brattleboro, VT 05301-6480
(802) 254-3457

**VERMONT INSTITUTE OF NATURAL SCIENCE**
Woodstock, VT 05091
(802) 457-2779

**VIRGINIA MARINE SCIENCE MUSEUM**
717 General Booth Boulevard
Virginia Beach, VA 23451
(804) 425-3476

**WORKMAN PUBLISHING COMPANY**
1 West 39th Street
New York, NY 10018
(800) 772-7202
(212) 398-9160

## Suppliers of Science Materials and Apparatus

The following is a briefly annotated list of commercial distributors of books and materials for hands-on science. It is meant not to be exhaustive but rather to serve as a guide for teachers or administrators implementing elementary programs. Readers are encouraged to seek out local sources for commercial products and recycled materials, and to consult the *NSTA Supplement of Science Education Suppliers*, published annually in the National Science Teachers Association periodicals (see Magazines listings).

### ACCENT! SCIENCE
301 Cass Street
Saginaw, MI 48602
(517) 799-8103

Astronomy and earth science models for use in the elementary classroom.

### ACTIVITY RESOURCES COMPANY, INC.
P. O. Box 4875
Hayward, CA 94540
(415) 782-1300

Chemistry materials for middle school and high school.

### AIMS EDUCATION FOUNDATION
P.O. Box 7766
Fresno, CA 93747
(209) 291-1766

Integration of math and science in activity books, grades K-9.

### ALBION IMPORT EXPORT, INC.
Coolidge Bank Building
65 Main Street
Watertown, MA 02172
(617) 926-7222

A kit of the human skeleton for children to assemble.

### BAUSCH AND LOMB OPTICAL SYSTEMS DIVISION
1400 North Goodman Street
P.O. Box 450
Rochester, NY 14692-0450
(716) 338-6005

Comprehensive collection of microscopes appropriate for elementary through college level classrooms.

### BURT HARRISON & COMPANY
P.O. Box 732
Weston, MA 02193-0732
(617) 647-0647
(617) 969-3330

Equipment and supplies for BATTERIES AND BULBS.

### CAROLINA BIOLOGICAL SUPPLY COMPANY
2700 York Road
Burlington, NC 27216-9988
(800) 334-5551

Science materials and equipment, including live organisms.

### CONNECTICUT VALLEY BIOLOGICAL SUPPLY COMPANY
Valley Road
P.O. Box 326
Southhampton, MA 01073
(800) 282-7757
(800) 628-7748

Science materials and equipment, including live organisms.

### CREATIVE LEARNING PRESS
P.O. Box 320
Mansfield Center, CT 06250
(203) 423-8120

Science materials and general education books and materials for use with gifted and talented population.

### CREATIVE LEARNING SYSTEMS, INC.
9889 Hilbret Street, Suite E
San Diego, CA 92131
(619) 566-2880

Resource books, materials, and equipment for science and technology.

## CUISENAIRE COMPANY OF AMERICA, INC.

12 Church Street
New Rochelle, NY 10802
(800) 237-3142

Materials and activity books to supplement science and math curriculums.

## DELTA EDUCATION, INC.

P.O. Box M
Nashua, NH 03061-6012
(800) 258-1302
(603) 889-8899

Kits and replacement materials for ESS, SCIS, SCIIS/85, SCISII, SAPA-II, OBIS, ISIS, and HAP, and items for specific publishers' kits.

## DENOYER-GEPPERT SCIENCE COMPANY

5711 North Ravenswood Avenue
Chicago, IL 60646
(312) 561-9200

Anatomical models, charts, biology materials, and materials in life science and health for upper elementary and middle school classrooms.

## EDMUND SCIENTIFIC

101 E. Gloucester Pike
Barrington, NJ 08007
(800) 222-0224

Science tools and equipment to refurbish hands-on science kits.

## ENERGY LEARNING CENTER
### Edison Electric Institute

1111 19th Street, NW
Washington, DC 20036
(202) 778-6400

Films, publications, and kits designed to give general information about energy sources.

## ENERGY SCIENCES, INC.

16728 Oakmont Avenue
Gaithersburg, MD 20877
(301) 770-2550

Educational materials, toys, and other solar-powered products.

## ESTES INDUSTRIES/HI-FLIER

1295 H Street
Penrose, CO 81240
(303) 372-6565

Kites Program—including kite sets and publications, and model rocket kits, engines, and other accessories.

## FORESTRY SUPPLIERS, INC.

205 West Rankin Street
Jackson, MS 39204
(601) 354-3565

Instruments and tools for biology, earth science, and environmental studies hands-on activities.

## FREY SCIENTIFIC

905 Hickory Lane
Mansfield, OH 44905
(419) 589-9905

Educational science laboratory equipment and supplies for chemistry, earth science, physics, astronomy, and general science teaching.

## HUBBARD SCIENTIFIC COMPANY

P.O. Box 104
Northbrook, IL 60065
(800) 323-8368

Materials for life science and earth science and Human Systems Activity Kits.

## IDEAL SCHOOL SUPPLY COMPANY

11000 South Lavergne Avenue
Oak Lawn, IL 60453
(312) 425-0800

Manipulatives, kits, and general science equipment appropriate for grades K-6.

## INSECT LORE PRODUCTS, INC.

P.O. Box 1535
Shafter, CA 93263
(800) LIVE BUG

Suppliers of painted lady butterfly kits and other science and nature activity kits.

## LAWRENCE HALL OF SCIENCE

University of California
Berkeley, CA 94720
(415) 642-7771

Science activity books with hands-on emphasis.

## LEARNING THINGS, INC.

68A Broadway
P.O. Box 436
Arlington, MA 02174
(617) 646-0093

Materials, books, and laboratory equipment.

## LEGO Systems, Inc.

555 Taylor Road
Enfield, CT 06082
(203) 749-2291

Manipulatives to teach physical science concepts.

## LET'S GET GROWING
## General Feed and Seed Company

1900-B Commercial Way
Santa Cruz, CA 95065
(408) 476-5344

Tools, seeds, supplies, and books for classroom gardening.

## METROLOGIC INSTRUMENTS

143 Harding Avenue
Bellmawr, NJ 08031
(609) 933-0100

Laser-optics accessories and instructions for use in elementary classrooms.

## NATIONAL GEOGRAPHIC SOCIETY

17th and M Streets, NW
Washington, DC 20036
(202) 857-7000

Multimedia kits, software, filmstrips, videos, and books.

## NATIONAL SCIENCE TEACHERS ASSOCIATION

1742 Connecticut Avenue, NW
Washington, DC 20009
(202) 328-5800

SCIENCE AND CHILDREN magazine and other printed materials concerning science education.

## NATIONAL WILDLIFE FEDERATION

1400 16th Street, NW
Washington, DC 20036
(800) 432-6564

RANGER RICK magazine, NatureScope activity guides for teachers, audiovisual programs on environmental science, and posters.

## NYSTROM/EYE GATE MEDIA

3333 North Elston Avenue
Chicago, IL 60618
(312) 463-1144

New hands-on programs for middle school, models, charts, and sound filmstrips for different grade levels.

## PLAY-JOUR, INC.

200 Fifth Avenue, Suite 1024
New York, NY 10010
(212) 243-5200

Capsela Scientific kit includes a guide with 25 lessons covering specific physical science concepts.

## RIGHT BEFORE YOUR EYES

136 Ellis Hollow Creek Road
Ithaca, NY 14850
(607) 277-0384

Natural history poster series covering common animals and plants of North America, appropriate for all elementary grades.

## SAVI/SELPH
## CENTER FOR MULTISENSORY LEARNING

Lawrence Hall of Science
University of California
Berkeley, CA 94720
(415) 642-8941

A series of science-enrichment activities designed for handicapped students that may be used with all children.

## THE SCIENCE MAN

P.O. Box 56036
Harwood Heights, IL 60656
(312) 867-4441

Science resource books.

## SOIL CONSERVATION SERVICE

U.S. Department of Agriculture
P.O. Box 2890
Washington, DC 20013
(202) 217-2290

Hands-on activities, such as making your own soil profile, education publications, posters, and transparencies for use in elementary and junior high school classrooms.

## SOUTHERN PRECISION INSTRUMENT COMPANY

3419 East Commerce
San Antonio, TX 78220
(512) 224-5801

Microscopes and microprojectors for use in the elementary classroom.

## THE TEACHER'S LABORATORY, INC.

214 Main Street
P.O. Box 6480
Brattleboro, VT 05301-6480
(802) 254-3457

Science 5/13 and Learning Through Science (from England) and other books and materials for teaching math and science.

## TOPS LEARNING SYSTEMS

10978 South Mulino Road
Canby, OR 97013
(503) 266-8550

Inexpensive science and math materials and idea books.

## WARD'S NATURAL SCIENCE ESTABLISHMENT, INC.

5100 West Henrietta Road
P.O. Box 92912
Rochester, NY 14692-9012
11850 East Florence Avenue
P.O. Box 2567
Santa Fe Springs, CA 90670-2502
East Coast Facility: (716) 359-2502
West Coast Facility: (213) 946-2439
(800) 962-2660

Specimens and materials for biology and biotechnology.

Centennial School District, Multnomah Education Service District, Portland, Oregon
*Photograph by Craig Walker*

# INDEX

The six indexes contained in this section are designed to allow easy access to materials and organizations described in Sections I, II, and III. Bibliographic entries are indexed by topic, title, and author/project. In addition, grade level and grade-level-by-category indexes enable readers to find materials appropriate to specific curriculum needs. All sources of information, publications, materials, or professional support are listed in the final index.

## Topic

4Mat, 92
16mm films, 105
absorbency, 71
absorption, 38, 50, 59, 71, 78
academies of science, 99
acceleration, 54, 57, 61-64, 71, 75, 84, 87-89
accident prevention, 35, 71
achievement tests, 101
acid rain, 28
acids and bases, 44, 50, 67, 81, 89
acorns, 18, 33
acoustics, 54, 59
activity-based instruction, 92-98
adaptations, 7-18, 20-24, 26-29, 31-33, 62, 70, 85
administration, 96, 101
advertising, 34, 60
aerodynamics, 45, 76
affective domain, 93-96, 98
age of dinosaurs, 83
air, 25, 35, 40, 43, 45, 48, 68, 70, 81-82, 88-90
air currents, 45
air pollution, 35
air pressure, 40, 43, 59, 70, 86, 89
air quality, 35
airplanes, 70, 76
algae, 15-16, 24-25
alloys, 70
aluminum, 70
amphibians, 13, 16, 21, 24, 32, 83, 86
amplitude, 45, 59
anatomy, 11, 82
animal behavior, 7-18, 20-24, 26-28, 30-31, 33, 73-75, 78, 83
animal care, 9-10, 12, 14-16, 22
animal coloration, 21-22, 25, 62-63, 85
animal communication, 21
animal sounds, 18, 24, 26
animal tracks, 21-22, 83, 85

animals, 7-28, 30-33, 44, 62-64, 70, 73-75, 77, 81-90, 103-107
ant farms, 21
anthropology, 104
ants, 8, 12, 17-18, 20-21, 26
approximation, 71
aquariums, 10, 15-16, 20, 22-27, 44, 90
aquatic animals, 7, 9, 11-13, 20, 22-24, 26-28, 30, 32, 77-78, 86, 105
aquatic insects, 23-24, 27
aquatic plants, 12-13, 20, 22, 24, 30, 32, 86, 105
architecture, 57, 60, 63, 67
area, 71
arid lands, 7, 13-14, 83
art, 10, 87
arthropods, 8-12, 14-18, 20-28, 30, 32, 82-83, 86, 88-89
assessment, 93, 95-96
asteroids, 38, 42
astronomy, 38-43, 87, 90, 92, 100-101, 103, 105-106
atmosphere, 38, 41-42, 48
atoms, 81, 92
attitudes, 90, 93, 96-98
attributes, 10, 36, 44, 51-52, 60, 65, 67-68, 71
auditory impairments, 97
autogyros, 70
averaging, 25, 35-36, 64, 69, 71, 76
babies, 88
backbones, 11
bacteria, 13, 23, 61, 81, 84
baking, 85
balance, 34, 82
balances, 53, 55-56, 63, 73-74, 77, 84
balloons, 42, 44, 56
balls, 47, 56, 75, 87
bark, 11, 30-31, 33, 90
barometers, 40, 43, 53
barometric pressure, 40, 43, 53
bats, 24, 83
batteries, 44, 46, 49, 51, 53, 60-61, 64, 66, 87
bays, 11-12, 17

beach animals, 9, 11-13, 15, 20, 28, 32
beach hoppers, 9, 28
beaches, 9, 11-13, 15, 20, 28, 32
beans, 22
beehives, 12, 21
bees, 12, 20-21, 24, 82, 86-88
beeswax, 12, 21
beetles, 9-10, 20-21, 24
behavior modification, 37
bending, 70
Bernoulli's Law, 45
bibliography, 99-103, 105
biochemistry, 58
biodiversity, 16
biogeography, 16
biographies, 82, 85
biological control, 20, 26
biology, 7-37, 61, 65, 73-78, 83-87, 90-92, 94, 97-98, 103-107
bird feeders, 18, 33, 82
birds, 8-13, 18, 23-24, 26, 28, 31, 33, 70, 78, 82-83, 85-87, 90
blackbirds, 24
blood, 35-36, 82
boats, 45, 59, 70, 89
bones, 11, 35-36, 81-83, 88, 91
boomerangs, 70
botany, 11, 14, 19, 22, 24-25, 29-32, 83, 99
bouncing, 56, 75
brain, 82
breathing, 34-35
bridges, 57, 63
brine shrimp, 11, 22
bubbles, 45, 59, 78, 82
budgets, 69, 77, 96
building materials, 39, 57, 60, 63, 67, 77, 79, 89
buildings, 39, 57, 60, 63, 67, 79, 89
bulbs, 44, 46, 53, 60, 64, 87
buoyancy, 45, 48, 50, 56, 59, 75, 84, 89
burning, 82
butterflies, 12, 20-21, 24
buzzers, 61, 87
calendars, 39, 66-67, 76-77

cameras,  53, 56
camouflage,  20-22, 25, 62-63, 85
candles,  77, 82
capillary action,  84
carbohydrates,  89
carbon dioxide,  15-16, 34
career education,  82-83, 97
carnivores,  8, 13, 26-27
cars,  75
caterpillars,  12, 20
cats,  9
cavities,  36
cells,  29, 64, 74, 79
censuses,  11
center of gravity,  34
center of mass,  34
centrifugal force,  57, 84, 87
centripetal force,  84
change,  9, 29, 31, 35, 39-40, 43, 45,
    47-48, 51-52, 54, 56-57, 61-65,
    67-68, 73-74, 77, 81, 85, 89-90
chemical bonding,  65
chemical elements,  70
chemical energy,  45
chemical reactions,  45, 53-54, 74,
    77, 81
chemical safety,  45
chemical systems,  49
chemistry,  44-46, 49-50, 53-54, 56,
    58, 61, 64-65, 67, 73-77, 81-82, 85,
    89-90, 104
chicks,  77
child development,  35, 79, 88, 94-97
children's literature,  93, 99-101
children's writing,  104
chocolate,  84
chromatography,  25, 46, 84, 90
chrysalis,  12
circles,  87
circuits,  44, 46, 49, 51, 53, 60-61,
    64, 73, 87, 90
circular motion,  57
circulation,  35-36, 59, 82
circulatory system,  35-36, 91
clams,  11
classification,  8, 13, 19, 39, 41-42,
    51-52, 60, 62-66, 68-69, 73-74, 78,
    90
classroom design,  62
classroom management,  62, 98
clay,  45
clay boats,  48
climate,  14, 31-32, 39-41, 43, 53,
    61, 66-67, 76, 83
clocks,  39, 77, 82, 87
clouds,  40, 42-43
coal,  39
coastal ecology,  11-13, 15, 17, 20,
    26, 28, 32
cockroaches,  82
codes,  87

cognition,  93-94
cognitive development,  88, 98
cognitive domain,  93-96
cold,  49, 59, 81, 83-84, 88
colloids,  54
color,  10, 25, 38, 42, 44-46, 50, 54,
    56, 62-64, 72-74, 76-77, 84-85,
    87-88, 90
comets,  38, 42
commercial fishing,  26
communication,  45
communities,  13, 26-27
community resources,  83, 101
comparison,  10, 36, 42, 44, 51-52,
    60, 63, 65, 68-69, 73-74, 77, 79
compasses,  40, 52-53, 82
compost,  31
compression,  86
computer-assisted learning,  97
computers,  87, 97, 100, 102-104, 106
condensation,  15-16, 56, 78, 89
conduction,  48-49, 66, 68, 70
conductivity,  44, 49, 60, 64, 70, 87
conservation,  9, 11, 13-17, 19,
    21-22, 27-28, 32, 78, 105
conservation of energy,  64-65
conservation of matter,  63
constellations,  38-39, 42, 92
construction,  60, 63
consumer education,  34, 63, 71-72,
    76
consumer science,  71
consumers,  13
contagious diseases,  35
continental drift,  38, 82
continents,  82
contour maps,  40
convection,  38, 68, 82
cooking,  61, 76, 85-86, 89
cooling,  48, 61
copper,  70
coral reefs,  15
cost-benefit analysis,  69, 71-72
counting,  11, 63, 66-67, 72
crabs,  11-12, 20
crawdads,  11, 30
crayfish,  9, 11, 14, 24, 30
creativity,  84
crickets,  9, 22
criminology,  46, 66
critical thinking,  90-91, 98
crustaceans,  11, 14, 16, 24
crystals,  39, 67
cultures,  104
currents,  17-18, 26, 28, 66
curriculum development,  32, 88, 92,
    94-98, 101-102
curriculum implementation,  94-95,
    97-98
curves,  87
daily living skills,  34-37

dams,  57, 89
damselflies,  9, 18, 30
day and night,  24, 39-40, 42-43
decay,  61, 79
decision making,  34, 37
decomposers,  13
dehydration,  73
density,  41, 45-46, 48, 50, 56,
    77-78, 88
dental health,  36, 84
dentistry,  83
depth perception,  35, 37
deserts,  7, 13-14, 83
design,  54, 57, 60, 62, 65, 77, 82,
    85-86, 91
diameter,  41
diet,  36, 84
diffusion,  38, 65, 81
digestion,  36, 82, 84, 91
dinosaurs,  9, 14, 83
dirt,  10, 19, 25, 29, 31, 39, 41-43,
    60, 87, 89
disease control,  35
diseases,  35
dissolving,  59, 61
distance,  40-41, 54
division,  48
dogs,  9
dolls,  75
dolphins,  19, 28
domes,  63
domestic animals,  13
dragonflies,  9, 18, 30
drainage,  42
driftwood,  79
drugs,  91
dyes,  62
early childhood science education,
    86, 88, 92
ears,  36-37, 45, 57, 65, 82, 91
Earth,  38-39, 41-42
earth science,  30-32, 38-43, 52-53,
    55, 66-68, 70, 72-76, 78, 82-83, 85,
    87-90, 92-94, 105-106
earthquakes,  39, 90
earthworms,  15, 17, 86, 89
echinoderms,  11, 20, 28, 32
echolocation,  28
eclipse,  39
ecology,  7-8, 10, 12-28, 30-33, 65,
    75, 78, 83, 85-86, 90, 92
ecosystems,  12, 15-17, 23, 32, 90
education suppliers,  100
educational research,  93
eggs,  11, 16
elasticity,  77
electrical circuits,  46, 49, 51, 53, 61,
    66, 73
electricity,  44, 46, 49, 51, 53, 60-61,
    64, 66, 73, 75, 87-88, 90, 99
electromagnetism,  46, 87

electromagnets,   44, 51, 60, 66
electrons,   51
elementary science methods,   7-33, 36-63, 65-79, 83-84, 86-88, 90-91, 92-98, 101-106
elevation,   40
emulsions,   50, 67, 89
endangered species,   9, 16
energy,   44, 46-48, 54-57, 61, 64-66, 68, 70, 82-85, 88-90
energy conservation,   48, 83
energy transfer,   47-48, 56, 64, 66, 83
energy transformation,   64
engineering,   45, 105
environment,   7-28, 30-33, 39, 41-42, 45, 62-63, 65, 70, 75, 77-78, 83-84, 86-87, 89-90, 92, 97-98, 101-103, 105
epidemics,   35
equations,   69
equilibrium,   55-56
equinox,   39
equity in education,   94, 97, 101
erosion,   30, 39, 42-43, 61, 75, 78
estimation,   41, 55, 60, 62, 64, 67, 69, 71-72, 74, 76-78
estuaries,   17
estuarine biology,   17
evaluation,   67, 73-75, 93-98,
evaporation,   15-16, 39, 40, 42, 53, 58-59, 73, 78, 82
evolution,   14
exceptional children,   97
excretion,   82
exercise,   34-36
exhale,   34
exhibits,   94
expansion,   70
extinction,   9, 14, 16, 83
extinction theories,   83
eye/hand coordination,   34
eyes,   24, 36-37, 53-54, 62, 65, 68, 74-75, 82, 88, 91
fabrics,   77
fall,   41
farming,   84
fatigue,   34
fats,   89
feathers,   11, 28
federal agencies,   99
feet,   70, 81, 91
fences,   63
fertilizer,   15-16
fiction,   100
field guide,   24, 78
field of view,   53
field of vision,   37
field trips,   85-86, 93-94
films,   100-101, 105
filmstrips,   100-101
filters,   83

filtration,   64, 68
fingerprints,   66
fingers,   36, 81
fish,   9, 13, 15-18, 22-24, 26, 32, 70, 84, 86, 89
fishing,   26
fitness,   34-37
flavorings,   86
fleas,   9, 28
flexibility,   35
flies,   12, 18, 24, 28
flight,   11, 28, 56, 70, 75-76, 89
floating,   45, 48, 50, 56, 59, 75, 84, 89
flowers,   10-12, 17-19, 22, 29, 31, 77-78
fluids,   38, 45-46, 50, 56, 68, 75, 84
fly traps,   12, 18, 28
focal length,   53
food,   12-13, 18, 23, 28, 36, 66-67, 69, 77, 81-82, 84, 86-89, 91, 97
food additives,   86
food chains,   8, 13, 15-18, 22, 24, 26-27, 32, 83
food coloring,   46
food gathering,   7, 10-11, 18
food preservation,   86
food webs,   15, 24-27, 32, 83
foot paths,   30
forces,   38, 47, 54-57, 61, 63-64, 69-70, 73-75, 77, 84, 87-90
forces and motions,   38, 47, 54-57, 61, 64, 69-70, 73-75, 84, 87-88, 90
forest ecology,   30
forests,   18, 30, 83, 85
fossils,   14, 39, 83
fractions,   25, 62, 65, 68, 72, 76-77
frame of reference,   40, 52, 55
freezing,   49, 59
frequency,   45, 59
freshwater animals,   13, 24, 26, 32, 86
freshwater ecology,   13, 24, 26, 32, 86
freshwater plants,   13, 24, 26, 32, 86
friction,   54, 63, 72, 84
frogs,   9, 21, 24, 85
fruits,   7, 19, 30, 78, 87
fulcrum,   55-56, 84
fungus,   13, 23-24, 81, 87
fuses,   46
galaxy,   38
games,   87
gardening,   19, 83
gardens,   19, 31, 84
gases,   15, 38-39, 44-45, 48, 56, 81, 84-85
gears,   49, 54, 56, 88, 91
generators,   51
genetics,   21-22, 24
geography,   12, 39-40, 43, 82, 105

geological time scale,   83
geology,   12, 39, 41-42, 83, 102
geometry,   52, 65, 67, 69, 71-77, 82
gerbils,   8-9
germination,   13, 21-22, 24-25, 29-30, 81
gifted and talented students,   92, 97-98
giraffes,   19
gliders,   70
globes,   39, 82
graphing,   19, 22, 30-31, 34-36, 39, 43, 50, 53, 58, 60-69, 71-77, 84-85
graphs,   22, 30, 34-35, 39, 50, 53, 58, 64-68, 73-77, 84-85
grasses,   24, 87
grasshoppers,   9, 20-21, 28
grasslands,   9
gravity,   39, 42, 54-56, 70, 75, 83-84, 87-89, 92
grouping,   51-52
growth,   11-12, 16, 19, 23, 29-31, 35, 65, 77, 91
growth patterns,   18, 35
guinea pigs,   73
guppies,   15, 24-25
habitat destruction,   16, 21
habitats,   7-10, 12-28, 31-32, 83, 85-86, 90
habits,   37
hamsters,   8, 22
handicapped students,   16, 30, 45, 50-51, 53, 66, 70, 75, 92, 97, 101, 133
hands,   91
hardness,   42, 70
health,   30, 34-37, 58, 61, 67, 71, 75, 77, 84, 89, 91, 100-101, 106
health education,   34-37, 91
health risks,   35-37
health services,   34
hearing,   37, 45, 57, 88, 91
hearing impairments,   97
heart,   35-36, 82, 91
heart rate,   30, 36, 75
heartbeat,   36
heat,   28, 37, 38, 40, 45, 47-49, 59, 61, 64-65, 68, 77, 81, 84-85, 90
heat loss,   37, 49
heat transfer,   38, 40, 47-49, 64-65, 68
heating,   48, 61
helicopters,   70
herbivores,   8, 13, 21, 23, 26-27
herps,   21
hibernation,   33, 83
high school science methods,   87, 95, 98, 106
histograms,   30, 58, 64
holes,   68
holidays,   66-67, 76

home range,   23
honeybees,   12, 20-21, 24, 82, 85-88
honeycombs,   12
human biology,   30, 34-37, 58, 65-67, 73-75, 81-84, 88-89, 91
human body,   30, 34-37, 66-67, 74-75, 81-82, 84, 88-89, 91
human development,   35
human sexuality,   88
humane education,   9, 22-23
humidity,   43
hunting,   16
hydras,   81
hydroponics,   84
hygiene,   34-37
ice,   49, 59, 64, 84, 92
ice cubes,   49, 59
immunization,   35
inclined planes,   54, 63
indicators,   44, 50, 58
inertia,   57, 75, 84
inference,   73-75
inhale,   34
injuries,   35
inks,   46, 64, 87, 89-90
insect communication,   21
insectivores,   8
insects,   8-10, 12, 15-18, 20-28, 32, 77, 82-83, 85-90
inservice,   96, 101
insulation,   25, 37, 48-49, 55, 62, 66
interdependence,   15, 26-27
intertidal zones,   15, 32
inventions,   84-85, 87, 91
inventors,   85
invertebrates,   8, 10, 12-13, 15-16, 20, 23-24, 27, 70, 78, 81-83, 86, 89
iodine,   56
isopods,   8-10, 16-17
jays,   8, 12, 18
junior high school methods,   106
Jupiter,   38, 41-42
kidneys,   82
kinetic energy,   48, 72
kitchen physics,   50, 61, 88
kites,   76
ladybugs,   21
lakes,   22, 26, 32, 87
language development,   31, 98
language of science,   31, 84
larvae,   12, 20, 23
lasers,   84
layering,   46
lead,   70
leadership,   96
leaf prints,   33, 87
learning cycles,   94
learning disabilities,   16, 30, 45, 50-51, 53, 66, 70, 75, 92
learning styles,   92

leaves,   11, 18-19, 22, 25, 29, 31, 66, 76-78, 85, 87-88, 90
lenses,   26, 29, 37, 50, 53-54, 56, 84
levers,   54, 63
lichens,   14, 18, 23
life cycles,   8, 10-12, 15-17, 19, 21-26, 29, 31, 33, 73-74, 77, 85
life science,   7-37, 41, 44, 58, 61, 65-66, 71, 73-78, 82-94, 97, 103-107
light,   8, 11-12, 24, 37-40, 49-51, 53-54, 56, 62-64, 68, 73-74, 76, 82-84, 87-88
lightning,   43
liquids,   10, 45-46, 50, 54, 56, 65, 68, 71, 76-77, 81, 83-84, 86, 88-90
lizards,   8-9, 14, 18, 21
locomotion,   22-23, 70, 78
logging,   79
logic,   72, 96, 98
lungs,   34-35, 82, 91
machines,   47, 54, 85-86, 91
magazine,   103-107
magma,   38-39
magnesium,   70
magnetism,   44, 46, 49, 51, 53-54, 64, 66, 70, 73-75, 87-90
magnets,   44, 46, 49, 51, 53-54, 64, 66, 70, 73-75, 87-90
magnification,   29, 50, 53, 84
mainstreaming,   97
mammals,   8-9, 13, 24, 27-28, 70, 83, 86
mapping,   22-23, 25, 40, 52, 55, 61, 72-76, 82, 92
maps,   22, 40, 52, 55, 82
marine biology,   8-9, 12-13, 15, 17, 20, 22-23, 27-28, 32, 83, 86, 100
marine science,   12-13, 26, 32, 105
marketing,   69, 77, 85
Mars,   38, 41-42
marshes,   32, 83
mass,   77-78
mathematics,   19, 25, 27-28, 35-36, 39, 41-43, 48, 52, 55-56, 60-62, 64-67, 69, 71-78, 89, 97-99, 104
maturity,   35
meadows,   20
mealworms,   10
measurement,   10, 19, 25, 28, 31, 35-37, 39, 41-43, 44-46, 52-53, 55-56, 60-74, 76-78, 82, 84-85, 90, 94, 96
mechanical systems,   49
mechanics,   28, 49, 56
media producers,   100
medicinal plants,   22
melting,   49, 59, 61, 82
Mercury,   38, 41-42
metacognition,   93-94
metals,   39, 61, 70, 77
metamorphosis,   9, 12, 20-22

meteorologists,   43
meteorology,   39-40, 43
metric system,   28, 69-70
mice,   8, 24
microbiology,   23, 29
microorganisms,   11, 23, 26, 29, 89
microscopes,   23, 26, 29, 64
middle school science methods,   87, 90, 95, 97, 106
migration,   28, 85
mineral properties,   39, 42, 70
minerals,   39, 41-42, 58, 65, 70, 92
mining,   70
minnows,   17-18, 26
minorities in science,   84, 94, 101, 133-134, 136
mirrors,   50, 52, 56
misconceptions,   95
mixtures,   46, 53
mobiles,   53, 63
mobility,   34-35
models,   38-39, 42, 56, 72, 87, 91
moisture,   23, 25
mold,   13, 23, 61, 74, 81, 84
molecular structure,   81
molecules,   56, 64, 81, 84, 88
mollusks,   11, 32
momentum,   56, 87
moon,   38-39, 41-43, 77, 87, 90, 92
mosquitoes,   20, 23
moths,   12, 20-21
motion,   38, 40, 47, 52, 54-57, 61, 64, 69-70, 73-75, 84, 87-90
motors,   51, 56
mountains,   39, 82, 92
mouth,   36
movement,   54, 57, 65, 70
mud,   89
muscles,   35-36, 82
museum organizations,   94
museum programs,   94
museums,   9, 12-13, 15, 17, 19, 22, 26, 32, 38, 40, 42, 46-48, 50-51, 57, 60, 94, 99, 103-104
music,   45, 54, 57, 59
musical instruments,   54, 57, 59
natural dyeing,   22
nature,   7-33, 41, 82, 85-86, 90, 103-107
navigation,   82, 87
Neptune,   38, 41-42
nervous system,   81-82
nests,   10-11, 23, 82, 89
neurology,   34
niche,   16
nickel,   70
night,   24, 39, 42-43
nocturnal animals,   25
nocturnal insects,   8, 12, 24
nose,   36, 70, 91
nutrition,   36, 58, 67, 81, 84, 89, 91

nuts,   18, 90
ocean currents,   15, 38
oceanography,   15, 38, 105
oceans,   11, 20, 22, 28, 32, 82
odors,   10, 33, 44-45, 73
oil,   39, 50
oil spills,   11, 20, 30
opacity,   50
opaque,   50
operational definition,   73, 75
optical illusions,   54, 74-75, 89
optics,   50, 52-54
oral hygiene,   36
orbits,   41
organs,   34-37, 82, 91
orientation,   71
ornithology,   8-13, 18, 23-24, 26-28,
    31, 33, 70, 79, 82-83, 85-87, 90
orthopedic handicaps,   97
osmosis,   64
outdoor education,   7-14, 16-18,
    20-21, 23-28, 30-33, 41, 78, 82, 85-
    87, 90, 103-105
outer space,   38-39, 41-42
oxidation,   48
oxygen,   15-16, 34-35, 48
oxygen-carbon dioxide cycle,   15
oysters,   12
paddle wheels,   91
paints,   87
paleontologists,   14, 83
paleontology,   14, 39, 83
paper airplanes,   70, 76
parachutes,   70, 76
parallax,   40
parasites,   31
parents and science,   92, 94, 101
parks,   26, 103
patents,   85
patterns,   22, 25, 41, 43, 67-69,
    71-72, 77-78
peas,   22
pedagogy,   40, 50, 67-68, 79, 83-84,
    87-88, 91-98
peer pressure,   37
pendulums,   42, 55, 75, 77
percentages,   77
perception,   35, 37, 62
peripheral vision,   35, 37
permutations,   72
perspiration,   37
pests,   88
petroleum,   39
pets,   91
phases of the moon,   39, 43
photograms,   10, 26
physical conditioning,   36
physical facilities,   78, 96-97
physical handicaps,   16, 30, 45,
    50-51, 53, 66, 70, 75, 97

physical science,   10, 31, 44-78,
    81-94, 97-102, 104-106
physiology,   82
Piaget, Jean,   79, 93-97
pigments,   25, 46
pinhole viewer,   37
pinwheels,   66
pipes,   59
pitch,   45, 59
planetary motion,   38-39
planets,   38-39, 41-43
plankton,   15, 17
plant propagation,   19, 30
plantcrafts,   22
plants,   7-8, 10-33, 41-42, 44, 57,
    61-66, 68, 73-75, 77-79, 81-88, 90,
    103-106
plaque,   36, 91
plastics,   62
plate tectonics,   39, 82
playgrounds,   31
plumbing,   59
Pluto,   38, 41-42
poaching,   16
pods,   29
point of view,   40, 52, 55
poisons,   91
pollen,   12, 81
pollination,   10, 17-18
pollution,   15-16, 20, 35, 90-91
polyhedrons,   65
pond life,   14, 16, 24-26, 29
ponds,   10, 14, 22, 24-27, 32, 86-87
population distribution,   32
populations,   11, 21-22, 26-28,
    32-33, 63-65
porpoises,   28
potential energy,   48
powders,   90
precipitation,   41-43, 78
preconceptions,   93-95
predators,   9, 12-13, 18, 20-21, 24,
    26-27, 31-33, 85
prehistoric life,   9, 14, 83
preschool science,   86, 92, 94
preservatives,   86
prey,   9-10, 12-13, 18, 20-21, 24,
    26-27, 31-33, 85
primary colors,   50
primates,   8-9
principals,   96
printing,   72
prisms,   38, 50, 56
probability,   64-65, 69, 71-72, 74-75,
    78-79
probability and statistics,   60, 62,
    64-65, 72, 78-79
product testing,   60, 6366, 69, 71-72,
    77
projectors,   53
propellers,   51

proportion,   40, 65
propulsion,   70, 75
protective coloration,   20-22, 25,
    62-63, 85
proteins,   84, 89
psychomotor skills,   34
puddles,   27, 32
pulleys,   49, 54, 88, 91
pulse rate,   36
pumps,   59, 75, 86
pupa,   12, 20-21, 24
pupil performance,   93, 95-96
puzzles,   87-90
questioning techniques,   40, 83,
    95-98
raceways,   87
rain,   41-43, 78
rainbows,   38, 42, 50, 76, 87
rainforests,   28
ratios,   65, 69, 71, 74
rats,   8, 82
reaction time,   34
reactions,   44-45, 49-50, 61, 63,
    73-75, 77, 81
recipes,   85
reference books,   99-102
reflection,   50, 52, 54
reflexes,   34
refraction,   54
relativity,   40, 52, 55
relaxation exercises,   37
reproduction,   13, 21-22, 30, 77, 82,
    85, 88
reptiles,   13, 21, 32, 83
resistance,   66
respiration,   34-35, 82
respiratory system,   34-35
revolution,   41-42
rhythms,   44
ribs,   11
rivers,   13, 30
rockets,   42
rocks,   8, 17, 39, 41-42, 75, 92
rocky intertidal zones,   11
rodents,   8
roofs,   63
roots,   19, 21-22, 29-31, 90
rotation,   41-42
rotting logs,   17-18
rotting wood,   79
rust,   48, 61, 70
safety,   34-35, 37, 68, 71, 77-78, 91
safety guidelines,   68
salt,   46, 50, 54
salt water,   15, 20, 22
saltmarshes,   12, 32
sand,   42-43, 77
sand timers,   42
sandpaper,   42
sandpipers,   28
saturated solutions,   50, 53

Saturn,   38, 41-42
scale,   40, 65, 82
scale models,   72
scavenger hunts,   12, 14
scents,   33
scheduling,   78
school law,   97
science activity books,   81-91, 102
science and technology centers,   99
science fairs,   86-87, 92, 101
science projects,   86-87, 101
science trade books,   99-103
scientific models,   53
scientific theories,   53, 56
scripts,   100
seabirds,   27-28
seals,   28
seashore,   20, 28
seasons,   27, 31, 33, 41-42, 66-67,
    76, 83, 87, 92
seaweed,   11-13, 15, 17, 20
secondary colors,   50
secondary science methods,   32, 61,
    95, 98
sediment,   43
sedimentation,   43
seed dispersal,   7, 10, 28-29
seeds,   7, 10, 13, 16, 19, 21-22,
    24-25, 28-31, 44, 64, 73, 75, 77,
    81-82, 84, 88, 90, 92
self-concept,   37
self-esteem,   84
senses,   12, 18, 23, 31, 36, 62-63, 65,
    68, 70, 73-75, 77, 88, 91
sensory perception,   64
sequences,   10, 44, 51-52, 72, 77
serial ordering,   10, 44, 51-52, 72, 77
sextant,   39
shadows,   39-40, 42, 50, 73-74, 92
shapes,   10, 41, 44, 52, 57, 60, 63,
    67, 70-71, 73-74, 77
shellfish,   11-12, 15, 20, 26
shorebirds,   28
shrimp,   11
shrubs,   11, 23, 30, 83
sifting,   42
sight,   37, 88
simple machines,   48-49, 55, 63, 72,
    75, 85, 88, 91
sinking,   45, 48, 50, 56, 59, 75, 89
siphons,   86
size,   63, 73-74, 77
skeleton,   11, 35-36, 81-83, 91
skin,   37, 81-82, 88, 91
skulls,   11
sky,   38-43
slugs,   82
smell,   70, 86, 91
smoking,   37
snacks,   36
snails,   9, 24-26, 30, 83

snakes,   13, 83
snow,   43, 87
soap bubbles,   82
social science,   60-63, 65, 69, 71-72,
    77, 83
sociology,   60-62, 71
software,   100, 102, 104, 106
soil,   10, 19, 25, 29, 31, 39, 41-43,
    60, 74, 89
solar energy,   38, 47, 51, 61, 66, 68,
    87
solar system,   38-39, 41-42, 92
solids,   54, 56, 81
solstice,   39
solubility,   46
solutions,   44-46, 50, 53-54, 58-59,
    64, 90
sorrels,   24
sorting,   10, 42, 44, 52, 58, 62, 68
sound,   10, 12, 21, 36-37, 44-45, 54,
    57, 59, 64-65, 68, 73-75, 84-85, 88,
    90
sound waves,   57, 84
space,   38, 40, 76, 92
space food,   84
space science,   38, 41-42, 90, 106
spatial relationships,   10, 41, 44, 73,
    83, 92
species diversity,   16
spectroscopes,   38, 40
speed,   54, 57, 61, 75, 84, 89
spheres,   47, 56
spider webs,   10, 12, 21, 24
spiders,   8, 10, 12, 21, 24, 77
spores,   23, 87
sportfishing,   26
sports,   84
springs,   57, 75
squirrels,   18, 24, 33, 82
stability,   34
staff development,   96
staffing,   78
standardized tests,   96
star maps,   39
starch,   64
stars,   38-40, 42-43, 87, 90, 92
static electricity,   51, 87-88
statistics,   60, 62-65, 68, 71-72,
    77-78, 83
stems,   19, 29, 90
stimulus/response,   9
stomach,   84
story books,   102
streams,   17-18, 22, 27, 30, 32, 43,
    85-87
strength,   35-36, 57, 62, 70, 91
stress management,   37
structures,   57, 60, 63, 67, 89
study skills,   86
submerged plants,   24
summer,   41

sun,   38-40, 42, 47, 61, 66, 68, 73,
    77, 85, 87, 90
sun prints,   10, 26
sundials,   39, 73
sunlight,   68
surface area,   48, 67
surface tension,   45-46, 50, 76, 78,
    84, 89
surface-volume ratio,   49
survival,   18, 31, 85
suspensions,   54
swamps,   32, 86
symbiosis,   15
symmetry,   52-53, 55-56, 67, 71-74,
    84
tadpoles,   16, 77, 86
tangrams,   71
tapes,   100
taste,   36, 86, 88-89, 91
teacher education,   95, 101
teacher inservice,   78, 101
teaching strategies,   92-98
technology,   99, 101-106
teeth,   36, 82, 91
telegraphs,   51, 87
telescopes,   53
temperature,   14, 16-18, 23, 28, 33,
    37-41, 43, 45, 47-49, 55, 62, 64, 66,
    68, 70, 73-74, 84
tension,   57
terrariums,   15-17
testing,   93, 95-96
textbook publishers,   100
textbooks,   96-97, 102, 105
texture,   10, 42, 44, 60, 70, 73
thermodynamics,   47-48
thermometers,   18, 37, 41, 43, 47, 49,
    64, 66, 68, 70, 73, 84
thermoregulation,   37
three-dimensionality,   40
tides,   15, 20, 28
timber,   79
time,   39, 41-42, 61, 73, 75, 77
timers,   77
tin,   70
titration,   58
tongue,   91
tools,   70, 78
tooth decay,   36
topography,   32
tops,   75
touch,   88
towers,   57
toys,   56, 75, 101
tracks,   30, 83, 87
trade books,   97, 99-102
traffic safety,   3561, 71, 78
trails,   30
trains,   75
transcriptions,   100
translucence,   50

transparency,   50
transportation,   61, 70, 78
tree rings,   18
trees,   11, 18, 30-31, 33, 78-79,
   81-82, 90
tunicates,   32
tunnels,   57
two-dimensionality,   40
unit-pricing,   71
Uranus,   38, 41-42
urban ecology,   26, 82
variables,   28, 46, 56, 58, 64, 68,
   73-74, 96
vegetables,   30
velocity,   56-57
Venn diagrams,   41, 65
Venus,   38, 41-42
vertebrae,   11
vertebrates,   13, 24, 27, 70, 81, 86
vibration,   45, 54, 57, 59, 64, 75, 90
videodisks,   104
videos,   105
vines,   23
viscosity,   50
vision,   34, 37, 54, 68, 74, 84, 91
visual communication,   12
visual impairments,   16, 30, 45,
   50-51, 53, 66, 70, 75, 97, 133
vitamin C,   58
vitamins,   58, 84
volcanoes,   39
voltage,   66
volume,   48, 67, 70-71, 78, 89
wasp nests,   21
wasps,   21
water,   7, 9, 10-17, 22, 24-25, 27, 32,
   38, 40, 43, 45-50, 54, 56, 59, 64-66,
   68, 78, 81, 84, 88-91
water currents,   7, 38, 43
water cycle,   15, 40, 53, 78
water flow,   43, 46, 59, 89
water holes,   10, 14
water level,   59
water play,   89
water pollution,   78
water pressure,   59, 86
water striders,   9, 30
water treatment,   78
waterwheels,   91
waves,   15, 38, 43
weather,   31, 39-43, 61, 66-67, 73,
   76, 87
weather instruments,   40-41
webs,   8
weeds,   16, 82, 87
weight,   41-42, 44, 51, 53, 64, 70-71,
   77, 88
weight control,   36
wetlands,   32, 83
whales,   28
wheels,   54, 63, 70, 88, 91

whole number operations,   41, 71-72,
   76-77
wildflowers,   82-83, 85
wind,   25, 38, 40-41, 43, 47, 66, 91
windmills,   91
winter,   41, 67, 76
wires,   44, 46, 51, 60, 64, 87
women in science,   84, 94, 101,
   130-131, 133-134, 136
women's centers,   101
wood,   79
workshops,   94
worms,   10, 15, 17, 81, 87
yeast,   50, 85
zinc,   70
zoos,   9, 13, 103

## Title

3-2-1 Contact,   103
4mat and Science—Towards Wholeness in Science Education,   92
AAAS Science Book List, 1978-1986,   99
AAAS Science Book List for Children, 3rd Edition,   99
AAAS Science Education Directory 1988,   99
Action/Reaction,   34
Activities in the Life Sciences,   81
Adaptations,   7
Adventures Along the Spectrum,   38
Adventures with Atoms and Molecules: Chemistry Experiments for Young People,   81
Adventures with Atoms and Molecules: Chemistry Experiments for Young People, Book II,   81
Advertising,   60
All Around,   8
Amazing Mammals, Part I,   8
Amazing Mammals, Part II,   8
American Biology Teacher,   103
Animal Activity,   8
Animal Behavior,   8
Animal Defenses,   9
Animals in Action,   9
Animals in the Classroom: A Guide for Teachers,   9
Appraisal: Science Books for Young People,   103
Aquatic Animal Behavior,   9
Archi-Teacher: A Guide for Architecture in the Schools,   60
Art-to-Zoo,   103
ASTC Member Staff Directory (1988),   99
Astronomy,   38, 103
Astronomy Adventures,   38
Attribute Games and Problems,   60
Audubon Adventure,   103
Audubon Zoo Activity Books,   9
Backyard,   10
Balance in Movement,   34
Balloons and Gases,   44
Batteries and Bulbs,   44
Batteries and Bulbs II,   60
Beastly Neighbors: All About Wild Things in the City, or Why Earwigs Make Good Mothers,   82
Beginnings,   10, 44
Behavior of Mealworms,   10
Best Books for Children: Preschool Through the Middle Grades,   99
Best Little Planet Money Can Buy,   38

Best Science Books for Children,   100
Bicycle Transportation,   61
Bio-crafts,   10
Birds, Birds, Birds!,   11
Blood and Guts: A Working Guide to Your Own Insides,   82
Bones,   11
Book of Where,   82
Breakwaters and Bays,   11
Breathing Fitness,   34
Brine Shrimp,   11
Bubble-ology,   45
Bubbles,   82
Budding Twigs,   11
Burglar Alarm Design,   61
Butterflies,   12
Buzzing a Hive,   12
Campsite,   12
Candles,   82
Change: Stages 1 and 2 and Background,   61
Change: Stage 3,   61
Changes,   61
Characteristics of a Good Elementary Science Program (Parts A and B),   96
Chem Matters,   104
Chemical Reactions,   45
Chesapeake Bay,   12
Chickadee,   104
Child's Play,   12
Children and Plastics: Stages 1 and 2 and Background,   62
Classification Fun,   62
Classroom Computer Learning,   104
Classroom Design,   62
Classroom Management,   62
Clay Boats,   45
Coastal Plain River Curriculum,   13
Colored Solutions,   45
Colour,   62
Coloured Things: Stages 1 and 2,   63
COMETS Profiles. Career Oriented Modules to Explore Topics in Science, Volume I,   82
COMETS Science. Career Oriented Modules to Explore Topics in Science, Volume II,   83
Communication,   45
Communities,   13
Computing Teacher,   104
Connect,   104
Connections,   13
Constructions,   63
Consumer Health Decisions,   34
Consumer Research—Product Testing,   63
Convection: A Current Event,   38
COPES Teacher's Guide for Kindergarten/Grade One,   63

COPES Teacher's Guide for Grade Two,   64
COPES Teacher's Guide for Grade Three,   64
COPES Teacher's Guide for Grade Four,   64
COPES Teacher's Guide for Grade Five,   64
COPES Teacher's Guide for Grade Six,   65
Crayfish,   14
Crime Lab Chemistry,   46
Curious Naturalist,   83
Daytime Astronomy,   39
Describing People,   65
Desert,   14
Designing for Human Proportions,   65
Dice Design,   65
Digging into Dinosaurs,   14
Dinosaurs: A Journey Through Time,   83
Discovering Density,   46
Discovering Deserts,   14
Diving into Oceans,   15
Down to Earth: Solutions for Math + Science,   39
Drops, Streams, and Containers,   46
Early Childhood and Science,   92
Early Experiences,   65
Earth,   39
Earth, Moon, and Stars,   39
Earthworms,   15
Ecosystems,   15-16
Educators Guide to Free Science Materials,   100
Eggs & Tadpoles,   16
Elaborations: Science Labs for Intermediate Students,   83
Electric Circuits,   46
Electric Company,   104
Electricity,   46
Electromagnet Device Design,   66
Electronic Learning,   104
Elementary School Science and How to Teach It,   92
Elementary Science Methods,   93
Endangered Species: Wild & Rare,   16
Energy,   47
Energy Sources,   47
Energy Transfer,   48
Environmental Energy,   66
Environmental Health and Safety,   35
Environments,   16-17
Estuarine Biology,   17
Everyday Science Sourcebook: Ideas for Teaching in the Elementary and Middle School,   83

Expanding Children's Thinking Through Science: CESI Sourcebook II,  84

Explorations & Investigations: Science for Primary Students,  84

Exploratorium Quarterly,  104

Faces,  104

Fall into Math and Science,  66

Fingerprinting,  66

Flexibility and Strength,  35

Floaters and Sinkers: Solutions for Math and Science,  48

Flowers and Pollination,  17

Foodworks: Over 100 Science Activities and Fascinating Facts That Explore the Magic of Food,  84

For 8-to-11-Year-Olds,  17

For Large Groups,  18

For Small Groups & Families,  18

Forest,  18

From Head to Toe: Respiratory, Circulatory, and Skeletal Systems,  35

Fun with Foods: A Recipe for Math + Science,  67

Fun with Physics,  84

Games and Simulations,  18

Gases and "Airs,"  48

Gee Wiz!,  84

Geo Blocks,  67

Geology: The Active Earth,  39

Glide into Winter with Math and Science,  67

Grow Lab: A Complete Guide to Gardening in the Classroom,  19

Growing Classroom,  19

Growing Plants,  19

Growing Seeds,  19

Growth Trends,  35

Guide and Index,  67

Habitats,  19

Hands-on Nature: Information and Activities for Exploring the Environment with Children,  85

Hard Hatting in a Geo-world,  67

Have You Been to the Shore Before?,  20

"The Having of Wonderful Ideas" and Other Essays on Teaching and Learning,  93

Heart Fitness,  36

Heat,  48

Heating and Cooling,  48

Hide a Butterfly,  20

Holes, Gaps and Cavities: Stages 1 and 2,  68

Hot Water and Warm Homes from Sunlight,  68

Human Impact,  20

Ice Cubes,  49

Idea Factory's Super Science Sourcebook,  85

Incredible Insects,  20

Incredible Insects (Discovery Pac),  20

Insects and Other Crawlers,  21

Interaction and Systems,  49

International Wildlife,  105

Interstellar Jones in Question the Answers,  40

Introduction and Guide to Teaching Primary Science,  93

Invention Book,  85

Investigate and Discover: Elementary Science Lessons,  85

Jaw Breakers and Heart Thumpers,  36

Kitchen Interactions,  50

Kitchen Physics,  50

Lawns and Fields,  21

Learning by Doing: A Manual for Teaching and Assessing Higher-order Thinking in Science and Mathematics,  93

Learning Cycle and Elementary School Science Teaching,  94

Learning in Science: The Implications of Children's Science,  94

Let's Hear It for Herps!,  21

Life Cycles,  21-22

Life of Beans and Peas,  22

Light and Color,  50

Light and Shadows,  40

Light, Color, and Shadows,  50

Like and Unlike: Stages 1, 2, and 3,  68

Liquid Explorations,  50

Living in Water,  22

Lunch Lines,  68

Magic of Electricity: A School Assembly Program Presenter's Guide,  51

Magnetism and Electricity,  51

Magnetism/Electric Models,  51

Making Do with Plants,  22

Management Guide,  68

Manufacturing,  69

Mapping,  40

Mapping Animal Movements,  22

Mapping Fish Habitats,  23

Match and Measure,  69

Material Objects,  51-52

Materials,  69

Math + Science, A Solution,  69

Mathematics and Science: Critical Filters for the Future of Minority Students,  94

Measurement,  70

Measurement, Motion and Change,  40, 52

Messing Around with Baking Chemistry,  85

Messing Around with Water Pumps and Siphons,  86

Metals: Background Information,  70

Metals: Stages 1 and 2,  70

Meteorology,  40

Microgardening, An Introduction to the World of Mold,  23

Minibeasts: Stages 1 and 2,  23

Mirror Cards,  52

Mixtures and Solutions,  53

Mobiles,  53

Modeling Systems,  53

Models: Electric and Magnetic Interactions,  53

More Science Experiments You Can Eat,  86

More Than Magnifiers,  53

Mosquitoes: A Resource Book for the Classroom,  23

Moving Around,  54

Museum of Science and Industry Basic List of Children's Science Books 1973-1984,  100

Museum of Science and Industry Basic List of Children's Science Books 1986 and 1987,  100

Museums, Magic & Children: Youth Education in Museums,  94

Musical Instrument Recipe Book,  54

Mystery Boxes,  70

Mystery Powders,  54

National Geographic World,  105

National Wildlife,  105

Nature Activities for Early Childhood,  86

Nature of Science,  94

Nature with Children of All Ages,  86

Neighborhood Woods,  23

Nighttime,  24

NSTA Supplement of Science Education Suppliers 1988,  100

Nutrition/Dental Health,  36

Nuts and Bolts: A Matter of Fact Guide to Science Fair Projects,  86

OBIS Lawn Guide,  24

OBIS Pond Guide,  24

OBIS Sampler,  24

Oceanus,  105

Odyssey,  105

On the Move,  70

Oobleck: What Scientists Do,  54

Optics,  54

Organisms,  24-25

Orientation,  71

Our Wonderful World: Solutions for Math + Science,  25

Ourselves,  36

Ourselves: Stages 1 and 2,  37

Out of Doors,  41

Out of This World,  41

Outdoor Areas as Learning Laboratories: CESI Sourcebook,  87
Outdoor Study Techniques,  25
Outstanding Science Trade Books for Children in 1987,  101
Overhead and Underfoot,  41
Owl,  105
Paints and Materials,  87
Paper Towel Testing,  71
Pattern Blocks,  71
Pavement and Parks,  26
Peas and Particles,  71
Pedestrian Crossings,  71
Pendulums,  55
People and the Sea,  26
Personal Health Decisions,  37
Pieces and Patterns: A Patchwork in Math and Science,  72
Planning Scientific Investigations at Age 11 (Science Report for Teachers: 8),  95
Play Area Design and Use,  72
Pond Water,  26
Ponds and Lakes,  26
Popping with Power,  55
Populations,  26-27
Practical Testing at Ages 11, 13, and 15 (Science Report for Teachers: 6),  95
Primarily Bears, Book 1: A Collection of Elementary Activities,  72
Primary Balancing,  55
Primary Science...Taking the Plunge,  95
Principal's Role in Elementary School Science,  96
Printing,  72
Project Seasons: Seasonal Teaching Ideas K-6,  27
Project WILD Aquatic Education Activity Guide,  27
Project WILD Elementary Activity Guide,  27
Projects: The World of Science,  87
Pupil as Scientist?,  95
Quadice,  72
Raceways: Having Fun with Balls and Tracks,  87
Rainforests,  28
Ranger Rick,  105
Reasons for Seasons,  41, 87
Relative Position and Motion,  55
Resources for Educational Equity 1988,  101
Rocks and Charts,  41
Rocks, Sand, and Soil,  42
Safe and Simple Electrical Experiments,  87
Sand,  42
School Zoo,  28
Schoolyard,  28

Science 5-16: A Statement of Policy,  95
Science and Children,  105
Science—A Process Approach, Part A,  73
Science—A Process Approach, Part B,  73
Science—A Process Approach, Part C,  73
Science—A Process Approach, Part D,  73
Science—A Process Approach, Part E,  73
Science—A Process Approach, Part F,  74
Science—A Process Approach, Part G,  74
Science...A Process Approach II, Level K,  74
Science...A Process Approach II, Level 1,  74
Science...A Process Approach II, Level 2,  74
Science...A Process Approach II, Level 3,  74
Science...A Process Approach II, Level 4,  75
Science...A Process Approach II, Level 5,  75
Science...A Process Approach II, Level 6,  75
Science Around the House,  88
Science at Age 11 (Science Report for Teachers: 1),  96
Science Book,  88
Science Books & Films,  105
Science Books for Children: Selections from Booklist, 1976-1983,  101
Science Education (ORYX Science Bibliographies, Volume 6),  101
Science Experiences for Preschoolers: CESI Sourcebook IV,  88
Science Experiences for the Early Childhood Years,  88
Science Experiments,  88
Science Experiments You Can Eat,  89
Science Fare,  101
Science from Toys: Stages 1 and 2 and Background,  75
Science from Water Play,  89
Science Fun with Mud and Dirt,  89
Science Helper K-8,  102
Science in Schools: Age 11 (Research Report: 4),  96
Science Magic Tricks,  89
Science, Models and Toys: Stage 3,  56
Science News,  105
Science on a Shoestring,  89

Science Scope,  106
Science Teacher,  106
Science Teaches Basic Skills,  96
Science Weekly,  106
Science with Children,  96
Scienceland,  106
Scienceworks,  89
Sciencing,  97
Scientific Reasoning,  75
Scientific Theories,  56
Seals, Spouts, and Sandpipers,  28
Seashore,  28
Seasoning Math and Science: Fall & Winter,  76
Seasoning Math & Science: Spring & Summer,  76
Secret of the Cardboard Rocket,  42
Seeds,  29
Seeds and Seedlings,  90
Seeds and Weeds,  29
Seeds on Safari,  29
Senior Balancing,  56
Sight and Sound,  37
Sink or Float,  56
Skin Temperature,  37
Sky and Space,  42
Sky Pirates,  42
The Sky's the Limit! With Math and Science,  76
Small Things: An Introduction to the Microscopic World,  29
Soft Drink Design,  76
Solids, Liquids, and Gases: A School Assembly Program Presenter's Guide,  56
Sound,  57
Sourcebook: Science Education and the Physically Handicapped,  97
Spinning Tables,  57
Spring into Math and Science,  76
Starting from Seeds,  29
Stream Tables,  43
Streams and Rivers,  30
Structures,  57
Structures and Forces: Stages 1 and 2,  57
Structures and Forces: Stage 3,  57
Structures of Life,  30
Subsystems and Variables,  58
Super Science Activities: Favorite Lessons from Master Teachers,  90
Tangrams,  77
Teaching and Computers,  106
Teaching Elementary School Science: A Laboratory Approach,  97
Teaching Modern Science,  97
Teaching Science as Continuous Inquiry: A Basic,  98
Teaching Science Through Discovery,  98

Teaching Science to Children: A Resourcebook,   102

Teaching Science with Everyday Things,   90

TESS (The Educational Software Selector),   102

Think About It! Science Problems of the Day,   90

Time, Growth and Change,   77

Time: Stages 1 and 2 and Background,   77

Towards a Science of Science Teaching: Cognitive Development and Curriculum Demand,   98

Tracks,   30

Traffic Flow,   77

Trail,   30

Treemendous Activities for Young Learners,   90

Trees Are Terrific!,   30

Trees: Stages 1 and 2,   31

Unconventional Invention Book,   91

Understanding the Healthy Body: CESI Sourcebook III,   91

Universe in the Classroom,   106

Urban Gardening,   31

Using the Environment 1: Early Explorations,   31

Using the Environment 2: Investigations, Part 1,   77

Using the Environment 2: Investigations, Part 2,   31

Using the Environment 3: Tackling Problems, Part 1,   31

Using the Environment 3: Tackling Problems, Part 2,   32

Using the Environment 4: Ways and Means,   32

USMES Design Lab Manual,   78

USMES Guide,   78

Vitamin C Testing,   58

Wading into Wetlands,   32

Water and Ice,   59

Water Flow,   59

Water Precious Water, Book A,   78

Water World,   32

Ways to Learn/Teach,   78

Weather Predictions,   43

Western New York Freshwater Ecology Study Guide,   32

What Research Says About Elementary School Science,   96

Wheels at Work: Building and Experimenting with Models of Machines,   91

Where Is the Moon?,   43

Which and What?,   78

Whistles and Strings,   59

Wild About Weather,   43

Wintertime,   33

With Objectives in Mind,   79

Wonderscience,   106

Working with Wood: Background Information,   79

Working with Wood: Stages 1 and 2,   79

Your Big Backyard,   106

Your Neighbors: The Trees,   33

Zoobooks,   107

## Author/Project

Activities to Integrate Mathematics and Science (AIMS),   25, 35-36, 39, 41, 48, 55, 66-67, 69, 72, 76, 78, 138
Adair, Robin,   66-67, 76
Adair, Stan,   76
Adey, Philip,   98
Agler, Leigh,   50
Ahouse, Jeremy John,   66
Aicken, Frederick,   94
AIMS,   See Activities to Integrate Mathematics and Science
AIMS Education Foundation,   138
Akers, Art,   35
Albright, Janis,   28
Alfving, Alberta M.,   67
Allen, Gwen,   78
Allen, Maureen,   72, 78
Allison, Linda,   82, 84, 87
Amburgey, Leonard L.,   13, 15, 17, 21, 25, 27, 40, 47, 49, 52-53, 58
American Association for the Advancement of Science (AAAS),   73-75, 144
Appel, Gary,   19, 142
Aquarium of Niagara Falls,   32
Aspinwall, Karen,   22
Assessment of Performance Unit,   95-96
Audubon Park and Zoological Garden,   9
Barber, Jacqueline,   45-46, 56, 58, 71
Barker, Bill,   76
Barrett, Katharine,   9, 22-23
Beakes, Norris,   25
Beane, DeAnna Banks,   94
Beattie, Rob,   90
Beck, Janet,   25
Bell, Neill,   82
Berdugo, Aviva,   72
Berger, Carl F.,   47, 53, 55, 58
Biological Sciences Curriculum Study (BSCS),   145
Bird, John,   82, 89
Bird, Mary D.,   28
Black, Paul,   96
Blackmer, Marilyn,   83, 85
Bland, Carol,   41, 55
Blough, Glenn O.,   92
Bodourian, Marilyn,   139
Brady, Charles,   87
Bredt, Diane,   90
Brookfield Zoo,   13
Brummett, Micaelia R.,   68
BSCS,   See Biological Sciences Curriculum Study
Buegler, Marion E.,   46

Buller, Dave,   24
Buller, David,   34-37
Bunshoft, Sylvia,   53, 58
Bybee, Rodger,   145
Cadoux, Margaret,   19
Cain, Sandra E.,   97
Calvert Marine Museum,   17
Campbell, Lee Anne,   22
Campopiano, John,   69
Caney, Steven,   85
Carin, Arthur A.,   97-98
Carter, Lynne,   34-37
CEPUP,   See Chemical Education for Public Understanding
Challand, Helen J.,   81
Chapman, Victoria,   145
Chase, Valerie,   22
Chemical Education for Public Understanding (CEPUP),   138
Children's Book Council (CBC),   101
Cobb, Vicki,   86, 89
Collea, Francis,   13, 15, 17, 21, 25, 27, 40, 47, 49, 52-53, 58
Collis, Margaret,   8, 31-32, 41, 67, 77
Conard, David,   15-16, 21, 26
Conceptually Oriented Program in Elementary Science (COPES),   63-65, 138
Conservation for Children,   139
Contant, Terry,   145
Cooper, Richard,   13, 15, 17, 21, 25, 27, 40, 47, 49, 52-53, 58
COPES,   See Conceptually Oriented Program in Elementary Science
Cornell Plantations,   141
Cossey, Ruth,   72
Council for Elementary Science, International (CESI),   84, 87-88, 91
Courtney, Barry,   36, 41, 67
Crossley, Helen,   36, 55, 67
Deal, Debby,   78
Department of Education and Science,   95
Deruiter, Henry Richard,   25
Dewey, John,   25
Diamond, Dorothy,   82, 90, 93
Dixon, Susan,   36, 41, 55, 67
Donev, Mary,   84
Donev, Stef,   84
Driver, Rosalind,   95
Duckworth, Eleanor,   93
Dumdie, Laura,   142
Dupree, Lois,   35
Echols, Jean C.,   9, 12, 20
EDC,   See Education Development Center
Education Development Center, Inc. (EDC),   139-140, 146
Educational Products Information Exchange (EPIE),   102
Eitzen, C. Lloyd,   67

Elementary Science Study (ESS),   8-12, 14-16, 19, 22-23, 26, 29-30, 39-43, 44-46, 48-50, 52-57, 59, 60-61, 67, 69, 71-72, 77, 139
Elstgeest, Jos,   95
Ennever, Len,   79, 143
Erickson, Sheldon,   39
ESS,   See Elementary Science Study
Evans, Jack M.,   97
Ewing, Jill,   66-67, 76
Faircloth, Shirley,   66-67, 76
Falk, John,   24
FAST,   See Foundational Approaches in Science Teaching
Faulds, Ann,   28
Fletcher, Sandra,   21, 24
Florida State University,   145
FOSS,   See Full Option Science System
Foundational Approaches in Science Teaching (FAST),   139
Franklin Institute Museum-To-Go,   15, 38, 40, 46-48, 50-51, 57
Fredericks, Anthony D.,   90
Freeman, Thomas L.,   25
Freyberg, Peter,   94
Full Option Science System (FOSS),   139
Gardner, Robert,   88
GEMS,   See Great Explorations in Math and Science
Ginocchio, Cherie,   76
Gipsman, Sandra,   34-37
Glasser, Daneen,   72
Glick, Lisa,   19, 142
Gold, Carol,   84
Gould, Alan,   38, 51, 68
Graeber, Janet,   90
Graf, Rudolph F.,   87
Great Explorations in Math and Science (GEMS),   9, 12, 20, 22-23, 38-39, 45-46, 50-51, 53-54, 56, 58, 66, 68, 71-72, 140
Greco, Jim,   35
Green, Bea,   84
Greene, Sean,   55
Gregg, David,   39
Griffith, Joe H.,   144
Haggard, Ruth,   76
Hale, Jack,   19
Hammond, Bill,   92
Hands-On Elementary Science,   140
Hansen Planetarium,   38, 40, 42
HAP,   See Health Activities Project
Haracz, Geraldine,   67
Harlan, Jean,   88
Harlen, Wynne,   79, 95-96
Health Activities Project (HAP),   34-37, 140
Helling, Frank,   39
Henson, Kenneth T.,   93

Herrera, Sharon,   10, 44
Hill, Loretta,   36, 41, 55, 67
Hillen, Judith A.,   69, 72
Hofman, Helenmarie H.,   97
Holve, Helen,   67
Hood College,   140
Horn, Mary,   62
House, Kathleen,   36, 41
Houston Museum of Natural Science,   145
Hyman, Joanne,   67
Iatridis, Mary D.,   102
Improving Urban Elementary Science (IUES),   140
Informal Science Study (ISS),   140
ISS,   See Informal Science Study
IUES,   See Improving Urban Elementary Science
Ivans, Dennis,   76
Jacobson, Mark,   34-37
Jaffe, Roberta M.,   19, 142
James, Albert,   57, 68
Janke, Delmar,   93
Jarvis, Seth,   40
Jelly, Sheila,   95
Jenkins, Sherry,   76
John Muir Elementary School,   139
Jones, Howard,   140
Jones, Susan,   72
Kahn, Gale,   78
Karplus, Robert,   10, 13, 16-17, 22, 25, 27, 44, 47, 49, 52-53, 55-56, 58, 72, 145
Katz, David,   84
Khaligh, Nasrin,   96
Kincaid, Doug,   8, 36, 39, 41-42, 46, 54, 62, 67, 69-70, 77
King, Morris W.,   39
Kinnear, John,   69
Knecht, Pam,   41
Knott, Robert C.,   10, 13, 15-17, 22, 25-27, 44, 47, 49, 52, 55-56, 58, 140, 143
Knowledge Utilization Project in Science (KUPS),   102, 141
KUPS,   See Knowledge Utilization Project in Science
Laidlaw, Walt,   48, 69
Lakeview Museum Planetarium,   143
Landon, Kathleen,   48
Lanier, Mary Ann,   13, 15, 26
Lawrence Hall of Science,   138-140, 143-145
Lawson, Chester A.,   10, 13, 15-17, 21-22, 24-27, 44, 47, 49, 52, 55-56, 58
LEAP,   See Learning About Plants
Learning About Plants (LEAP),   141
Learning Labs,   141

Learning Through Science,   8, 36, 39, 41-42, 46, 54, 62, 67, 69-70, 77-78, 142
Lee, Ed,   141
Lee, Rhona,   34-37
The Life Lab Science Program,   142
Lile, David,   48
Lind, Mary,   41
Lingelbach, Jenepher,   85
Lowery, Lawrence F.,   83, 139
Lyford, Jean,   90
Manomet Bird Observatory,   28
Marek, Edmund A.,   94
Marine Science Center,   142
Marine Science Project: FOR SEA,   142
Marine World Africa USA,   19, 28
Martinez, Jacinta,   90
Massachusetts Audubon Society,   83, 86
Matthews, Catherine L.,   83
Maxwell, Donald E.,   13, 15, 17, 21, 25, 27, 40, 47, 49, 52-53, 58
Mayor, John,   144
McCarthy, Bernice,   92
McConnell, Pat,   72
McDonald, Ed,   86
McGrath, Susan,   84
McIntyre, Margaret,   92
McKibban, Mike,   48
Mebane, Robert C.,   81
Mechling, Kenneth R.,   96
Missouri Botanical Garden,   41
Missouri Botanical Garden (Suitcase Science),   17, 22, 29, 31, 33, 62, 70
Mitchell, John,   83
Molitor, Loretta L.,   83
Montgomery, Marshall A.,   10, 13, 16-17, 22, 25, 27, 44, 47, 49, 52, 55-56, 58
National Aquarium in Baltimore,   22
National Assessment of Educational Progress (NAEP),   93
National Gardening Association,   19
National Geographic Kids Network,   142
National Learning Center,   141
National Science Resources Center (NSRC),   144
National Science Teachers Association (NSTA),   100, 101
Nelson, Bess J.,   83
Nelson, Philip,   67
New York University,   138
Newman, Alan R.,   101
Newton, Nancy,   76
Nichols, Martha,   22
Nickelsburg, Janet,   86
Nikoghosian, Janice,   66-67, 76
Noffsinger, Joe,   40

Northern New England Marine Education Project,   20
Noyce, Ruth (editor),   82
NSTA,   See National Science Teachers Association
OBIS,   See Outdoor Biology Instructional Strategies
Oliver, Donna L.,   96
Olsen, Gary L.,   60
Olsen, Michelle J.,   60
Olson, Betsy,   76
Ontario Science Centre,   84, 89
Osborne, Roger,   94-95
Oshita, Steven,   90
Outdoor Biology Instructional Strategies (OBIS),   7-12, 14, 17-18, 20-21, 23-26, 28, 30, 33, 143
Owen, Steve,   35
Palacio, David,   96
Paldy, Lester G.,   13, 15, 17, 21, 25, 27, 40, 47, 49, 52-53, 58, 145
Parker, Sheila,   23, 31, 63, 79
Pasley, Ann,   35
Patron, Rose Lee,   67
Peterson, Cynthia,   66-67, 76
Peterson, Gordon E.,   15
Pitman-Gelles, Bonnie,   94
Pranis, Eve,   19
Project for Promoting Science Among Elementary School Principals,   96
Project STARWALK,   143
Project WILD,   27
Radford, Don,   56, 61, 70, 75
Randle, Joan Coffman,   47, 49, 51, 53, 55
Ranger Rick's NatureScope,   8, 11, 14-16, 20-21, 30, 32, 38-39, 43
Rawitscher-Kunkel, Erika,   24
Rayfield, Helen,   41, 55
Renner, John W.,   94
Rice, Nancy,   69
Richards, Roy,   36-37, 39, 42, 46, 54, 62, 65, 67-70, 77-78, 142
Richter, Bernice,   100
Ricker, Kenneth S.,   97
Riddle, Bob,   143
Rights, Mollie,   82
Riley, Joseph W.,   13, 15, 17, 21, 25, 27, 40, 47, 49, 52-53, 58
Roberts-Worley, Wendy,   76
Rockcastle, Verne N.,   90
Rogers, George,   35
Rojas, Yolanda,   35
Rose, Mary,   90
Rowe, Mary Budd,   98, 141, 145
Rudig, Anne,   36, 41, 55
Russell, Terry,   96
Rybolt, Thomas R.,   81
Samples, Bob,   92
Sandler, Judith,   140

SAPA, See Science—A Process
 Approach
Saul, Wendy, 101
SAVI/SELPH, See Science Ac-
 tivities for the Visually Impaired/
 Science Enrichment for Learners
 with Physical Handicaps
Scharer, Jane, 146
Schatz, Dennis, 83
Schlichting, Sandi, 83-85
Schmidt, Victor E., 90
Schneider, Livingston, 34-37
Schofield, Beta, 95
Scholastic, Inc., 145
School Curriculum Development
 Committee, 142
Schools Council, 143
Schroeder, Eileen E., 101
Schwartz, Julius, 92
Science 5/13, 23, 31-32, 37, 56-57,
 61-63, 65, 68, 70, 75, 77, 79, 143
Science Activities for the Visually
 Impaired/Science Enrichment for
 Learners with Physical Handicaps
 (SAVI/SELPH), 16, 30, 45, 50-51,
 53, 66, 70, 75, 144
Science and Technology for Children
 (STC), 144
Science—A Process Approach
 (SAPA/SAPA II), 144
The Science Connection, 145
Science Curriculum Improvement
 Study (SCIS), 10, 13, 15-16, 21,
 24, 26, 44, 47, 49, 51, 53, 55, 58, 145
Science Curriculum Improvement
 Study (SCIS II), 13, 15, 17, 21, 25,
 27, 40, 47, 49, 52-53, 58, 145
Science Curriculum Improvement
 Study (SCIIS/85), 10, 13, 16-17,
 22, 25, 27, 44, 47, 49, 52, 55-56, 58,
 145
Science for Life and Living: Integrat-
 ing Science, Technology, and
 Health, 145
SCIS, SCIS II, SCIIS/85, See
 Science Curriculum Improvement
 Study
Sconiers, Zachary, 76
Scotchmoor, Judith, 90
Seaborg, Glenn T., 140
Self Help Elementary Level Science
 (SHELLS), 145
Shalit, Nathan, 89
Shattuck, Julie, 141
Shayer, Michael, 98
Sheehan, Charlyn, 13, 15-16
SHELLS, See Self Help Elementary
 Level Science
Shennan, Bill, 76
Sipkovich, Vincent, 78
Sisson, Edith A., 86

Smith, Darlene, 66-67, 76
Smith, Ellyn, 85
Smith, Walter L., 83
Sneider, Cary I., 23, 39, 51, 53-54,
 71
Stage, Elizabeth, 72
Stanish, Bob, 91
Starkweather, Jeri, 39
STC, See Science and Technology
 for Children
Stein, Sara, 88
Stewardship Institute, 27
Stewart, James, 146
Strongin, Herb, 89
Sumners, Carolyn, 145
Sund, Robert B., 85, 97-98
Super Science: A Mass Media
 Program, 145
Symington, David, 95
Taylor, Glenn, 40
Taylor, Ron, 87
Technical Education Research
 Centers, Inc. (TERC), 142
TERC, See Technical Education
 Research Centers, Inc.
Terman, Dorothy, 78
Thier, Herbert D., 10, 13, 16-17, 22,
 25, 27, 44, 47, 49, 51-52, 55-56, 58,
 72, 97, 138, 144-145
Tillery, Bill W., 85
Tillett, Martin, 22
Tinker, Robert F., 142
Trojcak, Doris A., 96
Trowbridge, Leslie W., 85
Unified Science and Mathematics for
 Elementary Schools (USMES), 19,
 28, 43, 60-63, 65-66, 68-69, 71-72,
 76-78, 146
University of Florida, 141
University of Hawaii, 139
University of Houston, 140
University of Wisconsin–Madison,
 146
USMES, See Unified Science and
 Mathematics for Elementary Schools
Van Deman, Barry A., 86
Virginia Marine Science Museum,
 12-13, 26, 32
Webb, Sylvester, 47
Webster, Vera R., 88
Welford, Geoff, 95
Welmers, Marney, 76
Welsh Office, 95
Wentz, Budd, 51
Wenzel, Duane, 100
Westly, Joan, 21, 29, 42, 50, 59, 63
Wiebe, Ann, 36, 41, 67
Wiebe, Arthur, 138
Wiebe, Sheila, 66-67, 77
Wiens, Gina, 36, 41, 55
Wight, Tom, 90

Williams, Ana, 41
Williams, Coe, 146
Williams, Nancy, 36, 41, 55, 67
Williams, Paul, 146
Wisconsin Fast Plants, 146
Women's Educational Equity Act
 Publishing Center, 101
Wood, Dean A., 140
Worth, Karen, 140
Wyler, Rose, 89
Young, Donald B., 139
Zahlis, Karen, 69
Zubrowski, Bernie, 82, 85-87, 91

# Grade Level

**Preschool**
Life Science,   12, 20, 29
Earth Science,   41
Multidisciplinary and Applied
  Science,   62, 70
Activity Books,   82, 86-90
Magazines,   106

**Kindergarten**
Life Science,   8-16, 19-21, 23,
  27-32
Health and Human Biology,   36-37
Earth Science,   38-43
Physical Science,   44, 50, 52-55, 59
Multidisciplinary and Applied
  Science,   60, 62-63, 65-77
Activity Books,   82-91
Magazines,   104, 106-107

**Grade 1**
Life Science,   8-16, 19-25, 27-32
Health and Human Biology,   36-37
Earth Science,   38-43
Physical Science,   44, 50-57, 59
Multidisciplinary and Applied
  Science,   60-63, 65-77
Activity Books,   82-91
Magazines,   104-107

**Grade 2**
Life Science,   8-9, 11-16, 19-23,
  27-32
Health and Human Biology,   36-37
Earth Science,   38-43
Physical Science,   49-50, 52-57, 59
Multidisciplinary and Applied
  Science,   60-65, 67-78
Activity Books,   82-91
Magazines,   104-107

**Grade 3**
Life Science,   8-9, 11-17, 19-23,
  26-32
Health and Human Biology,   36-37
Earth Science,   38-43
Physical Science,   45-46, 49-59
Multidisciplinary and Applied
  Science,   60-79
Activity Books,   82-91
Magazines,   103-107

**Grade 4**
Life Science,   7-33
Health and Human Biology,   34-37
Earth Science,   38-43
Physical Science,   44-59

Multidisciplinary and Applied
  Science,   60-79
Activity Books,   81-91
Magazines,   103-107

**Grade 5**
Life Science,   7-33
Health and Human Biology,   34-37
Earth Science,   38-43
Physical Science,   44-59
Multidisciplinary and Applied
  Science,   60-79
Activity Books,   81-91
Magazines,   103-107

**Grade 6**
Life Science,   7-12, 14-33
Health and Human Biology,   34-37
Earth Science,   38-43
Physical Science,   44-48, 50-59
Multidisciplinary and Applied
  Science,   60-79
Activity Books,   81-91
Magazines,   103-106

**Grade 7**
Life Science,   7-12, 14, 16-28,
  30-33
Health and Human Biology,   34-37
Earth Science,   38-41, 43
Physical Science,   44-46, 48, 50-51,
  53-54, 56-58
Multidisciplinary and Applied
  Science,   60-72, 74-78
Activity Books,   81-91
Magazines,   103-106

**Grade 8**
Life Science,   7-12, 14, 17-21,
  23-28, 30-33
Health and Human Biology,   34-37
Earth Science,   38-41, 43
Physical Science,   44-46, 48, 50,
  53, 56-57
Multidisciplinary and Applied
  Science,   60-63, 65-72, 74, 76-78
Activity Books,   81-91
Magazines,   103-106

**Grade 9**
Life Science,   9, 19-20, 28, 31-32
Earth Science,   38-39, 41
Multidisciplinary and Applied
  Science,   60-61, 72
Physical Science,   45, 50, 56
Activity Books,   81-84, 87, 90-91
Magazines,   103-105

**Grade 10-12**
Life Science,   9, 19, 28
Earth Science,   38-39

Physical Science,   45
Multidisciplinary and Applied
  Science,   61
Activity Books,   84, 87, 91
Magazines,   104-105

## Grade Level by Category

**Life Science**
Preschool,   12, 20, 29
Kindergarten,   8-16, 19-21, 23, 27-32
Grade 1,   8-16, 19-25, 27-32
Grade 2,   8-9, 11-16, 19-23, 27-32
Grade 3,   8-9, 11-17, 19-23, 26-32
Grade 4,   7-33
Grade 5,   7-33
Grade 6,   7-12, 14-33
Grade 7,   7-12, 14, 16-28, 30-33
Grade 8,   7-12, 14, 17-21, 23-28, 30-33
Grade 9,   9, 19-20, 28, 31-32
Grade 10-12,   9, 19, 28

**Health and Human Biology**
Kindergarten,   36-37
Grade 1,   36-37
Grade 2,   36-37
Grade 3,   36-37
Grade 4,   34-37
Grade 5,   34-37
Grade 6,   34-37
Grade 7,   34-37
Grade 8,   34-37

**Earth Science**
Preschool,   41
Kindergarten,   38-43
Grade 1,   38-43
Grade 2,   38-43
Grade 3,   38-43
Grade 4,   38-43
Grade 5,   38-43
Grade 6,   38-43
Grade 7,   38-41, 43
Grade 8,   38-41, 43
Grade 9,   38, 41
Grade 10-12,   38-39

**Physical Science**
Kindergarten,   44, 50, 52-55, 59
Grade 1,   44, 50-57, 59
Grade 2,   49-50, 52-57, 59
Grade 3,   45-46, 49-59
Grade 4,   44-59
Grade 5,   44-59
Grade 6,   44-48, 50-59
Grade 7,   44-46, 48, 50-51, 53-54, 56-58
Grade 8,   44-46, 48, 50, 53, 56-57
Grade 9,   45, 50, 56
Grade 10-12,   45

**Multidisciplinary and Applied Science**
Preschool,   62, 70
Kindergarten,   60, 62-63, 65-77
Grade 1,   60-63, 65-77
Grade 2,   60-65, 67-78
Grade 3,   60-79
Grade 4,   60-79
Grade 5,   60-79
Grade 6,   60-79
Grade 7,   60-72, 74-78
Grade 8,   60-63, 65-72, 74, 76-78
Grade 9,   60-61, 72
Grade 10-12,   61

**Activity Books**
Preschool,   82, 86-90
Kindergarten,   82-91
Grade 1,   82-91
Grade 2,   82-91
Grade 3,   82-91
Grade 4,   81-91
Grade 5,   81-91
Grade 6,   81-91
Grade 7,   81-91
Grade 8,   81-91
Grade 9,   81-84, 87, 90-91
Grade 10-12,   84, 87, 91

**Magazines**
Preschool,   106
Kindergarten,   104, 106-107
Grade 1,   104-107
Grade 2,   104-107
Grade 3,   103-107
Grade 4,   103-107
Grade 5,   103-107
Grade 6,   103-106
Grade 7,   103-106
Grade 8,   103-106
Grade 9,   103-105
Grade 10-12,   104-105

# Sources of Information and Assistance

Academy of Natural Sciences of Philadelphia,  109
ACCENT! Science,  152
Activities to Integrate Mathematics and Science (AIMS),  138
Activity Resources Company, Inc.,  152
Addison-Wesley Publishing Company,  84, 86, 89, 142, 147
AIMS,  25, 35-36, 39, 41, 48, 55, 66-67, 69, 72, 76, 78, 138
AIMS Education Foundation,  138, 147, 152
Albion Import Export, Inc.,  152
Allen Press, Inc.,  105
Alley Pond Environmental Center, Inc.,  109
Allyn and Bacon,  85
Amateur Astronomers Association of New York City,  130
American Association for the Advancement of Science (AAAS),  99-100, 105, 130, 144, 147
American Association of Physics Teachers (AAPT),  130
American Astronautical Society,  130
American Astronomical Society,  130
American Bryological and Lichenological Society,  130
American Chemical Society (ACS),  104, 106, 130
American Geological Institute (AGI),  130
American Geophysical Union,  131
American Institute of Aeronautics and Astronautics,  131
American Institute of Biological Sciences (AIBS),  131
American Institute of Chemical Engineers,  131
American Institute of Chemists,  131
American Institute of Physics,  131
American Library Association,  100-101, 147
American Meteorological Society,  131
American Museum of Natural History Hayden Planetarium,  109
American Museum of Science & Energy,  109
American Nature Study Society,  131
American Physical Society (APS),  131
American Science and Engineering (AS&E),  25, 27, 49, 147

American Society for Microbiology,  131
Anniston Museum of Natural History,  109
Aquarium of Niagara Falls,  32, 110, 147
Arizona Museum of Science and Technology,  110
Arizona-Sonora Desert Museum,  110
Arkansas Museum of Science and History,  110
Assessment of Performance Unit,  147
Association for Science Education,  147
Association for Supervision and Curriculum Development (ASCD),  131
Association for Women in Science (AWIS),  131
Association of Science-Technology Centers (ASTC),  94, 99, 132, 147
Astronomical Society of the Pacific,  106, 132
Audubon Park and Zoological Garden,  110
Audubon Zoo,  9, 147
Badlands National Park,  110
Bausch and Lomb Optical Systems Division,  152
Biological Sciences Curriculum Study (BSCS),  132, 145
Bishop Museum,  110
Boston University,  103
Bowers Museum,  110
Bowker, R. R., Company,  99, 147
Brookhaven National Laboratory, Exhibit Center—Science Museum,  110
Brooklyn Botanic Garden,  111
Buffalo Museum of Science,  111
Buhl Science Center,  111
Burt Harrison & Company,  152
Cabrillo Marine Museum,  111
California Academy of Science,  111
California Museum of Science and Industry,  111
Calvert Marine Museum,  17, 111, 147
Capital Children's Museum,  111
Carnegie Museum of Natural History,  111
Carolina Biological Supply Company,  152
Center for American Archeology, Kampsville Archeological Center,  111, 132
Center for Excellence in Education,  132
Center for Meteorite Studies,  112
Center for Multisensory Learning,  147

Center for Teaching and Learning,  132
Charleston Museum,  112
Chemical Education for Public Understanding (CEPUP),  138
Chicago Zoological Park (Brookfield Zoo),  112
Chicago Zoological Society,  13, 148
Children's Museum (Boston),  112
Children's Museum, Detroit Public Schools,  112
Children's Museum, Indianapolis,  112
Children's Museum of Utah,  112
Children's Press,  81, 88, 148
Children's Television Workshop,  103-104
Cincinnati Museum of Natural History,  112
City College Workshop Center,  132
Cleveland Children's Museum,  112
Cleveland Health Education Museum,  113
Cobblestone Publishing, Inc.,  104
Computer Museum (Boston),  113
Conceptually Oriented Program in Elementary Science (COPES),  138
Connecticut Valley Biological Supply Company,  152
Conservation for Children,  139
Cornell Plantations,  141
Council for Elementary Science, International (CESI),  132
Council of State Science Supervisors (CSSS),  132
Council on Interracial Books for Children,  133
Cranbrook Institute of Science,  113
Creative Company,  148
Creative Learning Press,  152
Creative Learning Systems, Inc.,  152
Creative Publications,  21, 29, 42, 50, 59, 63, 68, 90, 148
Cuisenaire Company of America, Inc.,  153
Cumberland Science Museum,  113
Dale Seymour Publications,  83, 90, 148
Dallas Museum of Natural History/Dallas Aquarium,  113
Delta Education, Inc.,  7-30, 33, 40-41, 43, 44-50, 52-60, 67, 69, 71, 74-75, 77, 87, 141, 143, 145, 148, 153
Denoyer-Geppert Science Company,  153
Denver Museum of Natural History, The Hall of Life,  113
Department of Education and Science,  95-96, 133, 148

Department of Marine Resources, 113
Detroit Science Center, 113
Diablo Valley College Museum, 113
Discovery Center, 114
Discovery Center of Science & Technology, 114
Discovery Place, 114
Discovery World Museum of Science, Economics and Technology, 114
Don Harrington Discovery Center, 114
Dover Publications, Inc., 148
Edmund Scientific, 153
Education Development Center, Inc. (EDC), 19, 28, 43, 54, 60-63, 65-66, 68-69, 71-72, 76-78, 101, 139-140, 146, 148
Educational Products Information Exchange (EPIE), 102, 133, 148
Educational Resources Information Center (ERIC), 84, 87-88, 133, 148
Educational Testing Service (ETS), 93
Educational Testing Service, National Assessment of Educational Progress, 148
Educators Progress Service, Inc., 100, 148
Elementary Science Study (ESS), 139
Energy Learning Center Edison Electric Institute, 153
Energy Sciences, Inc., 153
Enslow Publishers, Inc., 81, 148
Equals, 133
ERIC Clearinghouse for Science, Mathematics, and Environmental Education, 84, 87-88, 133, 148
Estes Industries/Hi-Flier, 153
Evansville Museum of Arts and Sciences, 114
Excel, Inc., 92, 148
Exploratorium, 104, 114
Explorers Hall, 114
Facts on File, 87, 148
Fairbanks Museum and Planetarium, 115
Fernbank Science Center, 115
Field Museum of Natural History, 115
Florida State University, 145
Fontenelle Forest Nature Center, 115
Forestry Suppliers, Inc., 153
Fort Worth Museum of Science and History, 115
Foundation for Science and the Handicapped, 133
Foundational Approaches in Science Teaching (FAST), 139

Franklin Institute Science Museum and Planetarium and the Museum-To-Go Resource Center, 15, 38, 40, 46-48, 50-51, 57, 115, 149
Frey Scientific, 153
Full Option Science System (FOSS), 139
Garland Publishing, Inc., 102, 149
Girls Clubs of America, Inc., Operation SMART, 133
Good Apple, Inc., 91, 149
Government Printing Office (GPO), 133
Great Explorations in Math and Science (GEMS), 140, 149
Gulf Coast Research Laboratory, J. L. Scott Marine Education Center, 115
Hands-On Elementary Science, 140
Hanford Science Center, 115
Hansen Planetarium, 38, 40, 42, 116, 149
Harper & Row, 89, 101, 149
Harvard University Museums, 116
Harvard-Smithsonian Center for Astrophysics, 133
Health Activities Project (HAP), 140
Health Adventure, 116
Heath, D. C., and Company, 97, 149
Heinemann Educational Books, 94-95, 98, 149
Her Majesty's Stationery Office, 95
Holt, Henry, and Co., 89, 149
Holt, Rinehart & Winston, Inc., 92, 149
Hood College, 140
Houston Museum of Medical Science, 116
Houston Museum of Natural Science, 145
Howard B. Owens Science Center, Prince George's County Public Schools, 116
Hubbard Scientific Company, 34-37, 140, 149, 153
Hunt Institute For Botanical Documentation, 116
Idea Factory, Inc., 83-85, 90, 149
Ideal School Supply Company, 153
Impression 5 Science Museum, 116
Improving Urban Elementary Science (IUES), 140
Informal Science Study (ISS), 140
Insect Lore Products, Inc. 153
Insights—El Paso Science Museum, 116
International Council for Computers in Education (ICCE), 104
James Ford Bell Museum of Natural History, 117
John G. Shedd Aquarium, 117

John Muir Elementary School, 139
John Young Museum and Planetarium, Orlando Science Center, 117
Kalmbach Publishing Company, 103, 105
Kansas City Museum, 117
Kansas Learning Center for Health, 117
Kids Can Press, 89, 149
Kirkpatrick Center Museum Complex, 117
Knowledge Utilization Project in Science (KUPS), 141
Lakeview Museum of the Arts and Sciences, 117
Lakeview Museum Planetarium, 143
Lawrence Hall of Science, 9, 12, 20, 22-23, 38-39, 45-46, 50-51, 53-54, 56, 58, 66, 68, 71-72, 117, 138-140, 143-144, 149, 153
Lawrence Hall of Science Center for Multisensory Learning, 16, 30, 45, 50-51, 53, 66, 70, 75
Learning About Plants (LEAP), 141
Learning Labs, 141
Learning Things, Inc., 154
Learning Through Science, 142
LEGO Systems, Inc., 154
Let's Get Growing, General Feed and Seed Company, 154
Life Lab Science Program, 19, 142, 149
Lincoln Park Zoological Garden, 117
Lippincott, J. B., Co., 86, 149
Little, Brown and Company, 82, 84-87, 149
Living Arts and Science Center, Inc., 118
Louisiana Nature and Science Center, 118
LSU Museum of Geoscience, 118
Lutz Children's Museum, 118
Macdonald, 8, 23, 31-32, 36-37, 39, 41-42, 46, 54, 56-57, 61-63, 65, 67-70, 75, 77-79, 82, 89-90, 93, 142-143, 149
Macdonald-Raintree, 87
Magic House, St. Louis's Children Museum, 118
Manomet Bird Observatory, 28, 150
Marine Science Center, 142
Marine Science Project: FOR SEA, 142
Marine World Africa USA, 19, 28, 118, 150
Maryland Academy of Sciences/ Maryland Science Center, 118
Mayo Medical Museum, 118
McGraw-Hill, Inc., 8-9, 11-12, 14, 22-23, 26, 29-30, 39-40, 42-43, 52, 60-61, 90, 93, 96, 98, 150

Memphis Pink Palace Museum and Planetarium,   118
Merrill, Charles E., Publishing Co., 88, 97-98, 150
Messner, Julian,   88-89, 150
Metrologic Instruments,   154
Metrozoo,   119
Miami Seaquarium,   119
Michigan Space Center,   119
Michigan State University Museum, 119
Mid-Atlantic Center for Race Equity,   94, 150
Mid-Atlantic Equity Center,   134
Milwaukee Public Museum,   119
Mississippi Museum of Natural Science,   119
Missouri Botanical Garden,   17, 22, 29, 31, 33, 41, 62, 70, 119, 150
Monmouth Museum,   119
Morrow, William, and Company, 87, 91, 150
Museum of Art, Science, and Industry,   119
Museum of Arts and Science (FL), 119
Museum of Arts and Sciences (GA), 120
Museum of History and Science,   120
Museum of Holography,   120
Museum of New Mexico,   120
Museum of Science and Industry, 60, 120, 150
Museum of Science and Space Transit Planetarium,   120
Museum of Science, Boston,   120
Museum of the Chicago Academy of Sciences,   120
Mystic Marinelife Aquarium,   120
National Academy of Sciences (NAS),   134
National Aeronautics and Space Administration (NASA),   134
National Air and Space Museum, Smithsonian Institution,   121
National Aquarium,   121
National Aquarium in Baltimore,   22, 121, 150
National Association for Research in Science Teaching (NARST),   134
National Association for Science, Technology, and Society (NASTS),   134
National Association of Biology Teachers (NABT),   103, 134
National Association of Elementary School Principals (NAESP),   134
National Association of Geology Teachers,   134
National Audubon Society,   103, 135

National Center for the Improvement of Science Teaching and Learning, 135
National Diffusion Network (NDN), 135
National Gardening Association, 19, 150
National Geographic Kids Network, 142
National Geographic Society,   84, 105, 142, 150, 154
National Learning Center,   141
National Marine Fisheries Service Aquarium,   121
National Museum of American History, Smithsonian Institution, 121
National Museum of Natural History, Smithsonian Institution,   121
National Museum of Science and Technology,   121
National Science Foundation (NSF), 135
National Science Resources Center (NSRC),   135, 144
National Science Supervisors Association (NSSA),   135
National Science Teachers Association (NSTA),   82-83, 92, 96-97, 100, 101, 105-106, 135, 150, 154
National Urban Coalition,   136
National Wildlife Federation,   8, 11, 14-16, 20-21, 30, 32, 38-39, 43, 105-106, 136, 150, 154
National Zoological Park, Smithsonian Institution,   121
Native American Science Education Association (NASEA),   136
Nature Science Center,   121
New England Aquarium,   122
New Mexico Museum of Natural History,   122
New York Aquarium,   122
New York Hall of Science,   122
New York University,   138
New York University, Center for Educational Research and Field Services,   63-65
New York Zoological Society— Bronx Zoo,   122
North Carolina Aquarium, Fort Fisher,   122
North Carolina Department of Agriculture—North Carolina Maritime Museum,   122
North Carolina Museum of Life and Science,   122
Northern New England Marine Education Project, University of Maine, 20, 150

Nystrom/Eye Gate Media,   154
Office of Elementary and Secondary Education, Smithsonian Institution, 103, 125
Ohaus Scale Corporation,   139
Ohio's Center of Science and Industry (COSI),   122
Omniplex Science Museum,   123
Ontario Science Centre,   123
Open University Press, Taylor and Francis,   95, 150
Oregon Museum of Science and Industry,   123
Oryx Press,   101, 150
Outdoor Biology Instructional Strategies (OBIS),   143
Pacific Science Center,   83, 123, 151
PC-SIG/IASC CD-ROM Publishing Group,   102, 141, 151
Peter Li, Inc.,   104
Planet Ocean,   123
PLAY-JOUR, Inc.,   154
Prentice Hall,   83, 86, 151
Project STARWALK,   143
Project WILD,   27, 151
Rand McNally,   13, 15-16, 21, 24, 26, 47, 51, 53, 55, 58, 151
Reading Public Museum and Art Gallery,   123
Red Mountain Museum,   123
Reuben H. Fleet Space Theater and Science Center,   123
Right Before Your Eyes,   154
Roberson Center for the Arts and Sciences,   124
Roper Mountain Science Center,   124
Sacramento Science Center and Junior Museum,   124
Santa Barbara Museum of Natural History,   124
SAVI/SELPH Center for Multi-sensory Learning,   154
Schenectady Museum,   124
Scholastic, Inc.,   104, 106, 145
School Curriculum Development Committee,   142
Schools Council,   143
Science 5/13,   143
Science Activities for the Visually Impaired/Science Enrichment for Learners with Physical Handicaps (SAVI/SELPH),   144
Science and Technology for Children (STC),   144
Science—A Process Approach (SAPA/SAPA II),   144
Science Center of Iowa,   124
Science Connection,   145
Science Curriculum Improvement Study (SCIS/SCIS II/SCIIS),   145

Science for Life and Living: Integrating Science, Technology, and Health,   145
Science Helper K-8,   141, 145, 151
Science Kit, Inc.,   151
Science Man,   86, 151, 154
Science Museum of Connecticut,   124
Science Museum of Long Island,   124
Science Museum of Minnesota,   124
Science Museum of Virginia,   125
Science Museum of Western Virginia,   125
Science Museums of Charlotte, Inc., Nature Museum/Discovery Place,   125
Science Place,   125
Science Resource Centre,   136
Science Service, Inc.,   105
Science Weekly,   106
Scienceland, Inc.,   106
Scripps Aquarium—Museum Scripps Institution of Oceanography,   125
Sea World, Inc.,   125
Seattle Aquarium,   125
Self Help Elementary Level Science (SHELLS),   145
Sigma Xi, The Scientific Research Society,   136
Silver Burdett & Ginn,   145
SMEAC Information Reference Center, The Ohio State University,   91, 151
Smithsonian Institution,   see
   National Air and Space Museum
   National Museum of American History
   National Museum of Natural History
   National Zoological Park
   Office of Elementary and Secondary Education
Society for the Advancement of Chicanos and Native Americans in Science,   136
Soil and Water Conservation Society,   136
Soil Conservation Service,   154
South Florida Science Museum,   125
Southern Precision Instrument Company,   155
Space Studies Institute,   126
Springfield Science Museum,   126
St. Louis Science Center and Science Park,   126
State of Maine Marine Resources Laboratory,   126
Stewardship Institute,   27, 151
Strecker Museum,   126
Sunburst Publications,   140
Super Science: A Mass Media Program,   145

Teachers College Press,   93, 151
Teacher's Laboratory, Inc.,   104, 142-143, 151, 155
Technical Education Research Centers, Inc. (TERC),   142
Thames Science Center,   126
TOPS Learning Systems,   155
Triangle Coalition for Science and Technology Education,   136
Tucson Children's Museum,   126
U.S. Department of Education,   136
Unified Science and Mathematics for Elementary Schools (USMES),   146
University of California,   145
University of Florida,   141
University of Hawaii,   139
University of Houston,   140
University of Kansas Museum of Natural History,   126
University of Nebraska State Museum of Natural Science,   126
University of Wisconsin–Madison,   146
Vermont Institute of Natural Science,   85, 151
Virginia Living Museum,   127
Virginia Marine Science Museum,   12-13, 26, 32, 127, 151
Ward's Natural Science Establishment, Inc.,   155
Washington Park Arboretum/Center for Urban Horticulture,   127
Wildlife Education, Ltd.,   107
Wildlife Society,   137
Willamette Science and Technology Center,   127
Wisconsin Fast Plants,   146
Workman Publishing Company,   85, 88, 151
Xerox Education Division,   73-74
Young Astronaut Council,   137
Young Naturalist Foundation,   104-105
Zoological Society of San Diego, San Diego Zoo and Wild Animal Park,   127

*Above:*
Centennial School District
Multnomah Education
Service District,
Portland, Oregon
*Photograph by Craig Walker*

*Right:*
School District 54,
Schaumburg, Illinois
*Photograph by James Furey*